Baedeker's
PORTUGAL

152 colour photographs
59 maps and plans
1 large road map

Text:
Rosemarie Arnold (History)
Walter R. Arnold (Music) ·
Monika I. Baumgarten (General, Plant and Animal
Life, Population, State and Administration, Literature,
Economy, Portugal from A to Z)
Werner Fauser (Folk Traditions)
Gerlad Sawade (Climate)
Christine Wessely (Art)

Editorial work:
Baedeker Stuttgart

English language: Alec Court

Cartography:
Ingenieurbüro für Kartographie
Huber & Oberländer, Munich

Design and layout:
HF Ottmann,
Atelier für Buchgestaltung und
Grafik-Design, Leonberg

Conception and general direction:
Dr Peter Baumgarten, Baedeker Stuttgart

2nd edition

English translation:
James Hogarth

ⓒ Baedeker Stuttgart
Original German edition

ⓒ The Automobile Association
United Kingdom and Ireland 57286

ⓒ Jarrold and Sons Ltd
English Language edition Worldwide

US and Canadian Edition
Prentice Hall Press

Licensed user:
Mairs Geographischer Verlag GmbH & Co.,
Ostfildern-Kemnat bei Stuttgart

Reproductions:
Gölz Repro-Service GmbH,
Ludwigsburg

The name Baedeker is a registered trademark

In a time of rapid change it is difficult to ensure that all
the information given is entirely accurate and up to
date, and the possibility of error can never be
completely eliminated. Although the publishers can
accept no responsibility for inaccuracies and omis-
sions, they are always grateful for corrections and
suggestions for improvement.

Printed in Italy By Sagdos, Milan

0–13–056135–5 US and Canada
0 86145 145 7 UK

Source of illustrations:

Many of the illustrations were supplied by the
Portuguese National Tourist Office in Frankfurt am
Main.

Air Portugal, Frankfurt am Main (pp. 12, 41, 43, 52,
53, 62 (below left), 63, 65, 68, 70 (two), 71, 72, 73,
74, 75, 77, 78, 81, 88, 89, 92, 95 (two), 99, 101,
102, 108, 110 (two), 111, 114, 115, 119, 120
(above, left), 129, 135 (two), 137, 139, 142
(above), 145, 149, 150, 151, 152, 153, 154, 155,
156 (two), 163, 164, 166, 168, 169, 171, 172, 174,
175, 177, 179 (below), 182, 186, 187, 192
(above), 194 (above), 197, 198, 200, 203, 205
(right), 207 (below, right), 225, 233, 240, 247,
250)

Allianz-Archiv (pp. 212, 224)
Anthony-Verlag, Stanberg (cover picture)
Bildagentur Mauritius, Mittenwald (pp. 52, 56, 64,
104, 113 (below, left), 178 (left), 181, 188 (above,
right), 199, 206)
Werner Fauser, Stuttgart (pp. 42, 44, 51, 106, 194
(below), 239)
Willi Fischer, Esslingen (pp. 10, 49, 58, 60, 102
(above), 120 (two, right), 142 (below, right), 143,
144)
Internationales Bildarchiv Horst von Irmer, Munich
(pp. 40, 178 (right), 184, 185 (three), 188, 251)
Klaus Möller, Praia do Carvoeiro (pp. 15, 62 (above,
left), 245)
Georg Schiffner, Lahr (p. 79)
Gernot Ruoff, Viernheim (p. 85)
Zentrale Farbbild Agentur GmbH, Düsseldorf (pp. 83,
97, 107, 113 (above, left), 128, 159, 207 (left),
214)

The drawing of the St Vincent polyptych by Nuno
Gonçalves on p. 141 is by George Schiffner, Lahr.

How to Use this Guide

The principal towns and areas of tourist interest are
described in alphabetical order. The names of other
places referred to under these general headings can be
found in the very full Index.

Following the tradition established by Karl Baedeker
in 1844, sights of particular interest and hotels and
restaurants of particular quality are distinguished by
either one or two asterisks.

In the lists of hotels and other accommodation
r.=rooms, b.=beds and SP=swimming pool. Hotels
are classified in the categories shown on p. 235.

A glossary of common Portuguese geographical and
topographical terms will be found on pp. 231–233.

The symbol ⓘ at the beginning of an entry or on a
town plan indicates the local tourist office or other
organisation from which further information can be
obtained. The post-horn symbol on a town indicates
a post office.

Only a selection of hotels and restaurants can be
given: no reflection is implied, therefore, on establishments not included.

This guidebook forms part of a completely new series of the world-famous Baedeker Guides to Europe.

Each volume is the result of long and careful preparation and, true to the traditions of Baedeker, is designed in every respect to meet the needs and expectations of the modern traveller.

The name of Baedeker has long been identified in the field of guidebooks with reliable, comprehensive and up-to-date information, prepared by expert writers who work from detailed, first-hand knowledge of the country concerned. Following a tradition that goes back over 150 years to the date when Karl Baedeker published the first of his handbooks for travellers, these guides have been planned to give the tourist all the essential information about the country and its inhabitants: where to go, how to get there and what to see. Baedeker's account of a country was always based on his personal observation and experience during his travels in that country. This tradition of writing a guidebook in the field rather than at an office desk has been maintained by Baedeker ever since.

Lavishly illustrated with superb colour photographs and numerous specially drawn maps and street plans of the major towns, the new Baedeker Guides concentrate on making available to the modern traveller all the information he needs in a format that is both attractive and easy to follow. For every place that appears in the gazetteer, the principal features of architectural, artistic and historic interest are described, as are its main areas of scenic beauty. Selected hotels and restaurants are also included. Features of exceptional merit are indicated by either one or two asterisks.

A special section at the end of each book contains practical information, details of leisure activities and useful addresses. The separate road map will prove an invaluable aid to planning your route and your travel within the country.

Contents

Introduction to Portugal

A typical Portuguese windmill

Portugal
República
Portuguesa
(Mainland)

Azores: see p. 67
Madeira: see p. 147
Macao: see p. 146

VIANA
DO
CASTELO
Viana do Castelo

BRAGA
Braga

VILA
REAL
Vila Real

Bragança

BRAGANÇA

OPORTO
Oporto

AVEIRO
Aveiro

VISEU
Viseu

GUARDA
Guarda

Coimbra
COIMBRA

CASTELO
BRANCO
Castelo
Branco

LEIRIA
Leiria

Nazaré

Peniche

SANTARÉM
Santarém

Portalegre

PORTALEGRE

LISBON

LISBON
Cabo
da Roca

Setúbal

Évora ÉVORA

SETÚBAL

Sines

Beja

BEJA

FARO
Lagos
Faro

Boundaries
of districts

After a period of uncertainty Portugal is now in process of recovering its attraction as a tourist country and revitalising its tourist trade. Portugal's tourist statistics show a steady increase in the number of visitors, including large numbers from northern Europe.

This relatively small country, which in earlier centuries was one of the European great powers and has lost its great overseas possessions only in quite recent times, offers a wide range of both scenic and cultural attractions which are still relatively little known.

Geographical regions and administrative districts	Area in sq. km	sq. miles	Population
Continente (Mainland)	88,944	34,332	9,292,000
NORTE (North)	31,592	12,195	4,001,000
Aveiro	2,808	1,084	620,000
Braga	2,673	1,032	706,000
Bragança	6,608	2,551	181,000
Guarda	5,518	2,130	205,000
Porto (Oporto)	2,395	924	1,553,000
Vila Real	4,328	1,671	264,000
Viano do Castelo	2,255	870	256,000
Viseau	5,007	1,933	421,000
CENTRO (Central)	29,710	11,469	3,748,000
Castelo Branco	6,675	2,577	233,000
Coimbra	3,947	1,524	441,000
Leiria	3,515	1,357	418,000
Lisboa (Lisbon)	2,761	1,066	2,066,000
Portalegre	6,065	2,341	141,000
Santarém	6,747	2,604	449,000
SUL (South)	27,642	10,610	1,339,000
Beja	10,225	3,886	184,000
Évora	7,393	2,854	178,000
Faro	4,960	1,915	326,000
Setúbal	5,064	1,955	651,000
Ilhas adjacentes (Islands)	3,041	1,173	502,000
AÇORES (Azores)	2,247	867	244,000
MADEIRA (Funchal) and Archipelago	794	306	258,000
Portugal (Mainland and Islands)	**91,985**	**35,506**	**9,794,000**
Território (Territory under Portuguese administration)			
MACAU (Macao) with Taipa and Coloane	15·5	5·98	249,000

The **Portuguese mainland has an enormously long Atlantic coastline, the finest parts of which are to be found at its climatically favoured southern end, in the Algarve with its beautiful sandy beaches and rugged cliffs. The country's cosmopolitan capital, Lisbon, on the broad estuary of the Tagus, is one of the most strikingly situated cities in the world. In the interior of the country, too, there are numbers of interesting and attractive towns, villages and old monasteries and a wide range of varied and beautiful scenery – hills, valleys and plateaux – in every region of Portugal; and there is a special interest in getting to know this country which is now preparing to become a member of the European Economic Community.**

In Portugal, a land still unspoiled by mass tourism and the hectic urgencies of modern life, visitors will meet a relaxed and friendly people, attached to their own country but hospitable to strangers and ready to make them feel at home. This is true not only of mainland Portugal but also of Madeira and the Azores, those groups of islands far out in the Atlantic which offer so much to appeal to the visitor.

Another great attraction of Portugal lies in its native folk traditions; these find expression throughout the year in a whole range of local feast-days and festivals, in country markets and in those characteristic Portuguese folk-songs, the *fados*.

Finally there are the attractions of Portuguese food and drink – a varied range of native dishes and excellent wines.

The **mainland** of Portugal, with an area of 88,944 sq. km/34,332 sq. miles, occupies roughly a sixth of the Iberian peninsula. Broadly rectangular in shape, measuring some 550 km/340 miles from N to S and averaging some 150 km/95 miles from W to E (greatest width 200 km/125 miles), the country lies in the extreme SW of Europe between lat. 42°8′ and 36°58′ N and between long. 6°49′ and 9°3′ W. Also included within the territory of Portugal are the "Ilhas adjacentes", the two Atlantic archipelagos of **Madeira** and the **Azores** (total area 3041 sq. km/1173 sq. miles), and the former colony of *Macao* on the southern coast of China, which is administered by Portugal but enjoys self-government in internal affairs.

The large overseas provinces of the old Portuguese colonial empire have been given up only quite recently. Portuguese India was annexed by India in 1961; Portuguese Guinea became independent, as Guinea-Bissau, in 1974; and in 1975 Mozambique, the Cape Verde Islands (Cabo Verde), the islands of São Tomé and Príncipe and finally Angola, one after the other, achieved independence. In 1975 Portuguese Timor was invaded by Indonesian troops. In 1976 the territory was officially incorporated in Indonesia.

Mainland Portugal has preserved its frontiers unchanged for almost eight centuries – a circumstance which can be attributed mainly to its geographical situation. As a frontier territory of the Old World, rather than an area of passage, the kingdom of Portugal remained after its foundation in the 12th c. a region of only marginal significance in the conflicts between European states. The country's military efforts were directed solely towards the consolidation of its frontiers, at first against the Moors, then being driven back during the Reconquest, and later against Spanish claims to sovereignty.

Bathing beaches on the Algarve coast

The principal mountains, rivers and lakes in Portugal
(Mainland)

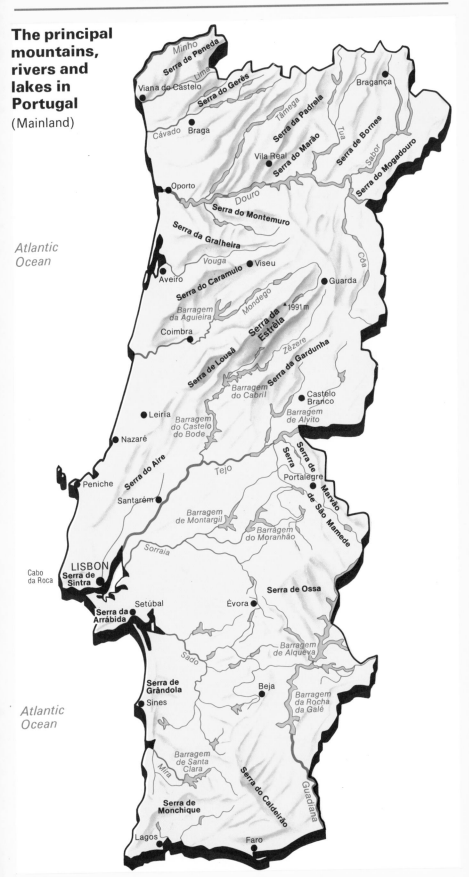

Portugal has a common frontier of some 1300 km/800 miles – more than half its total length of frontier – with Spain, its only neighbouring state. Most of this land frontier follows the course of three great Iberian rivers – the *Minho* (Spanish Miño) in the N, the *Douro* (Spanish Duero) in the NE and the *Guadiana* in the SE – or the rugged ranges of hills in the N of the country. Those sections of the frontier which are easily accessible and without natural barriers are nevertheless readily identifiable as frontier areas, since the maintenance of the same frontier for so many centuries and the building of castles and other fortifications during those centuries have led to a movement of population away from these areas.

The other half of Portugal's frontiers is formed by the Atlantic Ocean. It is not surprising, therefore, that throughout its history the whole country, including the inland as well as the coastal regions, should have shown a marked orientation towards the sea and should – thanks also to its traditional hankering for national independence – have differentiated itself so strikingly from its Spanish neighbour.

Geologically Portugal is the south-western part of the Iberian land mass, a region of gneisses, granites, quartzites, greywackes, limestones and Palaeozoic schists subjected to ancient folding movements which forms the Iberian mesetas, averaging some 700 m/ 2300 ft in height. It slopes gradually down from the higher hills in the N and has been much reduced and levelled by erosion.

These rump formations are overlaid in the N of the country by a number of massifs of early volcanic origin, often of imposing size, rising to heights of almost 2000 m/ 6560 ft. Only in a few places do the outliers of these hills reach down to the flat coastal region with its dunes and its lagoons, forming promontories such as the *Cabo da Roca*, the most westerly point in Europe.

Between the Minho, the frontier river which separates northern Portugal from the geographically similar Spanish province of Galicia, and the Mondego are the granite and schist hills and uplands of the provinces of *Minho*, *Trás-os-Montes* and *Beira Alta*: a region of extraordinary natural beauty and tourist interest (Peneda-Gerês National Park), with particularly wild and rugged scenery in the Serra de Soja, the Serra de Peneda and the Serra do Gerês.

To the S of the Mondego rises the mighty ridge of the *Serra da Estrêla* (Malhão da Estrêla, 1991 m/6532 ft), much broken up by erosion and battered by violent storms from the W – the highest mountain in mainland Portugal and the country's only major winter sports area.

These mountains of northern Portugal, the "Montanhas", are traversed by the lower course of the Douro. On the terraced slopes of the valley, in this "País do Vinho" ("Land of Wine"), are grown the grapes used in making port, which is carried down to the "lodges" of Oporto and shipped from there to countries all over the world.

The Serra da Estrêla is continued to the SW in the uplands of *Estremadura*, a region of beneficient climate and great fertility.

To the S of the Tagus is *Alentejo*, a great expanse of rolling country and level plateaux with occasional small ranges of hills (Serra da Ossa, etc.) rising to 700 m/ 2300 ft. This vast and featureless tract of arable country interspersed with heathland extends S to the *Serra de Monchique*, a range rising to some 900 m/2950 ft which forms a protective barrier against cold weather from the N and with its numerous streams provides an abundance of nourishment for the subtropical and tropical vegetation of the *Algarve*.

Windmills at Óbidos (Estremadura)

The rump formations of the Iberian land mass extend for some 15–20 km/9–12 miles out to sea at a shallow depth and then plunge steeply down to 300 m/1000 ft. Along the whole coastline they are overlaid by a fringe of Mesozoic sedimentary rocks deposited by the sea, then reaching farther inland. In the course of geological time these rocks were thrust upwards, forming the famous and exceedingly picturesque cliffs and stacks which are seen at their finest in the "Rocky Algarve", interspersed with bays and coves containing broad sandy beaches which shelve gently into the sea. In the estuaries of the Douro and Tagus in northern Portugal and of the Guadiana in the "Sandy Algarve" the sedimentary rocks have been much eroded and ground down, forming a landscape of dunes and lagoons.

In central and southern Portugal the Iberian rump formations are broken up by tectonic depressions. These are found particularly in the *Ribatejo* area and around the estuary of the Rio Sado, where the land is highly fertile as a result of the soil deposited by the river and the abundant water supply. These areas are still subject to earth tremors and contain numerous thermal springs. – Just before reaching the Atlantic the valley of the lower *Tagus* (Portuguese *Tejo*, Spanish *Tajo*) opens out into a kind of inland sea, forming a huge natural harbour for the country's capital, **Lisbon** (*Lisboa*).

Portugal has many perennial rivers, which play a major part in determining the climatic pattern and plant life. In recent years they have acquired additional importance as sources of hydroelectric power. Only a few of the larger rivers, including the Minho, Douro, Tagus, Sado and Guadiana, are navigable in the lower parts of their courses; there are few river ports of any size.

Portugal – Land of Water Mills and Windmills

In no other country in Europe are there so many water mills and windmills still working as in Portugal.

There are some thousands of **water mills** of different types (*azenhas* with vertical wheels, *sesicas* with horizontal wheels) on rivers, streams and reservoirs all over the country, used for grinding corn but more particularly, and increasingly, for irrigating fields and gardens.

In parts of the country with little water or wind power *winches* or gins are used, worked either by animal power or by an engine.

Visitors to Portugal are more likely, however, to be struck by the characteristic old windmills (first referred to in the 13th c.) which are still to be seen in considerable numbers, adding a picturesque touch to the landscape.

The mills are usually round, with a conical roof. The triangular sails are suspended between long wooden spokes which form a giant wheel. There are sometimes clay vessels attached to the ropes which make a whistling sound as the sails turn in the wind.

Climate

The climate of **mainland** Portugal, situated as it is on the Atlantic Ocean, is basically maritime, with fairly mild winters and summers that are not excessively hot. Towards the E, with increasing distance from the coast, continental influences become stronger, with a steadily greater range of variation between summer and winter temperatures. In the different parts of the country the climate is influenced by an area of high pressure from the Azores which moves N in spring and summer and returns S in autumn and winter. In consequence most of the rainfall comes in the winter, being particularly heavy in the N of the country, which between August or September and May or June falls within the zone of the western cyclones. In the Serra da Estrêla, which rises to almost 2000 m/6560 ft, the annual precipitation (including snow) may reach more than 3000 mm/120 in. Towards the S, Mediterranean influence increases, with higher temperatures and ever greater aridity, until on the Algarve coast there is practically no rain at all in the height of summer. The whole of the coastal region is relatively cool in summer as a result of the NW winds (*nortadas*) blowing from the area of high pressure over the Azores and the accompanying northerly currents in the sea. Because of this the surface temperature of the sea in summer reaches only 17–18 °C/62·5–64·5°F in the N and 19–20°C/66–68°F in the S, some 4–6°C/7–11°F less than on the E coast of Spain. Only the few stretches of coast running from E to W and sheltered from N and NW winds (around Lisbon and Setúbal and in the Algarve) are substantially warmer throughout the year. The port country in the lower Douro valley, also running from E to W, enjoys a similarly sheltered location.

Along the coast TEMPERATURES rise from N to S: Oporto annual average 14·8°C/58·6°F (January 8·7°C/47·7°F, July 21°C/70°F, annual range 12·3°C/22·1°F), Lisbon annual 15·9°C/60·6°F (January 11·2°C/52·2°F, August 21·7°C/71·1°F, annual range 10·5°C/18·9°F), Faro annual 17·3°C/63·1°F (January 11·8°C/53·2°F, July–August 23·8°C/74·8°F, annual range 12°C/21·6°F). In the more continental regions of the interior, where allowance has to be made for a fall of 0·3–0·5°C/0·54–0·9°F for every additional 100 m/330 ft of height, temperatures rise as follows: Guarda (alt. 1039 m/3409 ft, the highest town in Portugal, situated on the NE side of the Serra da Estrêla) annual 10·2°C/50·4°F (January 3·5°C/38·3°F, July 18·2°C/64·8°F, annual range 14·7°C/26·5°F), Serra da Estrêla (1386 m/4547 ft) annual 8·2°C/46·8°F (February 2·5°C/36·5°F, August 17°C/62·6°F, annual range 14·5°C/26·1°F), Coimbra (140 m/459 ft) annual 14·6°C/58·3°F (January 8·5°C/47·3°F, August 20°C/68°F, annual range 11·5°C/20·7°F), Évora (321 m/1053 ft) annual 14·8°C/58·6°F (January 8·2°C/46·8°F, July–August 22·3°C/72·1°F, annual range 14·1°C/25·4°F), Beja (284 m/932 ft) annual 15·3°C/59·5°F (January 8·2°C/46·8°F, August 23°C/73·4°F, annual range 14·8°C/26·6°F).

RAINFALL decreases from N to S. The annual rainfall in the S is only a third of the figure for the N; in November there is between two and two and a half times less rain in the S than in the N, in August anything up to fifteen times less. The annual average at Oporto is 1189 mm/47 in. (August 22 mm/0·87 in., November 160 mm/6·3 in.), at Guarda 1083 mm/43 in. (August 16 mm/0·63 in., November 160 mm/6·3 in.), at Coimbra 984 mm/39 in. (August 13 mm/0·51 in., December 135 mm/5·3 in.), at Lisbon 602 mm/24 in. (August 3 mm/0·12 in., November 100 mm/3·9 in.), at Beja 561 mm/22 in. (August 2 mm/0·08 in., November 82 mm/3·2 in.) and at Faro 363 mm/14 in. (July and August each 1·5 mm/0·06 in., November 65 mm/2·6 in.). The Serra da Estrêla (alt. 1386 m/4547 ft) has an annual rainfall of 2365 mm/93 in. (August 33 mm/1·3 in., December no less than 400 mm/16 in.). In the N of the country, in the rain shadow of the mountains of Trás-os-Montes, the annual rainfall is only 500–1000 mm/20–40 in.

The **Azores**, lying out in the Atlantic in the latitude of southern Portugal, have, thanks to the influence of the Gulf Stream, a much more equable climate than the mainland. On the frontier zone between polar and tropical air masses, they are exposed throughout the year to strong winds, which in summer blow mainly from the NE (the trade winds), bringing moderate rain, and in winter mainly from the SW, often rising to storm force. The heavy winter rainfall brought by the SW winds (in the mountains often falling in the form of snow) decreases markedly from W to E. – The annual average TEMPERATURE at Santa Cruz (on Flores), Horta (Faial) and Ponta Delgada (São Miguel) is 17·3–17·5°C/63·1–63·5°F, with a minimum (January, February or March) of 13·8–14°C/56·8– 57·2°F

and a maximum (August) of 21·7–22·2°C/71·1–72°F, i.e. an annual range of 7·8–8·8°C/14–15·8°F. On the pass of Achada das Furnas (São Miguel, alt. 550 m/1805 ft) the corresponding figures are 13·2°C/55·8°F, 7·5°C/45·5°F, 17·5°C/63·5°F and 7·5°C/13·5°F. – The annual RAINFALL decreases from W to E: Santa Cruz 1447 mm/57 in. (July 55 mm/2·2 in., January 170 mm/6·7 in.), Horta 1022 mm/40·2 in. (July 37 mm/1·5 in., January 120 mm/ 4·7 in.), Ponto Delgada 697 mm/27·4 in. (July 22 mm/0·87 in., November 87 mm/3·4 in.). On the Achada das Furnas pass the figure is 1730 mm/ 68·1 in. (July 57 mm/2·2 in., January 230 mm/ 9·1 in.); in the mountains, which rise to over 2300 m/7500 ft, it can be as high as 3000 mm/118 in.

The island of **Madeira**, lying 5–6° S of the Azores, almost in the latitude of Marrakesh, has an extreme oceanic climate, with a TEMPERATURE range which in places is no more than 5·5°C/9·9°F. While the August average at sea level is about the same as in the Azores (Funchal 21·5°C/70·7°F; the rocky bay of Lugar de Baixo, on the S coast, 23°C/73·4°F) and the annual figure is only 1–2°C/1·8–3·6°F higher (Funchal 18·2°C/64·8°F, Lugar de Baixo 19·3°C/66·7°F), the February average is up to 3·5°C/6·3°F higher (Funchal 15°C/59°F, Lugar de Baixo 17·5°C/63·5°F; Nice, on the Côte d'Azur, only 6·5°C/43·7°F). The much higher (425 m/1395 ft) and rainier Santana, in the N of the island, is cooler (annual average 15·5°C/59·9°F, January 12·9°C/55·2°F, August 18·5°C/65·3°F). On the hill of Areiro, at a height of 1610 m/5282 ft (with a drop in temperature of 0·5°C/0·9°F for every 100 m/330 ft of altitude), the annual average is 9·6°C/49·3°F (January 6·4°C/43·5°F, July 14·5°C/58·1°F). The island of Porto Santo, off the NE coast of Madeira, is particularly favoured, with an annual average of 19°C/66·2°F (January 16·3°C/61·3°F, August 22°C/71·6°F). – The surface temperature of the water is 20–23°C/68–73°F in summer, reaching its lowest figure in March (17·2°C/63°F). – RAINFALL (which often comes in the form of cloudbursts) varies between the relatively dry, and in summer almost rainless, S coast (Funchal annual 645 mm/25 in., July 1·4 mm/0·06 in., March 85 mm/3·3 in.) and the N coast, which can be very wet, particularly during the winter months (Santana annual 1314 mm/52in., July 27 mm/1·1 in., November 215 mm/8·5 in.). Rainfall is particularly heavy on the hills: Encumeada pass (950 m/3115 ft, to W of the centre; exposed to rain-bringing winds) annual 2675 mm/105 in., July 24 mm/0·94 in., November 300 mm/12 in., relatively dry only June–August; Arieiro (1610 m/5282 ft, to E of the centre) annual 2386 mm/94 in., June 13 mm/0·05 in., November 465 mm/18 in. The driest place in the archipelago is the island of Porto Santo (annual 338 mm/13 in., August 2·5 mm/0·1 in., November 62 mm/ 2·4 in.). – From time to time a hot, dust-carrying E wind from Africa, the *leste*, blows in Madeira; but here it remains within tolerable limits, driving away the clouds which form around midday and in June and July sometimes remain the whole day, at heights of 1200–1500 m/4000–5000 ft.

Plant and Animal Life

The natural **vegetation** of Portugal originally consisted of sparse forest. The trees now mainly found in the N of the country, with its harsher climate, are deciduous species, particularly oak, sweet chestnut, lime, maple, poplar and beech; in the S evergreens predominate, including cork-oaks and holm-oaks, together with eucalyptus. The dunes along the coast are fringed with pines.

The country's forests have been decimated by centuries of over-felling and neglect, and reforestation is now urgently necessary if the land is to be prevented from degenerating into a steppe-like waste. Accordingly in recent years there has been planned replanting in the dune and mountain areas. The original natural forests are now only to be found in the less accessible mountain regions.

In the undergrowth of the rainier regions of the NW, gorse and heather predominate; in the S and E large areas are covered by aromatic herbs and semi-shrubs, including broom, cistus, rosemary, thyme and lavender, with various colourful bulbous plants.

The equable climate and abundance of water in areas such as the Serra da Arrábida, the Serra de Sintra, the Buçao National Park and the Algarve have produced exceptionally rich vegetation, seen at its most colourful in spring, when the almond-trees are in blossom, and in early summer.

The **wildlife** of mainland Portugal is similar to that of Central Europe. In the wooded hills of northern Portugal are found not only species which occur N of the Alps including roe-deer, chamois and foxes, but also some surviving wolves, wild horses, golden eagles and aurochs. In the Peneda-Gerês National Park rare species enjoy full statutory protection.

The coastal lagoons are the haunt of numerous waterfowl, including flamingoes. Small game is abundant everywhere, and shooting is a popular sport. The rivers and lakes, including the many large reservoirs, are well stocked with trout, pike, salmon, carp and eels.

The Podengo (*Podengo ibizenco*) breed of dog, which is found both in Spain and Portugal, is a protected species on the Iberian Peninsula. The breed, the coat of which is brown and white, is believed to have originated in Ibiza and is related to the greyhound.

Almond-blossom (Algarve)

Population

Portugal's population of just under 10 million is very unevenly distributed over the country. The average density of 106 inhabitants per sq. kilometre (275 per sq. mile) is below the figure for other European countries. Some 35% of the population is concentrated in the large urban regions around Lisbon and Oporto, which have the very high densities of 677 and 662 per sq. km (1753 and 1715 per sq. mile). At the other extreme is Alentejo, with the very low density of 19 per sq. km (49 per sq. mile) in the Beja district and 24 per sq. km (62 per sq. mile) in the districts

of Évora and Portalegre. However, the drift of population from the rural to the rising industrial areas has halted.

Outside the large urban regions the predominant form of settlement is the densely built-up village which sometimes reaches the status of a small town. In the fertile valley basins scattered villages predominate. Villages built along one main street are rare, being found mainly in newly developed agricultural areas on the coast.

The birth rate (19 per 1000) is relatively high and fairly stable. The high rate of

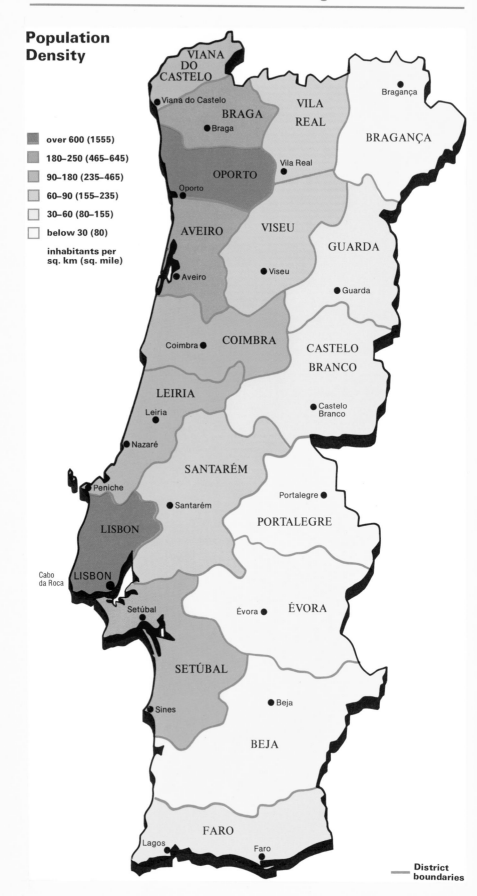

Population Density

- ▪ over 600 (1555)
- ▪ 180–250 (465–645)
- ▪ 90–180 (235–465)
- ▪ 60–90 (155–235)
- ▫ 30–60 (80–155)
- ▫ below 30 (80)

inhabitants per
sq. km (sq. mile)

VIANA
DO
CASTELO

Viana do Castelo

BRAGA

Braga

VILA
REAL

Bragança

BRAGANÇA

Vila Real

OPORTO

Oporto

AVEIRO

VISEU

GUARDA

Aveiro

Viseu

Guarda

COIMBRA

Coimbra

CASTELO
BRANCO

LEIRIA

Leiria

Castelo
Branco

Nazaré

SANTARÉM

Peniche

Santarém

Portalegre

PORTALEGRE

LISBON

Cabo
da Roca

LISBON

Setúbal

Évora

ÉVORA

SETÚBAL

Sines

Beja

BEJA

FARO

Lagos

Faro

District
boundaries

population increase which might be expected as a result is moderated by the traditionally high rate of emigration to the United States, Canada, France and South America (Brazil, Venezuela). During the last decade, however, large numbers of people have returned to Portugal from the country's former overseas possessions, so that on balance there has been a moderate increase in population.

The earliest inhabitants of Portugal were the Lusitanians, a Celtiberian people. The native population, particularly in the coastal region, received an admixture of blood at an early stage from visiting seamen and traders – Phoenicians, Carthaginians, Greeks, Jews. The 600 years of Roman rule not only left their mark on the ethnic composition of the population but gave Portugal its language. Evidence of the relatively brief stays of the Suevi and the Visigoths can still be seen in the N of the country, where tall, fair-skinned types are occasionally encountered. Particularly marked, and in the S of the country quite unmistakable, are the traces left by the Moorish period, which influenced both the physical type and the way of life of the population. During the Middle Ages the Inquisition drove large numbers of Jews out of Spain into Portugal, where – still persecuted and harried by pogroms – they became converts to Christianity and were absorbed into the Portuguese people.

Thus in the course of millennia this mingling between the native population and successive incomers, combined with the country's isolation from Spain and the rest of Europe, gave rise to a population structure which was homogeneous and distinctively Portuguese, both ethnically and culturally.

The Portuguese are predominantly dark-haired, of small to medium height and of sturdy, almost stocky, build. In contrast to the lively Spaniards they tend to be quiet, gentle, thoughtful, warm-hearted and friendly, strongly attached to their home and their family – a characteristic reflected in the return of so many emigrants. The relatively peaceful course of the 1974 revolution can also be ascribed to these qualities.

The small African minorities in the population are either descendants of former slaves or have come to Portugal from the country's former African possessions.

Some 99% of the population are Roman Catholics. Of the remainder an estimated 40,000 are Protestants and 6000 are Jews.

In Portugal the period of compulsory schooling is from 7 to 14. The shortage of schools and of teachers in rural areas is a serious problem. Elementary education is free, but fees are charged for secondary education, provided either in State schools or in private or church schools (which are subject to State supervision). A total of more than 80 universities and higher educational establishments, including famous and old-established institutions such as Coimbra University, train the academics, scientists and other specialists so urgently needed for the country's development.

State and Administration

The 1933 Portuguese constitution was swept away by the almost bloodless "Carnation Revolution" of April 1974 and replaced by a new one, promulgated on 25 April 1976. This in turn was revised by Parliament in 1982. The revision was not as far-reaching as the Centre-Right government would have wished because it had to enlist the qualified support of the opposition to secure the necessary majority. Thus the 1976 aim of "establishing a classless society" and "ensuring the transition to socialism through the creation of conditions for the democratic exercise of power by the working classes" remains enshrined in the revised version. But a major step was taken to strengthen civilian parliamentary rule with the abolition of the military Council of the Revolution. The constitution would henceforth be upheld by a Constitutional Tribunal of civilian judges elected by parliament, and the power to legislate on military matters was transferred to the latter.

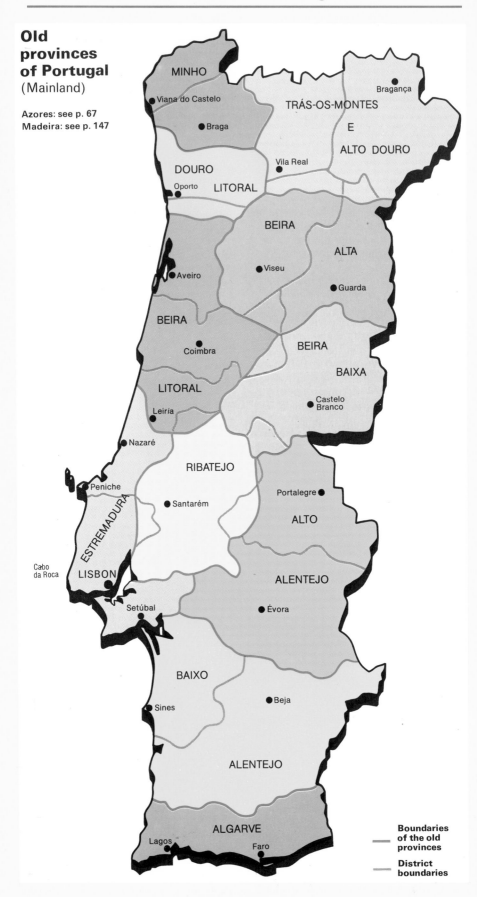

**Old
provinces
of Portugal**
(Mainland)

Azores: see p. 67
Madeira: see p. 147

MINHO

● Bragança

● Viana do Castelo

TRÁS-OS-MONTES

E

● Braga

ALTO DOURO

DOURO

● Vila Real

Oporto ●   LITORAL

BEIRA

ALTA

● Viseu

● Aveiro

● Guarda

BEIRA

BEIRA

Coimbra ●

BAIXA

LITORAL

● Castelo
Branco

Leiria ●

● Nazaré

RIBATEJO

ESTREMADURA

Peniche ●

Portalegre ●

Santarém ●

ALTO

Cabo
da Roca

LISBON

ALENTEJO

Setúbal ●

● Évora

BAIXO

● Beja

● Sines

ALENTEJO

ALGARVE

Lagos ●

Faro ●

Boundaries
of the old
provinces

District
boundaries

Likewise, the armed forces' role to ensure "the continuation of the 25 April 1974 Revolution" and "the conditions for the peaceful and pluralistic transition to democracy and socialism" was simplified to that of "ensuring the military defence of the Portuguese republic".

The head of state is the President, who is elected for a five-year term. The post is held at present by Mario A. Soares who was elected in February 1986. The revision of the constitution also curtailed his powers to a significant extent.

The Portuguese parliament, the Assembly of the Republic (Assembleia da República) is elected every four years and has 254 members including four representatives of Portuguese citizens living abroad. The President has the power to dissolve it and thus force a general election, but the revised constitution bars him from so doing during the first six months of a new parliament or in the last six months of his own term of office. Abiding by the verdict of the polls, the President appoints the leader of the government. Since 1985 this has been Anibal Cavaco Silva. The Christian Democrats (Centro Democrático Social; CDS), which had previously combined with the Social Democrats and the Monarchist People's Party to form the government, have lost their dominance.

Portugal is divided into 11 historical provinces (*provincias*) and 22 administrative districts (*distritos*), of which 18 are in mainland Portugal and 4 in the Azores and Madeira. The districts are subdivided into urban and rural councils (*concelhos*), made up of *municipios* and *freguesias*. Macao has a special status as an autonomous territory under Portuguese administration.

Portugal is a member of the United Nations, NATO, the Council of Europe, OECD and EFTA, and the European Community.

History

From prehistoric times to the emergence of the national state (*c.* 10000 B.C.–A.D. 1094).

The coastal regions of present-day Portugal were already occupied by man in the *Palaeolithic* period. The nature of the indigenous population was not yet clearly established: the Portuguese were probably, however, a mixture of Ligurians in the S, Iberians in the middle of the country and Celts in the N. Only at a very late period, in the 12th c. A.D., were they able to establish their position as a separate country with a history of its own and to assert their independence of Spain.

10000–5000 B.C. Evidence of *Mesolithic* occupation in large cemeteries (in one of which more than 200 skeletons were found).

2000–1600 Megalithic culture. Monumental cult structures erected in the *Chalcolithic* period (e.g. the well-preserved Dolmen da Barrosa, N of Vila Praia de Âncora).

From 2000 Iberians arrive in the peninsula, probably coming from North Africa.

From 1000 Phoenicians probably trading in amber and copper on the Portuguese coast.

From 700 Celtic peoples settle in Portugal and in subsequent centuries mingle with the Iberians to become *Celtiberians*. Some 30 tribes of **Lusitanians** settle in southern Portugal (the larger part of the country), building strongly fortified hilltop settlements (*castros, citânias*), some of which – e.g. the Citânia de Briteiros and the Castro de Sabroso, near Braga – are still occupied in Roman times.

From 500 Trading posts founded by Carthaginians and Greeks at a few places on the coast.

218–206 During the *Second Punic War* the **Romans** fight mainly on Carthaginian territories in the Iberian peninsula.

197–179 After the bitterly contested *Lusitanian War* Lusitania is incorporated in the Roman province of HISPANIA ULTERIOR.

147–139 The Lusitanians rebel against the Romans under the leadership of *Viriathus* (later honoured in literature and art as a national hero). Their resistance collapses only after the murder of Viriathus near Viseu in 139.

80–72 During the Roman civil war the Lusitanians support Sertorius against Sulla.

71 After the death of Sertorius (72) Pompey quells the Lusitanian rising.

61–45 Caesar finally subdues the province of Hispania Ulterior.

27–15 B.C. Under **Augustus** the peninsula is pacified (*Pax romana*) and Roman authority consolidated by the extensive settlement of colonists. The province of Hispania Ulterior is divided into the two provinces of BAETICA (Andalusia) and LUSITANIA.

Lusitania, a province of only marginal importance within the Roman Empire, comprises the whole of Portugal S of the Douro, together with the Spanish region of Extremadura and province of Salamanca. The region N of the Douro falls within the Roman province of GALLAECIA.

From A.D. 200 The *Christianisation* of Lusitania is believed to have begun at a very early stage, and the establishment of the bishoprics of Braga and Évora are attested in the 3rd c.

From 410 During the *great migrations* of the Germanic peoples the **Suevi** press into northern Gallaecia, the Asdingian **Vandals** into southern Gallaecia and the **Alans** into Lusitania.

About 414–418 The **Visigoths** defeat the Alans and the Vandals, who withdrew to the S of Spain (and later to Africa).

585 The Suevic kingdom is conquered by the Visigoths under their king *Leovigild* (568–586), who unites it with the powerful **Visigothic kingdom of Toledo**.

589 King *Reccared* and the Visigoths adopt the Roman Catholic faith. Soon afterwards the persecution of the Jews begins.

711 After the victory of the **Arabs** (Moors) over the last Visigothic king, *Roderick*, they occupy the whole of the Iberian peninsula except the mountainous regions in the N (713–718).

The territory of present-day Portugal becomes part of the Arab **Emirate** (later Caliphate) **of Córdoba**; although the only evidence of Moorish influence is in the southern part of the country (Algarve).

717 The **Reconquista** (the recovery of Arab-occupied territory) starts out from the Visigothic kingdom of Asturias.

From 722 Asturias recovers the territory between the Minho (Miño) and the Douro (Duero), with the stronghold of Portocale.

1035–65 Under King *Ferdinand I, the Great*, of Castile and León the reconquest of the main part of Portugal begins.

1064 Capture of Coimbra.

1094 King *Alfonso VI* of León (from 1065) and Castile (from 1072), after repeatedly advancing to the Tagus, is thrown back by the Moors at Lisbon.

From the emergence of Portugal as an independent state to the end of the Portuguese empire in the 16th c. (1095–1580). – After establishing its *independence* as a state Portugal achieves territorial *unity* at a very early state – the first European state to do so. In the 15th c. Prince Henry the Navigator initiates the Portuguese voyages of discovery in the Atlantic and along the African coast, and thus lays the foundations of the later Portuguese *empire*.

1095 Alfonso VI of León and Castile establishes the County of PORTUCALIA (named after the town of Portus Cale, now Oporto), between the rivers Douro and Mondego, and grants it as a fief to his son-in-law Count *Henry of Burgundy* (1095–1112), a Capetian.

1109 After the death of Alfonso VI, Henry of Burgundy frees Portugal for a time from its feudal dependence on León-Castile.

From 1112 Henry of Burgundy's widow *Teresa*, illegitimate daughter of Alfonso VI, acting as regent on behalf of her son *Afonso Henriques* (1112–85), takes advantage of the turbulent situation in Castile to gain greater independence for Portucalia.

1139 After a brilliant victory over the Moors at Ourique (Beja district) Afonso Henriques assumes the title of king as *Afonso I* and shakes off Castilian overlordship.

1143 Afonso I submits himself to the feudal superiority of the Pope. Alfonso VII of León-Castile recognises the independence of Portugal under the Burgundian dynasty.

1147 During the *Second Crusade* Afonso captures Lisbon from the Moors. – His successors extend the kingdom by further conquests in the S.

1179 Pope Alexander III recognises Portugal as a **kingdom**.

From 1200 Rapid progress in the development of towns (Lisbon, Oporto, Braga, Coimbra, Lagos, etc.), craft industry and maritime trade (thanks to Portugal's favourable situation on the Atlantic coast).

Circa 1250 With the help of the knightly order of Santiago *Afonso III* (1245–79) conquers the province of Algarve in southern Portugal. The Portuguese *Reconquista* is thus complete, and the frontier with Castile established on the Guadiana.

From 1254 The towns are represented in the Cortes (parliament).

1256 **Lisbon** becomes **capital**, displacing Coimbra.

1261 New taxes to be levied only with the agreement of the Cortes.

1279–1325 King *Dinis*, the "Farmer", promotes agriculture, afforestation, mining, trade and navigation.

1290 The first Portuguese university is founded in Lisbon (later transferred to Coimbra)

1297 The frontier between Portugal and Castile is definitively established.

1308 Treaty of friendship with England.

1355 The murder of Inês de Castro, to whom Pedro, the heir to the throne, is secretly betrothed, leads to a war between Afonso IV and his son, who becomes king as *Pedro I* (1357–67).

1383 In order to prevent Portugal from reverting to Castile after the extinction of the male line, the Cortes elect Pedro's illegitimate son as regent and later king. As *João I* (1383/85–1433) he becomes the founder of the **House of Avis**.

1385 João's decisive victory over Castile at Aljubarrota consolidates the independence of Portugal. His reign sees the beginnings of the colonial expansion in Africa and the voyages of discovery which prepare the way for Portugal's rise as the leading maritime and colonial power in western Europe.

With the rapid expansion of the merchant shipping fleet Lisbon develops into a major commercial city.

1386 The alliance with England is renewed.

1415 Capture of the trading post of Ceuta in Morocco.

The Great Portuguese Voyages of Discovery

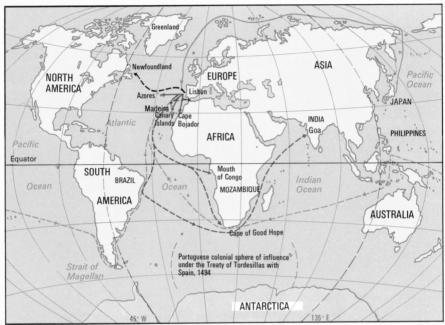

→ School of navigation founded at Sagres by Henry the Navigator (1394–1460); capture of Ceuta, 1415; Madeira, 1420; Azores, 1427; Gil Eanes at Cape Bojador, 1434.

- - - → Sea route to India:
Diogo Cão reaches the mouth of the Congo, 1482.
Bartolomeu Dias rounds the Cape of Good Hope, 1492.
(Columbus, sailing in the Spanish service, reaches the West Indies, 1492.)
Pedro Álvares Cabral reaches Brazil, 1500.
Vasco da Gama sails in 1497 from Belém, near Lisbon, rounds the Cape of Good Hope, calls in at Mozambique in SE Africa (1498) and reaches India. (The poet Luís de Camões describes the voyage in "The Lusiads".)

- - - → Gaspar Corte Real reaches Newfoundland, 1501.

- - - → Fernão de Magalhães (Magellan) sails in the Spanish service from Sanlúcar de Barrameda, crosses the S Atlantic and continues through the Strait of Magellan, at the souther tip of S America, into the Pacific, and is killed in 1521 during a fight with natives on the island of Mactan in the Philippines. One of his ships returns to Europe in 1522 by way of the Indian Ocean and the S Atlantic, thus completing the first circumnavigation of the globe.

→ David Melgueiro sails from Japan in a Dutch ship which makes the passage along the N of Asia and Europe and so to Portugal.

From **1418** João I's younger son **Henry the Navigator** promotes voyages of discovery along the West African coast and in the Atlantic. School of navigation founded at Sagres.

1419–57 Discovery and settlement of Madeira, the Azores and the Cape Verde Islands.
Beginnings of the negro slave trade (abolished by law only in 1850).

Circa 1470 Occupation of the coast of Guinea.

1471 *Afonso V*, the "African" (1438–81), takes Tangier and other coastal settlements.

1482 The Portuguese reach the mouth of the Congo. One member of the expedition is the Nuremberg merchant and cosmographer Martin Behaim, a friend of Columbus and Magalhães (Magellan).

1488 *Bartolomeu Dias* rounds the southern tip of Africa, the Cape of Good Hope.

1494 In the **Treaty of Tordesillas** Portugal and Spain agree on a demarcation line between their colonial spheres of interest in America.

1495–1521 **Manuel I**, *the Fortunate*, establishes Portugal's commercial power, with the foundation of trading posts in the East Indies, Eastern Asia, South Africa and Brazil.
Lisbon becomes a focal point of world trade.

1498 *Vasco da Gama* discovers the sea route to India.

1500 *Pedro Álvares Cabral* reaches Brazil.

From **1510** *Francisco de Almeida* and *Afonso de Albuquerque*, appointed viceroys in India, establish trading posts in India and SE Asia (Goa 1510, Malacca 1511, Ormuz, Diu, etc., 1514) and for a time hold the monopoly of the world spice trade.

Thanks to its worldwide trade Portugal enjoys an upsurge of prosperity during the reign of Manuel I. The contacts with other countries give a powerful stimulus to art and literature. Portugal's greatest poet, *Luís Vaz de Camões* (1524–80), glorifies the great voyages and conquests in his "Lusiads", in which he describes Vasco da Gama's voyage to India.

1518 Capture of Ceylon.

1521–57 Under *João III* there are the first signs of economic decline and the dissolution of the Portuguese colonial empire in the Far East.

1529 Treaty of Saragossa (Zaragoza), a further agreement between Portugal and Spain on the demarcation of their colonial spheres of interest. Taking of the Moluccas.

1536–58 The establishment of the Inquisition in Portugal and the foundation of a Jesuit university at Évora (closed 1759) promote the success of the *Counter-Reformation*.

1557 The Portuguese establish a trading post at Macao, the first European settlement in China.

1578 King *Sebastião I* (1557–78) undertakes a crusade against Morocco but is killed, along with many Spanish nobles, in the battle of Alcácer-Kibir.

1580 Death of King (and Cardinal) *Henrique II* (1578–80), the last ruler of the House of Avis.

From the union with Spain to the fall of the monarchy (1580–1910). – Although Portugal succeeds, with British help, in winning its *independence* it falls increasingly under British influence, politically and economically. In spite of the huge influx of money from its colonial possessions the country grows poorer, since it fails to establish a productive economy of its own. Civil war, political and constitutional conflicts, and financial and economic crises finally lead to the *fall of the monarchy*.

1580 *Philip II of Spain*, a grandson of Manuel I on his mother's side, occupies the whole of Portugal by force and expels the Portuguese claimant to the throne, António.

1581 The Cortes recognise Philip II of Spain as King *Filipe I* of Portugal. The country is ruled by viceroys; the colonies have a separate administration of their own.

1607–30 During the period of Spanish rule Portugal loses part of its colonial empire. The Dutch take the Moluccas (1607), Ceylon (1638), Malacca (1641) and NE Brazil (1630 onwards; recovered 1654).

1640 The heavy taxation imposed to finance Spanish wars, combined with much activity by French agents, leads to a successful *rising in Lisbon*. Its leader, the *Duke of Bragança*, descended from the old royal family through his grandmother, restores the **independent kingdom of Portugal** and is crowned king as *João IV* (1640–56).

1654 A treaty of friendship and commercial co-operation with Britain (ratified in 1656) ensures Portugal's independence of Spain but also guarantees British predominance in Portugal.

1661 Catherine of Braganze (Bragança), sister of King *Afonso VI* (1656–67), marries Charles II of Britain.

1668 Treaty of Lisbon: Spain recognises Portugal's independence.

1701 During the War of the Spanish Succession *Pedro II* (1683–1706) signs a treaty of alliance with France, but under British military pressure is forced to revoke it.

1703 Under pressure from Britain, Austria and Holland, Portugal is compelled to join the anti-French coalition.
The Methuen Treaty, a commercial treaty between Britain and Portugal, provides for the sale of Portuguese wine in exchange for British textiles. The Portuguese woollen industry is thus destroyed.

1750–77 The reign of King *José I* is the great age of enlightened *absolutism*. His chief minister, the *Marquês de* **Pombal** (1699–1782), carries through a series of reforms based on the principles of the Enlightenment and Mercantilism – the encouragement of manufactories and trading companies, the reorganisation of the fiscal and financial systems and of the army, the promulgation of a new code of laws, the secularisation of education, etc.

1755 After the devastating **Lisbon earthquake** (1 November), in which more than 30,000 people are killed, Pombal directs the rebuilding of the shattered capital.

1759 Expulsion of the Jesuits from Portugal and the Portuguese colonies and confiscation of their property.

1772 Refoundation of Coimbra University.

1777 After the death of José I the authoritarian Pombal is compelled to go into exile. During the reign of *Maria I*, the Mad (1777–1816) there is a clerical reaction and the Jesuits return. Most of Pombal's reforms are reversed, and the ideas of the Enlightenment are combated with the help of the Inquisition.

1792 *João VI* becomes Regent in place of his mentally disordered mother. During the *French Revolution* Portugal allies itself with Britain as a member of the anti-French coalition.

1805 João VI refuses to take part in the Continental System or to fight alongside the French against Britain.

1807 Under the Treaty of Fontainebleau (October) between France and Spain Napoleon gains the right to march his troops through Spain. The French General Junot is thus able to occupy the whole of Portugal. The royal family flees to Brazil under the protection of the British fleet (November).

1808–10 **War of National Liberation** against the French.

1808 General Arthur Wellesley (later Duke of Wellington) lands in Portugal with a British force and defeats Junot's French army (August). Under the Convention of Cintra (Sintra) on 30 August the French withdraw from Portugal.

1808–09 Napoleon himself, with 300,000 men, seeks to reconquer Spain and Portugal.

1810 Wellesley repels an attack on Lisbon by Marshal Masséna at Torres Vedras.

1811 After the complete liberation of Portugal, General William Carr Beresford remains in control of the country, the king being still in exile in Brazil.

1817 British forces quell a rising by Portuguese army officers.

1820 *Liberal revolution*, starting in Oporto.

1821 A new liberal constitution (modelled on the Spanish constitution of 1812) is proclaimed by the Cortes, confirming João as king on his return to Lisbon.

1824 With British help João VI defeats a conspiracy, directed against the new liberal measures, which is supported by his wife Carlotta (sister of Ferdinand VII of Spain) and their younger son Dom Miguel. Miguel is banished from Portugal.

1826 Since *Pedro I* of Brazil (Pedro IV of Portugal) is unable to unite his two kingdoms, he abdicates the Portuguese crown after his father's death in favour of his seven-year-old daughter Maria da Glória (Maria II), promulgating a moderate constitution and appointing Miguel as Regent.

1828 After a counter-revolution Miguel revokes the constitution and has himself elected king by the Cortes as *Miguel I*.

1832–34 *Miguelist Wars*. Pedro I of Brazil, having renounced the Brazilian throne in 1831 in favour of his son Pedro II, overthrows the reactionary regime of Miguel I, with British help. Miguel leaves Portugal.

1833–34 Land belonging to the Church is secularised and sold to nobles and wealthy middle-class citizens.

1834 On her father's death *Maria da Glória* becomes queen as Maria II, but is unable to prevent the continuance (until 1847) of party strife between conservatives ("Chartists", after the constitutional charter of 1826) and liberals ("Septembrists", after the constitution of 1822).

1836 The Queen marries *Duke Ferdinand of Saxe-Coburg-Koháry*, who is accorded the title of king in 1837.
After the *September Revolution* the 1822 constitution is reintroduced, but replaced only two years later by a more moderate constitution.

1839–46 *António Bernardo da Costa Cabral* restores the 1826 constitution and rules as a dictator.

1846–47 A popular rising is suppressed with Spanish and British help.

1851 After a *military revolt* Septembrists and some Chartists found a new party of "Regeneration" (Regeneração). They introduce direct elections, municipal self-government and a lower qualification for the vote.

1853 Construction of the first Portuguese railway line.

1853–61 During the reign of *Pedro V* Portugal is ruled by a dictator, *Saldanha* (until 1857). Repeated efforts to put the country's finances on a proper footing are unsuccessful.

Rulers of Portugal

House of Burgundy

Henrique
(Henry of Burgundy)
Count of Portucalia   1093–1112
   After Henry's death his widow
   Teresa acts as Regent during the
   minority of her son Afonso

Afonso Henriques, the Conqueror
King of Portugal   1139–85

Sancho I, the Populator   1185–1211

Afonso II, the Fat   1211–23

Sancho II   1223–45
(deposed 1245, d. 1248)

Afonso III, the Restorer   1245–79
(brother of Snacho II)

Dinis I, the Farmer   1279–1325

Afonso IV, the Brave   1325–57

Pedro I, the Cruel
or the Inexorable   1357–67

Fernando   1367–83

House of Avis

João I, Defender of the Kingdom
(illegitimate son of Pedro I;
Grand Master of the Order of Avis)
Regent   1383–85
King of Portugal   1385–1433

Duarte   1433–38
   His brothers are Pedro (Duke of
   Coimbra), Henrique (Henry the
   Navigator), Fernão (d. in Moorish
   captivity) and João (Grand Master
   of the Order of Santiago)

Afonso V, the African   1438–81

João II, the Perfect Prince   1481–95

Manuel I, the Fortunate   1495–1521

João III, the Pious   1521–57

Sebastião   1557–78
(grandson of João III)

Henrique II   1578–80
(brother of João III;
Cardinal Archbishop of Lisbon)

Spanish Kings of the House of Habsburg

Filipe I
(Philip II of Spain)
King of Portugal   1580–98

Filipe II   1598–1621
(Philip III of Spain)

Filipe III   1621–40
(Philip IV of Spain)

House of Bragança

João IV
(Duke of Bragança)
King of Portugal   1640–56

Afonso VI   1656–67

Pedro II   Regent 1667–83
(brother of Afonso VI)   King 1683–1706

João V, the Magnanimous   1706–50

José   1750–77

Maria I   1777–92
(wife of Pedro III, who d. 1786)

João VI   Prince Regent 1792–1816
   King 1816–26

Pedro IV   1826–28
(Emperor Pedro I of Brazil)

Miguel   1828–34
(brother of Pedro IV)

Maria II   1834–53
(daughter of Pedro IV; m. Duke Ferdinand
of Saxe-Coburg-Koháry 1836)
Duke Ferdinand rules as Regent during
the minority of his son Pedro   1853–55

Pedro V   1855–61

Luís   1861–89

Carlos   1889–1908
(assassinated in Lisbon in 1908
together with his heir Luís Filipe)

Manuel II   1908–10
(second son of Carlos I; leaves
Portugal 1910, d. in exile 1932)

1861–89 During the reign of *Luís I* the country is governed alternately by conservatives and liberals.

1875 Foundation of the first Portuguese Socialist Party.

1876 Foundation of the Republican Party and the Progressist Party.

1889–1908 King *Carlos I* extends Portuguese colonial possessions in Africa but is unable to overcome the country's increasing financial difficulties.

1890 A British ultimatum compels Portugal to abandon a colonial expedition aimed at linking Angola and Mozambique, and thus to give up its claim to the region linking the two colonies.

1891 Unsuccessful Republican revolt.

1892 A declaration of *national bankruptcy* severely damages the prestige of the crown.

1899 In the secret Treaty of Windsor Britain guarantees the security of the Portuguese colonies and receives in return the right to send troops through Portuguese territories in Africa.

1901 Carlos I is compelled to allow British, French and German representatives to participate in the control of the national budget.

1902/1906 Military and naval *risings*, underlining the crisis of the monarchy.

1906–08 The king attempts to rule without Parliament, with his minister *João Franco* exercising dictatorial powers, in order to maintain the monarchy in face of the rising wave of republicanism.

1908 Carlos is assassinated in Lisbon, along with the heir to the throne, *Luís Filipe* (1 February).

1908–10 Carlos I's younger son *Manuel II* is unable to save the monarchy, in spite of an amnesty and minor concessions.

1910 **Revolution** in Lisbon; Manuel is compelled to abdicate and flees to Britain.

From the foundation of the Republic to the present day (since 1910). – After the *abolition of the monarchy* continuing party strife prevents the necessary radical reforms (particularly land reform) from being carried through, and the new form of government is accordingly unable to achieve stability. Although Salazar overcomes the financial crisis, his authoritarian *Fascist regime* and colonial policy lead after the Second World War to the isolation of Portugal in the United Nations and the Western world. – After the *fall of the dictatorship* the development of a new pattern of government is hampered by political, economic and social problems resulting from the country's colonial wars. Conflicts between parties of the left and the right make it difficult to form a stable government.

1910 Proclamation of the **Republic** (5 October). The interim President, *Joaquim Teófilo Fernandes Braga*, forms an anti-clerical government.

1911 Separation of State and Church (20 April). Republican constitution comes into force (11 September); *Manuel d'Arriaga* becomes President (1911–15).
Reforms are carried through, but the urgently necessary land reform is not. Party strife among the Republicans, who are divided among themselves, together with revolutionary unrest, strikes, political corruption, the continuing financial crisis and other problems, prevent the formation of a stable government (between 1911 and 1926, under 8 Presidents, there are no fewer than 44 governments).

1912 The use of troops to repress disturbances in Évora leads to a general strike in Lisbon.

1914–18 During the **First World War** Portugal at first remains neutral.

1916 Portugal comes into the war on the side of the Allies.

1919–20 Social conflicts become more acute (frequent strikes).

1921 Foundation of the Portuguese Communist Party.

1926 After a military rising (28 May) under General *Manuel de Olveira Gomes da Costa* Parliament is dissolved and the constitution suspended. The Communist Party is banned.

1927 Gomes da Costa is displaced by General *António Oscar de Fragosa Carmona*, who represses an uprising in Oporto and Lisbon aimed at returning to a parliamentary regime.

1928 General Carmona is elected President (until 1951). He dissolves the Cortes and puts down several revolts against the **military dictatorship**. The economist *António de Oliveira Salazar* (1889–1970), finance minister in the new government, brings the national finances under control within a year and becomes the dominant political figure in Portugal.

1930 Salazar founds the National Union (União Nacional), the Fascist party of a one-party state.

1932 Salazar becomes prime minister.

1933 The new constitution is ratified by a national referendum (19 March). The Estado Novo (New State) is an authoritarian corporative state on the Fascist model. Strikes are prohibited and the trade unions dissolved.

1936–38 During the *Spanish Civil War* Portugal is officially neutral but favours General Franco by indirect means.

1939 Iberian Pact, a treaty of friendship and non-aggression with Spain (continued for another ten years in 1948). Renewal of the alliance with Britain. Concordat with the Vatican.

1939–45 During the **Second World War** Portugal remains neutral.

1943 Portugal gives Britain bases in the Azores, and breaks off diplomatic relations with Germany (6 May).

1944 Agreement with the United States permitting the establishment of American bases in the Azores.

1948 Portugal receives Marshall Aid and joins the Organisation for European Economic Cooperation (OEEC).

1949 Portugal becomes one of the founder members of the North Atlantic Treaty Organisation (NATO).

1951 Agreement with the United States (later extended several times) allowing the Americans and other NATO countries to establish military bases in the Azores.
On the death of President Carmona *Francisco Higino Craveiro Lopes* becomes President.
The Portuguese colonies are declared to be part of Portugal (overseas provinces).

1955 Portugal becomes a member of the United Nations. Treaty with Brazil providing for mutual consultation.

1958 Admiral *Américo de Deus Rodrigues Tomás* is elected President.

1960 Portugal becomes a member of the Organisation for Economic Cooperation and Development (OECD) and the European Free Trade Area (EFTA).

1961 Annexation by India of the Portuguese enclaves of Goa, Damão and Diu (not recognised by Portugal until 1974). Increasing unrest in Angola and Mozambique. The United Nations repeatedly condemn Portuguese colonial policy.

From 1967 Inflationary trend in Portugal as a result of the country's colonial wars and its entry to EFTA.

1968 Salazar retires on health grounds and is succeeded by *Marcelo José das Neves Álves Caetano*, a lawyer who has long been associated with him in the government. He tries briefly to take a more liberal line but is frustrated by steadily increasing opposition, particularly in the army.

1969 PIDE, the notorious secret police organisation, is renamed the Directorate General of Security (DGS).

1970 The period of compulsory military service is extended from two to three (in case of emergency four) years (5 February). The National Union becomes the National People's Action (Acção Nacional Popular: 21 Februaury).
Portuguese troops in Guinea-Bissau mount an unsuccessful secret raid on neighbouring Conakry the object of which was to overthrow President Sekou Toure.

1972 Treaty between the European Community and EFTA states not willing to join the Community providing for the reduction of duties on industrial products (22 July).

1973 Portuguese Guinea declares its independence as Guinea-Bissau (recognised by Portugal 1974). Earthquake in the Azores.

1974 The dictatorship is overthrown (25 April) in the "Carnation Revolution", an almost bloodless **coup d'état by the MFA** (*Movimento das Forças Armadas*, Armed Forces Movement). Tomás and Caetano are removed from office, and General *António Sebastião Ribeiro de Spínola* (whose book "Portugal and its Future" prepared the ground for the military putsch) becomes President. He is succeeded on 30 September by General *Francisco da Costa Gomes*.
The head of the left-wing democratic government is *Adelino da Palma Carlos*, a lawyer, who gives place on 15 July to Colonel *Vasco dos Santos Gonçalves*, A *Council of State* is established as an instrument of government, and a variety of parties are permitted. The government's domestic plans, which include the nationalisation of banks, insurance corporations and large companies and the expropriation of large estates as the first stage in land reform, give rise to violent political conflicts.
The country's acute economic problems are aggravated by the influx of refugees from the newly independent colonies. The overseas provinces are granted the right of self-determination (August).

1975 Unsuccessful attempt at a putsch by right-wing elements under the leadership of General Spínola (11 March); Spínola emigrates to Brazil. The Council of State is superseded by a **Council of the Revolution**, composed of military leaders, which initiates the nationalisation of the economy and land reform.
The elections for a new legislative assembly show a strong body of opinion in favour of a *pluralist democracy* (25 April). When the Council of the

Revolution takes no account of this there are bitter conflicts between the MFA and members of the socialist and communist parties.
Treaty of friendship with Romania.
The MFA sets up a "Triumvirate" of three military men (F. da Costa Gomes, V. dos Santos Gonçalves and Otelo Saraiva de Carvalho) as the highest political authority (end July). Vice-Admiral *José Baptista Pinheiro de Azevedo* becomes prime minister. Unsuccessful putsch by extreme left-wing paratroopers in which Carvalho plays an ambiguous role (end November); Carvalho is removed from office.
The former colonies of Mozambique, the Cape Verde Islands, the islands of São Tomé and Príncipe, and Angola become independent during 1975.

Mid 1975 to mid 1976 The effects of the world-wide *energy crisis* and economic *recession* aggravate Portugal's internal difficulties: increased inflation (35%), high unemployment (over 15%), a growing stream of refugees from the former colonies (nearly half a million), anti-communist riots in northern Portugal, occupation of large estates in the S by peasants, strikes and unrest in industry, flight of capital. Economic and financial collapse is averted only by financial help from the European Community and credits from Germany and other countries.

1976 The Constitutional Assembly promulgates (although the Social Democratic Center Party votes against it) the new **socialist constitution** establishing a democratic parliamentary Republic (2 April).
The Socialists are victorious in an election on 25 April, but without an absolute majority.
After a rising in Portuguese Timor the territory becomes part of Indonesia (24 June).
General *António Ramalho Eanes* is elected President (26 June) and appoints the Socialist *Mário Soares* as head of a minority government.
Portugal becomes a full member of the Council of Europe (22 September). – Resumption of relations with Angola (30 September).

1977 Foundation of a new party of the right, the Independent Movement for National Reconstruction (MIRN). Devaluation of the escudo (February) – the first devaluation since 1931. Extension of Portuguese territorial waters to 200 miles from the coast (11 March). The government officially applies for membership of the European Community (28 March). Second law on land reform, providing on the one hand for the return of illegally occupied land to the owner and on the other for further collectivisation of large estates (11 August); it gives rise to protests and unrest in the S. Government control of exchange rates is abandoned (August– September). Political and economic problems lead to the fall of the minority Socialist government (8 December).

1978 Coalition government of the Socialists and Social Democratic Center Party led by Mário Soares (12 February).
Portugal receives a large credit from the International Monetary Fund, with conditions as to restriction of imports and consumption; further devaluation of the escudo (May). Ten-year treaty of friendship and cooperation with Spain (5 May). – Fascist organisations banned (16 June).
After the dissolution of the coalition government President Eanes appoints the former minister of industry, *Alfredo Nobre da Costa*, head of a government of technocrats (28 August). After only 17 days Nobre da Costa's non-party government is defeated by the Socialists and Center Democrats

(14 September). The return to private ownership of nationalised land in the Alentejo wheat belt, which gives rise to protests, mainly from the Communists, leads to violent incidents in the agricultural areas (October). Mass demonstrations in Lisbon against the interim government formed by Nobre da Costa (November).

Carlos Mota Pinto, a non-party man with Social Democratic leanings, forms another government of technocrats, which takes the oath on 22 November. The Council of the Revolution rejects the electoral laws passed by Parliament as unconstitutional (14 December). Wave of resignations by Socialists (December).

1979 Mota Pinto demands State aid for the private sector. Country-wide demonstrations and strikes against the amendment of the land reform laws. Foundation of the Socialist Trade Union in Oporto (January). The government's plans for putting the country's finances on to a proper footing meet violent opposition. Mass demonstrations by both the left and the right face the government with another crisis (17 March). Split in the Social Democratic Party over the premature demand for an election by the party leader, Francisco Sá Carneiro. New electoral law passed by Parliament (April).

After no-confidence motions by the Communists and Socialists the Mota Pinto government resigns (6 June). – The parties of the central right – Social Democratic Center Party, Popular Monarchist Party, Social Democratic Party and breakaway Socialists – form a "Democratic Alliance" (5 July).

President Eanes asks *Maria de Lurdes Pintassilgo*, Portuguese representative at UNESCO, to form an interim government (19 July).

A special election on 2 December (in which 87·5% of the electorate vote) gives the conservative Democratic Alliance a clear majority. A liberal Social Democrat, *Francisco Sá Carneiro*, becomes prime minister.

1980 The escudo is revalued upwards by 6% (mid February).

Demonstrations and strikes by agricultural workers in Alentejo (March–April).

The Conservative "Democratic Alliance" also wins the normal elections (5 October). Sá Carneiro again forms the government. A little later he is killed in an aircraft crash (4 December).

General *Ramalho Eanes* is once more elected as President (12 December). Portugal's caretaker government under the acting Prime Minister Amaral resigns (8 December).

1981 The Social Democrat *Francisco Pinto Balsemão* (PSD) becomes prime minister (5 January). Mario Soares is confirmed as General Secretary of

the Socialist Party of Portugal (10 May). For the fourth time in 12 months the Council of the Revolution vetoes as unconstitutional a bill passed by parliament which would open parts of the nationalised sector to private enterprise (July). After disagreements within the PSD Pinto Balsemão resigns (11 August). Three weeks later he again forms a government (1 September). Inflation reaches 21·8% despite government's target of 16% (September).

1982 The year is dominated by the impending revision of the constitution. The Democratic Alliance makes no secret of its intention to rid the constitution of its Marxist traits.

President Eanes lets it be known that he may resign if the revision of the constitution curbs his powers. General 24-hour strike staged by the CGTP in support of the by now customary three-fold demand. On the same day (12 February) Lisbon police stop a car loaded with arms, explosives, a radio transmitter and tape recordings calling for insurrection. Elsewhere in the country police are fired on. There are numerous strikes by different groups of workers.

Parliament's revision of the constitution enters its final stage. Parliament drops any mention of the Council of the Revolution from the revised constitution, which effectively abolishing it. The revised version also deprives the President of the power to choose the armed forces' chiefs of staff. However, through lack of support from the Socialists, the classless society and the transition to socialism remain enshrined as goals in articles 1 and 2 of the constitution, which also retains the principle of the "irreversibility" of the nationalisations.

On the occasion of a pilgrimage to Fatíma Pope John Paul II escapes an attempt on his life (13 May). Changes in the cabinet (5 June).

1983 As a result of the early elections on 25 April the Socialists with 36·3% of all votes emerge as the strongest party. Together with the Social Democrats (PSD) they form a coalition of the left centre led by Prime Minister *Mario Suarez*. On the other hand the parties which have formed the Democratic Alliance coalition since 1979 suffer losses. At the meeting of the Spanish (Gonzalez) and the Portuguese prime ministers in Lisbon entry of both countries into the EEC is one of the topics discussed.

1984 Parliament accepts the abortion bill put forward by the Socialists, the Conservatives voting against (January). At the summit conference of EEC Heads of State at Fontainebleau the conditions for the entry of Spain and Portugal into the EEC are again discussed (June).

1986 Portugal (and Spain) become full members of the E.E.C. Mario Saores elected President.

Art

Until the 12th c. Portugal to a great extent Miguel deshared the destinies of its neighbour Spain. Although this old-established area of settlement, occupied by the stocky and dark-skinned Iberians and later by the mixed race of Celtiberians, lay on the outermost edge of Europe, remote from the rest of the Western world, it was already being visited in antiquity by seafaring Mediterranean peoples. At the mouth of the Tagus the Phoenicians established a staging point on the route to Britain which they called *Alis Ubbo*, later known as Olisipo and now as Lisbon. Thereafter Greeks and Carthaginians also settled at Alis Ubbo.

Under the **Romans** – who took almost 200 years (until A.D. 19) to subdue the Iberians – the Romanisation of the province of Lusitania proceeded relatively slowly (prehistoric and Roman antiquities in the Archaeological and Ethnological Museum at Belém, near Lisbon).
In Lisbon (*Felicitas Iulia*), which during the Roman period was apparently a place of no particular consequence compared with Mérida in Spain, few Roman remains have been preserved (Open-air Archaeological Museum in the church of the Carmo which was destroyed by the 1755 earthquake).
On the highest point in the town of Évora, which seems to have been a flourishing place in Roman times (*Liberalitas Iulia*), are the impressive remains, with 14 Corinthian columns, of a temple of the 2nd or 3rd c. A.D., traditionally ascribed to Diana. The temple, of which the cella is missing, was converted into a fortress in the Middle Ages and restored only in 1870.

During the period of Roman rule numbers of *villae rusticae* – country houses – were built by Roman landowners, the forerunners of the *quintas* which are so characteristic of Portugal. It may be appropriate to mention here one or two of the finest of these quintas, such as the famous Quinta das Lágrimas ("House of Tears") near Coimbra, in the gardens of which Pedro I's tragic bride Inês de Castro was murdered in 1355; the Quinta da Penha Verde, near Sintra, built in the 16th c. by Dom João de Castro, fourth Viceroy of India, with a beautiful park (round chapel in Renaissance style, with 17th c. faience, probably by Miguel de Arruda); and the Oriental-style Quinta de Monserrate, also near Sintra, built in 1856 for Sir Francis Cook, which likewise has beautiful gardens.

The site of *Conimbriga*, a Roman town originally founded in the 2nd c. B.C. and destroyed by the Suevi in A.D. 468, has yielded remains of walls, an aqueduct, fountains and baths with magnificent mosaics (Museu Monográfico, near the excavations). In Coimbra, which took over the name of Conimbriga after its destruction, Roman remains can be seen in the Museu Machado de Castro, housed in the former Bishop's Palace in the Largo da Feira, a picturesque old building originally dating from the Romanesque period (restored 1529).

There are also remains of Roman buildings at Beja (*Pax Iulia*; walls and an arched gateway) and at Milreu in the Algarve (*Ossonoba*, discovered 1529).

Between the 3rd and the 6th c. Portugal was largely Christianised.

The **great migrations** brought Germanic peoples into Portugal – the Vandals, the Suevi and the Visigoths, who originally settled in the Roman provinces as *foederati*. These were allies of Rome, who were granted land in return for the performance of certain services, but who established their own independent states after the fall of the Western Empire. Thus the Suevi established themselves in the N, with Braga as their capital and Oporto as their port, while the southern part of the country was incorporated in the Visigothic kingdom.

After the battle of La Janda in 711 Portugal fell into the hands of the **Moors**, but was of relatively minor importance compared with the Spanish part of the Caliphate. Lisbon, now known as Al Oshbuna or Lashbuna, probably changed relatively little under Moorish rule; the castle, originally built by the Visigoths in the 5th c. (now the Castelo de São Jorge), became the Moorish king's residence. Moorish rule seems to have left a more obvious mark on the Algarve, and certain features (house types, chimneys) are often ascribed to Moorish influence – though it must be said that this has not been established beyond doubt.
Buildings of the migration period and of the Moorish period are few and far

between in Portugal. The chapel of São Frutuoso, near Braga, built by Bishop Frutuoso around 660, is in Byzantine style, on a Greek cross plan; and the churches at Mértola and Lourosa (10th c.) are based on Moorish models.

The **Reconquesta**, the recovery of Christian territory from the Moors, left a distinctive imprint on Portugal. Starting from Asturias in the middle of the 8th c., it moved S stage by stage and was concluded by the occupation of the Algarve in 1249.

With the emergence of a Portuguese national consciousness in the reign of King Afonso Henriques (1139–85) there began also the country's independent artistic development – though political circumstances often involved a close relationship with Spain. Throughout its history Portuguese art reflects a great variety of influences: the old pre-Christian and pagan heritage, the Christian civilisation of Asturias, itself strongly influenced by France, Moorish culture, vigorous folk elements and later reminiscences of the cultures of Portuguese colonial territories in India, Africa and South America.

The art and architecture of the **Romanesque** period in Portugal were influenced both by the magnificent cathedral of Santiago de Compostela in NW Spain and by the architecture of France (particularly Auvergne and Normandy). Evidence of these influences can be seen in the cathedrals (originally designed as defensive structures) of Lisbon, Coimbra, Évora, Oporto and Braga.

Lisbon Cathedral (the Sé: Latin *sedes*, the "seat" of the bishop), the oldest church in the city, is said to have been built by Afonso Henriques in 1147 on the site of an earlier mosque. Over the centuries it was much altered and rebuilt, and its Romanesque lantern tower and Gothic choir were destroyed by the 1755 earthquake; but the Romanesque nave, triforium and aisles still survive. The fortress-like W front dates from 1380. The cloister contains a fine Romanesque wrought-iron screen.

Oporto Cathedral, also built in the 12th c. on the site of a Suevic castle, was originally Gothic but was completely rebuilt in the 17th and 18th c. There are remains of a late Romanesque cloister and its Gothic successor of 1385. The interior is notable for its richly decorated altars (silver Altar of the Sacrament, 1632–72).

The Old Cathedral of Coimbra, built by Afonso Henriques in 1170, has a sumptuously decorated W doorway surmounted by a balcony and a window. The richly decorated N doorway (Porta Especiosa, c. 1530), like the severe 12th c. façade, betrays French influence. The high altar, in Flamboyant style, is of polychrome carved wood (by Oliver of Ghent and John of Ypres, 1503); the Manueline font is by John of Rouen.

Braga Cathedral, begun in 1180, was much altered in later centuries, and the Romanesque cloister (1110) was demolished in the 18th c.

Évora Cathedral, with its beautiful tower and imposing interior, dates mainly from the 13th c. The last of the great Romanesque cathedrals, it already shows strong influence of French Gothic.

The order of **Templars**, which came to Portugal in 1126, began in 1160 to build a new stronghold at Tomar, which in the early 12th c. had stood on the frontier between Christendom and Islam. Little is left of this fortress but a commanding square watch-tower.

After the suppressions of the Templars the castle was taken over by the order of the **Knights of Christ**, which rose to great magnificence, particularly under their Grand Master Henry the Navigator. The wealthiest order in Christendom during the reign of Manuel I (1495–1521), this knightly order became a monastic one in 1523 and was dissolved in 1910.

The Convent-Castle of the Knights of Christ at Tomar is a large complex of buildings ranging in date from the 12th to the 17th c. and in style from Romanesque to Baroque. Following the model of the round church originally built by Constantine the Great over the Holy Sepulchre in Jerusalem, frequently destroyed and regularly rebuilt, the Templars built round Churches of the Holy Sepulchre all over Europe. The Templar church at Tomar is a sixteen-sided structure of Syro-Byzantine type on a centralised plan. It was begun in 1160 with a central octagon, which in the time of Manuel I became the high choir (*coro alto, capela-mór*) of the church of the Knights of Christ, the nave of which was enlarged in Manueline style by Diogo de Arruda after 1510. The magnificent S doorway was the work of João de Castilho (1510). The conventual buildings around the church have a number of interesting cloisters.

The **Cistercians**, who, like the Templars, were summoned to Portugal by Afonso Henriques, built a series of abbey churches which mark the final establishment of the **Gothic** style in Portugal. Gothic architecture was strongly influenced by France; but during the 13th and 14th c. different European countries evolved their own distinctive variants of the style. The cathedral at Évora, consecrated in 1204, already shows indications of the transition to a somewhat severe form of Gothic in Portugal.

The Franciscan convent at Santarém, completed in 1240 and now unfortunately in a state of considerable dilapidation, has a fine cloister of the 13th–15th c. with pointed arches and charming twin columns.

The Cistercian abbey of Alcobaça, founded by Afonso Henriques in 1153, was a daughter house of Clairvaux in Burgundy and is built on the same plan as Clairvaux. The church was consecrated in 1253 but the building of the abbey continued into the 14th c. Much rebuilding was required to make good the devastation caused by the 1755 earthquake, flooding and Napoleon's troops. The church – an austere hall-church in early Gothic style with pointed vaulting – contains the tombs of Pedro I and his beloved Inês de Castro, with a profusion of figural decoration along the sides and recumbent figures of Pedro and Inês, lying with their feet towards one another so that they would see one another at once on the day of resurrection (14th c.). Other notable features in the church are a 17th c. terracotta group depicting the death of St Bernard and two fine Renaissance doors by João de Castilho.

On the N side of the church is the impressive two-storey Claustro do Silêncio (or Claustro de Dom Dinis), a jewel of Cistercian Gothic built in 1311 (upper storey 16th c.), with pointed vaulting and triple windows, separated by twin colonettes and surmounted by rosettes, opening into the central garden. The two-storey hexagonal fountain-house has 16th c. relief decoration.

Notable, too, are the large kitchen of the abbey with its high fireplace, the three-aisled refectory, the dorter and the chapterhouse.

The octagonal Dominican church (consecrated 1267) at Elvas, with an azulejo-faced dome supported on columns, is the first master-work of Gothic architecture in Portugal. With its wide aisles and five chapels it is a marvel of simplicity and restrained elegance of proportion.

The steadily increasing refinement of Portuguese Gothic, originally somewhat severe, can be observed in the romantic remains of the convent of Santa Clara-a-Velha in Coimbra (1286), now partly silted up by the flooding of the River Mondego (W wall with fine rose window, Renaissance chapels).

In addition to the beautiful Gothic *cloisters* already referred to, which rank among the finest achievements of Gothic architecture in Portugal, with their two tiers of galleries, their sturdy pillars and their graceful arches, mention should also be made of the cloister of Lisbon Cathedral.

During this period King Dinis (1279–1325) caused a series of mighty *fortresses* to be built along the frontiers of his kingdom – the Torre de Menagem at Bragança, the castle of Leiria (originally founded by Afonso Henriques in 1135 and enlarged by Dinis; Gothic chapel attributed to Master Huguet of Batalha) and the castle at Beja.

The finest example of 14th c. Gothic architecture in Portugal is the church of Batalha Abbey (1388–1402), built to commemorate the decisive Portuguese victory over Castile at Aljubarrota in 1385. One of the great achievements of Christian architecture, the church is now a Portuguese national shrine.

The architects involved in building the Batalha church were Afonso Domingues (d. before 1402), Master Huguet, probably a Frenchman (attested until 1438), Martin Vásques (d. before 1448), Fernão d'Évora (d. 1477) and the famous João de Castilho (d. before 1553).

The interior of the church, with fine stained glass (particularly in the choir) and massive piers, is of impressive effect.

The square Founder's Chapel contains a number of notable tombs – the sarcophagus, supported on lions, of João I (d. 1433) and his English queen, Philippa of Lancaster, and the monuments of the Infante Fernardo (Calderón's "Steadfast Prince") and Henry the Navigator (d. 1460). The W front of the church with its sculptural decoration and the richly articulated S side are seen to particular effect, due to the open location of the church.

Adjoining the church are three cloisters – the Claustro de João III (destroyed in 1811), the 15th c. Claustro de Dom Afonso V with its simple lines and the Claustro Real, a truly royal cloister laid out around a garden-like court which is a masterpiece and a perfect exemplar of Portuguese Gothic, with arched galleries which range from the simplest forms to fantastic riots of Manueline ornament and offer charming glimpses of the fountain-house. – On the E side of the cloister is the chapterhouse, with pointed vaulting.

At the E end of the church are the Capelas Imperfeitas (Unfinished Chapels)., with seven funerary chapels enclosing a central octagon; the tombs include those of King Duarte I and his wife Eleanor of Aragon.

The period of prosperity and cultural flowering in the reign of Manuel I (1495–1521) led to the emergence of a

Manueline style (Belém)

"Batalha school" and the development of a distinctively Portuguese version of late Gothic. This **Manueline style** incorporates Early Renaissance features, elements taken over from the Moorish Mudéjar style and Oriental and Indian influences. It is notable for its delight in ornament, which – as in the Plateresque style of Spain – often includes naturalistic details, with a marked preference for the world of the sea and seafaring (e.g. twisted ropes, knots, shells, coral, etc.), symbolising the territories which Portugal had won under the leadership of Henry the Navigator.

The most striking example of the Manueline style is the Hieronymite convent at Belém (now a suburb of Lisbon), which miraculously survived the 1755 earthquake unscathed. Designed by an architect named at Boytac (Boitac, Boytaca, Boutaca, etc.), probably a Frenchman, it was begun in 1502.

The S doorway of the church has a profusion of sculptural decoration expressing the new power and wealth of Portugal. The W doorway, strongly reminiscent of a doorway at Champmol, near Dijon (Burgundy), was the work of Nicolas Chanterene. The interior of the church, of the type known as *igrejas salões* (saloon churches), is notable for its width and fine proportions and for the delicately carved decoration of the piers. The church contains the sarcophagus of Vasco da Gama and the cenotaph (empty tomb) of the poet Luís de Camões.

Adjoining the church is a magnificent two-storey cloister. Both the church and the cloister were completed by João de Castilho, the great master of the Manueline style.

Another splendid Manueline building is the Tower of Belém (Torre de Belém) commanding the Tagus estuary, built between 1515 and 1521 by Francisco de Arruda, brother of the famous architect Diogo de Arruda who worked at Tomar. With its flat domes, elegant loggias, Arab-style twin windows and intricate stone tracery the Tower is of strikingly Arab and Moorish style.

Other fine examples of the Manueline style at Batalha and Tomar have already been mentioned. Mention should also be made of the famous Manueline window of the old chapterhouse at Tomar (by Diogo de Arruda) with its striking and very typical ornament, here carried to excess.

Sintra, once the summer residence of the Portuguese kings, has three castles – the Castelo dos Mouros, the old Moorish castle (7th–8th c., much altered in later periods), the Palácio da Pena (19th c.) and the Paço Real or Royal Palace (14th–15th/16th c.), on the foundations of an earlier Moorish castle; it is built in a Manueline style which shows clear Mudéjar influence.

The **Mudéjar style** is the particular architectural and decorative style practised by the Moors who were allowed to

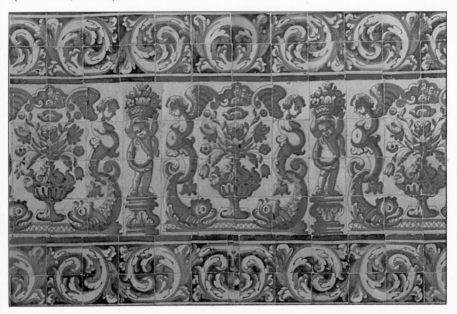

Azulejos – the favourite Portuguese form of architectural decoration

Everywhere in Portugal – in Madeira and the Azores as well as on the mainland – practically every church, chapel and convent, most palaces and country houses and the walls of countless other buildings are decorated with the glazed ornamental tiles known as **azulejos** (from *azul*, "blue").

Azulejos were originally imported into Portugal in the early 16th c. from Spain, where they were made by Moorish craftsmen in blue and other ground colours, with geometric patterns in relief. After the Moors were expelled from Spain towards the end of the 16th c. and Moorish-made tiles were no longer available numbers of azulejo manufactories were established in Portugal (particularly in Lisbon, Oporto and Coimbra), producing Portuguese tiles with new decorative motifs. These tiles, however, were no longer made in relief patterns but were flat, in the manner of Italian and Flemish majolica. They were now given a white tin glaze on which the designs were painted in metallic pigments.
What is probably the oldest tile picture in Portugal, dating from 1565, is to be seen in the Quinta de Bacalhoa, to the W of Setúbal.

Characteristic of the 17th c. are the "tile tapestries" (*tapetes*), with a great variety of patterns in blue, white and yellow. – Mass production of azulejos began with the establishment by King José I in 1767 of the Royal Manufactory (Real Fábrica do Rato) at Lisbon. Every conceivable surface – the walls of churches, staircases, fountains, benches, the exterior and interior walls of palaces, kitchens, etc. – was now covered with tiles.

In the early 19th c., when the court fled to Brazil and the country was convulsed by civil war, the production of azulejos ceased almost completely, but in the middle of the century they enjoyed a revival of popularity. Following the Brazilian model, tiles now began to be used for the decoration, both externally and internally, of ordinary middle-class houses and commercial, municipal and other public buildings throughout the country. – There was a final flowering of the art of the azulejo at the turn of the 19th c.

Tile-clad buildings have the advantage over stone or plaster surfaces that they retain a fresh, trim appearance – although the more recent azulejos, mass-produced in standard designs, are seldom of high artistic quality.

Present-day azulejo manufactories – notably three large firms in Lisbon – concentrate mainly on reproductions of old designs and export most of their output (mainly to the United States, Germany and Holland).

A good impression of the range and variety of Portuguese azulejos is provided by the Azulejo Museum in the Madre de Deus convent, the cloisters of the old Augustinian house of São Vicente de Fora and the Fronteira Palace, all in Lisbon.

stay on after the Reconquest and by Christians imitating them. It is basically a late Gothic style incorporating Moorish elements, and often with Manueline features. Particular marks of Moorish influence are the beautiful dark-coloured coffered ceilings and above all the use of **azulejos**, one of the most characteristic features of Portuguese art (see previous page).

Little *sculpture* of the Romanesque period has been preserved in Portugal, and much, even of the monumental sculpture, has been lost. The only item calling for mention is the tomb of Egas Moniz (1144) in the Romanesque church of the Benedictine monastery at Paço de Sousa near Oporto. The area in northern Portugal between Oporto and Vila Real is rich in Romanesque and Romanesque/Gothic churches, including those at Bustelo, Meinedo, Vila Boa de Quires, Cabeça Santa, Boelhe, Lufrei, Freixo de Baixo, Mancelos, Aboadela and Celorico de Basto.

Cistercian Gothic paid little attention to sculpture: only funerary sculpture flourished. Notable among tombs of the 14th c. are that of Archbishop Gonçalo Pereira (1336) in Braga Cathedral and the tombs of Pedro I and Inês de Castro at Alcobaça which have already been referred to. For the 15th c. there are the tombs of João I and Philippa of Lancaster in the Founder's Chapel at Batalha.

The Manueline style laid great stress on architectural sculpture, and Coimbra became the place of origin of two schools of sculpture, one of which, stimulated by influence from Rouen, played an important part in bringing the **Renaissance** to Portugal.

Nicolas Chanterene was responsible for the N doorway of the abbey church at Belém and for the tombs of Afonso Henriques and his son Sancho I in the church of the Santa Cruz convent at Coimbra, while to John of Rouen (João de Ruão) is attributed the Porta Especiosa of the Old Cathedral, Coimbra. Other notable foreign sculptors working in Portugal were Loguin and Oliver of Ghent (polychrome wood sculpture in the dome of the Rotunda at Tomar).

The other, more "national", school continued to work in the traditional style; a leading member of the school was Diogo Pires the Younger. Fine work was still produced in the field of funerary sculpture (tomb monuments), while the *goldsmith's art* which had long flourished in Portugal created some of its finest achievements.

Portugal's political and economic decline, beginning at the end of the heroic age after the disastrous Moroccan campaign of 1580, also had its effect on the country's artistic development.

The choir of the monastic church at Belém betrays the influence of the High Renaissance (marble choir-stalls; royal tombs, supported on marble elephants). But on the whole the Renaissance – its influence postponed and weakened by the great flowering of the Manueline style – never really established itself in Portugal, in spite of the country's intensive cultural and economic contacts with Italy, but remained a phenomenon of merely marginal importance.

An example of *Late Renaissance* architecture, though much influenced by the Manueline style, is the Claustro dos Filipes, the main cloister of the Convent-Castle of Tomar. This was begun by João de Castilho, but work was suspended after his death in 1551, and when it was resumed in 1562 the neo-classical Palladian style had come into fashion. The new architects were either trained in Italy,

---

Pelourinhos ("Pillories")

Between the 12th and the 18th c. the stone columns known as *pelourinhos* or pillories were erected in towns and villages all over Portugal. They were not, however, primarily designed for the punishment of thieves and other criminals but were emblems of municipal or feudal authority (*pelouro*=local authority).

This function explains both the form of the pelourinhos, which are often elaborately decorated, and the choice of site, usually near areas of secular or ecclesiastical authority such as town halls and bishop's palaces.

The pelourinhos erected in the 16th c. have the sumptuous decoration of the Manueline style. Columns of this type are particularly numerous, reflecting the large numbers of communities which were granted charters of privileges by Manuel I.

The shaft of the column, richly decorated, may be cylindrical, conical, prismatic or spiral in form; occasionally it may resemble an obelisk. The summit also has sculptural decoration, often including the sword of justice as a symbol of legal jurisdiction.

like Diogo de Torralva, or were themselves Italian, like Filippo Terzi.

Filippo Terzi built the church of São Roque in Lisbon (façade rebuilt after the 1755 earthquake), a fine example of the Jesuit style, with an impressive interior (trompe-l'œil painting). The church contains a masterpiece of the most sumptuous Italian **Baroque** in the form of the Chapel of St John the Baptist, originally built in Rome in 1742, then dismantled and re-erected in São Roque in the reign of João V. – The church of São Vicente de Fora in Lisbon (the tower of which collapsed in the 1755 earthquake) was also built by Terzi.

The influence of foreign artists remained considerable after the Portuguese revival (under Portuguese kings of the House of Bragança from 1640): the native power of artistic creation appeared to be exhausted.

The development of Portuguese *painting* followed a roughly parallel course to that of Spain. The first individual artistic personality emerged in *Nuno* **Gonçalves** (active between 1450 and 1480), whose principal work is the famous altarpiece, the "Adoration of St Vincent", a polyptych with numerous figures which clearly shows the influence of Flemish models (Museu Nacional de Arte Antiga, Lisbon). There followed a flowering of late medieval painting which lasted until the middle of the 16th c., its finest achievements being in the field of portraiture.
In addition to Gonçalves, leading figures of this period included *Jorge Afonso* (d. after 1540) who had a studio in Lisbon, *Guilherme de Belles, João Mestre* (d. 1528), *Luís de Velasco, António Taca* and

Vasco Fernandes (b. about 1542), known as **Grão Vasco**, who worked in Viseu (works in Museu Grão Vasco, Viseu).

During the reign of João III the Dutch "Romanist" school exerted still stronger influence on Portuguese painters including *Gregório Lopes* (d. 1550: "Salome", "St Augustine"), but particularly on *Cristóvão* **de Figueiredo** (attested between 1515 and 1540: retable on high altar of Santa Cruz church, Coimbra) and the *Master of Santa Auta* ("Martyrdom of the 11,000 Virgins", Museu Nacional de Arte Antiga, Lisbon).

The next generation of painters – represented, for example, by *Cristóvão Lopes* (1516–1606) – show Italian influence, now coming direct and no longer through Flemish intermediaries. The old tradition of portrait-painting, a notable practitioner of which was *Cristóvão de Morais*, declined in importance with the departure of *A. Sanchez Coelho* (1513–90) for the Spanish court.

During the Baroque period painting was of subordinate importance, being used mainly for the decoration of palaces and the vaulting of churches. Painters of this period include *Francisco Vieira Lusitano* (1699–1783), the fresco-painter *Domingos António de Sequeira* (1769–1837), *Francisco Portuense* (1765–1805) and *Pedro Carvalho Alexandrino* (1730–1810).

In the field of Baroque *architecture* a leading place is occupied by the massive complex at Mafra, planned on the model of the Spanish Escorial to include a royal palace, a church and a monastery in a unified group and built between 1717 and 1770. This enormous building, designed by two German architects, Johann Friedrich Ludwig and his son Johann Peter Ludwig, broke away from the severity of Spanish Baroque with its profusion of decoration and its chinoiserie and influenced a whole architectural generation in the late Baroque and **Rococo** periods, which became steadily more luxuriant and fantastic. At the same time there was a great flowering of azulejos.

Foreign architects also worked in Oporto, where an Italian, Nicolò Mazzoni, built the church of the Clérigos with its fine Capela-mór and famous tower (1732–48).

**Talhas douradas
(gilded wood sculpture)**

In the early Baroque period there first appears in Portugal an ornate form of decorative art which was to achieve its finest flowering here, though it was also practised in Spain and other countries. This was the wood sculpture covered with gold leaf known as *talhas douradas*, predominantly used in religious art.

In many 18th c. churches in Portugal altars, walls, recesses, domes and ceilings were covered either in whole or in part with carving of this kind, foliage and arabesques combining with figures in rich decorative patterns.

The French architect J. B. Robillon completed the royal palace at Queluz, which had been begun in 1758 by *Mateus Vicente* (1747–86) on the model of Versailles – a likeness which is enhanced by the park, laid out in the style of Le Nôtre. The interior is of great magnificence, the Throne Room and the Hall of the Ambassadors being particularly fine.

The great earthquake on All Saints Day in 1755, which laid Lisbon in ruins and spread alarm throughout Europe, offered a unique opportunity for architects and town planners, which José I's chief minister the *Marquês de* **Pombal**, ruling in the spirit of enlightened absolutism, was quick to grasp. Rebuilt under the direction of *Eugénio dos Santos*, Lisbon became one of the handsomest capitals in Europe.

The new town thus created (though the wide Avenida da Liberdade and the Praça do Marquês de Pombal, with the huge monument to Pombal, were not completed until the end of the 19th c.) is laid out on spacious lines. Streets intersect at right angles and there are three superb squares: the Praça da Figueira, the even larger Praça de Dom Pedro IV (Rossio) and the Praça do Comércio (Terreiro do Paça), one of the most famous squares in the world, with an equestrian statue of José I (by Joaquim Machado de Castro, 1755).

The uniform layout of the square and its three ranges of arcaded buildings with coloured façades contrast with the surprising width of the fourth side, and, attractively with its marble steps leading down to the Tagus, is reminiscent of St Mark's Square in Venice.

The *sculpture* of the Baroque period – affected, like architecture and painting, by Portugal's cultural decline in the 17th c. – can claim few artists of any importance apart from *Joaquim Machado de Castro* (1736–1828), whose vigorous work can be seen on the sumptuous façade of the late Baroque Basilica da Estrêla in Lisbon, built in the Roman style at the end of the 18th c.

After the catastrophe of the 1775 earthquake there was a general reaction against the decorative excesses of Baroque and Rococo, and a more sober **neoclassicism** came into vogue. In Lisbon work began in 1802 on the Palácio da Ajuda, which remained unfinished and has been completed only in recent years as a convention complex, and the Teatro Nacional de Dona Maria II was built on the Rossio in 1846. – In Oporto the church of the Third Order of St Francis was built (not to be confused with the adjoining church of São Francisco, originally Gothic, with a Renaissance doorway altered in the Baroque period).

Although the neo-classical school of architecture long remained dominant, the school known as **Historicism**, with its romantic leanings towards the past, became established in Portugal, as elsewhere in Europe, in the second half of the 19th c. French influence can be detected, but so, too, can influences from Britain and Germany, as in the Palácio da Pena at Sintra (1840–50), built for Ferdinand of Saxe-Coburg-Koháry by Baron Eschwege in the style of a medieval castle (borrowing some ideas from the extraordinary castles built for King Ludwig II of Bavaria). This fantastic mixture of styles – Arab, Gothic, Manueline, Renaissance, Baroque – has a curious charm. A striking and typical feature is the monstrous figure above the main entrance, a riot of fancy which is half man, half fish or tree.

Other examples of Historicist architecture are the Moorish-style bullring in the Campo Pequeno in Lisbon (1892) and the Palace Hotel in the beautiful Buçaco Forest (now a national park, with many rare trees), a neo-Manueline structure built at the end of the 19th c. as a royal summer residence.

Portugal is especially rich in fine *parks* and *gardens*, illustrating the development of landscape architecture from the Moorish style by way of the formal gardens of the Baroque period to the more natural English style.

Modern art and architecture were slow to establish themselves in Portugal. Gustave Eiffel, best known for the Eiffel Tower in Paris, built the Ponte de Dom Luís I in Oporto, the famous two-storey bridge which spans the Douro at an impressive height (1877–78), and was also responsible for the Elevador de Santa Justa, the lift which links the upper and lower towns of Lisbon. About 1940 the massive complex of the University City (Cidade Universitária) was built in

Lisbon. The monumental style of an authoritarian regime found expression in the huge figure of Christ the King (1959) on the left bank of the Tagus near Lisbon and the 52 m/170 ft high Monument of the Discoveries (Padrão dos Descobrimentos, 1960) on the banks of the Tagus at Belém. The Ponte do 25 de Abril (originally Ponte Salazar, 1966), a suspension bridge 2227 m/2436 yd long which provides a rapid link between Lisbon and southern Portugal, is an impressive technological achievement.

In *painting*, developments in the 19th c. followed the general European pattern. Notable figures during this period were the portrait-painter *Miguel Lupi* (1826–83), *Tomás de Anunciação* (1818–79) and the landscapist *António Carvalho da Silva* (1850–93).

The "Grupo de Leão", established in 1881, had close affinities with Impressionism. The portraitist and fresco-painter *Columbano* (1867–1929) remained within the romantic tradition. Other schools also had their adherents, including Fauvism, Cubism – a leading representative of which was *Amadeu de Souza Cardoso* (1887–1918) – and a rather strident revolutionary Naturalism.

Between the two world wars the Futurist *Almada Negreiros* gained a considerable reputation with his tapestries and frescoes.

The Salazar regime discouraged artists with unduly progressive leanings, and only after the "Carnation Revolution" of 1974 did Portuguese art fall into line with the international movements of the day. A great reputation is enjoyed by the Franco-Portuguese woman painter *Maria Helena Vieira da Silva* (b. 1908). *Lourdés Castro* (b. 1930 in Funchal, Madeira) is a sculptress whose figures are mounted on coloured plastic panels.

House Types in Rural Portugal

Situated as it is on the western margin of Europe, exposed to influences from other countries only on the N and E, Portugal has developed its own distinctive house types, particularly in rural areas. As in many southern countries, building is mostly in stone. The peasants' houses and farmhouses usually have no more than two storeys.

In Minho the two-storey house type is common, with stables and working areas on the lower floor and living accommodation on the upper storey, usually opening on to a balcony and reached by an external stair. Characteristic features of this northern region are the *espigueiros*, small granaries or storehouses built on piles and constructed either of granite or timber.

Farther S, where Moorish influence can be detected, the house fronts are mostly whitewashed, with the doors and window-frames painted in vivid colours. Depending on the local topography, single-storey farmhouses become more common. The doors and windows are smaller in order to keep out the heat of summer.

Since the winters become more severe with increasing distance from the moderating influence of the Atlantic, open fires are more usual in the inland regions and the chimney becomes a prominent feature of the house.

In the deep south of the country, the Algarve, the single-storey house is predominant, frequently in the shape of a cube. Flat roofs are sometimes used to collect rainwater, which is then stored in a cistern.

Particularly characteristic of the Algarve are the richly decorated chimneys with their lantern-like tops.

Literature

The development of literature in Portugal went in step with the formation of the Portuguese nation-state and the sense of national and linguistic identity in the Portuguese people. Throughout this period of development and down to modern times the characteristic features of Portuguese literature have been a rather melancholy sensibility, marked national feeling and a leaning towards criticism of the society of the day; and this Portuguese sensibility is underlined by the soft and gentle tonal colouring of the language.

The earliest *courtly lyric poetry*, found in the neighbouring region of Galicia as well as in Portugal, had its leading practitioners in King Alfonso X of Castile (d. 1284) and Kings *Sancho I* (1185–1211) and *Dinis I* (1279–1325) of Portugal. This poetry consists exclusively of songs in Provençal style, some 2000 of which –

love songs (*cantigas de amor*), women's songs (*cantigas de amigo*) and satirical songs (*cantigas de maldizer*) – are preserved in three collections, the "Cancioneiro da Ajuda", the "Cancioneiro da Vaticana" and the "Cancioneiro Colocci-Brancuti".

In the 14th c. this poetry rapidly declined in quality and the first cautious beginnings of prose writing appeared, at first taking the form of works written for a practical purpose: genealogical registers recording the lineage of noble families (*livros de linhagem*) and dry *chronicles* of modest literary pretension but great documentary value. During this period translations of religious and edifying works from Latin, French and Spanish were also produced. Then towards the end of the century lyric poetry enjoyed an astonishing renaissance under the influence of the Galician troubadour *Macias o Enamorado* ("Macias the Enamoured").

The beginning of the 15th c. brought a temporary decline in the literary use of Portuguese, and Castilian usage increasingly asserted itself in the written language. The work of the "palace poets" (*poetas palacianos*) who now came into fashion was collected by *Garcia de Resende* in his "Cancioneiro geral".

With the Renaissance and the great voyages of discovery by Portuguese navigators the ideas of humanism gained entry to the court; and literature, particularly prose writing, enjoyed generous royal patronage, prominent in this respect being King *Duarte I* (1391–1438) and his brother *Dom Pedro* (1392–1449) – themselves the authors of treatises on moral philosophy of no great literary merit. *Historical writing* was institutionalised by the creation of the post of historiographer royal, and *Fernão Lopes* (*c.* 1384–*c.* 1460), *Gomes Eanes de Zurara* (*c.* 1410–73), *Rui de Pina* (*c.* 1440–*c.* 1522) and *João de Barros* (*c.* 1496–1570) wrote works showing a very modern objectivity. Unofficial chronicles of a more speculative and picturesque character were written by *Damião de Góis* (1502–74), *Caspar Correia* (*c.* 1495–*c.* 1565), *Fernão Lopes de Castanheda* (*c.* 1500–59) and *Fernão Mendes Pinto* (*c.* 1510–*c.* 1583).

Other genres which now established themselves were the bucolic poems of *Bernardim Ribeiro* (1482–1552;

"Saudades") and *Cristóvão Falcão*, whose existence in the first half of the 16th c. is still the subject of dispute, and the *pastoral plays* of *Gil* **Vicente** (*c.* 1465–*c.* 1540), who thus introduced the drama to the court and into Portuguese literature, always taking his subjects from popular life. During this period, too, *Francisco Sá de Miranda* (*c.* 1481–1558) introduced Italian stylistic features in his sonnets, *cançones* and comedies; and while these, like the sensitive lyric poetry of *António Ferreira* (1528–69) and *Diogo Bernardes* (1530–1600), enjoyed great success they did not displace the more popularly written works of other contemporaries such as *Gonçalo Eanes Bandarra*.

In the second half of the 16th c. Portuguese literature gained international status with the appearance of the country's greatest writer, *Luís Vaz de* **Camões** (b. late 1524 or early 1525, d. 1580). After a life of adventure and many vicissitudes he glorified the achievements of the Portuguese people in the national epic "Os Lusiadas" ("The Lusiads", 1572; after Lusus, the legendary ancestor of the Portuguese), which exerted a powerful influence on the Portuguese literature of the day and later periods. Camões' wide-ranging and sensitive work, often reflecting his own experiences, attracted numerous imitators, who treated similar national themes with markedly inferior talent, setting the pattern for Portuguese literature until the beginning of the 17th c.

The period of decline during the Baroque age in the 17th c. brought a return to the old forms of bucolic poetry and religious and moralising prose. The personal union with Spain, seen by the Portuguese as the imposition of foreign rule, led to an increase in the cultural and linguistic influence of Castile and a decline in the writing of Portuguese. Only *Francisco Rodrigues* **Lobo** (1580–1622), with his idyllic pastoral poems, *Francisco Manuel de Melo* (1608–66), *Manuel de Sousa Coutinho*, known as **Frei Luís de Sousa** (*c.* 1555–1632), and the Jesuit preacher *António de Vieira* (1608–97) achieved reputations which outlasted their own day.

At the turn of the 17th c. the Enlightenment, coming from France, began to make headway in Portugal, where it took on a curiously melancholy note. The 18th c.

was the heyday of various literary societies committed to the renewal of literature, the most notable being the "Arcádia Lusitana" (1757–74) and the "Nova Arcádia" (1790–94), with such figures as *Francisco Manuel do Nascimento* (1734–1819), a committed opponent of rhyme in poetry, *António Correia* (1724–72), *José Agostinho Macedo* (1761–1831) and *Manuel Maria Barbosa do* **Bocage** (1765–1805). All these writers sought to renew Portuguese drama in the classical style.

The prose writing of the later 18th c. consisted mainly of reports, letters and didactic works by such writers as the diplomat *Francisco Xavier de Oliveira* (1702–82), *António da Costa* (d. 1780), *António Nunes* (d. 1783) and *Luís António Verney* (1718–92). – *António José da Silva* (1705–39) wrote liberettos for puppet operas on popular themes.

After 1825 the *Romantic movement*, coming from Germany, France and Britain, began to make rapid headway in Portugal. Fostered and emotionally reinforced by the serious and sentimental cast of mind of the Portuguese, it soon led to a new flowering of the national literature.

The first Portuguese Romantics and the most brilliant representatives of the movement were *João Baptista de Silva Leitão de* **Almeida Garrett** (1799–1854), author of romances, epics and lyrical dramas, and *Alexandre* **Herculano** *de Carvalho Araújo* (1810–77), a historian who also wrote historical novels. Historical novels and novels of manners were written by *Camilo Castelo Branco* (Visconde de Correia Botelho, 1825–90), *Augusto Rebelo da Silva*, *Pinheiro Chagas* and others, novels of country life and love by *Júlio Dinis* (pseudonym of Joaquim Guilherme Gomes, 1839–71).

The excesses of Romanticism were countered from 1865 onwards by the "Coimbra school", the leader of which was *João de Deus Nogueira Ramos* (1830–96). Towards the end of the century this developed into a *Realist* school, with such writers as *Antero de Quental* (1842–91), *José Maria Eça de Queirós* (1845–1900) and *Teófilo Braga* (1843–1924).

The first decades of the 20th c. were notable for their lyric poetry. *Symbolism*, largely concerned with patriotic themes, was represented by *António Nobre* (1867–1900), *Camilo Pessanha* (1867–1926), *Eugénio de Castro e Almeida* (1869–1944) and *Mário de Sá-Carneiro* (1890–1916), who founded the review "Orpheu" in 1915. The "Saudosismo" of *Teixeira de Pascoaes* (1877–1952) took on an almost messianic tone.

The literary review "Águia", published between 1910 and 1932, provided a forum for the writers of the period.

One of the major lyric poets of recent times was *Fernando António Nogueira* **Pessoa** (1888–1935), who grew up in South Africa and wrote some of his work in English. Like his contemporaries he had a strong sense of mission; and with his linguistic virtuosity and profundity of content he exerted an influence which extended beyond the bounds of Portugal.

Together with *José Régio* (pseudonym of José Maria dos Reis Pereira, 1901–69) Pessoa introduced the *modern movement* in Portuguese literature, which found a mouthpiece in the review "Presença" (1927–40).

Other representatives of this trend are *Vitorino Nemésio* (Vitorino Nemésio Mendes Pinheiro da Silva, b. 1901), *José Sobral Almada-Negreiros* (b. 1893) and *Miguel Torga* (pseudonym of Adolfo Correia da Rocha, b. 1907).

In more recent times there has been a trend, in both poetry and prose, towards neo-realism and social criticism. Among notable lyric poets are *José Gomes Ferreira* (b. 1900), *Eugénio de Andrade* (b. 1923) and *Alberto de Lacerda* (b. 1928); among novelists and short story writers *Raul Brandão* (1867–1930), *Aquilino Ribeiro* (1885–1963), *José Maria Ferreira de Castro* (b. 1898), *António Álves Redol* (1901–69), *Fernando Namora* (b. 1919) and *Carlos de Oliveira* (b. 1921).

Since the revolution of 1974, which put an end to a long period of authoritarian government, liberal and more particularly socialist ideas have increasingly found expression in literature: thus *Manuel Alegre* (b. 1936), while actively engaged in politics, has also made a name for himself as a writer.

Until the end of the 18th c. BRAZILIAN LITERATURE was a mere offshoot of Portuguese literature and wholly under the influence of mainland Portugal. At the turn of the century there were signs of a distinctively Brazilian approach, particularly in religious writings, and with the separation of Brazil from Portugal in the mid 19th c. this trend was strengthened.

Music

From the earliest days of Portugal's existence as an independent state there is evidence in both literature and art of a distinctive Galician/Portuguese musical culture.

Composed music (as distinct from folk music) went through the same phases of development in Portugal as in other European countries. Various song-books of the 12th–14th c. ("Cancioneiro da Ajuda", "Cancioneiro de Colocci-Brancuti", "Cancioneiro da Vaticana") have been preserved, but these give only the texts, not the music. During this period the art of the *troubadours* flourished at the courts, particularly in Lisbon, producing distinctively Portuguese genres in the *cantares de amigo* and *cantares de escarnio e maldizer*. The songs of the troubadours were accompanied on various instruments, including the fiddle, the psaltery, the harp, the rattle, the tambourine and the gittern (a seven-stringed plucked instrument with a cranked neck).

During the 15th c. Portuguese music was exposed to increased influence from other countries (England, Burgundy, the Low Countries) as a result of the royal family's foreign alliances and the growth in trade. Singing to the accompaniment of a guitar or a keyboard instrument enjoyed a considerable vogue. Two song-books of this period, "De Palacio" and "Da Biblioteca Publia Hortênsia", contain part-songs with Galician/Portuguese texts. Music also played an important part in theatrical performances (singspiels).

At the court of Manuel I, *Gil* **Vicente** (*c.* 1465–1540) performed his famous *autos* (Corpus Christi plays) and *tragi-comedies*, in which both instrumental and vocal music figured prominently, using such musical forms as the *vilancico*, the *chacota*, the *folia* and the *entrada*, the forerunner of the early Baroque toccata.

In the 16th and 17th c. polyphonic instrumental and vocal music enjoyed a great flowering (motets, cantatas, masses, psalms), influenced by the Dutch music of the period. Notable names include *Damião de Goes* (1502–74), *António Pinheiro* (*c.* 1530–90), *Vicente Lusitano* (*c.* 1550–1610), *Cosme Delgado* (1540–1603), *Manuel Mendes* (*c.* 1547–1605), *D. Lobo* (1565–1646) and *J. L. Rebello* (1609–61).

Fine music for keyboard instruments (organ, harpsichord) was written by *António Carreira* (1590–1650) and *Duarte Lobo* (*c.* 1570–1643). *Manuel Cardoso* (1571–1650), *Pedro Vaz* (*c.* 1585–1640) and *Alejandro de Aguiar* (*c.* 1590–1645) wrote mainly for the guitar.

In 1620 *Manuel Rodrigues* **Coelho** (*c.* 1580–after 1633) published his "Flores de Música para o instrumento de Tecla e Harpa" – the first printed instrumental music in Portugal.

During the 18th c., in spite of increasing Italian influence, the instrumental music of *José António Carlos de Seixas* (1704–42), *Frederico Jacinto* (1700–55) and *João de Sousa Carvalho* (1720–98) shows a characteristically Portuguese lyrical sensibility.

The main contribution to the music of the 18th c. was made by *opera*. In 1733 the poet *António José* **da Silva** (1705–39), known as "O Judeo" ("the Jew"), and the composer *António Teixeiras* founded a musical puppet theatre where they put on popular shows (satires, parodies) resembling singspiels. Da Silva wrote pieces such as "Os Encantos", "O Labirinto de Creta" and the puppet opera "Guerras do alecrim e da mangerona" ("Wars of Rosemary and Marjoram", first performed during the Carnival in 1737). Accused by the Inquisition of heresy, da Silva was burned at the stake in 1739 at the age of 34.

King João V (who married Maria Ana of Austria in 1708) was a great lover of

Italian opera, and accordingly this came to dominate the musical scene in Portugal as it did in other countries. The king sent Portuguese composers to Italy to study and brought Italians to his court as teachers. Among them was Domenico Scarlatti, who was court harpsichordist at Lisbon from 1721 to 1725 and composed many of his famous sonatas there. – In 1732 the first Italian touring company came to Portugal.

The leading representative of Portuguese opera in the Italian style was *Francisco António de* **Almeida** (d. about 1765; "Il Pentimento de Davide", "La Finta pazza"), whose opera buff "La Pazienza di Socrate" was performed in the Teatro Paco da Ribeira in 1733 – the first opera written by a Portuguese composer. *Marcos da Fonseca Portugal* (1762–1830; "La morte di Semiramide", "Le nozze di Figaro", "Zaira"), long-time director of the Teatro de São Carlos in Lisbon, also made a major contribution to the creation of opera in Portuguese.

The 1755 earthquake destroyed Lisbon's five opera-houses, and it was nearly 40 years before the new Teatro de São Carlos was built on the initiative of *Diogo de Pina Manique*. It was opened in 1793 with a performance of Domenico Cimarosa's work "La Ballerina amante", and is still Portugal's leading opera-house. Famous foreign singers and instrumentalists (including Franz Liszt in 1845) performed there, and by 1910 more than 60 operas by Portuguese composers had been produced. The great majority of the operas were performed in Italian, but Gounod's "Faust" was sung in French in 1884 and Wagner's "Ring" in German in 1909.

In the 19th c. Portuguese composers turned mainly to the romantic opera, reflecting both French and German (Wagner, from 1850) influence in their work. The foundation of the Philharmonic Academy (1838) and the Lisbon Conservatoire by *João Alberto Rodrigues da Costa* (1798–1870) and *João Domingos Bomtempo* (1775–1842) enriched the quality of Portuguese musical life in an enduring fashion.

Francisco Xavier Migone (1811–61) wrote two operas ("Sampiero", "Mocana") which were performed in the Teatro de São Carlos. *Francisco Norberto dos Santos Pinto* (1815–60) composed much music for the theatre and ballet as well as church music. *Eugénio Ricardo Monteiro d'Almeda* (1826–98) wrote operas and sacred music, including a "Libera me" which was highly praised by Rossini.

Francisco de Freitas Gazul (1842–1925) composed one opera ("Fra Luigi di Sousa") and numerous operettas, symphonies, oratorios and overtures. *Domingos Ciriaco de Cardoso* (1846–1900) ranks as the leading Portuguese operetta composer ("Girofle-Girofle").

Representatives of the Portuguese *Romantic* school were the composers *Augusto* **Machado** (1845–1924) and *Alfredo* **Keil** (1850–1907).

Machado's main work was in the field of lyric opera, sometimes showing French influence ("Laureana", "Os Dorias"), and in operettas of considerable musical quality "Ticão Negro", "O Rapto de Helena", "Venus").

Both in his piano music and his songs Keil shows strong national feeling. His song "A Portuguesa" was chosen as the national anthem on the proclamation of the republic in 1910. He also wrote operas ("Serrana", "Irene"), cantatas and symphonic poems ("Uma Caçada na Corte").

At the beginning of the 20th c. Portuguese music was in a state of stagnation, having become unduly subject to the influence of Italian music. *J. Vianna da Motta* (1868–1948), a pupil of Liszt, turned away from Italianism and gave fresh vitality to instrumental music.

With *Luís de Freitas Branco* (1890–1955) the music of the modern age came to Portugal. In his extensive œuvre ("Vathek 1914", "Artificial Paradises", symphonies and sonatas for violin and piano) he showed affinities with the atonality of the school of Schönberg and gave a major stimulus to the development of Impressionism in Portuguese music.

Rui Coelho (b. 1892) also followed in the footsteps of Schönberg's twelve-tone music ("Camoniana"; "Inês de Castro", 1926), while *Frederico de Freitas* (b. 1902; "Wall of Contention", "Nazaré") adopted the linear polytonality of Milhaud and Honegger for the first time in his sonata for violin and piano.

Fernando Lopes Graça (b. 1905) represents a Portuguese classical style, devoting himself mainly to the folksong and developing a very personal technique of harmonisation, particularly in the treatment of a cappella voices ("Prayer for the Souls of the Departed", "Traditional Portuguese Christmas Music").

Successful recent composers include *Claudio Carneiro, Luís Costas, Ivo Cruz* and *António Fragoso. Filipe Peres, Armando Santiago, Vitorino de Almeida* and *Correia de Oliveira* are among composers working in the fields of concrete and electronic music.

The leading figure among younger Portuguese composers is *Jorge* **Peixinho** (b. 1940), who studied in Venice with Luigi Nono and in Basle with Pierre Boulez with the aid of a scholarship from the Gulbenkian Foundation and worked with Karlheinz Stockhausen in Darmstadt. In 1970 he founded the Contemporary Music Group in Lisbon.

The leading Portuguese orchestra, consisting exclusively of professional musicians, is the National Radio Symphony Orchestra (Emissora Nacional), established in 1934. The Lisbon Opera House, the Teatro São Carlos as well as the Gulbenkian Orchestra, the Gulbenkian Choir and the Gulbenkian Ballet also make their contribution to the musical life of Portugal.

In contrast to Spain, the FOLK MUSIC of Portugal shows little Arab or Moorish influence except in the southerly region of Algarve. The folk dances performed at the numerous religious and secular festivals are usually accompanied by singing and a musical accompaniment on traditional instruments such as the guitar (*guitarra, viola*), fiddle (*rabeca*), flute (*flauta*), bagpipe (*gaita*), drum (*tambor*) and *reque-reque*, a percussion instrument, probably of African origin, consisting of reed pipes which are struck with a wooden rod.

The *folk dances* show considerable regional variation. In the northern coastal regions between the Minho and the Douro the commonest dance is the *vira*, a lively round dance. The Galician *gota* is danced to an even faster tempo. In the *malhão* and *cana verde* the women wear beautiful traditional costumes.

In the hill country of Trás-os-Montes, Beira Alta and Beira Baixa the most popular dance is the *chula*. The *dança dos*

pauliteiros which is also danced in these regions is performed by men bearing staves – probably substitutes for the sabres used in the old warlike dances.

The *vira*, performed at Nazaré on the coast of Estremadura, is a graceful fisherfolk's dance. In the Ribatejo region men dance the solo *escovinho* and *fandango*.

Folk-dancers, Ribatejo

To the S of the Tagus, where the people are of a more serious cast of mind, the dances are stately, almost melancholy. The best known folk dances of Alentejo are the *saia* and the *balha*. In the Algarve, on the other hand, the lively and vigorous *corridinho* is danced.

A specifically Portuguese form of folk music is the type of song known as the **fado**.

The word *fado* comes from the Latin *fatum*, "fate", with which the Portuguese associate the ideas of misfortune, unhappiness, disaster and destruction. In many fados the word *saudade* occurs: originally derived from the Latin *solitudo*, "loneliness", this has acquired connotations of desolation, homesickness, nostalgia, melancholy and longing for an apparently unattainable happiness.

The genuine fado always has a note of melancholy. The melody is usually in a minor key, but even in the major has a tinge of sadness. The elaborate cadences express selfless devotion on the one hand, theatrical self-pity on the other. Although it is difficult to define in words the distinctive character of the fado, it always involves an outpouring of passionate emotional feeling.

The **Lisbon fado**, which can be heard in late evening sessions in the *casas de fado* of the old town, is always sung by a solo *fadista*, either female or male. The fadista, usually wearing black, is accompanied by two guitarists, one playing the melody on the silvery-toned twelve-stringed *guitarra*, the other supplying the rhythm on the six-stringed *viola*, alternating between tonic and dominant sevenths.

The fado was for long confined to the more disreputable quarters of Lisbon, and it was only from about 1870 that it began to reach a wider public. Its origins are still the subject of dispute: some authorities maintain that it was derived from the Moors, others seek its beginnings in the negro music of Africa or Brazil, while others again believe that it originated among seamen – a theory to which the rhythms of the fado would seem to lend some support. But since it is known that Lisbon had a long tradition of singing and dancing to a guitar accompaniment the most widely accepted view is that the origins of the fado are to be looked for in the folk music of the capital.

Thanks to its geographical situation, its importance as a seaport and its status as the national capital Lisbon was always receptive to influences from outside. Thus as early as the 16th c. an exotic dance known as the *batugue* was popular in the town; and there are other dances including the *oitavado*, the *arrepia* and the *charamba* in 1734. About the middle of the 18th c. the *lundum* was danced in the streets of Lisbon to the accompaniment of guitars, and this was soon afterwards followed by a melancholy type of song called the *modinha*. The fado may well, therefore, have developed in the late 18th c. and early 19th c. out of these two forms.

Fado singer, Lisbon

There is also much difference of opinion about the qualities of the fado. The writer Ventura de Abrantes calls it "the most authentic of all Portuguese songs" and refers to "this liturgy of the popular soul", while José Maciel Ribeiro Forte sees it as "a rogues' song, a hymn to crime, an ode to vice, an incitement to depravity".

The most celebrated fadistas of the 19th c. were *José Dias* (1824–96) and the legendary *Maria Severa* (around 1840). In our own day radio and the record-player have made the fado known far beyond the frontiers of Portugal, so that it has developed into a king of pop music. The best known contemporary fado singer, with an international reputation, is *Amália Rodrigues*.

The **Coimbra fado** is very different from the ballad-like Lisbon fado. In this old university town the students sing their own traditional form of fado, reminiscent of the serenades of the southern European countries.

Economy

Portugal is still predominantly an agricultural country, but also has a number of rapidly developing industrial complexes ("industry parks" in the province of Minho and round Oporto, Lisbon and Sines), the contribution of which to the national economy far exceeds that made by agriculture.

Some 45% of the country's total area is devoted to **agriculture**, which employs roughly 27% of the working population.

The proportion of the gross national product contributed by the primary sector of the economy (including fisheries), which in 1980 amounted to 640 million US dollars, is falling sharply. This decline is due on the one hand to the extreme fragmentation of land ownership in the fertile north-western regions which makes economic working of the land impossible. Of a total of around 800,000 farm holdings more than 80% are concentrated on only a third of the total cultivable area, mainly in the NW. On the other hand there are the great expanses of land in Alentejo which are mainly in the hands of large landowners but are largely incapable of intensive agricultural development because of their aridity.

Here the expropriations carried out after the 1974 revolution and the working of the land by cooperatives, which in the early days were poorly organised and inefficient, led to significant falls in output.

The situation should be improved by the large irrigation projects which are planned to bring 4196 sq. km (1620 sq. miles) into cultivation with water from the Tagus and 298 sq. km (115 sq. miles) with water from the Mira. Medium-sized holdings, between the extremes of the tiny plots of the N and the great latifundia of the S, are found only in a few areas, for example in Estremadura. A general problem, in Portugal as in other countries, is the drift of population from the agricultural areas into industry.

The principal agricultural crop is wheat, cultivated by dry farming methods. In the wetter NW this gives place to maize (for feeding to livestock), potatoes and pulses, in the hill regions to rye and barley. Much land is devoted to viticulture; the best known Portuguese wine is, of course, port, but increasing quantities of other wines are now also being exported. In recent years there has been an increase in the production of citrus fruits, figs, pears, almonds, olives, early vegetables and onions, which are also exported.

Portugal is, like other south European countries, a considerable producer of rice, with extensive paddy fields in the lagoons of Aveiro and the Sado estuary and along the Algarve coast.

Stock-farming is concentrated mainly in the damp N and NW. Cattle are also reared in Ribatejo. Sheep and goats are kept on the dry hills; and large numbers of pigs are reared, particularly in the extensive cork-oak forests, many of them grazed by large herds of free-ranging pigs. The transhumant system of herding (seasonal movement of stock from one region to another) formerly widely practised in the N is now very much in decline.

Some 40% of the area of Portugal is covered by *forest*, about half of it coniferous; and this area is to be increased, for ecological reasons, by a large reforestation plan.

Of particular economic importance are the large expanses of cork-oak forests in southern Portugal, partly managed by the State and partly in private ownership; these supply half the total world production of cork. – The resin of the pines is a valuable raw material used in the production of turpentine, tar and rosin.

In recent years the **fisheries** of Portugal have suffered a considerable decline as a result of the fall in fish stocks in coastal waters and the reduction in whaling. The main catches are now of sardines, anchovies and tunny, principally for canning, and of cod, fished off the Newfoundland coasts and marketed as stockfish (dried cod), one of the national dishes of Portugal.

Fish laid out to dry (Nazaré)

A specialised branch of the fishing industry is the gathering of seaweed, particularly in the Azores, for the manufacture of agar-agar (gelatine).

The extension of Portuguese fishing zones to 320 km (200 miles) from the coast and the expansion and modernisation of the fishing fleet and processing facilities are now matters of urgency if this traditional branch of the Portuguese economy is to develop its full potential.

Portugal possesses a variety of workable **minerals** – pyrites in eastern Alentejo (São Domingos); uranium (the second largest deposits in Europe after those of France) in Beira Alta; haematite and iron around Torre de Moncorvo in the province of Trás-os-Montes; lead, zinc, wolfram and manganese in Beira Alta; and marble in eastern Alentejo and below the N and NE sides of the Serra de Sintra.

In the plains around the mouths of the Vouga, the Tagus and the Sado and on the Algarve coast (around Faro) are salt-pans which supply salt for the domestic canning industry.

Ores are still exported in crude form; but there is an old-established industry manufacturing high-quality steel products (blades, scissors, tools) based on the iron-mines around Torre de Moncorvo; and the blast furnace which came into operation at Seixal, near Lisbon, at the beginning of the 1960s has led to the development of an iron and steel industry in that area.

Coal is mined in the coastal region between Oporto and Figueira da Foz, providing fuel for a thermal power station – though this makes only a small contribution towards meeting the country's energy requirements.

In this respect the *hydroelectric power* available in northern Portugal, with its numerous rivers, is of great importance. The numerous hydroelectric projects carried through in this region – some of them joint projects with Spain – have so far been sufficient to meet the increasing demand for electricity.

No oil has so far been found on the mainland of Portugal, though test borings are being carried out on the continental shelf off the coast. The rich deposits of uranium in Portugal should, however, play an important part in the provision of energy in future. The construction of nuclear power stations is at present under discussion.

The industrialisation of Portugal is making progress, thanks to government measures designed to provide employment for the refugees from the former Portuguese colonies: a group notable in any event for entrepreneurial qualities.

Industry is concerned mainly with processing the produce of agriculture, forestry and fishing – i.e. the foodstuffs and textile industries, woodworking and cork-processing. In addition, however, the number of firms manufacturing chemicals and pharmaceuticals, electrical appliances and machinery is steadily increasing. Most firms are still small, often using inefficient methods which hamper industrial expansion. The large undertakings (particularly in textiles) were previously for the most part in foreign ownership; Portuguese undertakings were, however, expropriated after the 1974 revolution and are now under State control.

The Minho region is the main headquarters of the textile industry, with numerous small woollen and linen mills, which produce blankets and fine woollens under licence for British firms. The woollen industry has also been established for many centuries in the Serra da Estrêla to the S.

Around the large industrial ports of

Fishermen on the beach at Sesimbra (Estremadura)

Lisbon, Oporto (Leixões) and Sines there are now developing industrial areas with a variety of industries – engineering (shipyards at Lisbon), electrical apparatus, chemicals, pharmaceuticals, building materials. Along the central section of the Atlantic coast are both traditional industries such as ceramics, glass and foodstuffs and recently established industries including papermaking and the manufacture of fertilisers, building materials and petrochemicals. In southern Portugal are the main areas of cork-processing (Setúbal, Faro) and fish canning.

Madeira and the Azores are predominantly agricultural, supplying mainland Portugal with fruit (pineapples, bananas, citrus fruits, etc.) and wine.

Some 20% of Portugal's **exports** are accounted for by textiles and another 20% by machinery and chemicals.
The country's main trading partner is Britain, with which it has centuries-old commercial relations. After Britain come Germany, the United States and other EEC countries.
Portugal is a member of the European Free Trade Area (EFTA) and has applied for membership of the European Community.

Portuguese **communications** are not in all respects comparable with those of Central and Northern European countries.

The railways are run by the State-owned Companhia dos Cominhos de Ferro Portugueses (CP), with a total network of some 3500 km/2175 miles. Of this total 765 km/475 miles in the hilly country of northern Portugal are narrow-gauge (1000 mm/39·37 in.), the rest broad-gauge (1670 mm/65·75 in.), as in Spain. With the extension of hydro-electric plants progress is being made in the electrification of the railway system. The most important route in the country is the Lisbon–Oporto line, which carries almost half the total railway traffic.

The Portuguese road system (34,000 km/ 21,000 miles) is, on the whole, in reasonable condition. A superhighway is under construction between Lisbon and Oporto, and some sections have already been completed. The secondary roads, however, are not yet sufficiently adapted to the needs of the modern driver.

Buses also play an important part in the transport system for shorter journeys and connections with rail and air services.

Shipping traffic is confined to the lower stretches of the larger rivers and coastal waters. On account of the very variable water levels in the rivers only small or flat-bottomed boats can be used, carrying goods from places lying farther up the rivers to the large seaports at the mouths. There are no large inland ports. There is

Sunset, Nazaré beach

considerable ferry traffic in the estuary of the Tagus, but this is falling as the capacity of the bridge increases.

Portugal has, of course, a long seafaring tradition, and its ships formerly played an important role in maintaining links with its overseas possessions. Some 90% of the present Portuguese merchant fleet is based on Lisbon, which has the country's major shipyards. Other important seaports are Oporto (Leixões), Matosinhos, Setúbal, Aveiro and Sines. Vila Real de Santo António, on the S coast, handles the shipment of copper ore. The ports of Funchal on Madeira and Ponta Delgada and Horta in the Azores are of importance for trade between the islands and mainland Portugal and as ports of call for shipping in the North Atlantic.

Air transport is steadily increasing in importance. Lisbon airport, an important staging point on the routes linking Europe with South America (Brazil) and West Africa, is used by 20 international airlines. Oporto, as a major industrial town, has its own airport; and the airport at Faro serves the busy holiday traffic to the Algarve. The Azores provide a valuable staging point for transatlantic air traffic, both civil and military.
The national airline AIR PORTUGAL (Transportes Aéreos Portugueses, TAP) flies scheduled services to the principal European airports, to the former overseas possessions and to South America (Brazil) and North America.

Tourism. – Portugal has an old-established tradition as a holiday country, at any rate in certain areas. During the 19th c. Lisbon and the neighbouring resorts of Estoril, Cascais and Sintra, the beaches of the Algarve and the island of Madeira attracted many visitors, particularly from Britain.
The Portuguese spas – Caldas da Rainha, Caldas de Monchique, Caldas de Gerês, etc. – have long enjoyed an international reputation.

Of the almost 9 million foreigners who took their holidays in Portugal in 1983, about three-quarters were Spaniards, followed by English, German, French, American and Dutch. Most tourists travelled overland. Thanks to its long coastline Portugal is especially suitable for water-sports and bathing.
In addition to the popular coastal stretches, the Costa de Prata ("Silver Coast") and the Costa Verde ("Green Coast"), facing the Atlantic north of Lisbon, are gaining in popularity – even with foreign holidaymakers – in spite of the somewhat more severe climate and relatively low water temperatures.

Connoisseurs of architecture and art will find much of interest both in the coastal regions and inland.

Portugal
A to Z

Rocky coast, Algarve

Abrantes

Historical province: Ribatejo.
District: Santarém.
Altitude: 190 m/623 ft.
Population: 11,000.
Post code: P-2200.
Telephone code: 0 41.
ⓘ **Turism,**
Largo da Feira;
tel. 2 25 55.

ACCOMMODATION. – *Turismo de Abrantes*, II, 48 r.;
Tubuci, P II, 19 r.; *Central*, P III, 18 r.; *Aliança*, P IV,
49 r.; *Abrantes*, P IV, 24 r.

RESTAURANT. – *O Pelicano.*

**An old-world little town of white
houses and streets gay with flowers
perched high above the N bank of the
Tagus, Abrantes occupies an exposed situation which made it a key
point in the defence of the old Beira
provinces.**

A local speciality is *palha de Abrantes*
(sweet egg floss).

SIGHTS. – Above the town are the
remains of the once mighty **Castelo**, built
by King Dinis in 1303. It was destroyed by
an earthquake in 1533 and finally demolished in 1807 by French troops under
Marshal Junot, whom Napoleon created
Duke of Abrantes.

From the ruined keep, the *Torre de
Menagem*, there are magnificent *views of
the Tagus valley and the surrounding hills.

Within the castle precincts is the *church of
Santa Maria do Castelo* (originally built
1215; restored in 15th c.), now housing
the **Museu Dom Lopo de Almeida**,
which contains, in addition to the fine
late Gothic monuments of the Almeida
family (15th–16th c.), valuable old tiles
(16th c.), Gothic sculpture, a Gothic head
of Christ and two Roman statues of the
1st c. A.D.

Other features of interest in the town are
the *church of São João Baptista* (founded
1300, rebuilt 1589), with a Renaissance
coffered ceiling and rich woodcarving,
and the *church of the Misericórdia* (16th
c.) which has a Renaissance doorway
and paintings of the 16th c. Portuguese
school. – Also worth seeing is the *Convento de São Domingos* (originally 1472;
much altered and rebuilt), with a beautiful
two-storey cloister.

SURROUNDINGS. – 12 km/7½ miles W on a beautiful
road running above the right bank of the Tagus, with
fine views, is **Constância** (alt. 20 m/65 ft), the
Roman *Pugna Tagi*, a little market town charmingly
situated at the junction of the Rio Zêzere with the
Tagus. Church of the Misericórdia, with tile decoration, and the parish church (1636) which was restored
in 19th c. (ceiling painting of 1890).

5 km/3 miles SW of Constância, on a rocky islet in the
Tagus, stands the Templar *castle of Almourol, one
of the finest 12th c. castles in Portugal (restored in
19th c.).

Almourol Castle

10 km/6 miles N of Constância is the **Barragem do
Castelo do Bode**, the lowest of a series of dams
which form a string of lakes nearly 100 km/65 miles
long on the *Rio Zêzere* and its tributaries.

30 km/19 miles E of Abrantes, on the right bank of the
Tagus, lies the little town of **Belver** (alt. 220 m/720 ft;
pop. 2000), dominated by a castle begun in 1194, in
the reign of King Sancho I, and completed in 1212
(restored in 14th c.).
In the castle chapel is a beautiful carved reredos
(13th c.).
From the viewpoint known as "Sancho I's Balcony"
there is a beautiful prospect of the Tagus valley.

Albufeira

Historical province: Algarve.
District: Faro.
Altitude: 0–35 m/0–115 ft.
Population: 8500.
Post code: P-8200.
Telephone code: 0 89.
ⓘ **Turismo,**
Rua 5 de Outubro;
tel. 5 54 28.

ACCOMMODATION. – *Balaia*, 5 km/3 miles E in
Praia Maria Luisa, L, 193 r., SP; *Montchoro*, I, 362 r.,
SP; *Alfamar*, I, 264 r.; *Sol e Mar*, I, 74 r.; *Boavista*, I,
51 r.; *Do Cerro*, I, 51 r.; *Mar à Vista*, I, 29 r.; *Rocamar*,
II, 91 r.; *Da Aldeia*, 3 km/2 miles E, II, 68 r.; *Baltum*
(with annexe), III, 48 r.; etc. – Apartment hotels:
Auramar, II, 90 r.; *Turial*, II, 122 r.; *Albufeira Jardim*,
NW of the town, II, 36 r.

HOLIDAY COLONIES. – *Aldeia das Açoteias*, 8 km/5 miles
E, 392 r., SP; *Alfamar*, in Vale de Cerros de Baixo,
185 r.; *Jacarandá*, 165 r., *Da Aldeia*, 117 r., SP, both
in Areias de São João; *Quinta da Balaia*, 147 r., SP;
Montchoro, 144 r., SP; *Vilanova*, 108 r., SP; etc.

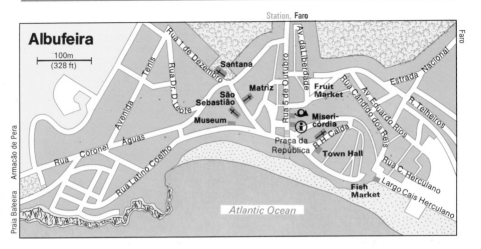

RESTAURANTS. – *Alfredo*, Rua 5 de Outubro; *Borda d'Agua*, on the Praia da Oura.

RECREATION and SPORT. – Water-skiing, windsurfing; tennis, riding; golf-courses at Vilamoura (18 holes) and in Vale do Lobo (18 holes).

The fishing village of *Albufeira, beautifully located in a bay on the S coast of Portugal in the shelter of bizarrely shaped cliffs (Ponta da Baleeira), has developed in recent years into one of the busiest seaside resorts in the Algarve.

A favourite haunt of artists and flatteringly known as the "St Tropez of the Algarve", Albufeira has contrived to retain, in spite of the swarms of visitors, something of its original Moorish character as a picturesque *little town of white houses and steep, narrow streets.

SIGHTS. – *Parish church* (18th c.) of Santana (St Anne); *church of Misericórdia*, originally Gothic, with a beautiful doorway in Manueline Renaissance style. – Small archaeological and historical *Museum*.

Visitors will enjoy a stroll through the old town with its narrow winding streets and inviting cafés, shops and little boutiques.

From the observation terrace Bem Parece a magnificent view over the town and the beach may be enjoyed.

Below the town, reached by a tunnel 50 m/55 yd long, is the **beach**, the E end

Albufeira: general view

of which also serves as a harbour for numerous brightly painted fishing boats. The busy activity of the local fishermen and the more leisurely pursuits of the holidaymakers complement each other in this attractive setting.

Other beaches are the *Praia Baleeira, Praia de São Rafael* and *Praia do Castelo* (picturesque cliffs) to the W and the *Praia da Oura* to the E.

Alcácer do Sal

Historical province: Alentejo.
District: Setúbal.
Altitude: 30 m/100 ft.
Population: 13,500.
Post code: P-7580.
Telephone code: 0 65.
ⓘ **Turismo,**
Câmara Municipal.

ACCOMMODATION. – *Herdade da Barrosinha,* 3 km/2 miles SE on N5, I, 10 r. – *Pousada de Vale de Gaio,* 27 km/17 miles SE in Vale de Gaio, near the Barragem Trigo de Morais, 6 r.

The ancient little town of Alcácer do Sal ("castle of salt"), the Roman Salacia, lies above the right bank of the Rio Sado, which here opens out into a wide estuary. The banks of the river are lined with the salt-pans which have given the town its name.

A number of fine old buildings bear witness to the town's earlier prosperity, achieved from medieval times onwards by its flourishing trade in salt and corn and by the growing of rice in the warm low-lying marshland along the river.

SIGHTS. – Above the town is a ruined castle (*view), within the walls of which is the *church of Santa Maria do Castelo* (12th–13th c.), it has a Renaissance doorway to the Chapel of the Sacrament and beautiful 17th c. tile decoration.

On the far side of the main road is the former **Convent of Santo António** (16th c.). This church, too, has a beautiful Renaissance doorway and lavish marble decoration in the *Chapel of the 11,000 Virgins* (16th c.). – The former *church of the Espírito Santo* (Manueline windows) houses the **Archaeological Museum** (*Museu Municipal*), with Stone Age and Roman material, relics of the Moorish period and coins.

1 km/¾ mile W of the town is the Romanesque and Gothic **church of the Senhor dos Mártires** (13th–14th c.), with the stone sarcophagus of Diogo Pereira (1427).

SURROUNDINGS. – 12 km/7½ miles NE is a dam on the rivers *Alcáçovas* and *Sítimos*.

Alcácer do Sal at sunset

23 km/14 miles SE a dam, the **Barragem Trigo de Morais**, converts the *Rio Xarrama* into an attractive lake. At its NE end is **Torrão** (church in Manueline style), birthplace of Bernardim Ribeiro (*c.* 1482– *c.* 1552), famous for his poem "Saudades" (published 1554, probably posthumously).

23 km/14 miles S is the little country town of **Grândola** (alt. 95 m/312 ft; pop. 4000; pensions Vila Morena, P II, 23 r.; Paraiso do Alentejo, P II, 12 r.; Fim do Mundo, P IV, 46 r.), a hub of the Portuguese cork industry.

Alcobaça

Historical province: Estremadura.
District: Leiria.
Altitude: 42 m/138 ft.
Population: 5000.
Post code: P-2460.
Telephone code: 0 62.
ⓘ **Turismo,**
Praça 25 de Abril;
tel. 4 23 77.

ACCOMMODATION. – *Corações Unidos*, P II, 16 r.; *Mosteiro*, P II, 13 r.; *Bau*, P III, 15 r.

EVENT. – *Feira de São Bernardo* (end August), an industrial and agricultural show.

Alcobaça, the Roman Eburobriga, is charmingly set between two little rivers, the Alcoa and the Baça, below the ruins of a Moorish castle. Its principal attraction is a magnificent Cistercian ** abbey, once one of the most prosperous and influential religious houses in Portugal and now one of its outstanding architectural monuments.

Alcobaça is the cultural and economic heart of a large and fertile agricultural region (fruit canning), first brought under cultivation by St Bernard's monks in the 14th c. – The town is noted for its blue painted pottery.

HISTORY. – The history of the town is bound up with that of the abbey, the Real Abadia de Santa Maria de Alcobaça. King Afonso (Henriques) I granted land in this area, recovered during the liberation of Santarém from the Moors (15 March 1147), to Bernard of Clairvaux – who had supported him in the long-drawn-out negotiations for Papal recognition of the newly established kingdom of Portugal – for the foundation of a Cistercian abbey. In 1148 the king himself laid the foundation stone of the first church, and work began on the monastic buildings in 1187, the influx of monks from Burgundy having made the provision of accommodation for them urgently necessary. The structure was substantially complete by 1222, but was much altered in subsequent centuries, the new buildings combining with the old to form an ensemble of notable harmony.

In accordance with the rules of the order there were always 999 monks ("one less than a thousand"), who cultivated fruit and vines in the valleys of the Alcoa and the Baça, thus laying the foundations of what is still the largest area of orchards and vineyards in Portugal. Here, too, in the 13th c., the monks established the first public school in the kingdom, and this later played a part in securing the establishment of the first Portuguese university at Coimbra. The abbot of Alcobaça, who styled himself "Counsellor to His Majesty and Almoner of the Crown", had dominion over thirteen towns and villages, three ports and two castles; and between the 13th and the 18th c. the abbey was one of the country's leading intellectual and spiritual institutions, providing the Portuguese kings not only with a refuge in case of need but also with a place for retreat and meditation.

The 1775 earthquake severely damaged the abbey, and in 1811 it was occupied by French troops under Marshal Junot and plundered of many of its treasures. In 1834 the abbey was secularised and the buildings converted to various uses (barracks, stables, etc.). Finally, after long neglect, the importance of this national monument was recognised and it was given statutory protection. Some of the monastic buildings are now occupied by government offices and a school.

THE ABBEY. – The layout of the ** **Real Abadia de Santa Maria de Alcobaça** is modelled on that of the mother house at Cluny, and its excellent state of preservation makes it the finest example of Cistercian architecture in Europe.

The abbey, basically Gothic in structure, is approximately square in plan. In addition to the mighty church and the usual offices it contains five cloisters, seven dorters (dormitories), accommodation for guests, a library and a huge kitchen.

The *main front* of the abbey, 221 m/725 ft long, is dominated by the Baroque façade (1725) of the **church** with its two low towers and its numerous statues. Of the original Gothic façade there survive

Souvenir shop outside Alcobaça Abbey

only the doorway (also decorated with Baroque sculpture) and the large rose window.

The *INTERIOR of the early Gothic hall-church is of Cistercian clarity, austerity and simplicity. The most spacious church interior in Portugal (106 m/348 ft long, 21·5 m/71 ft wide and 20 m/65 ft high), it is divided into three aisles of equal height, the lateral aisles being very narrow. Twenty-four massive piers, recessed on the inner side to take the choir-stalls (which were burned by the French), support twelve bays of Gothic vaulting. Around the choir are nine chapels and the high altar is surrounded by eight columns.

In the transepts are the sumptuous *tombs of King Pedro I (S transept) and his beloved Inês de Castro (N transept), who was murdered at the behest of Pedro's father King Afonso IV. After his accession Pedro had her exhumed and crowned in due form at Coimbra as queen. The tragic story of the unhappy lovers and the bloody vengeance which Pedro exacted on the murderers after he became king, earning him the style of Pedro the Cruel, are celebrated by Camões in the third canto of his "Lusiads". – By Pedro's desire the tombs were so placed that when they arose on the Day of Judgment the two lovers would see each other at once. The sarcophaguses, hewn from soft Ançâ sandstone, with rich figural decoration, are in the Flamboyant style of the second half of the 14th c. They were damaged by Junot's troops in 1811.

On the sarcophagus of Inês de Castro, which is supported by crouching figures, is the recumbent figure of the dead woman, surrounded by six praying angels. Along the sides are scenes from the life of Christ, at the foot the Last Judgment, at the head Christ on Calvary. – The stone sarcophagus of King Pedro, borne by six lions, has the recumbent figure of the king, also surrounded by praying angels. Along the sides are scenes from the life of St Bartholomew, and at the head is a wheel of fortune with 18 episodes from the life of the two lovers, including the murder of Inês.

In the transept chapels are painted terracotta figures of unnamed monks (17th c.) and a fine representation of the death of St Bernard. – To the E of the ambulatory the two fine Manueline *doorways (16th c.) are by João de Castilho. In the antechamber of the sacristy is the only example of reticulated vaulting in the abbey.

On the W side of the S transept is the Sala dos Túmulos, a funerary chapel containing a number of tombs.

On the N side of the church are the medieval monastic buildings. – A doorway in the N aisle leads into the beautiful two-storey *Claustro do Silêncio or Claustro de Rei Dinis. The lower cloister was built by Domingo and Diogo Domingues between 1308 and 1311; the upper gallery (by the Castilho brothers) was built for King Manuel in the 16th c.

On the N side of the cloister stands a Gothic fountain-house. Here, too, is the entrance to the **Refectory** (fine reading-desk), one of the oldest parts of the abbey. Adjoining is the large Kitchen, 18 m/60 ft high, with a huge open fireplace and a fish-tank supplied with water from the Alcoa – once an important feature of the abbey, since the Cistercians were forbidden to eat meat.

On the E side of the cloister is the Chapterhouse (Sala do Capítulo, 14th c.), at the SW corner the Sala dos Reis (Royal Hall), the walls of which are decorated with azulejos depicting scenes from the history of the abbey. Also on the walls are terracotta statues (probably by monks) of most of the Portuguese kings down to

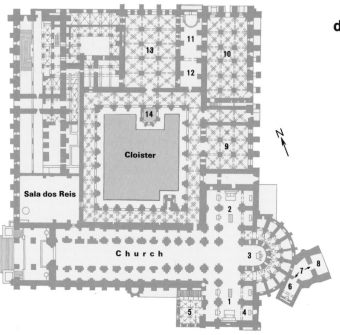

Real Abadia de Santa Maria de Alcobaça

Alcobaça Abbey

1 Tomb of Pedro I
2 Tomb of Inês de Castro
3 Choir
4 "Death of St Bernard" (terracotta)
5 Sala dos Túmulos
6 Chapel of the Sacrament
7 Manueline doorways
8 Sacristy
9 Chapterhouse
10 Dorter (upper floor)
11 Kitchen
12 Pantry
13 Refectory
14 Fountain-house

José I. On the upper floor are the *Dorters*, the *Library*, etc.

In the square in front of the abbey there are numerous shops and stalls selling craft articles, particularly the blue Alcobaça pottery. – From here various narrow lanes run up to the ruined **Castle** (*view).

SURROUNDINGS. – 2 km/1¼ miles SW is the village of **Vestiaria**, which has a church with a fine Manueline doorway.
2 km/1¼ miles N is the little spa of **Termas da Piedade** (Hotel Termal de Piedade, IV, 60 r.).
7 km/4½ miles NE is **Aljubarrota** (Estalagem do Cruzeiro, I, 26 r.), the scene of a famous battle on 15 August 1385 in which a Portuguese army commanded by Nuno Álvares Pereira won a decisive victory over the Spaniards. In token of thanksgiving King João I founded Batalha Abbey (see p. 81). – Aljubarrota has a number of handsome 17th and 18th c. houses and the church of Nossa Senhora dos Prazeres (originally Romanesque).

Alenquer

Historical province: Estremadura.
District: Lisboa.
Altitude: 160 m/525 ft.
Population: 8000.
Telephone code: 063.
ⓘ **Turismo Lisboa,**
Avenida António Augusto de Agviar 86
P-1000 Lisboa (Lisbon)
Tel. (01) 57 50 91

ACCOMMODATION. – None in town. See under LISBON and SANTARÉM.

The ancient little town of Alenquer clings picturesquely to the slopes of a hill 45 km/28 miles N of Lisbon. Its population is mainly employed in the woollen and papermaking industries.

HISTORY. – Alenquer was the birthplace of the navigator and pilot *Pero de Alenquer*, who was with Bartolomeu Dias when he discovered the Cape of Good Hope and with Vasco da Gama on his expedition to discover the sea route to India. Pero, a man of humble origin, won a great reputation for his extraordinary achievements, earning the name of "prince of pilots" and being welcomed at court. His exploits were vividly described in the writings of the diplomat and chronicler *Damião de Góis* (1507–71), scion of a noble family of Alenquer.

SIGHTS. – Above the town is the long range of buildings of the **Convent of São Francisco**, the oldest Franciscan house in Portugal, founded in 1222, during the saint's lifetime. Notable features of the convent, now falling into dilapidation, are the two-storey *cloister*, originally Romanesque but rebuilt in Manueline style, and the Manueline doorway of the refectory.

The sundial in the NW corner of the cloister was presented by Damião de Góis.

In the **church of São Pedro** is the tomb of Damião de Góis, with a long epitaph which he composed himself. – The *Museu de Hipólito Cabaço* contains archaeological (particularly Stone Age) material.

Alentejo

Historical province: Alentejo.
Districts: Portalegre, Évora, Beja and Setúbal.
Area: 23,514 sq. km/9079 sq. miles.
Population: 370,000.
Chief town: Évora.
ⓘ **Turismo Évora,**
Praça do Giraldo 71,
P-7000 Évora;
tel. (00 66) 2 26 71.

The southern Portuguese province of Alentejo extends to the SE of the Tagus ("além Tejo", beyond the Tagus) over a seemingly endless tableland as far as the Algarve, bounded on the E by the Spanish frontier and on the W by the Atlantic Ocean. This lonely, barren and almost featureless expanse seems to have strayed here from more northerly latitudes, forming a remarkable contrast to the hilly terrain and luxuriant vegetation of most of the Portuguese provinces.

The chief town of **Alto Alentejo** (Upper Alentejo, to the N) and of the province as a whole is **Évora** (see p. 114). The main town of **Baixo Alentejo** (Lower Alentejo, to the S) is **Beja** (p. 83).

Alentejo is a region of very ancient settlement, with numerous remains of Stone Age occupation (standing stones and megalithic chamber tombs, known as *antas*, being particularly common in Alto Alentejo) and of the Roman and Moorish periods.

The purely agricultural character of the region is reflected in the architecture: here the seafaring motifs common in the architectural ornament of the Manueline period give place to agricultural motifs (ears of corn, plants, farming equipment).

Geologically Alentejo is a continuation of the Castilian Meseta, a residual expanse worn down and levelled by erosion, resting on Palaeozoic rocks of the Iberian basement. The land rises to average heights of between 150 and 350 m/ 500 and 1150 ft, reaching barely 400 m/ 1300 ft at its highest point in the SW and with its only "real" mountains in the NE, the **Serra de São Mamede** (1025 m/ 3365 ft).

The *climate* is Mediterranean, but with some continental features – a cold but snow-free winter, a short spring with little rain, a hot, dry summer and frequent showers of rain in the autumn. The rainfall is relatively low, an annual average of 600–700 mm/24–28 in.

Given this climatic pattern, the natural *vegetation* is confined to modest evergreen heaths and oaks and sclerophyllous evergreens (woody plants with small leathery leaves). The few trees mostly grow in isolated clumps. The cork-oak is widely distributed, and makes an important contribution to the economy of the region.

With only 370,000 inhabitants – barely a tenth of the total population of Portugal – spread over a quarter of the country's area, Alentejo is very sparsely populated, with a density of 27 to the sq. km/70 to the sq. mile. There are concentrations of population in a few smallish towns and large villages, but for the rest the rural population is widely dispersed, living in and around large isolated farms (*montes*). These are often on low hills and consist of the farmhouse itself, the houses of the farm workers and the various farm buildings and are usually surrounded by great expanses of farmland. The buildings, with walls of beaten earth, are carefully white-washed, and with their flat roofs and intricately decorated openwork chimneys have preserved many Moorish features.

Farms of this kind, which with the addition of day labourers and seasonal workers can amount to settlements of considerable size, are characteristic of the old type of large estate which has long given rise to social tensions in Portugal. The expropriation measures introduced after the 1974 revolution – some of them since revoked or mitigated by compensation payments – still present the government with serious domestic problems.

Typical Alentejo scenery near Estremoz

The *towns* of Alentejo have been from time immemorial markets for the agricultural areas surrounding them, as well as having importance for communications and administration and for culture and education. Along the Tagus and the Guadiana there are also a series of towns established many centuries ago to provide defence against Spain.

Although Alentejo has a fifth of Portugal's total coastline the life and activities of the region revolve around the interior. Less than 1% of the country's total catch of fish comes from here, and the endless stretches of broad beach are empty and scarcely known to tourists. The people of the Alentejo region live almost exclusively from *agriculture*. In spite of the sparse population and the extreme aridity, almost the whole area is carefully cultivated. In the W, on poor soils, extensive monoculture predominates (corn, grown by dry-farming methods); in addition pastoral farming (with a third of the total Portuguese stock of cattle) is carried on throughout the year, together with the growing of cork-oaks (*montados*), pig-farming and charcoal-burning. The wet and fertile coastal areas and the land on the weather side of the hills in the NE are the granary of Portugal – growing in addition to grain (wheat, rye, maize) large quantities of fruit and olives.
Alentejo is also the home of a celebrated breed of horses, the Alter Real, which has been reared here since the mid 18th c. and is particularly prized for the purposes of dressage.

The problem of *irrigation* is of fundamental importance in this agricultural province. The rivers which flow through the region are almost dry in summer and are thus of little use for irrigation; but there is an ambitious plan to build a series of dams on the Tagus and Guadiana and the Guadiana's left bank tributary the Rio Chança and pump the water throughout the region in a dense network of canals.

Algarve

Historical province: Algarve.
District: Faro.
Area: 5072 sq. km/1958 sq. miles.
Population: 277,000.
Telephone code: 0 89.
Chief town: Faro.

ⓘ **Comissão Regional de Turismo do Algarve,**
Rua Ataide de Oliveira 100,
P-8000 Faro.
tel. 2 40 67.

ACCOMMODATION. – IN SAGRES, LAGOS, PRAIA DA ROCHA, PORTIMÃO, SILVES, ALBUFEIRA, FARO, OLHÃO, TAVIRA AND VILA REAL DE SANTO ANTÓNIO: see the entries for these places. – IN MONCHIQUE: see under Serra de Monchique.

IN VILA DO BISPO: *Mira Sagres*, P III, 12 r.; *Casal da Vila*, P IV, 10 r.

IN MONTES DE ALVOR: *ˣGolfe da Penina*, L, 202 r., SP, golf-courses (18 and 9 holes).

IN LAGOA: *Levante*, in Vale do Olival, I, 37 r., SP; *Alagoas*, I, 22 r., SP; *Parque Algarvio*, II, 42 r., SP.

ON THE PRAIA DA LUZ: *Conjunto Turístico Luz Bay Clube*, 1200 r., SP (holiday colony).

IN PRAIA DE ALVOR: *Dom João I*, I, 213 r., SP; *Torralta-Torrec*, II, 76 r.; *Apartamentos de Torralta*, 910 r., SP; *Conjunto Turístico da Torralta*, 107 r., SP (holiday colony).

IN BEMPOSTA: *Conjunto Turístico Bemposta*, 181 r., SP (holiday colony).

IN PRAIA DO CARVOEIRO: *Solférias*, I, 192 r., SP; *Dom Sancho*, I, 47 r. – Holiday colonies: *Conjunto Turístico Quinta do Paraíso*, 160 r., SP; *Conjunto Turístico Solférias*, 66 r., SP.

IN ARMAÇOÃ DE PÊRA: *Viking*, I, 184 r., SP; *Garbe*, I, 109 r., SP; *Cimer*, I, 21 r.; *Algar*, I, 19 r.; *Hani*, P II, 30 r.; *Conjunto Turístico Vila Lara*, in Alporchinhos, 94 r.; SP (holiday colony).

IN QUARTEIRA: *Quarteira Sol*, I, 98 r., SP; *D. José*, II, 134 r., SP; Apartment hotel *Atis*, III, 90 r.; *Mário*, P II, 36 r.; *Triângula*, P II, 34 r.; *Miramar*, P II, 19 r.; *Batista*, P II, 16 r.; *Romeu*, P III, 12 r.

IN VILAMOURA: *ˣAtlantis*, L, 109 r., SP; *Dom Pedro*, I, 261 r., SP; *Cegonha*, I, 7 r.; *Golf Vilhamoura*, II, 52 r., SP. – Holiday colonies: *Conjunto Turístico Aldeia do Mar*, 112 r., SP; *Conjunto Turístico Golférias*, 112 r.; *Conjunto Turístico Aldia do Golfe*, 226 r., SP; *Conjunto Turístico Clube de Golfe de Vilamoura*, 110 r., SP, golf-course.

IN ALMANSIL: *Conjunto Turístico Quinta do Lago*, 50 r., SP (holiday colony).

IN VALE DO LOBO:ˣ *Dona Filipa*, L, 129 r., SP; *Conjunto Turístico Vale do Lobo*, 213 r., SP, golf-course.

IN MONTE GORDO: *Vasco da Gama*, I,165 r., SP; *Alcazar*, I, 95 r., SP; *Monte Gordo*, I, 25 r.; *Navegadores*, II, 214 r.; *Caravelas*, II, 87 r.; *Residência Catavento*, PI, 63 r.; *Espanhola*, P IV, 12 r.; Apartamentos Turísticos *Guadiana*, 150 r.; *Monte Sol*, 92 r.

RECREATION and SPORT. – Swimming, diving, sailing, water-skiing, rowing;ˣ golf, riding, tennis.

Casinos in Alvor, Vilamoura and Monte Gordo.

GOLF-COURSES. – *Palmares*, Lagos (27 holes); *Alvor/Penina*, 5 km/3 miles W of Portimão (27 holes); *Dom Pedro* (18 holes) and *Vilamoura Golf Club* (18 holes), both at Vilamoura; *Vale do Lobo* (18 holes); *Quinta do Lago*, Almansil (27 holes).

EVENTS. – *Carneval*, Loulé (four days before Ash Wednesday); *Romaria da Senhora da Piedade*, Loulé (end of March); *Festival de Folclore do Algarve*, at several places in the Algarve, with a grand finale in Vilamoura (beginning of September); *Feira de Santa Iria*, Faro (end of October).

The southern Portuguese province of the ****Algarve, lying in the extreme SW corner of Europe, is a broad strip of land, some 155 km/95 miles long and up to 50 km/30 miles wide, on the southern Atlantic coast of Portugal, extending from the Cabo de São Vincente (Cape St Vincent) in the W to the Rio Guadiana, the frontier with Spain, in the E. Sheltered on the N by a mountain range, increasing in height from E to W, which isolates it from the rest of Portugal, the Algarve has preserved its own distinctive character and is very different – in scenery, climate and culture – from the more northerly parts of the country.**

Although the Algarve is much poorer in art and architecture than other parts of the country, it has developed into the most popular tourist and holiday region in Portugal thanks to its equable climate, its luxuriant subtropical vegetation and its beautiful beaches of fine sand, enclosed by bizarrely shaped cliffs and crags of golden-yellow rock.

In spite of the rapid growth of tourism, a prudent development policy has largely preserved the Algarve from the over-building which has spoiled some stretches of the Spanish Mediterranean coast. Most of the new developments are spaciously and attractively laid out, and of course more costly because of this; but the holiday visitors (most of them British) who come to this part of Europe seem more concerned than in other tourist regions for the preservation of its natural beauty and way of life and are prepared to meet the extra cost. – To explore the beauties of this enchanting part of Portugal a car is an advantage.

The sparsely populated northern part of the province, the **Alto Algarve** (Upper Algarve), is occupied by a hilly region of schists and sandstones, overlaid in the W by the intrusive rocks of the Serra de Monchique. Apart from one or two features there is little here to interest the ordinary visitor.

The coastal region, the **Baixo Algarve** (Lower Algarve), a Mesozoic tableland of limestones and sandstones, has two aspects. The western half, from Cabo São Vicente to Val do Lobo (just W of Faro), is the better known and scenically more

Typical rock formations on the Algarve coast

striking**Rocky Algarve**, world-famous for its picturesque golden-yellow cliffs, slashed by crevices and caves, its sheltered beaches of fine sand, its emerald-green water and its deep blue sky. To the E, from Faro to the Spanish frontier, is the *Sandy Algarve, with endless expanses of sandy beach, dunes and pine-groves but without any outstanding scenic beauties. This area has been less extensively developed for the tourist trade.

The purplish-red soil of the Algarve supports flourishing plantations of almond-trees, olives, figs and carob-trees. The carob-tree grows to heights of 15–20 m/50–65 ft, with a short trunk and dense foliage; the carob beans are edible. In the irrigated valleys are orange-groves, cotton plantations and fields of rice and sugarcane. Most of the gardens and orchards are enclosed by hedges of agaves. Camellias and oleanders make an attractive show, and the almond-trees, which flourish in the mild Mediterranean climate, come into blossom as early as January or February.

The Algarve has one of the most settled climates in the world, with 3000 hours of sunshine in the year. The climate on the coast is similar to that of North Africa. Sheltered on the N and NW by the hills of the Alto Algarve and exposed to the moderating influence of the Atlantic, the Algarve escapes climatic extremes.

Winter temperatures rarely fall below 10°C/50°F; the summers are dry and hot, but there is always a light sea breeze to bring a pleasant coolness. Temperatures fall rapidly in the evening, and visitors will do well to include some warm clothing in their luggage.

Rainfall is low (an annual 350–600 mm/ 14–24 in.) and mostly concentrated in November; but there are abundant resources of ground water which is used for irrigation and makes it possible to take three or four crops a year off the land.

In choosing where to go for their holiday visitors should consider wind conditions. The farther W they go the less protection there is from the winds blowing off the Atlantic and the more bracing the climate. The bathing resorts in the most westerly quarter of the Algarve are for the hardier souls, or for diving enthusiasts and anglers, since in this area there is usually a brisk, cool wind and the sea tends to be rough. The W coast of the Algarve has only limited facilities for visitors, but has a number of sheltered (though less easily accessible) bays and is a paradise for sub-aqua (scuba) divers.

HISTORY. – Shut off by a barrier of hills in the N, the Algarve developed on its own. The fertility of the soil and the pleasant climate attracted human settlement from an early period. It is known that the Phoenicians and later the Greeks established colonies here, though only scanty remains have survived. In the 6th and 5th c. Celts settled in this region, followed soon afterwards by Carthaginians: it is said that Portimão was founded by Hannibal. In Roman times the

Almond-blossom in the Algarve

A cove in the Rocky Algarve

Algarve, then known as *Cyneticum*, was a prosperous and flourishing region, and evidence of the busy trade carried on here has been recovered by excavation.

After the Romans came the Visigoths, who controlled the region for almost 300 years. The Visigoths in turn gave way to the Moors, who remained for 500 years and left an enduring mark on the population and way of life of the Algarve. The physical type of the inhabitants – swarthy, short and stocky – bears

witness to a Moorish ancestry, the local style of building and the traditional costumes show clear Moorish features, and the language and place-names include many elements of Arab origin. The name **Algarve** itself is Arabic, from *Al-Gharb*, "the West" – referring to the situation of this region at the extreme western end of the Islamic empire.

The capture of Faro by King Afonso III of Portugal in 1249 marked the first stage in the recovery of the territory from the Moors. The Algarve then became the last element to be incorporated in Portugal, an independent kingdom subject to the Portuguese crown in a personal union.

In the 15th c. the Algarve attracted worldwide interest, when Henry the Navigator founded his famous school of seamanship at Sagres and with his systematic technical research laid the foundations for the great voyages of discovery of the following century.

The inhabitants of the Algarve are concentrated in the towns and villages along the coast, earning their living from three main sources of roughly equal importance – tunny and sardine fishing and processing; agriculture, with up to four crops a year, principally of citrus fruits, wine, vegetables, almonds, rice and cotton; and the tourist trade, which continues to grow in importance.

A local speciality is *medronho*, a brandy made from the fruit of the strawberry-tree (arbutus). It is also combined with honey (*medronho mel*) as a liqueur. – The full-bodied wines of Lagoa, Portimão and Lagos are much esteemed.

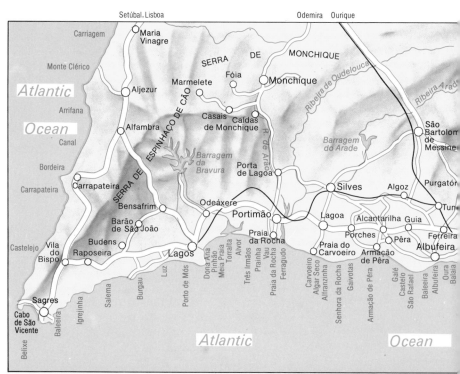

Names of beaches are shown in red

The **Algarve coast** extends from Cabo de São Vicente (Cape St Vincent) to Vila Real de Santo António, on the Portuguese–Spanish frontier, a distance of 185 km/115 miles.

At the western tip of the coast is the windswept *Cabo de São Vicente, a rocky headland rising 60 m/200 ft above the sea, familiar in British history as the scene of the naval victory of Cape St Vincent over a Spanish fleet in 1797. Here in the 12th c. a ship bearing the body of St Vincent came ashore.

On the cape is a lighthouse 24 m/80 ft high, with a light which is visible at a distance of 35 km/22 miles. Tourists can visit the lighthouse, from which there is a fine *view.

From Cape St Vincent the coast road runs NE over a windy heath.

1 km/¾ mile: *Fort Beliche* (tea-room).

5 km/3 miles: **Sagres** (see p. 186).

10 km/6 miles: *Vila do Bispo*. The 17th c. parish church is richly decorated with blue azulejos and gilded woodcarving.
3·5 km/2 miles W is the *Torre de Aspa* (159 m/522 ft), the highest cliff on the Algarve coast.

2 km/1¼ miles: *Raposeira*.

2 km/1¼ miles: to left, the Romanesque and Gothic *chapel of Nossa Senhora de Guadalupe* (13th c.).

12 km/7½ miles: *Espiche*. Beyond this a road goes off on the right to the seaside resort of **Luz de Lagos**.
The main road continues through increasingly sheltered and fertile country.

7 km/4½ miles: **Lagos** (see p. 125).

Beyond Lagos the road crosses the Rio Alvor.

4 km/2½ miles: road on right to *Montes de Alvor*, with a large sandy beach.

2 km/1¼ miles: road on right to ***Praia da Rocha** (see p. 182), with magnificent beaches between picturesque cliffs.

7 km/4¼ miles: road on right to *Penina Golf Hotel* (two golf-courses, 18 and 9 holes).

15 km/9 miles: **Portimão** (see p. 181). Road on left running N via Porto de Lagos and Caldas de Monchique to Monchique and from there to the summit of Mt Fóia (see under Serra de Monchique).
Leaving Portimão by the suburb of *Vila Nova de Portimão*, the road crosses the Rio Arade on a long viaduct.

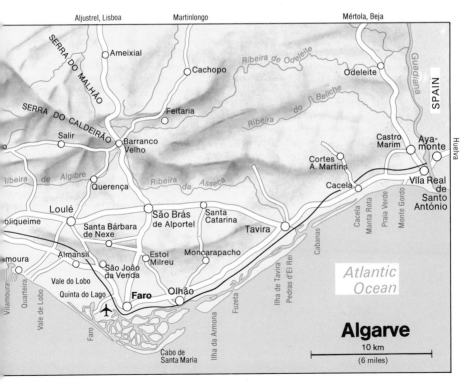

8 km/5 miles: **Lagoa** (pop. 6000), a modest little country town with wine-making establishments. Road on left to **Silves** (see p. 194); road on right to *Praia do Carvoeiro*, a picturesque little fishing village which is now also a pleasant resort with attractive vacation villas.

> During the summer there are fascinating *sightseeing flights over the beautiful Algarve coast.
>
> Information from the tourist offices in Portimão and other major resorts.

11 km/7 miles: *Alcantarilha*. Road on right to the resort and salt-water spa of **Armação de Pêra**, 3 km/2 miles S (sub-aqua and wind-surfing courses); 2 km/1¼ miles W, on a high crag, is the 13th c. chapel of Nossa Senhora da Rocha.

Rock arch near Praia do Carvoeiro

Hotel Dom Pedro, Vilamoura

10 km/6 miles: road on right to *Albu-feira (see p. 50), one of the most attractive resorts in the Algarve.

8 km/5 miles farther on the road forks. The main road, to the right, continues through a fertile region, passing a side road to the fishing village and seaside resort of *Praia da Quarteira* (6 km/4 miles S), adjoining which is the vacation complex of **Vila-moura** (yachting harbour, casino, riding school), and continues to **Almansil**, from where roads lead to the *Hotel Dona Filipa* (18- and 9-hole golf-courses) and the charming resort of *Quinta do Lago*, and Faro (18 km/11 miles).

The left-hand road runs through attractive country to the picturesque town of **Loulé** (alt. 170 m/560 ft; pop. 15,000), 13 km/8 miles E on one of the southern foothills of the Serra de Malhão. The town has a Gothic and Manueline parish church (13th c.) and the ruins of a medieval castle. It is famous for its curious old openwork chimneys. Nearby, at *Abicada*, are Roman remains (mosaics).

From Loulé the road continues SE and in 8 km/5 miles reaches *São João da Venda*, where it rejoins the main road.

8 km/5 miles: **Faro** (see p. 117), chief town of Algarve province.

The coast road runs E from Faro over the irrigated plain, which resembles one enormous fertile garden. To the right is the *Ria de Faro*, and, on a sandy spit of land, the **Cabo de Santa Maria** (lighthouse), the most southerly point on the Portuguese mainland. From here to the Spanish frontier extends a long succession of broad sandy *beaches, interrupted by stretches of pine forest and holiday settlements.

8 km/5 miles: side road on right to the fishing town of **Olhão** (see p. 166).

Beyond this *Monte São Miguel* (408 m/1339 ft) can be seen to the left.

22 km/14 miles: **Tavira** (see p. 199).

19 km/12 miles: road on right (500 m/550 yd) to the resort of **Monte Gordo** (casino), much favoured by British and Dutch visitors, with a good beach, along which there is a beautiful road to Vila Real de Santo António. The main road runs at some distance from the coast.

4 km/$2\frac{1}{2}$ miles: **Vila Real de Santo António** (see p. 206), on the Rio Guadiana, which forms the frontier between Portugal and Spain (car ferry to Ayamonte).

Amarante

Historical province: Douro Litoral.
District: Porto (Oporto).
Altitude: 125 m/410 ft.
Population: 4000.
Post code: P-4600.
Telephone code: 0 55.
ⓘ **Turismo,**
  Rua Cãndido dos Reis;
  tel. 42 29 80.

ACCOMMODATION. – *Silva*, IV, 22 r.; *Príncipe*, P II, 18 r.; *Caçador*, P III, 22 r.; – *Pousada de São Gonçalo*, in Serra de Marão, 15 r.

EVENT. – *Romaria de São Gonçalo* (first Saturday in June), festival in honour of the town's patron saint, who is also patron of married couples and lovers. The celebrations, which are uninhibited and sometimes almost obscene, may be a survival of some pre-Christian fertility cult.

The little town of Amarante, well known for its wine, lies picturesquely above the right bank of the Rio Tâmega, on the NW slopes of the Serra de Marão.

SIGHTS. – The 16th c. **Convento de São Gonçalo** is dominated by its *church*, with a fine tile-clad central dome. The convent, originally founded by King João III and his queen, Catherine of Castile, was enlarged in the reign of Filipe III in the "Philippine" style of the Renaissance period. The exterior, with arcades decorated with sculpture on the granite façade,

is reminiscent of Italian Renaissance architecture.

INTERIOR of church. – To the left of the high altar is the *tomb of São Gonçalo* (d. about 1260), in an over-decorated chapel. – Fine carved *organ-case* (17th c.). – In the *sacristy* are paintings (damaged by French troops) of scenes from the saint's life.

The front *cloister*, though dilapidated, is very attractive.

On the upper floor of the rear cloister, now occupied by the *Town Hall*, is the **Museu de Albano Sardoeira**, a museum of modern Portuguese painting of about 1900 (including works by the Cubist painter Amadeu de Sousa Cardoso, a native of the town), sculpture and archaeology.

Near the convent is the beautiful *Ponte de São Gonçalo* (1790), a three-arched granite bridge spanning the Tâmega. From the left side of the bridge there is a fine view of the convent.

The round **church of São Pedro** (17th c., with a façade of 1725) has fine talha dourada and azulejo decoration.

In the old part of the town there are a number of handsome *burghers' houses* of the 16th–18th c., most of them roofed with shingles and surrounded by continuous wooden balconies.

SURROUNDINGS. – 6 km/4 miles NW is **Freixo de Baixo**, with the fine Romanesque church of São Salvador (1210).

17 km/10 miles SW is the spa of **Caldas de Canaveses**, with hot springs of water containing sulphur and arsenic.

There is a very attractive excursion (50 km/30 miles) eastward through the wooded **Serra do Marão** (1415 m/4643 ft), reaching a height of 1020 m/3347 ft at the *Alto do Espinho* pass (*view) and then descending past the *Pousada de São Gonçalo* (885 m/2904 ft) to **Vila Real** (see p. 205).

In a large chestnut wood near **Rebordela**, 10 km/6 miles SE of Amarante, are numerous prehistoric remains, including rock engravings.

Travança Abbey: see under Oporto.

Church of São Gonçalo, Amarante

Arraiolos

Historical province: Alto Alentejo.
District: Évora.
Altitude: 275 m/900 ft.
Population: 5000.
Post code: P-7040.

ⓘ **Turismo Évora,**
Praça do Giraldo 71,
P-7000 Évora;
tel. (0 66) 2 26 71.

ACCOMMODATION. – None in town. – IN
MONTEMOR-O-NOVO: *Sampaio*, P II, 7 r.; *Monte
Alentejano*, P III, 9 r. – See also under ÉVORA.

**The ancient little town of Arraiolos,
referred to by the Alexandrian geographer Ptolemy under the name of
Arandia, is set on a low hill above the
wide Alentejo plain, with magnificent views.**

The town is noted for its brightly coloured
woollen carpets with geometric patterns,
a craft inherited from the Moors and
practised here since the 16th c. – *Palos*
(ham sausages) are a local culinary
speciality.

SIGHTS. – Above the white houses of the
town, with their coloured (mostly blue)
window-frames, rise the massive ruins of

the 14th c. **Castle**, with two gates and six
square towers, from which there is a
superb *view.

The *church of the Misericórdia* has
beautiful azulejo decoration (18th c.) and
some notable paintings.

Outside the town, to the N, stands the old
Convento (now **Quinta**) **dos Lóios**
(16th c.). Its *church* has a Manueline
doorway and is completely faced with
azulejos (*c.* 1700); the size of the interior
is apparently increased by trompe-l'œil
painting. In the two-storey *cloister* is a
beautiful marble basin of 1575.

SURROUNDINGS. – 4 km/2½ miles SE, the **Solar da
Sempre Noiva**, a country house in late Gothic and
Manueline style, was built in the 16th c. as a hunting
lodge for Archbishop Afonso de Portugal. It contains
fine stellar vaulting in the tower room and the chapel
and has architectural detail of notable quality.

6 km/4 miles NW is the church of *Santa Ana do
Campo*, built on the site of a Roman temple.

23 km/14 miles SW lies **Montemor-o-Novo** (alt.
291 m/955 ft; pop. 9000), a little town of Moorish
appearance, its white houses rising up the slopes of a
hill. High above the town are the ruins of a medieval
castle, occupying the site of a Roman fortress.
Montemor-o-Novo was the birthplace of St John of
God (São João de Deus, 1495–1550), founder of the
order of Brothers Hospitallers.

Arraiolos (Alentejo)

Aveiro

Historical province: Beira Litoral.
District: Aveiro.
Altitude: sea level.
Population: 20,000.
Post code: P-3800.
Telephone code: 0 34.
ⓘ **Turismo,**
   Praça da República;
   tel. 2 36 80.
   A.C.P.
   Avenida do Dr Lourenco Peixinho 89
   tel. 2 25 71.

ACCOMMODATION. – *Imperial,* II, 52 r.; *Arcada,* II, 152 r.; *Afonso V,* III, 84 r.; *Pomba Branca,* P II, 19 r.; *Beira* (with annexe), P III, 40 r.; *Palmeira,* P III, 28 r.; *Aveirense,* P IV, 51 r.

IN OVAR: *Rosa,* P IV, 12 r. – *Pousada da Ria,* at Murtosa, 10 r. (restaurant).

IN VILA DA FEIRA: *Santa Maria,* I, 32 r.; *Ferreira,* P IV, 17 r.

IN ÍLHAVO: *Arimar,* I, 22 r.; *Galera,* P III, 6 r.

IN PRAIA DA BARRA: *Barra.* II, 64 r.; *A Marisqueira,* P II, 18 r.

IN CACIA (7 km/4½ miles NE): *Cacia,* I, 27 r.

CAMP SITES on São Jacinto beach and at Murtosa.

RESTAURANTS. – *Centenário* and *Galo d'Ouro.*

EVENTS. – *Festa de São Sebastião* at Vila da Feira (end January); *Carnival* at Ovar; *Feira de Março,* industrial and trade fair in Aveiro (end March); *Procissão dos Terceiros,* religious procession, Ovar (March); *Festas da Semana Santa,* Holy Week celebrations at Ovar, with fireworks; **Festa da Ria** (second half of July: see adjoining box); *Romaria da Senhora da Saúde da Serra* at Castelães (mid August); *Romaria de São Paio da Torreira,* religious procession to the sea, with "holy bath", blessing of boats and popular festival, Praia da Torreira (beginning of September).

RECREATION and SPORT. – Swimming and water sports on the Costa de Prata (see p. 105).

The old port and fishing town of Aveiro, traversed by canals, is attractively situated on the E side of the Ria de Aveiro, a lagoon 47 km/ 29 miles long and up to 7 km/4½ miles wide, well stocked with fish, with many branches and windings which earn it the local name of the "pólipo aquático" ("sea polyp"). The town is the see of a bishop.

Aveiro has preserved many medieval features. With its numerous canals it is reminiscent of Amsterdam, but the perpetually blue sky and the white houses give it a typically southern charm.

The people of Aveiro and the surrounding area live chiefly from the production of salt, obtained from the salt-pans on the shores of the Ria de Aveiro, the gathering of seaweed for use as a fertiliser and the manufacture of porcelain and ceramics, an industry established here in the early 19th c. – A popular local sweet is *ovos moles* (candied eggs).

HISTORY. – In Roman times the town, then known as *Talabriga,* lay directly on the sea. In the course of time, however, alluvium brought down by the Rio Vouga

---

The Seaweed-Fishers of Aveiro

An unusual harvest is gathered by the *moliceiros* of Aveiro, the **seaweed-fishers** with their characteristic boats, the *barcos moliceiros;* they fish up seaweed (*moliço*), used as a natural fertiliser, from the Ria de Aveiro.

The moliceiros sail their wooden boats, with naive pictures painted in bright colours on the high prow and the stern, through the many branches of the ria, gathering the seaweed with large rakes. When the shallow vessels have a full load the "crop" is brought to land or loaded into ox-carts in the shallows at the edge of the ria.

The boats are up to 15 m/50 ft long and 2–2·2 m/ 6½–7 ft wide. If there is sufficient wind a trapezoid sail is hoisted; otherwise the boats are propelled by long poles or towed along narrow channels by long topes.

In recent times the number of boats has fallen from its original total or more than a thousand to no more than thirty or so. The once busy and profitable trade of seaweed-gathering is now gradually dying out as a result of the increasing use of artificial fertilisers in agriculture. As the demand for seaweed has fallen the moliceiros have begun to harvest wrack-grass (*junco*), which is dried and used as litter for livestock. The difficulty of making a living and the drift of young people to the towns, however, mean that few young men are now prepared to take up this old trade.

During the **Festa da Ria,** held annually in the second half of July, the last of the moliceiros take part in a regatta, with contests of skill and a competition for the finest paintings on the boats.

A *barco moliceiro* in the Aveiro lagoon

built up a spit of land off the coast, leaving only a narrow channel to the sea, the Barra. The town thus acquired one of the most sheltered harbours on the W coast of the peninsula, and enjoyed a period of high prosperity in the 15th and 16th c. as a result of the voyages of discovery which set out from here. The town still preserves many fine old buildings dating from this period.

In 1575 a violent storm devastated the town and closed its outlet to the sea. The harbour was now land-locked and useless, and all attempts to reopen the passage to the sea were unsuccessful; the fishermen, deprived of their livelihood, migrated in the 18th c. to the new port of Vila Real de Santo António at the mouth of the Guadiana, founded by Pombal. – A further storm in 1808 opened up the old channel to the sea, and this is now protected from silting-up by dykes and weirs. Aveiro harbour now ranks once again among the finest harbours in Portugal.

SIGHTS. – In the Praça da República, opposite the *Town Hall*, stands the **church of the Misericórdia** (16th–17th c.), with a fine Baroque doorway and beautiful 19th c. azulejo decoration on the façade.

To the E is the **Cathedral** (*Sé de Nossa Senhora da Glória*), presented to the Dominicans by the Infante Dom Pedro and consecrated in 1464.
It was much altered in the 18th c., and the porch dates from the beginning of that century.

The Cathedral contains the tomb of Catarina de Atalíde (d. 1551), celebrated by Camões in his sonnets under the name of Natércia – in consequence of which the poet was compelled to make a hasty departure from Portugal. – In front of the Cathedral is a beautiful Gothic cross, the *Cruzeiro de São Domingos.

Opposite the Cathedral, to the S, is the **Convento de Jesús**, formerly a house of Dominican nuns, which the Infanta Joana, daughter of King Afonso V, entered in 1472, against her father's will. She died in the convent in 1490 at the age of only 38 and was buried in the church. Her readiness to endure privation and her renunciation of all privileges won her many admirers, and she is now much revered as the town's patron saint.

The convent now houses the well-stocked ***Museu de Aveiro**, which gives an excellent and almost complete survey of Portuguese Baroque art and also displays pictures of the 15th to 20th c., sculpture and archaeological material. In the vestibule of the church, which is richly decorated with talha dourada and azulejos, is the Baroque tomb of St Joana (by João Antunes, 1699–1711).

Beside the Fish Market is the octagonal *chapel of São Gonçalo*, with a richly

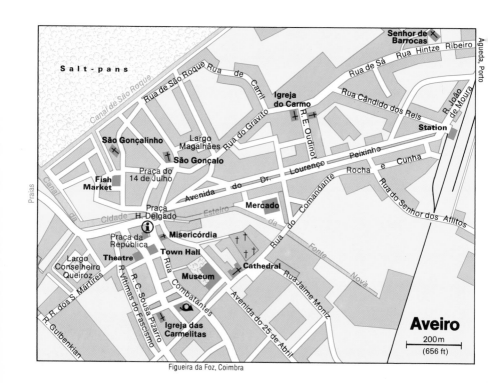
Figueira da Foz, Coimbra

decorated doorway, and in the N of the town, near the station, the **chapel of the Senhor de Barrocas**, also octagonal (by João Antunes, *c.* 1730).

The town's many handsome *burghers' houses* are best seen on a *boat trip on the canals (recommended).

SURROUNDINGS. – A very attractive trip from Aveiro is a *cruise on the lagoon (angling, wildfowling). Interesting features are the pile-dwellings designed to cope with varying water levels and the racks for drying the cod (stockfish) landed by the deep-sea fishermen. The brightly painted boats of the *moliceiros* (seaweed-gatherers) will also be seen.

At the N end of the Ria de Aveiro is **Ovar** (pop. 14,000; timber trade), famous for its Carnival, with splendid processions through the streets of the town. The Calvário, with six chapels, is a scheduled national monument. An interesting local museum contains modern painting, folk art and ethnographical material. – 5 km/2½ miles farther NW is the pretty little resort of *Praia do Furadouro* (good beach), where, as at Nazaré, the fishermen use oxen to haul in their full nets. – Farther S, also on the spit of land between the ria and the sea, are the village of *Torreira* and the *Pousada da Ria.*

12 km/7½ miles NE of Ovar, the little market town of **Vila da Feira** (pop. 3000) is dominated by the imposing ruins of a castle built in the 11th c. and later much altered and enlarged.

7 km/4½ miles S of Aveiro in the old fishing port of **Ílhavo** (pop. 6500), now completely silted up, there is an interesting Museu Marítimo e Regional. – 1 km/¾ mile farther SW **Vista Alegre** has a famous porcelain manufactory founded in 1824. Interesting conducted tour of the manufactory, with porcelain museum. In the little chapel of Nossa Senhora da Penha de França (17th c.) is the tomb of Bishop Manuel de Moura (1699), by the French sculptor Claude Laparde.

Along the coast W of Aveiro are beautiful sandy beaches – **São Jacinto**, 8 km/5 miles W, and **Barra** and **Costa Nova do Prado**, farther S. They offer not only good bathing but excellent facilities for water sports (sailing, rowing, motorboats, water-skiing).

Costa de Prata: see p. 105.

Avis (Aviz)

Historical province: Alentejo.
District: Portalegre.
Altitude: 200 m/655 ft.
Population: 2000.
Post code: P-7480.
Telephone code: 0 45.
ⓘ **Turismo Portalegre,**
Rua 19 de Junho 40,
P-7300 Portalegre;
tel. (00 45) 2 18 15.

ACCOMMODATION. – None in town. See under PORTALEGRE.

The little town of Avis (formerly spelt Aviz), with fine old buildings bearing witness to a glorious past, lies at the junction of the Ribeira de Avis and the Ribeira de Sêda. 10 km/6 miles SW of the town is the dam supplying the Maranhão hydro-electric station, which converts the river into a long, straggling lake with numerous arms.

HISTORY. – The military order of the Freires de Évora was founded by Afonso Henriques in 1147 to fight the Moors – the first **knightly religious order** in Europe. In 1211 its headquarters were moved to Avis by Afonso II and it became the order of São Bento. Thereafter the splendour and influence of the Knights of Avis lasted into the late 18th c. With the coronation of the Grand Master of the order as King João I in 1385 Avis became the cradle of a royal dynasty which ruled Portugal until 1580, during which period (particularly in the regency of João II and the reign of Manuel I) the country flourished as never before and became the leading seafaring nation in the world.

SIGHTS. – Of the fortifications of the **Castle** of the Knights (founded 1214) there remain a gateway and three towers.

The **church** (rebuilt in the 17th c.) contains a number of 15th c. tombs and a valuable gilt reliquary. From the sacristy there is a fine *view.

SURROUNDINGS. – 25 km/15 miles E is the little town of **Fronteira** (pop. 2500), with a late 16th c. parish church and burghers' houses of the 17th and 18th c. In the main square stands a handsome 17th c. marble pillory column. There are fine views from the tower of the Town Hall.
Above the town is the church of Nossa Senhora da Vila Velha, entirely clad with 17th c. azulejos.

Azores/ Ilhas dos Açores

Autonomous Region of the Azores
(Região Autónoma dos Açores).
Area of islands: 2247 sq. km/867 sq. miles.
Population: 244,000.
ⓘ **Turismo Ponta Delgada,**
Avenida do Infante Dom Henrique,
P-9500 Ponta Delgada;
tel. (via operator): 2 57 43.

AIR SERVICES. – Inter-continental airport on **Santa Maria**; airport on **São Miguel** (connections with Lisbon and with Santa Maria, Terceira, Faial and Madeira); air-strips on *Terceira* and *Faial*. – Local services are flown by the Azorean airline SATA.

BOAT SERVICES. – Regular services two or three times a month from *Lisbon* via *São Miguel* and *Terceira* or *Faial* to *Madeira* and back. – Local services between islands; also attractive round trips and cruises.

The archipelago of the *Azores (Ilhas dos Açores, "Islands of the Hawks"), still little involved in the tourist trade, lies in the Atlantic 1400–1800 km/870–1120 miles W of the Cabo da Roca on the mainland of Portugal and 1800–2500 km/1120–1550 miles E of Newfoundland, between lat. 39° 43′ 23″ and 36° 55′ 43″ N and long. 24° 46′ 15″ and 31° 16′ 24″ W.

The nine largest islands lie in three widely separated groups. To the E are **Santa Maria**, with the little *Formigas Islands*, and **São Miguel**, the principal island of the whole archipelago; in the middle are the islands of **Terceira**, **Graciosa**, **São Jorge**, *Faial* and *Pico*, with Portugal's highest mountain (Pico, 2351 m/7714 ft); and to the NW **Flores** and **Corvo**. Two broad arms of the sea, more than 2000 m/6500 ft deep and respectively 137 km/85 miles and 222 km/138 miles wide, separate the three groups, the farthest points on which are 635 km/395 miles apart.

HISTORY. – The Azores were known to the *Phoenicians* in the 6th c. B.C., and many centuries later were visited by *Norsemen*. Thereafter they were forgotten for centuries, first reappearing on an Italian map of 1351.

The islands were rediscovered in 1427 by Portuguese seafarers sent out by Henry the Navigator. In 1432 *Gonçalo Velho Cabral* landed on Santa Maria, in 1444 a Portuguese vessel put in at São Miguel, and by 1452 the other islands were also known. From 1439 the archipelago, until then uninhabited, began to be settled and colonised by the Portuguese. In 1466 Afonso V made the islands over to his aunt Duchess Isabella of Burgundy, and thereafter there was a considerable influx of *Flemish* settlers. – As an

important port of call on the voyages of exploration of the 15th and 16th c. the islands enjoyed a period of great prosperity. From 1580 to 1640 the Azores, like the rest of Portugal, were under Spanish rule. They played an important part in the constitutional conflicts in Portugal between 1829 and 1832.

During both world wars, in spite of Portugal's neutrality, the United States established important naval and air bases in these strategically situated islands. A recently signed agreement provides for the presence of United States army units and the maintenance of the bases until 1984.

For some time there has been a movement for Azorean independence from Portugal (Frente de Libertação dos Açores, FLA, and other groups). – The Azores are represented in the Portuguese Parliament. Since 1980 they have issued their own stamps.

Like other groups of islands in the Atlantic, the Azores are of volcanic origin, consisting of basaltic lavas, mainly of Tertiary date, and trachytes overlying the

Porto Formosa (São Miguel)

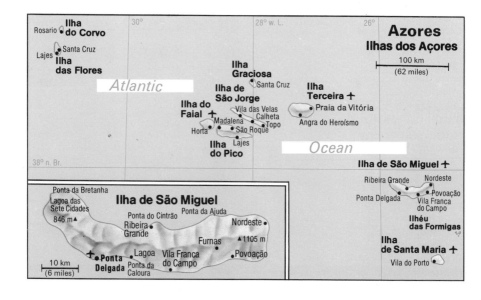

Central Atlantic anticline. There are numbers of huge calderas, some of them (particularly on São Miguel) containing lakes of considerable size. The general topography of the islands is strikingly impressive, with a variegated pattern of hills and uplands, deeply slashed gorges, steep coastal cliffs and numerous hot springs. Some islands have frequent earthquakes (São Miguel was completely destroyed in 1522, and there was a severe earthquake on Terceira, São Jorge, Faial and Pico on New Year's Day 1980), while others (Santa Maria, Graciosa) are almost free from seismic activity. Sea-quakes are of frequent occurrence in the offshore waters.

The *vegetation* of the Azores, thanks to the high humidity content of the air, is of almost tropical abundance, though it falls short of the luxuriance and variety found on Madeira. The flora is mainly of either European or African origin. In spite of excessive felling of trees since the colonisation of the islands the hillsides are still covered with fine coniferous forests. Plans are now under way for replanting the deforested areas. Laurels, chestnuts and eucalyptuses are frequently found, either in fair-sized stretches of woodland or in smaller groves. The undergrowth includes bamboos and ferns. Palms are rare, and olive-trees are found in large numbers only on Terceira.

Apart from a few native species of birds and bats the animal life is of European origin. Curiously, the sparrow so ubiquitous elsewhere has never established itself in the Azores. Rabbits, mice and rats – common everywhere, and in some places so numerous as to have become pests – were brought in by ships.

Thanks to their oceanic location and the influence of the Gulf Stream, which flows past the islands to the N, the Azores have a very equable subtropical *climate*.
The annual variation of temperature is scarcely greater than on the more southerly island of Madeira (January average at Ponta Delgada 14·1°C/57·4°F, August 21·9°C/71·4°F), but the rainfall is higher than on Madeira and the summers in particular are not so dry (average annual rainfall at Ponta Delgada 1083 mm/43 in.; average duration of sunshine in the year 1579·1 hours).
The islands are exposed throughout the year to strong winds, in summer blowing mainly from the NE (trade winds), in winter often violent, mostly coming from the SW.

The Azores are of great importance to weather forecasters, since very stable zones of high pressure frequently build up in the area, particularly to the S and W, from which they move NE towards Europe, bringing a settled period of good weather.

Visitors to the Azores, at any time of year, should be sure to take with them adequate rainproof clothing.

The *population* of the Azores is predominantly of Portuguese origin, with some admixture of Irish, Flemish and Breton blood and small numbers of negroes and mulattoes. The overwhelming majority of the population professes the Roman Catholic faith.
In the past an unduly high population density and the unequal distribution of the land, most of which during the colonial period was held by a few large landowners, led to a high rate of emigration, particularly to North and South America.

The *economy*, now as in the past, depends mainly on agriculture. All the islands are well cultivated, producing grain (wheat, maize), fruit (apricots, pomegranates, bananas, figs, citrus fruits; pineapples on São Miguel), tea and tobacco for export, mainly to mainland Portugal. Wine is produced on all the islands.
There is also a considerable amount of stock-farming (cattle, pigs, sheep, goats). – There are productive fisheries off the coasts. Whaling, long based on Faial and Pico, is now very much in decline. – A contribution is also made to the economy by the gathering of seaweed, which produces the agar-agar used in the manufacture of gelatine.

There is practically no industry in the Azores apart from a few recently established textile plants on Terceira and São Miguel. Linen and woollen goods, lace and pottery are made at home or in small workshops, and – like the brandies which are distilled at a number of places in the islands – make popular souvenirs.

São Miguel/ Ilha de São Miguel

*São Miguel, the largest and most populous island in the archipelago (area 747 sq. km/288 sq. miles; pop. 155,000), is the economic and cultural hub of the Azores, with more features of tourist interest and better facilities for visitors than any of the other islands.

São Miguel, 65 km/40 miles long and up to 16 km/10 miles wide, is known as the "green island" by virtue of its extraordinary fertility. Most of the population live on the steep S coast. The highest points on the island are the Pico da Vara (1105 m/3626 ft) in the E and the *Pico da Cruz* (846 m/2776 ft) in the W; in the middle of the island, between these two peaks, are many basalt cones ranging in height between 200 m/650 ft and 500 m/ 1650 ft.

The volcanic character of this hilly island is reflected in the countless extinct craters, large and small, and the severe earthquakes and volcanic eruptions which have racked São Miguel since the 15th c. – Some of the largest *craters are now occupied by beautiful mountain lakes (Caldeira das Sete Cidades, Lagoa das Furnas, Lagoa do Fogo) which are now among the island's main tourist attractions.

Warm and mineral springs are found, particularly in the valleys of Ribeira Grande near the N coast, and at Furnas near the S coast.

The large areas of agricultural land on the island produce maize, figs, pineapples, oranges, wine and tea.

Ponta Delgada

Autonomous Region of the Azores.
Island: São Miguel. – District: Ponta Delgada.
Altitude: sea level.
Population: 22,000.
Post code: P-9500.
Telephone code: 096.
ⓘ **Turismo,**
    Avenida do Infante Dom Henrique;
    tel. 2 57 43.

ACCOMMODATION. – *Avenida*, I, 80 r.; *São Pedro*, I, 30 r.; *Albergaria Casa das Palmeiras*, I, 9 r.; *Infante*, III, 39 r.; *Central*, P II, 40 r.; *América*, P II, 23 r.; *São Miguel*, P II, 20 r.; *O Casarão*, P 11, 15 r.; *Roma*, P III, 7 r. – IN FURNAS: *Terra Nostra*, II, 38 r., SP.

EVENTS. – Festival of the *Senhor Santo Cristo dos Milagres* (5th Sunday after Easter), with folk events, singing competitions (Cantadores ao Desafio) and traditional costumes; *Cavalhadas de São Pedro* (end June), medieval equestrian games in Ribeira Grande; *Festas do Divino Espírito Santo* (beginning of August), folk festival.

Ponta Delgada, capital of the autonomous region of the Azores and the chief town and port of the whole archipelago, lies in a wide bay on the S coast of the island of São Miguel.

The town is built on gently rising ground between green hills, and with its many churches, its trim white houses and the lush gardens on its outskirts presents an attractive *spectacle to visitors arriving by sea.
Since 1975 Ponta Delgada has been the seat of the University of the Azores, which is still in process of development.
The airport is to the W of the town.

Beach of volcanic sand, Ponta Delgada

Ponta Delgada harbour (São Miguel)

Caldeira das Sete Cidades (São Miguel)

SIGHTS. – The **Harbour** (mainly handling fruit and vegetables) is protected by a breakwater 1544 m/1690 yd long, from which there are fine views. At the landward end of the breakwater is *Fort São Braz* (1553), behind which stands a former *Franciscan convent* (now a hospital), with the beautifully decorated **church of São José** (15th–18th c.).

In the middle of the town are three linked squares. The first of these, as one comes from the harbour by way of the three-arched *Town Gate* (1783), is the Praça de Gonçalo Velho, with a *monument to Gonçalo Velho Cabral*, discoverer and first governor of the Azores; then comes the Praça da República, with a *statue of St Michael* (São Miguel) in front of the **Paços do Concelho** (Town Hall, 17th–18th c.); and finally the Largo da Matriz, with the **church of São Sebastião** (founded 1533, in the reign of João III), mainly Baroque, with a tall tower which is a prominent landmark. The beautiful main doorway, on the W front, is in Manueline style. The church has a beautiful high altar of carved cedarwood (18th c.) and fine choir-stalls. The adjoining *Museum* is devoted to religious art, in particular 16th c. vestments.

The former *Convento de Santo André* (16th c.; chapel with azulejo decoration) now houses the interesting **Museu Carlos Machado**, with extensive collections illustrating the folk traditions, culture and natural history (birds, fishes) of the Azores.

From here Rua Guilherme Poças leads to the **Igreja do Colégio** (1592), built for the Jesuits (who were expelled in 1759). The church has a sumptuous Baroque doorway and a magnificent Baroque *altar.

On the outskirts of the town are a number of attractive gardens and parks, some of them privately owned (seen on application), including the **Municipal Park**, formerly the *Jardim António Borges* (wild-life enclosure).
Also worth a visit are the *pineapple-houses* just outside the town.

SURROUNDINGS. – There are superb panoramic *views from the hills around the town – the *Pico Salomão* (3 km/2 miles N), the *Pico da Lima* (6 km/4 miles NE) and the *Pico do Fogo* (10 km/6 miles NE).

17 km/11 miles NW of Ponta Delgada is the *Caldeira das Sete Cidades** ("Cauldron of the Seven Cities"), in which legend has it that seven towns founded by expelled Spanish bishops were sunk. This is a volcanic crater which collapsed during some mighty eruption in prehistoric times and was given its present form, with a diameter of some 7 km/4½ miles and a circumference of 17 km/10½ miles, by another violent eruption in 1445.
The caldera is occupied by three small and two large crater lakes, the latter two – the *Lagoa Grande* or *Lagoa Verde*, with clear green water, and the *Lagoa Azul*, with deep blue water – being separated only by a narrow strip of land.
The walls of the crater, falling steeply down for some

300 m/1000 ft, are surrounded by a fringe of woods, ferns and laurels.

18 km/11 miles NE of Ponta Delgada, on a lava plateau above the N coast of São Miguel, is the town of **Ribeira Grande** (pop. 9000), with a town hall of the 16th–18th c. and a 17th c. parish church.
From Ribeira Grande a road climbs to the SE via *Caldeira da Ribeira* (6 km/4 miles), a small spa with hot mineral springs containing carbonic acid and hydrogen sulphide, and *Lombadas* (11 km/7 miles), which produces a mineral water esteemed throughout Portugal, to the **Lagoa do Fogo** ("Lake of Fire"), a crater lake 2 km/1¼ miles long by 1 km/¾ mile wide, surrounded by high hills, which was formed during an eruption in 1563. – It is worth climbing the *Pico da Barrosa* (949 m/3114 ft) for the sake of the extensive *views it affords over the whole island.

Lagoa do Fogo (São Miguel)

25 km/15 miles E of Ponta Delgada, on the S coast, is the former capital of the Azores, **Vila Franca do Campo**, birthplace of the navigator *Bento de Góis*, which was completely destroyed by an earthquake in 1522 (several 16th c. churches; pottery workshops). From Vila Franca do Campo a road runs inland, passing the *Lagoa das Furnas*, a crater lake 2 km/1¼ miles long, to *Furnas, a popular summer resort (fine gardens, villas) in a beautiful forest-fringed valley basin (alt. 200–275 m/650–900 ft). Here after a violent volcanic eruption in 1630 there emerged a whole series of springs of various kinds (hot springs, mud springs, sulphur and mineral springs), some of which are used for medicinal purposes, either internally or in baths. There is magnificent luxuriant vegetation.

12 km/7½ miles SE of Furnas on a beautiful road is **Povoação** (pop. 4000), one of the oldest settlements in the Azores, in a wide bay on the S coast.

Santa Maria/
Ilha de Santa Maria

Santa Maria, the most southerly of the Azores, lies 85 km/53 miles S of São Miguel in lat. 37° N and long. 25° 5′ W.

This rocky but fertile island, 17 km/11 miles long and up to 8 km/5 miles wide, has an area of 97 sq. km/37 sq. miles and a population of 9000, who live mainly by crop-farming, stock-rearing and fishing, with pottery as a common subsidiary activity.

Some of the inhabitants are now also employed by the Portuguese and United States air forces and navies, which have maintained important bases here (and on Terceira) since 1944.

The island is hilly, becoming flatter towards the W, with steep coasts fringed by long stretches of cliffs. The highest point is the double summit of *Pico Alto* (590 m/1836 ft). There are no calderas on Santa Maria.

Some 35 km/22 miles NE of Santa Maria is the *Formigas Bank*, a subterranean ridge which emerges from the water to a height of up to 11 m/36 ft in a series of bare cliffs known as the **Rocas Formigas**.

SIGHTS. – **Vila do Porto** (pop. 6000; Hotel Aeroporto de Santa Maria, III, 47 r.), the chief town on the island, is a small port in a wide, open bay on the S coast, surrounded by cliffs. The town, defended by two forts, is believed to have been the first settlement founded by Portuguese colonists in the 15th c. It has a number of 16th and 17th c. churches, including the church of Nossa Senhora da Assunção (15th c.; partly rebuilt in 1832), with a fine tower. – The airport lies NW of the town.

From Vila do Porto an attractive excursion (12 km/7½ miles S) can be made, passing below the Pico Alto, to **São Lourenço**, which enjoys a beautiful *setting above a sheltered bay on the E coast.

On the S side of the bay is the little islet of *Romeiro*, with a beautiful stalactitic cave.

Terceira/
Ilha Terceira

Terceira, the "third" island, was the third to be discovered and is also the third largest in the Azores. The most important of the islands after São Miguel, it lies 157 km/98 miles NW of that island and 56 km/35 miles E of the neighbouring island of São Jorge.

Terceira is 31 km/19 miles long and up to 18 km/11 miles wide, with an area of 397 sq. km/153 sq. miles. Its highest point is the *Caldeira de Santa Bárbara* (1067 m/3501 ft), in the western half of the island. The eastern half consists mainly of a great volcanic plateau surrounded by high mountains. The coasts are steep, with many stretches of cliff, protected here and there by forts.

The 80,000 inhabitants, many of them descended from the first Flemish settlers in the 15th c., live by crop-farming, stock-rearing and seaweed-gathering. Thanks to the extraordinary fertility of its soil Terceira is the largest grain-producer in the archipelago. – Some of the inhabitants find employment as civilian personnel at the *Lajes* air base in the NE of the island.

On 1 January 1980 the island was shaken by a severe earthquake which caused considerable damage to buildings and installations and a number of deaths.

Angra do Heroísmo

Autonomous Region of the Azores.
Island: Terceira.
District: Angra do Heroísmo.
Altitude: sea level.
Population: 14,000.
Post code: P-9700.
Telephone code: 095.
ⓘ **Turismo,**
Rua de Lisboa;
tel. 2 33 93.

ACCOMMODATION. – IN ANGRA DO HEROÍSMO:
Albergaria Cruzeiro, I, 47 r.; *De Angra*, II, 86 r.

IN CABO DE PRAIA: *Motel das Nove Ilhas*, II, 18 r.

IN SERRETA: *Estalagem da Serreta*, I, 12 r.

Angra do Heroísmo, the fortified chief town of its district and of the island of Terceira and the see of the Bishop of the Azores, lies in an open bay 2 km/1¼ miles wide on the S coast of the island.

On the W side of the bay is a peninsula, with *Monte Brazil* (210 m/689 ft). The attractive little town, which has a good harbour, was founded in 1534 and owes the second part of its name to its heroic resistance to the Spanish conquerors in the late 16th c., falling into Spanish hands only in 1583. Until 1832, when it was displaced by Ponta Delgada on São Miguel, Angra do Heroísmo was the

capital of the Azores, and it still ranks as the cultural heart of the archipelago.

SIGHTS. – From the **Harbour** the busy Rua de Lisboa (or Rua Direita) leads past the **church of the Misericórdia**, an imposing twin-towered Renaissance church, to the Praça da Restauração, the hub of the town's life. On the E side of the square is the 19th c. *Câmara Municipal* (Town Hall). The Rua de Lisboa ends in the Largo Prior do Crato, to the N of the Praça da Restauração, in which is the former *Jesuit College*; the **church** (1652) has a richly decorated Baroque interior.

To the E of the Praça da Restauração, in Rua de João de Deus, stands the *church of São Francisco* (15th c., rebuilt in 17th c.). The convent buildings of the former Franciscan friary now houses the **Municipal Museum** (*Museu Municipal*: folk traditions, coins, militaria, ships and the sea, art).
The Franciscan friary is believed to contain the remains of Paulo da Gama (d. 1499), brother of the great navigator

Angra do Heroísmo (Terceira, Azores)

An attractive trip can be made to the volcanic western part of Terceira and the **Caldeira de Santa Bárbara** (1022 m/3353 ft; *view), the highest point on the island, a volcano with a number of explosion vents and collapsed craters.

NE and E of the volcanic plateau, between *Pico Alto*, *Pico da Bagacina* and *Furnas do Enxofre*, are several crater lakes and fumeroles.

On a broad lava flow in the N of Terceira is the little wine-making town of **Biscoitos**.

Porto Martins (Terceira)

Vasco da Gama, who fell ill during the return voyage from the West Indies and died on Terceira; his tomb has not been identified.

SW of the Praça da Restauração, in Rua da República, is the twin-towered **Cathedral** (*Sé*), built in 1568 on the site of an earlier church; 1983 completely destroyed by fire.

NE of the Praça da Restauração, higher up, is an *obelisk* commemorating Pedro IV, from which there are far-ranging *views of the town.

To the E of the Praça da Restauração, at the end of Rua Rainha Dona Amélia, is the 17th c. *church of the Conceição* (Conception), with rich talha dourada decoration in the interior.

Fort São João Baptista, above the town to the NW, at the foot of Monte Brazil, was built by the Spaniards in the 17th c. It affords a magnificent panoramic *view of the town.
From the fort it is an easy climb up *Monte Brazil* (210 m/689 ft), a crater formed in a submarine eruption. From the rim of the crater there are superb *views.

SURROUNDINGS of Angra do Heroísmo. – 21 km/ 13 miles NE of the town, in a wide bay on the E coast of Terceira, lies the old fortified port of **Praia da Vitória** (pop. 9000), named in commemoration of the Liberals' victory over the Royalists on 11 August 1829. The town has several times suffered earthquake destruction (1641, 1841; severe damage in 1980), and only two old buildings survive – the church (15th c.) in the upper part of the town, which has a rich Manueline doorway, and the 16th c. Town Hall. There is a fine long sandy beach.
25 km/16 miles NW of Praia da Vitória is **Lajes** (pop. 6500), a busy little town which depends almost entirely on the nearby air base for its subsistence.

Graciosa/
Ilha Graciosa

Graciosa, the most northerly island in the central Azores group, lies some 70 km/45 miles NW of Terceira and 55 km/35 miles N of São Jorge in lat. 39° 3′ N and long. 28° W. It owes its name to its unusual abundance of *flowers.

The island is 13 km/8 miles long and up to 7 km/4½ miles wide, with an area of 62 sq. km/24 sq. miles. Unlike the other islands in the Azores, it is not particularly hilly but, like them, it has steep and rocky coasts. Its highest point is the rim of the *Caldeira do Enxofre* (411 m/1348 ft).

The island's 7500 inhabitants live by crop-farming, fruit-growing and stock-rearing.

SIGHTS. – **Santa Cruz** (pop. 2000), chief place on the island and its principal port, lies in a small plain on the NE coast. The little town was founded in 1485.
The parish church (1701) has a fine altar.

5 km/3 miles SE of Santa Cruz is the little port of *Praia da Graciosa*, from which it is a 1½ hours' climb to the **Caldeira do Enxofre**, 4 km/2½ miles S. This is a crater 1200 m/1300 yd long, 600 m/650 yd across and some 300 m/1000 ft deep, with a crater lake and several eruption vents. There are extensive views from the rim of the crater.

On the floor of the crater is the *Furna do Enxofre*, a cavern some 150 m/165 yd long, 100 m/110 yd wide and over 20 m/ 65 ft high formed by the collapse of a layer of solidified lava after the outflow of the molten lava below. In the cavern are a small warm lake and several fumeroles of carbonic acid.

São Lourenço (São Miguel, Azores)

At the foot of the Caldeira, in the extreme S of the island, is the little spa of **Termas do Carapacho**, with subterranean mineral springs.

São Jorge/ Ilha de São Jorge

Roughly in the middle of the central group of the Azores is the long narrow island of São Jorge (St George), 55 km/35 miles W of Terceira and separated from the islands of Pico to the SW and Faial to the W by the 18 km/11 mile wide Canal de São Jorge.

São Jorge has an area of 246 sq. km/95 sq. miles and consists of one long narrow ridge of forest-covered volcanic hills, 45 km/28 miles from end to end, which reaches its highest point in the *Pico da Esperança* (1066 m/3498 ft) and falls down to the sea in steep and rugged cliffs.

The 13,000 inhabitants live by crop-farming, stock-rearing, fishing and timber-working.

The island was shaken by a severe earthquake on New Year's Day 1980.

SIGHTS. – The chief settlement on the island is the little port of **Vila das Velas** (pop. 1100), in a sheltered bay on the SW coast.

22 km/14 miles SE of Vila das Velas is *Calheta* (pop. 1500; canning plant), a modest coastal village with a small harbour, from which the **Pico da Esperança** (1066 m/3498 ft) can be climbed. This is a now quiescent volcano which last erupted in 1808; from the top there is a superb ** view of the whole archipelago.

At the eastern tip of the island is **Topo**, which is noted for its brightly coloured woollen blankets and cloth.

Faial/ Ilha do Faial

Faial ("Beech Island"), the most westerly island in the central group of the Azores, is so called after a scrub tree (*Myrica faya*) resembling the beech which grows on the island. It is separated from the neighbouring island of Pico to the SE by the 7 km/4¼ mile wide Canal do Faial, and from São Jorge to the E by the 18 km/11 mile wide Canal de São Jorge.

This hilly island, with a greatest length of 22 km/14 miles and a greatest width of 15 km/9 miles, has an area of 172 sq. km/66 sq. miles. Its highest point is the *Pico Gordo* (1043 m/3422 ft), a volcano which has been quiescent since 1672.

The 18,000 inhabitants live by farming and stock-rearing. The whaling industry which has been based on Faial for many centuries is now uneconomic and is dying out.

In the early years of this century the island was also important as an intermediate station for transatlantic cables.

The island has a soil of remarkable fertility and is covered with a luxuriant growth of vegetation. It is famous for an abundance of* hydrangeas, which form dense hedges along the island's roads and tracks. The main town, Horta, is said by some to derive its name from the hydrangea (*Hydrangea hortensia*) – although in fact the flower is of Eastern Asian origin.

Faial has been frequently devastated by earthquakes, as in 1759–60, 1862, 1926, 1958 and most recently on New Year's Day 1980.

The Nuremberg cosmographer *Martin Behaim* (1459–1507), who made major contributions to nautical and geographical knowledge in the age of the great discoveries, lived on Faial from 1486 to 1490.

Horta

Autonomous Region of the Azores.
Island: Faial.
District: Horta.
Altitude: sea level.
Population: 7500.
Post code: P-9900.
Telephone code: 092.
ⓘ **Turismo,**
Rua Conselheiro Medeiros;
tel. 2 22 37.

ACCOMMODATION. – *Faial*, I, 83 r., SP; *Estalagem de Santa Cruz*, I, 25 r.; *São Francisco*, P II, 29 r.; *Infante*, P III, 19 r.

Horta, **the fortified main town of Faial, lies facing the imposing cone of Pico in a wide bay on the SE coast of the island, with a beach of black volcanic sand.**

The town is probably named after Josse van Hutere, who settled Flemish colonists here at the behest of the Infante Dom Henrique. (For an alternative derivation of the name see under Faial.)

The Parliament of the Azores usually meets in Horta. The town with its well-protected harbour is the most frequent port of call in the North Atlantic for transatlantic sailors of every nation.

SIGHTS. – The town is attractively situated on gently rising ground, surrounded by handsome villas and beautiful gardens. The inhabitants, many of them of Flemish descent, live by trade and the sale of fine embroidery and basketwork.

The **harbour,** one of the best in the Azores, is protected by a breakwater 750 m/820 yd long. (Note the "painting wall", on which the seamen immortalise themselves.) The bay is closed on the S by the *Guia* peninsula (148 m/486 ft), formed by a submarine crater, which is linked to the island by a narrow isthmus.

There is an attractive walk (or boat trip from the harbour) around the peninsula to the water-filled **Caldeira do Inferno** on the S side, continuing to *Porto Pim* (former whaling station), on the seaward side of the isthmus.

SURROUNDINGS. – A road (18 km/11 miles NW) ascends to the rim of the* **Caldeira do Pico Gordo,** in the middle of the island. On the floor of the crater, which is 2 km/1¼ miles in diameter and some 400 m/ 1300 ft deep, is a small lake. There is an attractive walk with magnificent* views around the rim.

The western tip of Faial is formed by the **Volcão dos Capelinhos,** a submarine volcano which emerged from the sea in 1957, burying under its ash the fishing village of *Comprido* and partly covering the old lighthouse. When the volcano subsided in 1958 the island was larger than before.
There is a small museum containing relics of the eruption and explanations of the formation of the volcano.

The *trip around the island* from Horta is also very rewarding.

Pico/
Ilha do Pico

Pico, the most southerly island in the central group of the Azores, lies E of Faial and SW of São Jorge, from which it is separated by the 18 km/ 1 mile wide Canal de São Jorge.

View of the island capital of Horta (Faial, Azores)

The rugged and mountainous island of Pico, 48 km/30 miles long and up to 15 km/9 miles wide, with an area of 433 sq. km/167 sq. miles, rises at its western end to the prominent *Pico Alto* (2351 m/7714 ft), the highest peak not only in the Azores but in the whole of Portugal. The highest point in the eastern half of the island is the *Pico Topo* (1633 m/5358 ft).

The volcanic soil, of recent formation and over large areas without any covering of humus, affords little scope for agriculture, and the 18,000 inhabitants have to import much of their food from the neighbouring islands. The only extensive areas of cultivation are the vineyards which have been created with much labour on the slopes of the Pico Alto. The once considerable whaling industry has now much declined. There is an airport on the island.

The island was shaken by a severe earthquake on New Year's Day 1980.

SIGHTS. – The chief town of the island and its oldest settlement is the whaling port of **Lajes** (pop. 2500) on the S coast, with a town hall and parish church built of black lava.

Two other little ports are **Cais do Pico** or *São Roque* (fish-canning plant) on the N coast and **Madalena** (regular boat connections with Horta, on the island of Faial) on the NW coast. The three places are linked by a road encircling the island, which also gives access to a number of stalactitic caves, some of them only recently discovered, of which the *Furna de Frei Matias* at the NW foot of the Pico Alto is the best known.

The main tourist attraction on the island is the * **Pico Alto** (2351 m/7714 ft), a still active volcano with an unusually steep-sided summit which is frequently shrouded in clouds. The most violent recorded eruptions took place in 1562 and 1718.
The ascent of the volcano (guide advisable) should be undertaken only in clear weather. The best starting-point is Madalena. From the summit there is a superb *view of the whole of the central group of the Azores.

In the caldera, some 300 m/330 yd in diameter and 30 m/100 ft deep, are numerous hot fumeroles (temperatures up to 74°C/165°F) and the *Pico Pequeno*, a bare eruption cone 70 m/230 ft high (difficult but rewarding *climb on SE side).

Flores/
Ilha das Flores

Flores, the "Island of Flowers", the most westerly of the Azores, lies 230 km/145 miles NW of Faial and 20 km/12½ miles S of the neighbouring island of Corvo in lat. 39° 25′ N and long. 31° 15′ W.

The island of Flores owes its name to the luxuriant *vegetation which makes it one of the most beautiful of the Azores. As on Faial, the hydrangea grows in profusion here.
17 km/11 miles long and up to 14 km/9 miles wide, Flores has an area of 142 sq. km/55 sq. miles. Its highest point, the *Morro Grande* (942 m/3091 ft), is in the northern part of the island. The whole of the central and southern parts is made up of volcanic heights, with numerous crater lakes, waterfalls and hot springs.

The 5000 inhabitants live by farming and stock-rearing, producing abundant yields for domestic consumption and for export.

Anglers, Vila Franca do Campo (São Miguel)

SIGHTS. – The main town on the island is the little port of **Santa Cruz das Flores** (pop. 2000), half-way along the E coast, which has several small 18th c. Baroque churches. In a small bay on the SE coast is the even smaller port of *Lajes* (pop. 800).

There are very attractive trips into the lush green interior of the island with its numerous crater lakes (*Funda*, *Lomba*, *Rasa*, etc.), inhabited by carp which are used as bait by the deep-sea fishermen.

Corvo/
Ilha do Corvo

Corvo ("Crow Island"), the most northerly and the smallest (17·5 sq. km/6¾ sq. miles) of the Azores, lies 15 km/9 miles NE of Flores in lat. 39° 42′ N – i.e. in roughly the same latitude as Palma de Mallorca in the Balearics and Corfu in the Ionian Islands.

The island, 7 km/4½ miles long and up to 4·5 km/3 miles wide, is made up of a single extinct volcano, *Monte Gordo* (777 m/2549 ft), the crater of which, over 1·5 km/1 mile wide, contains a lake with nine small rocky islets.

The 500 inhabitants of the island gain a modest subsistence from stock-farming and fishing. The women weave excellent woollen cloth for domestic consumption. In recent years the gathering of seaweed for the production of agar-agar (gelatine) has made an increasing contribution to the economy.

SIGHTS. – With its rugged and cliff-fringed coasts, which are particularly steep on the W side of the island, Corvo has no proper harbour. Boats put in at **Rosário** on the S coast, the island's only settlement, with a radio station and meteorological observatory on the hill above the village.

Barcelos

Historical province: Minho.
District: Braga.
Altitude: 40 m/130 ft.
Population: 5000.
Post code: P-4750.

Telephone code: 0 53.
ⓘ **Turismo,**
Rua dos Duques de Bragança;
tel. 8 28 82.

ACCOMMODATION. – IN BARCELOS: *Albergaria Condes de Barcelos*, I, 30 r.; *Arantes*, P III, 23 r.; *Bagoeira*, P IV, 38 r.
IN ESPOSENDE: *Estalagem do Zende*, L, 14 r.; *Nélia*, II, 42 r.; *Suave Mar*, III, 60 r., SP.

YOUTH HOSTEL. – *Pousada de Juventude*, Rua do Dr Henriques Barros de Lima, 20 b.

IN OFIR: *Estalagem do Parque do Rio*, L, 36 r.; *Ofir*, I, 220 r., SP; *Pinhal*, I, 90 r., SP.

EVENTS. – *Romaria ao Senhor Bom Jesús de Fão* (end April), church festival in Fão, with procession and fireworks; *Festas das Cruzes* (beginning of May), a popular festival lasting several days, with picturesque processions; *Festa da Senhora da Saúde e Soedade* (mid August), traditional fishermen's festival, with contests on the Rio Cávado; *pilgrimage of St Bartholomew* (end August) in Esposende.

The very picturesque old town of *Barcelos, once capital of the first County established in Portugal (1298), lies on the right bank of the Rio Cávado 18 km/11 miles W of Braga. It is famous for the brightly coloured pottery cockerels which have become a ubiquitous emblem of Portugal.

SIGHTS. – The life of the town revolves around the spacious *Campo da República*

The Cockerel of Barcelos

in the UPPER TOWN, one of the largest squares in Portugal (very interesting market on Thursdays), with a number of fine old buildings.

On the N side of the square is the **church of Nossa Senhora do Terço**, belonging to a Benedictine house founded in 1705. It has a fine coffered ceiling with many painted panels and azulejo-clad walls (18th c.).

On the S side of the square is the **Torre de Menagem** or *Porta Nova*, a relic of the town's 16th c. fortifications. Opposite this is the former Capuchin *convent of the Misericórdia* (1649), now a hospital.

The handsome Baroque church of the **Bom Jesús da Cruz** (16th–17th c.), an octagonal structure on a centralised plan with an imposing granite dome and a richly decorated interior, shows clear Italian influence.

In the LOWER TOWN, near the five-arched Gothic *bridge* (14th c.) over the Cávado, are the ruins of the **Paço dos Duques de Bragança**, seat of the Counts of Barcelos and later of the Dukes of Bragança (15th–16th c.). On the wide terrace (*view) is the **Archaeological Museum** (*Museu Arqueológico*), an open-air lapidarium with inscribed stones and sculpture from the Roman period to the Middle Ages. A particularly notable item is the Cruzeiro do Senhor do Galo, a 14th c. wayside cross.

On the lower floor of the palace is the **Regional Museum of Ceramics** (*Museu Regional de Cerâmica*), with a fine collection of the colourful pottery of Barcelos, in particular the "Cock of Barcelos", which has become a symbol and emblem for the whole of Portugal.

The Cockerel of Barcelos (*O Galo de Barcelos*). – The story goes that a pilgrim travelling to Santiago de Compostela who had been wrongly accused of theft and condemned to death was saved from the gallows when he appealed to St James to make the hangman's roast cock crow in proof of his innocence. The grateful pilgrim then offered a pottery cockerel to St James in token of thanksgiving.

Opposite the Paço dos Duques de Bragança is the **Solar dos Pinheiros** (1448), a granite-built mansion with two towers and a beautiful arcaded courtyard. In front of it is a Gothic *pelourinho*

(15th c.), symbolising the jurisdiction of the municipal authorities.

Behind the Solar dos Pinheiros stands the Romanesque and Gothic **parish church** (*Igreja Matriz*; 13th–14th c., remodelled in 18th c.), with a Romanesque doorway and fine azulejo decoration in the interior.

On a hill on the left bank of the Cávado, beyond the outlying district of BAR-CELINHOS, are the ruins of the *Castelo da Faria* (1373) and remains of a pre-Roman settlement.

SURROUNDINGS. – 5 km/3 miles NW is the Romanesque and Gothic **Abade de Neiva**, with a well-preserved church and a free-standing fortified belfry.

14 km/9 miles W, near the mouth of the Cávado, lies the seaside resort of **Esposende** (pop. 1500), with a beach of fine sand.

S of Esposende, on the far side of the Cávado, is the recently developed resort of **Ofir**.

6 km/4 miles SW of Barcelos stands the **pilgrimage church of Nossa Senhora da Franqueira** (12th c., with later alterations), situated on the summit of Monte Franqueira (298 m/978 ft; *view).

8 km/5 miles E of Barcelos, at **Areias de Vilar**, is the Benedictine abbey of Vilar de Frades (now a home for the mentally handicapped: not open to the public), with a curious late Romanesque doorway (12th c.). Here, too, is the Manueline church of São Lóios, with 18th c. azulejo pictures in two side chapels and a 15th c. Gothic copper cross in the sacristy.

3 km/2 miles NE of Barcelos, the spa of **Termas de Eirogo** has alkaline and radioactive sulphur springs which are used in the treatment of disorders of the digestive system and high blood pressure.

On a hill above the Cávado at **Manhetes**, 6 km/4 miles NE of Barcelos, stands a fine 12th c. Romanesque church.

Batalha

Historical province: Beira Litoral.
District: Leiria.
Altitude: 70 m/230 ft.
Population: 7000.
Post code: P-2240.
Telephone code: 0 44.
ⓘ **Turismo,**
Largo Paulo VI;
tel. 9 61 80.

ACCOMMODATION. – *Estalagem do Mestre Afonso Domingues*, L, 20 r.; *São Jorge*, II, 10 r., SP.

EVENT. – *Festas da Senhora da Vitória* (mid August), popular festival.

The unpretentious little town of Batalha, in a fertile basin of the

Lena valley between Lisbon and Coimbra, possesses in its famous Dominican **abbey one of the great monuments of Christian architecture and a splendid memorial to the liberation of the Portuguese people.

Batalha Abbey, the *Mosteiro de Santa Maria da Vitória*, was founded in 1388 by King Joâo I in fulfilment of a vow he had made on 14 August 1385, at the beginning of the battle of Aljubarrota, in which he defeated King Juan I of Castile and re-established Portuguese independence.

The architects involved in the building of the abbey were *Afonso Domingues* (d. before 1402) and *Huguet, Houet* or *Huet* (until 1438), Martin Vasques (d. before 1448) and *Fernão de Évora* (d. 1477) for the building of the second cloister, later *Mateus Fernandes the Elder* (from 1480; d. 1515) and *Mateus Fernandes the Younger* (d. 1528), and finally João de Castilho, the architect of the Hieronymite convent at Belém (see p. 143)

Part of the abbey was destroyed by the French in 1810. The monastery was dissolved in 1834 and declared a national monument in 1840. It was restored during the 19th c.

Batalha Abbey

THE ABBEY. – The *church*, built during the reign of João I, is a finely conceived example of the noblest Gothic style. Particularly notable are the W front with its rich sculptural decoration (partly restored) and the lively articulation of the S side.

The *INTERIOR (80 m/260 ft long, 32·5 m/107 ft high) is of impressive effect with its tall stained-glass windows (some of the glass, particularly in the choir, is old) and its massive piers. Set in the floor immediately inside the main entrance is the tomb-slab of Mateus Fernandes the Elder, one of the builders of the abbey.

Batalha Abbey

Mosteiro de Maria da Vitória

1 W doorway (entrance)
2 Founder's Chapel (Capela do Fundador)
3 Nave
4 Choir
5 Vestibule
6 Unfinished Chapels (Capelas Imperfeitas)
7 Chapterhouse (Sala do Capítulo)
8 Fountain-house (Pavilhão)
9 Refectory (Museum of Unknown Soldier)

From the S aisle a magnificent *doorway* leads into the *Founder's Chapel* (*Capela do Fundador*), almost 20 m/65 ft square, with many fine tombs. In the middle is the sarcophagus, supported on eight lions, of *Joâo I* (d. 1433) and his English wife *Philippa of Lancaster* (d. 1416).
In recesses on the S side of the chapel are the tombs of four of the royal couple's children: at the left-hand end the tomb of the Infante *Dom Fernando*, the "steadfast prince" of Calderón's tragedy, who died in Moroccan captivity in 1443; next to this the double tomb of the Infante *Joâo* (d. 1442) and his wife *Isabella*; and the tombs of the Infante *Dom Henrique* (1394–1460), known to history as Henry the Navigator, although he himself never took part in any voyages of discovery, and the Infante Dom Pedro (1392–1449).
On the W wall of the chapel are the tombs of King *Afonso V* (d. 1481) and his wife, King *Joâo II* (d. 1495) and his son Afonso.

On the N side of the church is the **Royal Cloister** (*Claustro Real*), a masterpiece of Portuguese Gothic with its richly decorated arcades overlooking a garden-like courtyard. Here can be seen the whole range of Gothic in Portugal, from the simplest and plainest forms to the fantastic profusion of ornament of later periods. The stone tracery is mostly modern. – From the cloister there is a fine view of the richly decorated N side of the church. In the NW corner of the cloister is the chapel-like fountain-house (Pavilhão), from which, too, there are attractive glimpses of the abbey.

The *Chapterhouse (*Sala do Capitulo*), on the E side of the cloister, has imposing doorway and fine stained glass. It contains the *tomb of two unknown soldiers* of the First World War.

The **Refectory**, on the W side of the cloister, beyond the fountain-house, now houses the *Museum of the Unknown Soldier*.

A doorway at the NW corner of the Claustro Real gives access to the **Claustro de Dom Afonso V**, with simple double windows and a plain pillared gallery (15th c.) on the upper floor. To the E of this cloister is the Claustro de João III, destroyed by fire in 1811.

The *Unfinished Chapels *Capelas Imperfeitas*) were built on to the E end of the church in the reigns of Duarte and Manuel I in the richest Manueline style. Surrounding a central octagon are seven large chapels, one of which contains the *tomb of King Duarte* and his wife *Eleanor of Aragon*. – The massive buttresses around the inside of the octagon were designed to support the dome, which was left unfinished.

On the W side is a large vestibule, with a magnificent *doorway almost 15 m/50 ft high and above this a gallery opening on to the octagon.

From the Claustro de Dom Afonso V it is possible, with special permission, to climb up to the roof of the church and to ascend the tower (160 steps) adjoining the N aisle. From the top there are magnificent panoramic * views of the abbey and the well-cultivated surrounding countryside.

A short distance from the Unfinished Chapels are a number of old houses (17th–18th c.) and the **parish church of Santa Cruz** (1512), which has a superb doorway.

SURROUNDINGS. – 5 km/3 miles SW, on the edge of the *battlefield of Aljubarrota*, the little *chapel of São Jorge* was built on the spot from which Nuno Álvares Pereira directed the battle. At the entrance to the chapel there still stands a jug of fresh water, originally set there for the thirsty warriors.

9 km/5½ miles S of Batalha Abbey, on the slopes of an isolated hill above the Rio Lena, is **Porto de Mós**,

dominated by a massive castle, the origins of which go back to the 9th c. After recovering the castle from the Moors King Sancho I had it restored, but much of it was again destroyed in the 1755 earthquake. Since then it has been restored on a number of occasions, most recently in 1956. From the castle there are magnificent panoramic * views.

10 km/6 miles SE of Porto de Mós, near the village of *Mira de Aire*, are three remarkable *stalactitic caves* (open to the public).

The **Grutas dos Moinhos Velhos** contain interesting stalactites and stalagmites and an underground lake. A flight of steps leads down into the caves; the return is by elevator.

The **Grutas de Alvados**, on the NW side of the *Pedra do Altar*, contain numbers of small lakes in which the golden-brown walls of the caves are reflected. The caves can be seen only on a conducted tour.

The **Grutas de Santo António**, on the upper slopes of the S face of the Pedro do Altar, contain large numbers of curiously shaped stalagmites; in three of the chambers the rock face has a reddish gleam. These caves, too, can only be seen on a conducted tour.

Beira

Historical provinces: Beira Alta, Beira Baixa and Beira Litoral.
Districts: Viseu, Guarda, Castelo Branco, Aveiro and Coimbra.
Area: 27,398 sq. km/10,578 sq. miles.
Population: 2,209,000.
Principal towns: Guarda, Castelo Branco and Coimbra.

(i)   **Turismo Guarda,**
Praça de Luis de Camões,
P-6300 Guarda;
tel. (0 71) 2 22 51.
Turismo Castelo Branco,
Alameda da Liberdade,
P-6000 Castelo Branco;
tel. (0 72) 2 10 02.
Turismo Coimbra,
Largo da Portagem,
P-3000 Coimbra;
tel. (0 39) 2 37 99.

The region of Beira (="edge", "shore") in northern Portugal is a great tract of land between the Douro in the N and the Tagus in the S, consisting mostly of rugged mountain country and bleak plateaux. In this frontier territory, long disputed between Christians and Moors, the towns were always stoutly fortified.

Beira is made up of three old provinces of very different characters, Beira Alta, Beira Baixa and Beira Litoral. **Beira Alta** (Upper Beira) takes in the wooded highlands – geologically the continuation of the cordilleras of central Spain – which extend from the highest peaks on the Portuguese mainland, the * **Serra da Estrêla** (1991 m/6532 ft: see p. 189), to

Washing-day on the banks of the Tagus, in Beira Baixa

the valleys of the Douro and Mondego. The climate is hot and dry in summer and cold in winter, with a great deal of snow at the higher altitudes.

This is a region of extensive agriculture and pastoral farming (sheep). Excellent wine is produced, particularly in the Dão and Mondego valleys. – The population is sparse, reflecting the low fertility of the soil and the limited area of land suitable for cultivation.

The main town of Beira Alta is **Guarda** (pop. 15,000: see p. 121), its largest town **Viseu** (pop. 20,000: p. 207).

Beira Baixa (Lower Beira), with **Castelo Branco** (p. 95) as its capital, extends over an infertile plain between the southern foothills of the *Serra da Estrêla* and the Tagus. The economy is similar to that of Alentejo; the predominant type of farming is monoculture (single-crop farming, in this case grain) on large estates, with mixed farming of Mediterranean type (grain, vegetables, fruit, including citrus fruits, olives) in the river valleys. In the extreme western part of the region the fragmentation of land holdings makes it difficult to achieve efficient and

profitable working of the land. – The rivers of Beira Baixa are famous for their abundance of fish.

Beira Litoral (*Coastal Beira*) occupies a swathe of land extending along the coast from Ovar to Monte Real – relatively narrow in the N but becoming broader about the latitude of the chief town, ****Coimbra** (see p. 99). It is bounded on the E by the heights of the *Serra do Caramulo*, the *Serra da Estrêla and the *Serra de Lousã*.

This is a landscape of dunes with pine-woods planted to consolidate them, marshy river estuaries (Vouga, Mondego) and salt-pans (Ria de Aveiro). Only in the inland parts of the region are grain and vegetables grown.

Beja

Historical province: Baixo Alentjo.
District: Beja.
Altitude: 282 m/925 ft.
Population: 20,000.
Post code: P-7800.
Telephone code: 0 84.

ⓘ **Turismo,**
Rua do Capitão João Francisco de Sousa 25;
tel. 2 36 93.

ACCOMMODATION. – IN BEJA: *Cristina*, P I, 31 r.; *Santa Bárbara*, P I, 26 r.; *Coelho*, P II, 28 r.; *Bejense*, P II, 28 r.; *Planicie*, P II, 8 r.; *O Lidador*, with annexe, P II, 22 r.; *Rocha*, P III, 13 r.; *Tomás*, P III, 9 r.; *Pax Júlia*, P IV, 8 r. – YOUTH HOSTEL: *Pousada de Juventude*, Rua de Pedro Álvares Cabral 8, 16 b. – CAMP SITE.

IN SERPA: *Pousada de São Gens*, 17 r.

EVENTS. – *Feira de São Lourenço e Santa Maria* or *Feira de Agosto* (August), fair with programme of events and bullfights in Beja; *Romaria da Senhora de Aires* (end September), church festival with bullfights, Viana do Alentejo.

The old town of Beja, the Roman Pax Julia (of which some remains survive – foundation of walls on the N side of the town and a gate on the S side), is commandingly perched on a hill in the fertile plain of Baixo Alentejo. – Near the town is a Portuguese air base, also used by the German air force for training purposes.

Beja was the birthplace of two Portuguese kings during whose reigns the country achieved splendour and renown, *João I* and *Manuel I*.

SIGHTS. – The focus of the life of the town is the *Praça da República*, in which·is a Manueline *pelourinho* (pillory column).

At the NW end of the square stands the **church of the Misericórdia**, which was originally built by the Infante Dom Luís in 1550 as a market hall and was later converted, by the addition of a chapel, into a church with a very spacious portico. The original function of the building, with its nine bays of vaulting which are borne on columns, can still be recognised.

To the SE of the Praça da República is the Praça da Conceição, with a modern *statue of Queen Eleanor* (1958). In this square is the surviving part of the *Convent of the Conception* (Nossa Senhora da Conceição), a small house of Poor Clares founded by the Infante Dom Fernando and his wife Dona Brites and built between 1459 and 1506. It shows clear Manueline features. The cloister has beautiful 16th c. azulejo decoration.

The convent now houses the rich archaeological and local collections of the *Museum da Rainha Dona Leonor (Queen Eleanor Museum: religious art, pictures, one of the finest private collections of azulejos in Portugal, coins, folk art, furniture).

Opposite the convent is the unusual **church of Santa Maria** (13th c.), built of light-coloured stone, with five towers.

> One resident in the Convent of the Conception who attained some literary reputation (probably spurious) in the 17th c. was a nun named *Mariana Alcoforado* (1640–1723), the supposed author of the "Letters of a Portuguese Nun" – love letters addressed to the Chevalier de Chamilly – which were published in Paris in 1669. The letters are now thought to have been written by Gabriel-Joseph Guillergues (1628–85).

Above the town to the N rises the massive **Castle**, built by King Dinis about 1300 on the remains of a Roman fortress; it has a handsome crenellated tower partly of marble; *view. In the inner courtyard is the **Military Museum of Lower Alentejo** (*Museu Militar do Baixo Alentejo*).

Near the castle, beyond the Roman *Évora Gate*, stands the early Romanesque **church of Santo Amaro**, which now houses a Visigothic Museum.

Below the castle, to the SE, is the former *Cathedral*, in Renaissance style (1590; restored 1940).

In the old town there are many handsome old *burghers' houses*, many of them with interesting details (wrought-iron grilles, windows, doorways, flying buttresses, arcades, etc.).

To the NW of the town is the **Ermida de Santo André**, founded in 1162 in thanksgiving for the recovery of the town from the Moors.

SURROUNDINGS. – 8 km/5 miles SW are the excavated remains of a Roman settlement at **Pisões** (baths, with mosaics, atrium, etc.).

25 km/15 miles W lies the little town of **Ferreira do Alentjo** (alt. 141 m; pop. 6000; Estalagem Eva, I, 16 r.; Santo António, P II, 28 r.), with a 16th c. parish church and the church of the Misericórdia (16th c. retable).

30 km/19 miles SE is the quaint little walled town of **Serpa** (alt. 230 m/755 ft; pop. 8000), still known by the name it bore in Roman times. Above the town are the ruins of a 13th c. castle (*view). The Gothic church of·Santa Maria (13th c.) has polychrome azulejo decoration (17th c.) in the interior. The narrow lanes of the old town are lined with white houses (pretty windows), many of them faced with azulejos. Other features of interest are the former convents of São

Paulo and São António (15th–16th c.; cloister) and the remains of an ancient aqueduct at the Porta de Beja.

Belmonte

Historical province: Beira Baixa.
District: Castelo Branco.
Altitude: 610 m/2000 ft.
Population: 2000.
Post code: P-6250.
Telephone code: 0 75.

ⓘ **Turismo Castelo Branco,**
Alameda da Liberdade,
P-6000 Castelo Branco;
tel. 2 10 02.

ACCOMMODATION. – *Pensão-Restaurante Altitude*, P III, 18 r.

The charming little hill town of Belmonte, on a commanding eminence at the foot of the Serra da Estrêla, was the birthplace of the navigator Pedro Álvares Cabral, who discovered Brazil in 1500.

SIGHTS. – Above the town are the remains of the massive **Castle**, built at the beginning of the 13th c., in the reign of King Dinis (restored 1940). There are extensive * views of the Beira hills.

Opposite the castle gate, still bearing the arms of the Cabral family, is the little Romanesque and Gothic **church of Santiago** (restored 1971).

The interior of the church is notable for its simplicity. It contains the tomb of Cabral's mother, the remains of old frescoes in the choir and the tombs of Fernão and Henrique Francisco Cabral (17th c.). It also preserves the Gothic image of Nossa Senhora da Esperança (Our Lady of Hope) which Cabral took with him on his voyage to Brazil and later bequeathed to a Franciscan friary he founded near Belmonte. On the dissolution of the friary the image was transferred to the church of Santiago.

In the main street of the town can be seen a *monument to Pedro Álvares Cabral*, erected in 1963 on the 500th anniversary of his birth.

There are a number of handsome old *mansions* in the town, witnesses to its past prosperity and dignity.

SURROUNDINGS. – In a field 2 km/1¼ miles outside the town is the *Torre Centum Cellas*, a well-preserved Roman watch-tower (square in plan, with two storeys and a crenellated roof) which is said to have been built in the 2nd c. A.D. as a place of banishment for a Roman bishop named Cornelius.

From Belmonte attractive excursions can be made into the * **Serra da Estrêla** (see p. 189).

Berlenga Islands/ Ilhas Berlengas

Historical province: Estremadura.
District: Leiria.
Altitude: 0–88 m/0–289 ft.
Population: 50.

ⓘ **Turismo Peniche,**
Rua de Alexandre Herculano,
P-2520 Peniche;
tel. (0 62) 7 22 71.

ACCOMMODATION. – *Abrigo para Pescadores*, 31 r. (summer only; crayfish a speciality).

Facilities for CAMPING.

The rugged Ilha da Berlenga

RECREATION and SPORT. – Swimming, sea angling; good scuba diving.

12 km/7½ miles NW of the rugged and imposing Cabo Carvoeiro the *Ilhas Berlengas – bizarrely shaped masses of granite which seem to have been violently broken off the mainland – rear out of the shimmering green waters of the Atlantic.

This little archipelago consists of the main Ilha da Berlenga (4·5 km/3 miles long and up to 800 m/½ mile wide), the neighbouring Estelas, Forcadas and Farilhões islands and numerous reefs and isolated rocks, offering magnificent opportunities for scuba divers. – The main island can be reached by boat from Peniche in about an hour (regular services in summer).

SIGHTS. – On the highest point of the main island stands a prominent *light-house*, and below this, on a crag above the sheltered bay on the SE side of the island, is a **castle** built in the reign of João IV, now containing an inn (the only one on the island).

From here a waymarked footpath (1½ hours) runs round the island, giving access to picturesque caves and tunnels, deep gorges and rocky coves lashed by the sea. Particularly fine is the *Blue Grotto* below the castle, which can stand comparison with the better known Blue Grotto on Capri. To the S of the castle is the *Furado Grande*, a natural tunnel 70 m/75 yd long which leads to the *Cova do Sonho*, a tiny rocky cove.

A *boat trip* around the island (enquire at the harbour or the inn) provides a memorable experience, with constantly changing views of the rugged and dramatic scenery.

Borba

Historical province: Alto Alentejo.
District: Évora.
Altitude: 416 m/1365 ft.
Population: 4500.
Post code: P-7150.
Telephone code: 0 68.
ⓘ Turismo Évora,
  Praça do Giraldo 71,
  P-7000 Évora.
  tel. (0 68) 2 26 71.

ACCOMMODATION. – None in town. See under ESTREMOZ.

The handsome and old-world little town of Borba, half way between Évora and Elvas, owes its evident prosperity to the white marble quarried in the nearby Montes Claros, a popular building material. Excellent wine is produced in the area.

SIGHTS. – The life of the town revolves around the Praça do Cinco de Outubro, in which are the *Town Hall* (1797) and *parish church*.

The most notable building in the town is the **church of São Bartolomeu** (16th c.), in Renaissance style, with a fine doorway, brightly painted stone vaulting and rich azulejo decoration.

Also of interest is the two-storey cloister of the *Convento das Servas de Cristo* in the middle of which is a fountain faced with azulejos. Visitors will be impressed by the number of roadside chapels.

At the intersection, where the road to Vila Viçosa branches off, stands a marble fountain, the *Fonte das Bicas* (1781).

Braga

Historical province: Minho.
District: Braga.
Altitude: 185 m/607 ft.
Population: 49,000.
Post code: P-4700.
Telephone code: 0 53.
ⓘ Turismo,
  Avenida da Liberdade;
  tel. 2 25 50.
  ACP,
  Avenida da Liberdade 466;
  tel. 2 70 51.

ACCOMMODATION. – IN BRAGA: *Turismo Dom Pedro*, I, 132 r., SP; *João XXI*, III, 28 r.; *Francfort*, IV, 15 r.; *Grande Residência*, P II, 21 r.; *Económica*, P III, 25 r.; *Oliveira*, P III, 20 r.; *Comercial*, P III, 11 r.; *Inácio Filho*, P III, 8 r.; *A Marisqueira*, P III, 8 r.

IN BOM JESÚS DO MONTE: *Elevador*, P I, 25 r.; *Parque*, III, 32 r.; *Sul Americano*, IV, 28 r.; *Águeda*, P IV, 12 r.

IN VILA NOVA DE FAMALIÇÃO: *Francesa*, P II, 40 r.; *Ferreira*, P II, 24 r.; *Garantia*, P III, 29 r.

EVENTS. – *Holy Week* processions; *Midsummer* celebrations (23–25 June), with processions and folk events, Braga; *Feira Grande do São Miguel* (end September), agricultural and livestock show, Vila Nova de Famalição.

The old-world town of Braga, situated in an extensive depression between the rivers Cávado and Este, is one of the largest towns in the country and the seat of the Primate of Portugal, with many fine Manueline and Baroque buildings.

Braga is also a busy industrial town ("industry park" in course of development), producing motor vehicles, electrical appliances, leather goods and textiles. The showrooms of the local Craft Corporation provide an excellent opportunity of seeing (and buying) the varied handicrafts of the Minho.

HISTORY. – The site seems to have been inhabited in prehistoric times. Later it was the Roman *Bracara Augusta*, chief town and military headquarters of the territory of the Callaeci Bracarii, linked by five military highways with other military posts in Lusitania. – During the great migrations Braga became capital of the Suevic kingdom. In 716 it was occupied and devastated by the Moors. In 1040 Fernando I, the Great, of Castile recovered the town, which at the beginning of the 12th c. became the residence of the Portuguese kings. This was the beginning of an age of splendour, to which many buildings of the period still bear witness.

When, after the great voyages of discovery, attention was increasingly focused on the coastal ports and the sea, the power and prosperity of the town began to decline and it sank back into the role of a provincial town.

SIGHTS. – Braga's many handsome noble palaces and beautiful fountains have earned it the flattering title of the "Portuguese Rome". In the middle of the town is the *Cathedral (Sé)*, built in the 11th c. on the site of an earlier Romanesque church, enlarged in later

centuries and remodelled in Manueline style in the early 16th c.

The most notable features of the exterior are the W porch, with three bays of groined vaulting and a beautiful iron grille, and a charming figure of Nossa Senhora do Leite (Our Lady of Milk), probably by the French sculptor Nicolas Chanterene, on the rear wall of the choir.

INTERIOR. – Above the richly ornamented Manueline *font* is a magnificently carved *organ-case*. In the Coro Alto (raised choir) are fine 15th c. choir-stalls. On the *high altar* is a 14th c. figure of the Virgin.
Among the many monuments in the church is the very fine *tomb of the Infante Dom Afonso*, João I's natural son (15th c.).

On the N side of the Cathedral are two cloisters. The first of these (18th c.) has on the N side the 14th c. **Capela da Glória**, decorated with azulejos and heraldic frescoes, which contains the *tomb of Archbishop Gonçalo Pereira* (1336), who commanded the Minho forces in the battle of the Rio Salado with the Arabs.
In the **Capela dos Reis** (*Nossa Senhora do Livramento*), built on to the nave, are the 16th c. *tombs of Henry of Burgundy* (d. 1112) and his wife *Dona Teresa* and the mummified body of Archbishop *Lourenço Vicente Coutinho* (14th c.).
From the second cloister a flight of steps leads up to the *Treasury, richly stocked with precious objects, and a small *Museum of Religious Art* (fine talha dourada and azulejo decoration of the 17th–18th c., etc.).

Particularly notable among Braga's more than thirty churches are the Renaissance **church of the Misericórdia** (1562); the **church of Santa Cruz**, with a 17th c. Rococo façade; the **church of the Pópulo** (16th c.), which also has a handsome façade; and the **church of São João do Souto** (18th c.), with the adjoining *Capela da Conceição* or Capela dos Coimbra, founded by João Coimbra in 1525 (fine statues).

To the NE of the Cathedral stands the former **Archbishop's Palace** (*Antigo Paço Episcopal*),

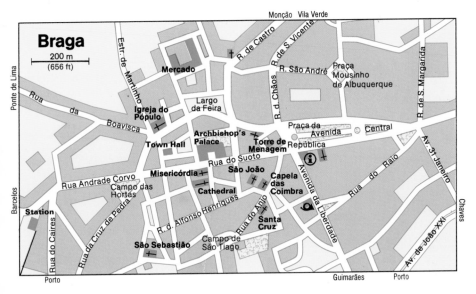

consisting of three ranges of buildings dating from the 14th–17th c.; these now house the Public Library, one of the finest old libraries in Portugal, with more than 300,000 volumes and over 10,000 valuable manuscripts (the earliest dating from the 9th c.).

Everywhere in the old town visitors will encounter handsome fountains and fine old burghers' houses and noble mansions, built of granite in an imposing style characteristic of Braga. Among the most striking are the *Casa das Gelosias* (17th c.) and the *Palácio do Raio* or *Casa do Mexicano* (18th c.), with an azulejo-decorated façade.

At the NE corner of the old town is the **Torre de Menagem** (1378), a relic of the medieval fortifications.

SURROUNDINGS. – In the suburb of *São Jerónimo Real*, 3 km/2 miles NW of the town, is one of the oldest Christian buildings in Portugal, the *Capela de São Frutuoso*, founded by and named after an early bishop of Braga, Frutuoso de Dume (second half of 7th c.). The central part of the chapel and the E end date from the late 7th c. and show Byzantine influence – an unusual feature in Portugal. Other parts of the chapel were rebuilt or added after its destruction by the Moors in the 11th c.
The simple interior shows a variety of styles (Visigothic, Romanesque, Lombard). – Against the rear wall of the chapel is the sarcophagus of São Frutuoso. The saint's remains are now in the adjoining Baroque church of the former Franciscan convent, in which the chapel, which has a fine carved pulpit, was incorporated in the 18th c.

6 km/4 miles E of Braga (reached by car, trolley-bus or funicular) is the *pilgrimage church of Bom Jesús do Monte* (alt. 401 m/1316 ft), on the western slopes of *Monte Espinho* (564 m/1850 ft), which draws thousands of pilgrims at Whitsun (Pentecost). A Way of the Cross leads up to a terrace from which a monumental Baroque staircase ascends to the church (originally 15th c.; rebuilt in 18th and 19th c.). From the top there are extensive *views.
The church is surrounded by beautiful gardens.

3 km/2 miles farther S, on *Monte Sameiro* (582 m/ 1910 ft), is another pilgrimage church, likewise affording magnificent views. – Another 3 km/2 miles beyond this is the Baroque *chapel of Maria Madalena*

The pilgrimage church of Bom Jesús do Monte, Braga

(mid 18th c.), from which, too, there is a fine view of Braga. In the vicinity are the remains of the Ice Age settlement *Citânia de Briteiros (see entry).

18 km/11 miles SW of Braga is the little industrial town of **Vila Nova de Famalição** (watchmaking), with the imposing church (formerly monastic) of São Tiago de Antas (13th c.).

Bragança

Historical province: Trás-os-Montes.
District: Bragança.
Altitude: 670 m/2198 ft.
Population: 15,000.
Post code: P-5300.
Telephone code: 073.
(i) **Turismo,**
Avenida 25 de Abril;
tel. 2 22 72.

ACCOMMODATION. – *Albergaria Santa Isabel*, I, 14 r.; *Bragança*, II, 42 r.; *Grande Pensão Moderna*, P II, 25 r.; *Santo António*, P II, 6 r.; *Cruzeiro*, P III, 30 r.; *Poças*, P III, 19 r.; *Casa Nova*, P III, 9 r.; *Internacional*, P III, 9 r. – *Pousada de São Bartolomeu*, SE of the town, 16 r.

The attractive old town of Bragança, the Roman Iuliobriga, lies in a pleasantly cool setting on a hill above the valley of the Rio Sabor, in the extreme NE corner of Portugal.

The town was the original seat of the House of Bragança, which ruled in Portugal from 1640 to 1910 (for the last part of the period in the female line of Saxe-Coburg-Bragança) and in Brazil (as Emperors) from 1822 to 1889.

Bragança is notable for its many fine burghers' houses and noble mansions of the Renaissance period, with handsome granite façades. As capital of the district of Bragança (area 6545 sq. km/ 2527 sq. miles; pop. 185,000) it is the cultural and economic heart of the surrounding country, mainly agricultural in character. The traditional local craft of silk-weaving still flourishes.

SIGHTS. – In the middle of the newer part of the town, in the long Largo da Sé, stands the **Cathedral** (*Sé de São João Baptista*), originally a Jesuit church – a plain and sturdy Renaissance building with the air of a secular building rather than a church.
The aisleless interior is partly clad with azulejos. The choir has reticulated vaulting with bosses bearing coats of arms. – The sacristy has a coffered ceiling and

painted panels with scenes from the life of St Ignatius Loyola on the walls. – Adjoining the church is an unusual brick-built cloister.

Outside the main entrance to the Cathedral is a *pelourinho* (pillory column) of 1689, the symbol of municipal authority.

From the Cathedral Rua do Conselheiro Abilio Beça leads to the former *Bishop's Palace*, now occupied by the **Museu do Abade de Baçal** (archaeology, fine art, folk traditions, handicrafts). – Nearby is the *church of the Misericórdia*.

Above the town is the massive *Castle (Fortaleza)*, an imposing stronghold, long regarded as impregnable, which was built by King Sancho I in 1187 and later strengthened by João I.
Originally the castle enclosed within its double circuit of walls and 18 towers the whole of the medieval town. Contemporary views, however, show that by the 15th c. the town had expanded well beyond the castle walls. – In front of the castle gateway is a modern *statue of Dom Fernando*, Duke of Bragança and governor of Ceuta, erected to commemorate the 500th anniversary of the ceremonial granting of a charter to the town in 1464.

Within the walls are the remains of the *Ducal Castle* (12th c.), seat of the Dukes of Bragança. The 34 m/112 ft high keep, the **Torre de Menagem**, with two fine Gothic twin windows on the S and E sides, was built in the 15th c. Nearby is a 6 m/20 ft high *pelourinho* (pillory column), with a Gothic shaft based on a granite figure of a wild boar, probably dating from the late Iron Age.

Also within the precincts of the castle is the **church of Santa Maria do Castelo** (16th c.), with a fine Renaissance doorway.

The most interesting building within the castle walls is the Romanesque *Domus Municipalis** (Town Hall), a severe granite structure of the 12th c., built over a Roman cistern. In form an irregular pentagon, it has a dwarf gallery under the roof ridge (recently restored). This is one of the few secular buildings of the Romanesque period in Portugal.

SURROUNDINGS. – 5 km/3 miles S is the **Capela de São Bartolomeu**, from which there is a superb *view of the castle and the town.

Domus Municipalis (town hall), Bragança

6 km/4 miles NE, in the village of **Castro de Avelãs**, are the remains of a 12th c. Benedictine abbey. Parts of the abbey church, the only brick-built church in Portugal, have been incorporated in the present parish church.

Briteiros

Historical province: Minho.
District: Braga.
Altitude: 336 m/1102 ft.

ⓘ **Turismo Braga,**
Avenida da Liberdade
P-4700 Braga;
tel. (0 53) 2 25 50.

12 km/7½ miles E of Braga on Monte São Romão, surrounded by the pleasant hills of the Serra Falperra, are the remains of the *Citânia de Briteiros, an Iron Age settlement.

The settlement, discovered in 1874 and excavated from 1875 onwards under the direction of Francisco Martins Sarmento (1833–99), was probably established about 500 B.C.; its most flourishing period was in the 4th c. B.C. and, as the excavations have shown, it continued to be occupied into late Roman times.

THE SITE. – The settlement was enclosed within three rings of ramparts and contained some 150 single-roomed dwellings, round, oval or rectangular in plan. The streets were paved with stone slabs.

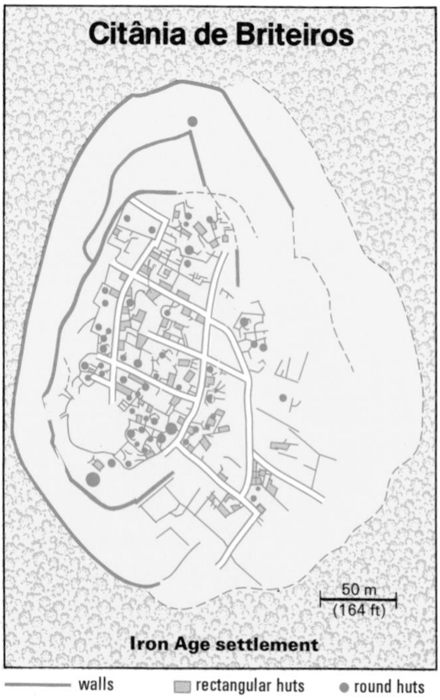

Two of the round huts were reconstructed on the model of the *trulli* of Apulia or the Sardinian *nuraghi*, on the theory that the circular dwelling with a conical roof was the basic type of human habitation. There remains considerable doubt, however, about the authenticity of the reconstructions.

From the small *chapel of São Romão* on top of the hill there is an excellent general *view of the remains.

On another hill (278 m/912 ft) a short distance away are the remains (less well preserved) of another prehistoric settlement, the **Castro de Sabroso**, surrounded by a massive wall of dressed stone. Sabroso, which was also excavated by Francisco Martins Sarmento, is older (c. 800–300 B.C.) and smaller than Briteiros.
There are the remains of numerous circular huts on this site, too, some of them with a block of stone in the middle which may have supported the roof.

These two sites are the oldest known settlements in Portugal. Fragments of pottery (much of it painted), carved stones, weapons, implements and jewelry recovered during the excavations are now in the Museu de Martins Sarmento in Guimarães (see p. 124).

Citânia de Briteiros

50 m
(164 ft)

Iron Age settlement

——— walls   ▦ rectangular huts   ● round huts

Buçaco National Park/ Parque Nacional do Buçaco

Historical province: Beira Litoral.
District: Aveiro.
Altitude: 220–541 m/722–1775 ft.
Area: 105 hectares/260 acres.

ⓘ **Turismo Luso,**
Rua de António Granjo,
P-3050 Luso;
tel. (0 31) 9 31 33.

ACCOMMODATION. – IN BUÇACO FOREST: *Palace Hotel do Buçaco*, L, 60 r.

IN LUSO: *Estalagem do Luso*, I, 10 r.; *Grande Hotel das Termas do Luso*, II, 157 r., SP; *Serra*, IV, 41 r.; *Alegre*, P II, 21 r.; *Imperial*, P II, 19 r.; *A Regional*, P II, 16 r.; *Astória* (with annexe), P III, 36 r.; *Lusa*, P III, 31 r.;

Avenida, P III, 21 r.; *Central,* P III, 16 r.; *Portugal,* P III, 10 r.

EVENTS. – *Festa da Senhora da Vitória em Comemoração da Batalha do Buçaco* (end September), celebrations commemorating Wellington's victory over the French in 1810, with processions in period costumes.

**Buçaco Forest, which vies with Sintra in scenic beauty and the

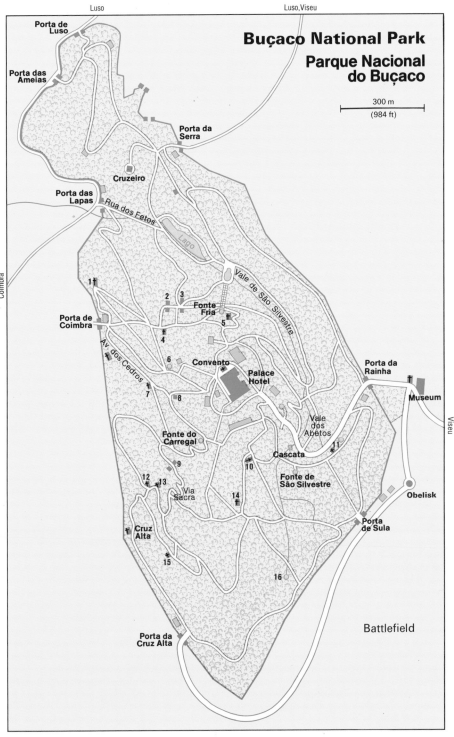

Luso   Luso, Viseu

Buçaco National Park

Parque Nacional do Buçaco

300 m
(984 ft)

Porta de Luso
Porta das Ameias
Porta da Serra
Cruzeiro
Porta das Lapas
Rua dos Fetos
Lago
Coimbra
Vale de São Silvestre
Porta de Coimbra
Fonte Fria
Av. dos Cedros
Convento
Palace Hotel
Porta da Rainha
Museum
Fonte do Carregal
Vale dos Abetos
Cascata
Porta de Sula
Fonte de São Silvestre
Obelisk
Viseu
Via Sacra
Cruz Alta
Porta da Cruz Alta
Battlefield

1 Capela de Caifas
2 Porta de Siloé
3 Porta de Cedron
4 Capela de Annas
5 Ermida de Nossa Senhora da Assunção
6 Fonte da Samaritana
7 Ermida de São José
8 Casa de Pilatos
9 Porta Judiciária
10 Ermida de Nossa Senhora da Conveição
11 Ermida and Fonte de São Elias
12 Ermida do Sepulcro
13 Ermida do Calvário
14 Ermida de São Miguel
15 Ermida de São João Baptista
16 Fonte de São Miguel

magnificence and variety of its vegetation, lies 27 km/17 miles NE of Coimbra on the northern slopes of the Serra do Buçaco. The older spelling, Busaco, is familiar in British history as the scene of Wellington's victory in 1810.

The charm of this forest, which has been protected for many centuries by royal and papal decree, lies in the great range of native and exotic species of trees to be seen here and in the network of attractive footpaths leading to idyllic spots in the forest, to picturesque fountains and springs and to magnificent viewpoints.

In the 6th c. the Benedictine monks of Lorvão established a *hermitage* in the forest on the eastern slopes of the Cruz Alta hill. In the 11th c. this passed into the hands of the Augustinian canons of Coimbra, who always strenuously upheld their claim to the area and maintained it with great care. In 1622 women were forbidden to enter the area.

In 1628 a Carmelite *convent* was established in the forest and enclosed by the **wall**, fully 5 km/3 miles long, with nine gates, which is still to be seen today. Here the monks planted an *arboretum which quickly became famous and was continuously enriched by exotic species brought back by the Portuguese navigators from their wide-ranging voyages.

The forest now contains some 400 native and 300 exotic species. Its special pride is its array of gigantic cedars from Lebanon, Mexico, India and Africa; other outstanding specimens include mighty cypresses, ancient ginkgo trees, sequoias, araucarias and palms. – A papal decree of 1643 prohibited the felling or damaging of any of the trees.

But the monks did not confine themselves to looking after the trees. They built a whole series of chapels, hermitages, oratories and grottoes, constructed ponds and fountain basins and laid out the dense network of paths which still allow visitors to explore the beauties of the forest.

An *obelisk* just outside the walls at the SE corner of the park commemorates the battle of Buçaco (1810), in which a British and Portuguese army commanded by Wellington frustrated Napoleon's third attempt to conquer Portugal. A *Military Museum* contains relics and mementoes of the Franco-Portuguese war and the battle of 1810.

After the secularisation of all religious houses in Portugal in 1834 the property passed to the crown. Adjoining the remains of the convent, then in a state of dilapidation, the Italian architect Luigi Manini built (1888–1907) a summer residence and hunting lodge for Carlos I – a sumptuous palace in neo-Manueline style, with a great deal of sculpture and azulejo decoration, which now has a certain nostalgic charm. Since 1909 the *Palace (Palácio)* has housed the luxurious *Palace Hotel do Buçaco* (alt. 357 m/1171 ft). All that remains of the old convent is the little **church** (with sculpture and paintings illustrating the history of the convent), the *cloister* and a number of cells (small Wellington memorial).

From the hotel a Way of the Cross (also a road, 6 km/4 miles) leads up the hill to the SW, the *Cruz Alta* ("High Cross", 541 m/1775 ft), from which there are superb panoramic *views extending to the Serra da Estrêla and the Atlantic Ocean.

There are numerous *springs in the forest, with basins and fountains constructed by the monks: e.g. the *Fonte Fria* ("Cold Spring") to the N of the hotel, with a cascade of 144 steps descending to a basin surrounded by beautiful flowering shrubs and conifers, and the *Fonte do Carregal* to the S of the hotel, flowing out of a grotto.

SURROUNDINGS. – Some 500 m/550 yd NW of the park, in a picturesque setting at the foot of the Cruz Alta hill, is the little spa of **Luso** (alt. 380 m/1247 ft), with chalybeate and radioactive mineral springs.

Palace Hotel, Buçaco Forest

Caldas da Rainha

Historical province: Estremadura.
District: Leiria.
Altitude: 50 m/165 ft.
Population: 16,000.
Post code: P-2500.
Telephone code: 0 62.

(i) **Turismo,**
Praça da República;
tel. 2 24 00.

ACCOMMODATION. – *Olhos Pretos,* P II, 31 r.;
Pensão Portugal, P II, 28 r.; *O Telheiro,* P II, 17 r.;
Estremadura, P III, 22 r.; *Central,* IV, 40 r.

EVENT. – *Midsummer* celebrations, with "holy bath"
(23–25 June).

Casino.

RECREATION and SPORT. – Swimming and water
sports in Atlantic (see under Costa de Prata).

**Caldas da Rainha ("Queen's Spa")
is one of Portugal's leading spas,
with hot sulphur springs (34·5°C/
94·1°F) which are particularly
recommended for the treatment of
rheumatism.**

Local delicacies are *cavacas, trouxas de
ovas* and *lampreias,* sweets made from
yolk of egg and sugar.

SIGHTS. – The story goes that the virtues
of the mineral springs were discovered by
Queen Leonor, wife of João II, who
observed the local peasants bathing in
the water to cure pains in their joints.
Thereupon she sold her jewels and used
the money to found a hospital (1484), to
which she herself came to take the cure. In
1504 she built the *bath-house* which still
survives.

Adjoining the bath-house is the **church
of Nossa Senhora do Pópulo,** also
founded by the queen and built by the
famous architect Boytaca. It has a
separate *tower,* the lower part of which is
square and the upper part octagonal.
Notable features of the interior are a fine
triptych and a Manueline chancel arch.
The little *baptistery* and the font are richly
decorated with azulejos.

The beautiful **Parque da Copa,** also
established by Queen Leonor, was altered
and enlarged in the mid 18th c. by João V,
who came here to take the cure. In the park
is a pavilion containing the **Museu de
José Malhoa** (modern Portuguese
painting, sculpture and ceramics).

Near the park is a **majolica manufactory,** one of the leading Portuguese
establishments, founded in the 19th c. Its
colourful – sometimes rather crudely
coloured – wares are very different from
those of northern Portugal.

SURROUNDINGS. – 7 km/4½ miles SW is the
fascinating old town of *Óbidos (see p. 165), and 25
km/15 miles farther W the little fishing port of
Peniche (p. 177).

Resorts on the coast: see under **Costa de Prata.**

Caminha

Historical province: Minho.
District: Viana do Castelo.
Altitude: 30 m/100 ft.
Population: 2000.
Post code: P-4910.
Telephone code: 0 58.

(i) **Turismo,**
Rua Ricardo Joaquim de Sousa;
tel. 92 19 52.

ACCOMMODATION. – IN CAMINHA: *Albergaria Santa
Rita,* P II, 5 r.; *Gala de Ouro,* P III, 12 r.; CAMPING
SITE.

IN MOLEDO DO MINHO: *Ideal,* P II, 21 r.

IN VILA PRAIA DE ÂNCORA: *Meira,* III, 45 r.; *Sereia da
Gelfa,* P II, 6 r.

RECREATION and SPORT. – Swimming and water
sports (see below under Surroundings).

EVENTS. – *Festas de Santa Rita de Cássia* (mid
August), with processions in traditional costume,
Caminha; *Festas da Senhora da Bonança* (beginning
of September), fishermen's festival with blessing of
boats, Vila Praiai de Âncora.

**The frontier town of Caminha, once
strongly fortified, is charmingly set
on a tongue of land between the
rivers Coura and Minho, just above
the mouth of the Minho.**

Once a bulwark in the defence of northern
Portugal against Galicia, and strategically
situated opposite the Spanish stronghold
of Santa Tecla, Caminha is now a modest
little fishing town, with handicrafts and
lace-making as flourishing subsidiary
activities.

SIGHTS. – In the main square, the Praça
do Conselheiro Silva Torres, stands the
Town Hall (*Paços do Concelho,* 15th
c.), with a beautiful coffered ceiling in the
council chamber. The adjoining 15th c.
Clock-tower is a relic of the town's
medieval fortifications.

On the S side of the square can be seen the Gothic *Casa dos Pitas* (1490), and in the middle of the square, opposite the Town Hall, is a Renaissance *fountain* (16th c.), in granite.

The town's most notable building is the three-aisled **Collegiate Church** (*Igreja Matriz*), built between 1488 and 1565, which has a Renaissance façade with an imposing main doorway and a beautiful rose window.
The church has a carved wood ceiling in Mudéjar style by a Spanish master. The apse and the charming octagonal font are Manueline.

SURROUNDINGS. – SW of the town, along the Atlantic coast to the S of the Minho estuary, are a number of fine broad beaches – the *Praia de Moledo*, in the little resort of **Moledo do Minho**, S of this the *Praia do Pirata* and the beach of *Vila Praia de Âncora*. All these beaches are well kept, with fine sand and dunes, and are fringed by beautiful pinewoods.

Cascais

Historical province: Estremadura.
District: Lisboa (Lisbon).
Altitude: 0–20 m/0–65 ft.
Population: 30,000.
Post code: P-2750.
Telephone code: 01.
(i) **Turismo Estoril,**
   Arcadas do Parque,
   P-2765 Estoril;
   tel. 2 68 01 13.

ACCOMMODATION. – *Estoril-Sol*, L, 400 r., SP; *Albatroz*, L, 40 r.; *Cidadela*, I, 130 r., SP; *Albergaria Valbom*, I, 42 r.; *Farol*, I, 11 r.; *Baía*, II, 87 r.; *Nau*, II, 57 r.; *Dom Carlos*, P I, 9 r.; *Casa Lena*, P II, 7 r.; *Residência Vista Alegre* , P II, 7 r.; *Avenida*, P IV, 6 r. – Apartment hotels: *Equador*, 117 r., *Miradouro*, 30 r., *Três Porquinhos*, 18 r.

CAMP SITE.

RESTAURANTS. – *Baluarte, O Pipas, Beira Mar*. Local speciality: *caldeirada* (fish soup).

EVENT. – *Feira de Cascais* (mid to end July) in Municipal Park.

RECREATION and SPORT. – Swimming, windsurfing, sailing, motorboats, water-skiing; tennis; golf-course (18 holes) at Estoril.

The picturesque old fishing port of *Cascais, now one of the most popular and elegant resorts on the W coast of Portugal, is beautifully set amid luxuriant parks and gardens on the W side of a wide rocky bay on the Costa do Sol, sheltered from N winds by the Serra de Sintra.

There was a settlement here in Roman times. The town was granted a charter in the 14th c. The 1755 earthquake devastated Cascais, destroying most of its old buildings. As the summer residence of the kings of Portugal (from 1870) and now of the President of the Republic, Cascais has developed since the end of the 19th c. into a fashionable *seaside resort which still caters for the discriminating individual visitor rather than for mass tourism.

Although the town has grown at a frenetic rate and has now almost joined up with Estoril (see p. 111), the central part of the old town with its trim white houses and narrow lanes bustling with activity has preserved much of its original atmosphere.

SIGHTS. – Above the SW side of the bay stands the 17th c. **Citadel**, now the President's summer residence.
NW of the Citadel is the Manueline *church*

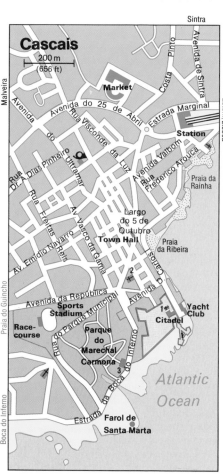

1 Nossa Senhora da Nazaré
2 Church of Nossa Senhora da Assunção
3 Former Palace of the Condes de Castro Guimarães (now a museum)

of *Nossa Senhora da Assunção*, with 18th c. azulejos.

To the W of the Citadel extends the **Parque do Marechal Carmona**, with the *Stadium* and other sports grounds beyond it.
On the SE side of the park is the **Palace of the Condes de Castro Guimarães**, now housing a small *Museum* (18th c. pictures, furniture, silver; library).

From the N side of the Citadel the Avenida de Dom Carlos I follows a winding course NE above the **Praia da Ribeira** (sandy beach), affording beautiful views of Cascais Bay. Beyond this are the little beach of **Praia da Rainha**, picturesquely framed by rocks, and, still farther NE in the direction of Estoril, the beach of *Praia da Duquesa, with fine sand and excellent facilities for bathers.

Boating harbour, Cascais

Palace of the Condes de Castro Guimarães, Cascais

SURROUNDINGS. – 2 km/1¼ miles W along the picturesque rocky coast is a viewpoint above the *Boca do Inferno ("Mouth of Hell"), a cliff 15–20 m/50–65 ft high in which the sea has hollowed out a number of caves. The pounding of the waves gives an impressive demonstration of the power of the Atlantic.

A trip along the *Costa do Sol (see p. 106) from Lisbon via Cascais to Sintra provides a memorable experience.

5 km/3 miles N of Cascais on the road to Alcabideche is a *monument to Ibn Mukau*, the 10th c. Arab poet who was born here, the first writer to celebrate the windmills of Portugal.

*Estoril: see p. 111.

Castelo Branco

Historical province: Beira Baixa.
District: Castelo Branco.
Altitude: 472 m/1549 ft.
Population: 25,000.
Post code: P-6000.
Telephone code: 0 72.
(i) **Turismo,**
Alameda da Liberdade;
tel. 2 10 02.

ACCOMMODATION. – IN CASTELO BRANCO: *Caravela*, P II, 26 r.; *Arraiana*, P II, 25 r.; *Império*, P II, 14 r.; *Lisbonense*, P III, 15 r. – On the N18 11·5 km/7 miles SW: *Motel de Represa*, 24 r.

IN FUNDÃO: *Estalagem da Neve*, I, 6 r., SP; *Samasa*, III, 50 r.; *Tarouca*, P II, 20 r.; *Central Amaval*, P IV, 10 r.

EVENTS. – *Romaria à Senhora do Almurtão* (end April), church festival celebrated in Beira Baixa, particularly impressive at Idanha-a-Nova (30 km/19 miles NE of Castelo Branco); *Festa das Cruzes* or *Festa do Castelo* (beginning of May), with folk events, Monsanto.

Castelo Branco, formerly capital of the old province of Beira Baixa and now chief town of the district which bears its name, is a very picturesque old town, with remains of a circuit of walls and towers dating from the reign of King Dinis, charming and colourful old lanes and handsome old burghers' houses.

Lying so near the Spanish frontier, the town was of great military and strategic importance. Of the medieval Templar castle (*castelo branco*, the white castle), probably built in the reign of King Dinis, only scanty remains survive. In spite of its defensive walls Castelo Branco suffered throughout its history from enemy assaults and raids, most recently in 1807, when French troops did much damage.

Castelo Branco has been celebrated since the 17th c. for the brightly coloured embroidered bedspreads known as *colchas*. Other local products much esteemed in Portugal are goat's milk cheese and olive oil.

SIGHTS. – The town's principal tourist attraction is the former **Bishop's Palace** (*Antigo Paço Episcopal*) with its Baroque garden, the *Jardim Episcopal**.

The terraced gardens of the palace, laid out in the early 18th c. for Dom João de Mendonça, are a showpiece of Baroque extravagance and fantasy, with carefully clipped trees and shrubs, elaborately patterned flowerbeds and a profusion of basins and fountains. There is also a lavish display of Baroque sculpture – archangels, evangelists, apostles, fathers of the church, allegorical figures, animals and, flanking a flight of steps, the complete series of Portuguese kings; the Spanish kings (1580–1640) being represented by much smaller figures.

The Bishop's Palace itself (originally Gothic, remodelled in Baroque style in 1726) houses the **Museu de Francisco Tavares Proença Júnior**, with prehistoric and Roman material from the Castelo Branco area, pictures by Portuguese artists of the 16th, 18th and 19th c.,

tapestries, coins, furniture and arms and armour.
In front of the palace is a *pelourinho* (pillory column) with a twisted shaft. Nearby is the *church of the Misericórdia* (1519), with a fine doorway.

Also of interest are the Baroque **churches** of *Nossa Senhora da Piedade*, with beautiful azulejo decoration, and *Santa Isabel* (paintings).

Above the town are the ruins of the *Templar castle* and the little *church of Santa Maria do Castelo*. From here a flight of steps leads up to the **Miradouro de São Gens**, a viewpoint from which there is a far-ranging* prospect of the town and surrounding area.

SURROUNDINGS. – 5 km/3 miles E is the Gothic **pilgrimage church of Nossa Senhora de Mércoles** (15th c.).

6 km/4 miles SE is the prehistoric **Castrum São Martinho**.

Castelo Branco is a good base for excursions in the **Serra de Guardunha**, a range of hills N of the town which in places takes on an almost Alpine character, with bizarrely shaped rock formations bearing such names as the Cabeça de Frade ("Monk's Head") and Pedra Sobreposta ("Piled-Up Rock").
The chief place in the area is the little town of **Fundão** (alt. 496 m/1627 ft; pop. 5500), 45 km/28 miles N of Castelo Branco in a fertile fruit-growing region on the northern slopes of the hills, with an old-established textile industry. It has two attractive churches, the parish church of the Misericórdia (18th c.) and the chapel of São Francisco.

45 km/28 miles SW of Fundão, under the summit of a rocky hill, is the picturesque little town of **Monsanto da Beira**, dominated by the ruins of a medieval castle. With its trim white houses, sometimes hewn out of the rock, its steep and narrow lanes and its Celtic remains it is one of the most interesting and characteristic old settlements in Beira Baixa.

30 km/19 miles from Castelo Branco on the road to Fundão is the pretty little hill town of **Alpedrinha** (alt. 555 m/1855 ft), the Roman *Petrata* (remains of which can be seen in the area). From here there is a pleasant walk to the *Penha da Senhora da Serra* (hermitage), with beautiful panoramic* views, and from there to the summit of the *Pirâmide* (1223 m/4013 ft), the highest point in the Serra de Guardunha.
The Pirâmide can also be climbed from the picturesque hill village of **Castelo Novo** (700 m/2300 ft), below the hermitage.

30 km/19 miles SW of Castelo Branco the Tagus has carved out a magnificent rocky gorge, 45 m/150 ft wide, the ***Portas de Ródão**. The best view of the gorge is from the bridge at *Vila Velha de Ródão* (pop. 3000), to the E.

Castelo Branco

Castelo de Vide

Historical province: Alto Alentejo.
District: Portalegre.
Altitude: 462–628 m/1510–2060 ft.
Population: 5000.
Post code: P-7320.
Telephone code: 0 45.

ⓘ **Turismo,**
Rua de Bartolomeu Álvares da Santa 81;
tel. 9 13 61.

ACCOMMODATION. – *Albergaria Jardim*, I, 44 r.;
Casa do Parque, P II, 23 r.; *Cantinho Particular*, P IV,
8 r.

On the NW side of the bleak Serra de
São Mamede, clustering in steps and
stairs around the summit of a hill,
the little town of Castelo de Vide has
preserved all its medieval character
and atmosphere. Its maze of narrow
streets, trim whitewashed houses
with their characteristic chimneys,
charming little squares and unexpected nooks and corners are all
dominated by the massive ruins of
the old castle.

Castelo de Vide has cold mineral springs
containing Glauber's salt and many
visitors come here in summer to take the
cure.

SIGHTS. – In the middle of the town is the
Praça de Dom Pedro V, with its Baroque
palaces, churches and *Town Hall* forming
a harmonious pattern. In the middle of the
square stands a *statue of Dom Pedro V.*
The square is dominated by the Baroque
church of Santa Maria with its squat
pyramidal central tower.

From the Praça de Dom Pedro V picturesque lanes lead up to the **Castelo de**

Castelo de Vide

São Roque (1327), with a massive *keep*
(damaged by an explosion in 1705) and
the *church of Nossa Senhora da Alegria,*
which is completely covered with 17th c.
azulejos. From the Moorish castle which
once stood here there survives an
ingenious ventilation system. There are
fine * views from the castle's bastions and
tower.

Below the castle huddles the *Judearia,
the old Jewish quarter, a labyrinth of
narrow lanes and little squares full of
atmosphere, with numerous Gothic and
Manueline windows and doors.
Below the Judearia is an attractive square
with a Renaissance fountain-house, the
Fonte da Vile.

Other features of particular interest are the
beautiful cloister of a former Franciscan
convent, now the *Asilo dos Cegos* (Blind
Asylum), and, outside the town, the
church of Salvador do Mundo (13th c.;
17th c. azulejo decoration).

SURROUNDINGS. – 4 km/2½ miles S is the **Monte
da Penha** (700 m/2300 ft; chapel), from which there
is a charming view of the town.

14 km/9 miles NW is the **Barragem de Póvoa e
Meada** (reservoir: water sports).

25 km/15 miles NW is the little town of **Nisa**, on the
Rio Nisa (a tributary of the Tagus), with a Baroque
parish church.

Also within easy reach of Castelo de Vide are the little
town of **Marvão** (12 km/7½ miles SE), with its castle,
and **Portalegre** (20 km/12½ miles S: see p. 180).

Castro Verde

Historical province: Baixo Alentejo.
District: Beja.
Altitude: 245 m/804 ft.
Population: 6000.
Post code: P-7780.
Telephone code: 0 86.

ⓘ **Turismo Beja,**
Rua do Capitão João Francisco de Sousa 25;
P-7800 Beja;
tel. (0 84) 2 36 93.

ACCOMMODATION. – None in Castro Verde. See
under BEJA.

EVENT. – *Fair* (mid October).

The modest little market town of
Castro Verde ("Green Castle") lies
60 km/37 miles SW of Beja, surrounded by pastureland and forests
of cork-oak.

SIGHTS. – The aisleless church of **Nossa Senhora da Conceição** has an interior completely clad with early 18th c. azulejos depicting scenes from the battle of Ourique (see below, Surroundings).

Also of interest is the *church of the Chagas do Salvador*, decorated with azulejos in a style typical of the region, which was built by Philip II of Spain in the 16th c. on the site of an earlier church.

SURROUNDINGS. – 5 km/3 miles SW is the **Campo de Ourique**, traditionally the scene of the battle of Ourique (1139), in which Afonso I Henriques won a decisive victory over the Moors.

10 km/6 miles SW of the battlefield, on a low hill rising out of the plain, is the modest little village of **Ourique** which gave its name to the battle.

6 km/3 miles farther SW, at *Aldeia dos Palheiros*, are the remains of a settlement of the early historical period, the **Castro de Cola** (known in Roman times as *Ossonoba*). Roughly rectangular in shape, it is surrounded by a rampart 5 m/16 ft high.

21 km/13 miles S of Castro Verde, in the little town of **Almodôvar** (alt. 289 m/948 ft; pop. 2500), are a 17th c. Franciscan convent, with a beautiful cloister, and a Gothic and Manueline parish church.

23 km/14 miles N of Castro Verde lies the busy little town of **Aljustrel** (alt. 200 m/655 ft; pop. 10,000), with copper-mines, some of which have been worked since ancient times.

Chaves

Historical province: Trás-os-Montes.
District: Vila Real.
Altitude: 324 m/1063 ft.
Population: 15,000.
Post code: P-5400.
Telephone code: 076.

ⓘ **Turismo,**
Terreiro de Cavalaria
tel. 2 10 29.
Information bureau
tel. 2 14 45.

ACCOMMODATION. – *Estalagem Santiago*, I, 31 r.; *Jaime*, P II, 60 r.; *Trajano*, III, 39 r.; *Comércio*, P III, 17 r.; *Imperial*, P III, 13 r.; *Chaves*, IV, 31 r.; *Rito*, IV, 14 r.; *Flávia*, P IV, 7 r.

CAMP SITE.

EVENT. – *Feira dos Santos* (end October).

The old-world little town of Chaves, the Roman Aquae Flaviae, lies on a plateau near the Spanish frontier, in an area watered by the Rio Tâmega which has been cultivated since ancient times. The town's hot springs (73°C/163°F) have been used for medicinal purposes since Roman times.

The town has a history dating back to pre-Roman times. With a substantial stone bridge over the Rio Tâmega built in the reign of Trajan (98–117), it became an important staging point on the road between *Asturica Augusta* (Astorga) and *Bracara Augusta* (Braga). During the Middle Ages it was a stronghold defending Portuguese territory against Spain.

The powerful castle of Chaves, rearing above the white houses of the town with their balconies and arcades, still presents a sturdy defensive face to the world.

A local gastronomic speciality is *presunto* (ham dried in the air).

SIGHTS. – The Rio Tâmega is spanned by a well-preserved *Roman bridge of twelve arches, 140 m/155 yd long, dating from the 2nd c. A.D. In the middle of the bridge are two Roman *milestones*, still preserving their inscriptions.

Near the bridge stands the Baroque church of **São João de Deus**, an octagonal structure with a handsome granite façade.

The life of the town revolves around the Praça da República, with the **parish church** (*Igreja Matriz*). Originally Romanesque, this was rebuilt in the 16th c., only the tower and part of the doorway surviving from the earlier church.

Also in the Praça da República is the Baroque **church of the Misericórdia** (17th c.), with *azulejo pictures (Biblical scenes) covering the interior walls and fine 18th c. ceiling paintings. – Near the church is a *pelourinho* (pillory column) in Manueline style.

The **Municipal Museum** (*Museu Municipal*) contains archaeological material found in the area, coins, azulejos and folk art.

Above the town is the massive **Castle** (*Castelo*), built on the site of a Roman fortress; it was strengthened after the Moorish conquest, badly damaged during the Reconquista and rebuilt by King Dinis. The medieval castle with its imposing keep, the *Torre de Menagem*, was the residence of the first Duke of Bragança, a natural son of King João I. – In the 17th c. bastions in the style of Vauban were built on to the castle, but these were later destroyed.

SURROUNDINGS. – 4 km/2½ miles N stands the **church of Nossa Senhora da Azinheira**, an aisleless Romanesque building with unusual figural decoration in Romanesque style and medieval frescoes (much altered) in the interior.

4 km/3½ miles NW, on a difficult road, is the prehistoric cult site of **Abobeleira**, with Bronze Age rock engravings, mainly of human figures and warriors.

Coimbra

Historical province: Beira Litoral.
District: Coimbra.
Altitude: 75–100 m/250–330 ft.
Population: 56,000.
Post code: P-3000.
Telephone code: 0 39.
ⓘ **Turismo,**
Largo da Portagem;
tel. 2 55 76.
ACP,
Avenida de Emídio Navarro 6;
tel. 2 68 13.

ACCOMMODATION. – *Bragança*, Largo das Ameias 10, II, 83 r.; *Astória*, Avenida de Emídio Navarro 21, II, 61 r.; *Oslo*, Avenida de Fernão de Magalhães 23, II, 33 r.; *Larbelo*, Largo da Portagem 33, P II, 53 r.; *Kanimambo*, Avenida de Fernão de Magalhães 494, P II, 44 r.; *Residência Almedina*, Avenida de Fernão de Magalhães 203, P II, 29 r.; *Rivoli*, Praça do Comércio 27, P II, 21 r.; *Infante Dom Henrique*, Rua do Dr Manuel Rodrigues 43, P II, 20 r.; *Residência Moderna*, Rua de Adelino Veiga 49, P II, 20 r.; *Avis*, Avenida de Fernão de Magalhães 64, P II, 16 r.; *Residência Domus*, Rua de Adelino Veiga 62, P II, 15 r. *Jardim*, Avenida de Emídio Navarro 65, P III, 21 r.; *Gouveia*, Rua de João 21, P III, 20 r.; *Antunes*, Rua do Castro Matoso 8, P III, 19 r.; *Atlântico*, Rua de Sargento-Mor 42, P III, 13 r. *Mondego*, Largo das Ameias 4, IV, 35 r.; *Avenida*, Avenida de Emídio Navarro 37, IV, 25 r.; *Internacional*, Avenida de Emídio Navarro 4, IV, 20 r.

CAMP SITE.

RESTAURANTS. – *Dom Pedro*, Avenida de Emídio Navarro 58; *Piscinas*, Rua de D. Manuel; *Império*, Rua da Sofia 165; *Funchal*, Rua das Azeiteiras 20; *O Alfredo*, Rua João das Regras 32; *Tritão*, Praça da República 25. – IN MONTE FORMOSA (2 km/1 mile away): *Lung Wak* (Chinese).
A local delicacy is the *pastel de Santa Clara*, a pastry made from eggs and almonds.

EVENTS. – **Queima das Fitas** (second half of May), a student festival; *Festa da Rainha Santa* (first half of June in even-numbered years), festival in honour of St (Queen) Isabel, the town's patron saint.

SHOPPING. – Azulejos and ceramics, wrought-iron work.

The old university town of **Coimbra, main town of a district and the see of a bishop, lies half-way between Lisbon and Oporto in the hilly country of Beira Litoral. It is built on the right bank of the Rio Mondego, here skirting the chalk hills of the Serra de Lavrão.

Coimbra

From the more modern *Lower Town* on the banks of the Mondego steep lanes climb to the *Upper Town*, with the extensive buildings of the University, on a hill 100 m/330 ft above the river.

With its fine old buildings, many of them dating from the time of Manuel I, and many other art treasures Coimbra is a town which should be included in any visit to Portugal.

> The students of Coimbra University wear a long black robe (*batina*) and over this a black cape (*capa*), with facings of different colours for the various faculties; they wear nothing on their heads.
>
> Many of the students live in communal residences (*repúblicas*) in order to keep down costs. Visitors are usually welcome in the residences, and can thus form some impression of the student way of life.

HISTORY. – Archaeological material found on the site carries the history of the town back to prehistoric times. It was known to the Romans as *Aeminium*, but later, having become the see of a bishop, it took the name of the nearby Roman town of **Conimbriga** (see below, Surroundings), which was destroyed by the Suevi in 468.

The area fell into the hands of the Moors in the 8th c., but the town was temporarily won back in 872 and finally recovered by Fernando the Great of Castile in 1064.

In the 12th c. Coimbra became capital of the new Portuguese kingdom. It lost this status to Lisbon in 1260, but was compensated by the foundation (1307–08) of the University – which with interruptions was until 1911 the only university in Portugal – which became a major element in the town's cultural and intellectual life.

SIGHTS. – The central feature of the LOWER TOWN is the Praça do Oito de Maio (8th May Square). On the E side of the square is the former Augustinian *Monastery of Santa Cruz, founded in

1131 and much altered and enlarged in later centuries. In particular much new building was carried out in the reign of Manuel I by the celebrated architect Boytaca, and after his death by Nicolas de Chanterene.

The whole of the N wing of the convent is now occupied by the **Town Hall** (*Câmara Municipal*).

The S wing contains the aisleless convent **church** (1131–32), which has a Manueline façade with rich sculptural decoration.

INTERIOR. – On the N wall is a magnificent *pulpit (1522), a relic of the rich furnishings which are referred to in the chronicles.

In the *Capela-mór* are the **tombs** (mainly in late Gothic style) of the first Portuguese kings; they were commissioned by Manuel I from Nicolas de Chanterene: on left the recumbent figure of

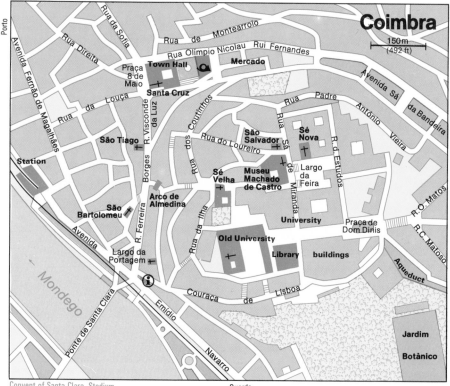

Coimbra

Afonso Henriques (1139–85), on right *Sancho I* (1195–1211), each surrounded by seven saints.

In the *Sacristy*, a Renaissance structure of 1622 with coffered barrel vaulting and polychrome azulejo decoration on the walls, are a number of notable pictures by Portuguese artists ("Pentecost", by Cristóvão de Figueiredo; "Calvary", by São Bento).

In the *Gallery* are fine 16th c. *stalls*, the only ones of that period in Portugal, carved with representations of Vasco da Gama's voyages and scenes from Camões' "Lusiads".

Adjoining the church is the picturesque *Claustro do Silêncio (16th c.), a two-storey Manueline cloister with magnificent reliefs (scenes from the Passion) in the SW and NE corners and on the S side. In the middle is a beautiful Renaissance *fountain*. – To the E is the *Jardim da Manga*, all that is left of a later cloister built by João III as a place for prayer and undisturbed meditation.

From the Praça do 8 de Maio the Rua do Visconde da Luz and its continuation Rua de Ferreira Borges, the town's principal traffic and commercial artery, lead S to the Largo da Portagem. From this square the **Ponte de Santa Clara** (fine general view of the town) crosses the Mondego to the *Convent of Santa Clara*, on the left bank of the river.

Attractive promenades run along the embankment on the right bank of the river, N and S of the bridge.

About half-way between the Town Hall and the Santa Clara bridge, below the W side of Rua Visconde da Luz at its intersection with Rua Corpo de Deus, stands the Romanesque **church of São Tiago**, founded by Fernando the Great in the 11th c. in thanksgiving for the reconquest of the town from the Moors. The church has a plain timber ceiling.

The UPPER TOWN of Coimbra can be reached either on a road which branches off at the Town Hall, ascends the N side of the hill and then turns right to reach the square in front of the University (1·5 km/ 1 mile), or (on foot) by turning off Rua de Ferreira Borges near its northern end (beside No. 75), passing under the **Arco de Almedina**, a relic of the Moorish town walls which was occupied in the 16th c. by a municipal court and now houses a *Museum of Ethnography*, and continuing up a stepped lane.

Half-way up is the *Old Cathedral (Sé Velha), a fortress-like structure built in the reign of Afonso Henriques (12th c.), with a plain exterior, crenellated walls and a massive Romanesque W doorway. Only the *Porta Especiosa*, a richly decorated early Renaissance doorway on the N side of the church, relieves the sombre effect of the exterior.

The Romanesque INTERIOR, with three aisles, is strikingly impressive. The most notable features are a number of fine **tombs**, including that of Bishop Almeida (16th c.); the large late Gothic **high altar**, with representations of the Assumption by two Flemish masters, Oliver of Ghent and John of Ypres; and the Renaissance *font* (16th c.).

From the S aisle a flight of steps leads up to the Early Gothic *cloister* (13th c.).

In the square in front of the Old Cathedral Dom João I was proclaimed King of Portugal in 1385.

From the N side of the Old Cathedral the steep Rua do Cabido leads up to the former Bishop's Palace and the Romanesque *church of São Salvador* (1169); then through the *Arco do Bispo* and into the **Largo da Feira**, which has been considerably enlarged in recent years.

Old Cathedral   Coimbra
Sé Velha

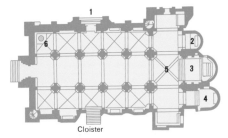

1 Porta Especiosa
2 N apse (tomb of Bishop Almeida)
3 Choir
4 S apse
5 Crossing
6 Font

Old Cathedral, Coimbra

The inner courtyard of the Old University, Coimbra

On the N side of the square is the **New Cathedral** (*Sé Nova*), built for the Jesuits in 1554 and raised to cathedral status in 1772; it has a handsome Early Baroque façade.

On the W side of the square, in the former *Bishop's Palace* (rebuilt in the late 6th c.), is the very fine *Museu Nacional de Machado de Castro**, with Roman material from excavations, medieval sarcophaguses, Romanesque and Gothic sculpture in stone and wood, goldsmiths' work, furniture, tapestries, porcelain, paintings of the 16th–18th c. (including some notable Flemish pictures) and a special section devoted to work by modern Portuguese painters.
From the double loggia in the beautiful courtyard there is a very fine *view of the town. – The *church of São João de Almedina* adjoining the museum contains its department of religious art.

To the S of the Largo da Feira, within the area once occupied by the castle, are the imposing modern buildings of the *University**; to the E the **Faculty of Medicine**; adjoining it on the right the **Faculty of Arts**, with a small archaeological museum, and the **Library** (*Biblioteca Geral*).

To the W, on the highest point of the upper town, where the royal palace (now represented only by a Manueline doorway) once stood, is the **Old University**,

partly rebuilt in the 17th and 18th c., with the earlier Porta Férrea ("Iron Gate", 1634) leading into the fine *courtyard. To the right are the *Colégio* (lecture theatres) and the colonnade of the "Via Latina".
On the E side of the courtyard is situated the *Observatory*, on the W side the **University Church**, built in 1517–52 as the palace chapel, with a 33 m/110 ft high *tower* (1733).

Adjoining the Old University is the sumptuous *Old Library**, built 1716–23 on the model of the Court Library in Vienna (João V's queen, Ana Maria, being Austrian).
The library has ceiling and wall paintings

Roman Mosaic, Conimbriga

by António Simões Ribeiro and valuable furniture with intarsia decoration. Its 120,000 books and manuscripts come from all parts of Portugal.
From the terrace at the SW corner of the courtyard there is a magnificent *view.

To the SE the Largo da Feira the *Botanic Garden (*Jardim Botánico*) is laid out in terraces on the slopes of a side valley of the Mondego, with large numbers of subtropical plants.

On the left bank of the Mondego, to the left of the Lisbon road, are the ruins of the Gothic *Convent of Santa Clara-a-Velha*, founded in 1286, which has gradually been destroyed by the flooding of the river. Here the saintly Queen Isabel spent the last ten years of her life and here she was buried, as was the murdered Inês de Castro, Pedro I's unhappy bride. Their remains were moved elsewhere after the destruction of the convent.

To the right, on the *Monte da Esperança*, stands the *Convent of Santa Clara-a-Nova*, built between 1649 and 1696 to replace the original building and now

used as a barracks. The Renaissance **church** is dedicated to St Isabel, wife of King Dinis, who is Coimbra's patron saint.

INTERIOR. – The church contains the silver **shrine** of St Isabel (1614), originally in the old convent, and which was transferred to the new one by Pedro II.
In the choir is the polychrome *cenotaph* of the saint, borne on six crouching lions. The recumbent figure of the queen is dressed in the simple habit of the Poor Clares, but the crown on her head bears witness to her rank; she is flanked by apostles and saints.

Near the old convent is the **Quinta das Lágrimas** ("House of Tears"), in which Inês de Castro is said to have been murdered in 1355.

On the road to Varzea is *Portugal dos **Pequenitos**, a miniature village ("The Children's Portugal") established in 1940, with reproductions of major buildings and monuments from Portugal and the former colonies.

SURROUNDINGS. – 2 km/1¼ miles E, in the suburb of *Celas*, is the former **Benedictine abbey of Celas**, founded in the 13th c. by Dona Sancha, daughter of Sancho I, and much altered in the 16th c. It has a fine *cloister of the late 13th c.
Farther E is the church of the Franciscan convent of

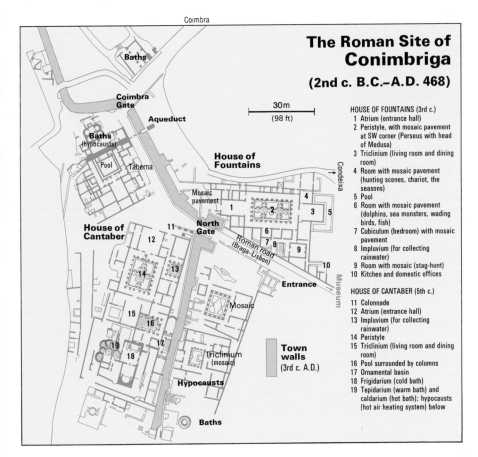

Coimbra

The Roman Site of Conimbriga
(2nd c. B.C.–A.D. 468)

Baths

Coimbra Gate

Aqueduct

30m
(98 ft)

Baths
(hypocausts)

Pool   Taberna

Mosaic pavement

House of Fountains

North Gate

Roman road
(Braga–Lisbon)

House of Cantaber

Entrance

Condeixa

Museum

Mosaic

Triclinium
(mosaic)

Hypocausts

Town walls
(3rd c. A.D.)

Baths

HOUSE OF FOUNTAINS (3rd c.)
1 Atrium (entrance hall)
2 Peristyle, with mosaic pavement at SW corner (Perseus with head of Medusa)
3 Triclinium (living room and dining room)
4 Room with mosaic pavement (hunting scenes, chariot, the seasons)
5 Pool
6 Room with mosaic pavement (dolphins, sea monsters, wading birds, fish)
7 Cubiculum (bedroom) with mosaic pavement
8 Impluvium (for collecting rainwater)
9 Room with mosaic (stag-hunt)
10 Kitchen and domestic offices

HOUSE OF CANTABER (5th c.)
11 Colonnade
12 Atrium (entrance hall)
13 Impluvium (for collecting rainwater)
14 Peristyle
15 Triclinium (living room and dining room)
16 Pool surrounded by columns
17 Ornamental basin
18 Frigidarium (cold bath)
19 Tepidarium (warm bath) and caldarium (hot bath); hypocausts (hot air heating system) below

Santo António dos Olivais, which was burned down in the middle of the 19th c. St Antony is said to have lived in the convent (founded at the beginning of the 13th c.) about 1220. – From here it is well worth climbing to the *Penedo da Meditação* for the fine* views from the top.

15 km/9 miles SW of Coimbra lies the market village of **Condeixa** (pop. 2000), with the 17th c. Palácio Lemos.

2 km/1¼ miles SE of Condeixa is the extensive site of the Roman town of** **Conimbriga**, founded in the 2nd c. B.C. and destroyed by the Suevi in A.D. 468. There are remains of the town walls (3rd c. A.D.), an aqueduct, fountains (some of them restored), baths and mosaics.
In the *Museu Monográfico* adjoining the site is displayed material recovered by the excavators (mosaics, pottery, marble busts, a colossal head of Augustus, etc.).

15 km/9 miles SE of Condeixa, picturesquely situated on a spur of high ground, in **Penela**, with a massive castle (11th–12th c.).

15 km/9 miles W of Coimbra can be found the sole relic of the Hieronymite **Convent of São Marcos**, the convent church (1510), which contains some notable 15th and 16th c. sculpture.

A pleasant excursion from Coimbra is to the *Buçaco National Park** (see p. 90), to the NE. The road up the Mondego valley via *Penacova* passes the convent of **Lorvão**, in a wooded valley a little way off the road 24 km/15 miles from Coimbra. The convent first appears in the records in 878; the present buildings, originally dating from the 10th c., were remodelled at the Renaissance. In the imposing church (late 16th c.) are 18th c. silver shrines, with elaborate intarsia decoration, containing the remains of Sancho I's daughters Sancha and Teresa (13th c.). The church also has fine choir-stalls. The cloister is enclosed by an intricately wrought grille. The other conventual buildings are now occupied by a mental hospital and are not open to the public.

Costa de Lisboa

Historical province: Estremadura.
District: Setúbal.
(i) **Comissão Municipal de Turismo de Lisboa,**
Rua Portas de Santo Antão
P-1100 Lisboa;
tel. (01) 32 70 58.
Turismo Sesimbra,
Largo do Município,
P-2970 Sesimbra;
tel. (01) 2 23 33 04.
Turismo Setúbal,
Largo do Corpo Santo,
P-2900 Setúbal;
tel. (0 65) 2 42 84.

ACCOMMODATION. – IN LISBON, SESIMBRA AND SETÚBAL: see the entries for these places.

IN COSTA DA CAPARICA: *Colibri*, I, 25 r.; *Rosa dos Ventos*, I, 25 r.; *Praia do Sol*, III, 54 r.; *Residência Dóris*, P I, 18 r.; *Tá-Mar*, P II, 37 r.; *Mar e Sol*, P II, 33 r.; *Santo António*, P II, 26 r.; *Capa Rica*, P II, 20 r.;

Real, P II, 10 r.; *Casa de São João*, P III, 30 r.; *Copacabana*, P IV, 11 r.; *Acácias*, P IV, 8 r. – CAMP SITE.

IN PORTINHO DA ARRÁBIDA: *Santa Maria da Arrábida*, P II, 33 r.

ON TRÓIA PENINSULA: *Tróia Mar* tourist village, 1597 r., SP.

EVENT. – *Fishermen's Festival* (beginning of October) on Cabo de Espichel.

RECREATION and SPORT. – Water sports; scuba diving at Portinho da Arrábida; golf-course at Tróia Mar tourist village.

The Costa de Lisboa ("Lisbon Coast") is the name given to the coast of the peninsula formed by the *Serra da Arrábida and its northern outliers between the estuaries of the Tagus and the Rio Sado – an area very popular with the people of Lisbon.

Although this stretch of coast is not yet fully equipped to cater for the international tourist trade and has only limited accommodation for holiday visitors, the beautiful scenery, fine beaches and the friendly atmosphere of its few small holiday resorts are greatly attractive.

RESORTS. – **Costa da Caparica**, an old fishing village 15 km/9 miles SW of Lisbon which is now a rapidly developing seaside resort. – From here the *Praia do Sol*, a broad beach fringed by dunes, with wooded hills lying just inland, runs S for some 22 km/14 miles. A narrow-gauge beach railway brings the remoter beaches within easy reach.

On **Cabo Espichel**, the western tip of the peninsula, formed by a westerly outlier of

Cabo Espichel

the Serra da Arrábida, is the pilgrimage chapel of Nossa Senhora do Cabo (traditional fishermen's festival at beginning of October). Extensive *views from the lighthouse.

Sesimbra: see p. 192.

Sétubal: see p. 193.

Portinho da Arrábida, a tiny fishing village, now attracting increasing numbers of holiday visitors, is idyllically situated in a small sandy cove under the S side of the Serra da Arrábida, which here falls steeply down to the sea.
There is excellent *scuba diving to be had in the many little rocky coves along this section of coast.

Tróia, a holiday village, is situated at the northern tip of the *Peninsula de Tróia*, a spit of land extending into the lagoon at the mouth of the Rio Sado, opposite Setúbal (ferry and fast motor-launch services).
The peninsula, which boasts the longest sandy beach in Portugal (30 km/ 19 miles), great stretches of dunes and areas of woodland but little in the way of roads, is ideal walking country.
Half-way along the peninsula are the remains of the Roman town of *Cetobriga*, destroyed by a tidal wave in A.D. 412.

There are pleasant excursions into the solitude of the hills in the beautiful *Serra da Arrábida**, with luxuriant vegetation which includes many rare species.
In a remote and sequestered situation in the hills is the Franciscan *Convento da Arrábida* (founded 1542), an extensive range of buildings surrounded by a wall.

Costa de Prata

Historical provinces: Beira Litoral and Estremadura. Districts: Aveiro, Coimbra, Leiria and Lisboa (Lisbon).

(i) **Turismo Ericeira,**
Rua de Eduardo Burnay 33A,
P-2655 Ericeira;
tel. (0 61) 6 31 22.
Turismo Torres Vedras,
Rua do 9 de Abril,
P-2560 Torres Vedras;
tel. (0 61) 2 30 94.

Turismo Peniche,
Rua de Alexandre Herculano,
P-2520 Peniche;
tel. (0 62) 7 22 71.
Turismo Nazaré,
Rua de Mouzinho de Albuquerque 72,
P-2450 Nazaré;
tel. (0 62) 4 61 20.
Turismo Figueira da Foz,
Rua do 25 Abril,
P-3080 Figueira da Foz;
tel. (0 33) 2 26 10.
Turismo Aveiro,
Praça da República,
P-3800 Aveiro;
tel. (0 34) 2 36 80.
Turismo Espinho,
Angulo das Ruas 6 e 23,
P-4500 Espinho;
tel. (02) 72 09 11.
Turismo Porot,
Praça do General Humberto Delgado,
P-4000 Porot;
tel. (02) 31 27 40.

ACCOMMODATION. – IN ERICEIRA: *Turismo da Ericeira*, I, 150 r., SP; *Morais*, I, 40 r., SP; *Pedro-o-Pescador*, I, 18 r.; *Fortunato*, P II, 15 r.; *Gomes*, P III, 17 r.

IN PRAIA DE SANTA CRUZ: *Santa Cruz*, I, 32 r., SP; *Mar Lindo*, P II, 7 r.; *Miramar*, P III, 27 r.

IN PRAIA DO PORTO NOVO: *Golf-Mar*, II, 284 r., SP; *Promar*, P III, 18 r.

IN VIMEIRO: *Termas do Vimeiro*, III, 88 r.; *Santa Isabel*, P II, 19 r.; *Braga*, P III, 21 r.; *Leopoldina*, P III, 11 r.; *Ludovino*, P IV, 39 r.

IN PENICHE, NAZARÉ, FIGUEIRA DA FOZ AND AVEIRO: see the entries for these places.

IN ESPINHO: *Praia Golfe*, I, 119 r., SP; *Oceano*, P II, 12 r.; *Luso-Brasileira*, P II, 10 r.; *Do Porto*, P II, 9 r.; *Particular*, P III, 48 r.; *Espinho*, III, 32 r.; *Mar Azul*, III, 24 r.; *Beira-Mar*, P IV, 12 r.; *Palmeira*, P IV, 8 r. – CAMP SITE.

IN PORTO (OPORTO): see p. 167.

RECREATION and SPORT. – Water sports; golf-courses at Vimeiro and Espinho; airfield for light aircraft at Espinho.

The Costa de Prata ("Silver Coast"), the long central stretch of the Portuguese Atlantic coast between the Cabo da Roca and the mouth of the Douro, has long been a favourite holiday area with the people of Portugal.

This is a region of long sandy beaches, fringed by dunes or edged by cliffs, of pinewoods and olive-groves, with old windmills adding a picturesque touch in many areas; but with its fairly cold sea and its bracing and windy climate the Costa de Prata is not the place for those whose only holiday activities are swimming and sunbathing.

Cliffs near Ericeira (Costa de Prata)

RESORTS. – *Ericeira* (pop. 3000), a little fishing town (crayfish) situated above a steep and rocky coast with numerous clefts and caves. At some distance from the town, connected to it by a narrow-gauge beach railway, are a number of small beaches where one can bathe, and long stretches of beach without such facilities.

Around **Praia de Santa Cruz** and **Praia do Porto Novo** are extensive beaches of fine sand, bordered by rocks and green hills.
4 km/2½ miles inland is the spa of **Vimeiro** with a golf-course.

Peniche, *Nazaré, **Figueira da Foz** and *Aveiro**: see the entries for these places.

Espinho, a seaside resort 15 km/9 miles S of Oporto with a broad beach of coarse sand and a fine seafront promenade. Developed solely as a resort, it has a wide range of facilities for recreation, including an 18-hole golf-course and an airfield for light aircraft.

*Oporto: see p. 167.

Costa do Algarve
See Algarve.

Costa do Sol

Historical province: Estremadura.
District: Lisboa (Lisbon).
ⓘ **Turismo da Costa do Sol,**
Arcadas do Parque,
P-2765 Estoril;
tel. (01) 2 68 01 13.

ACCOMMODATION. – IN PAÇO DE ARCOS: *Habiturismo Equador*, II, 182 r.; *Moreira*, P III, 16 r.

IN OEIRAS: *Conde de Oeiras*, I, 22 r.; *Continental*, II, 140 r., SP. – YOUTH HOSTEL: *Pousada de Juventude Catalazete*, Santo Amaro de Oeiras, 84 b. – CAMP SITE.

IN CARCAVELOS: *Praia Mar*, I, 160 r., SP.

IN ESTORIL AND CASCAIS: see the entries for these places.

ON THE PRAIA DO GUINCHO: *Do Guincho*, L, 36 r., SP; *Forte Muchaxo*, L, 24 r., SP; *Mar do Guincho*, II, 14 r. – CAMP SITE.

RECREATION and SPORT. – Water sports; golf-course (18 holes) at Estoril.

The *Costa do Sol ("Sunshine Coast"), to the W of Lisbon, is one of the most beautiful stretches of Portugal's W coast, known with some justification as the "Portuguese Riviera". Sheltered from the N and W winds, with excellent beaches, a mild climate and a luxuriant growth of vegetation, the towns and resorts on the Costa do Sol attract large numbers of holiday visitors, being particularly favoured by well-to-do Portuguese.

Lisbon to the *Cabo da Roca via Estoril and Cascais** (56 m/35 miles). – Leave Lisbon by the Avenida da Índia, which runs W following the Tagus and passing the port installations.

6 km/4 miles: *Belém** (see under Lisbon). Continue on the coast road (Estrada Marginal, No. 6).

2·5 km/1½ miles: *Algés*, with a large and very popular beach.

1 km/¾ mile, on right: the very interesting **Aqúario de Vasco da Gama**, with King Carlos I's oceanographical collection and a large collection of fishes from Portuguese coastal waters and the former overseas territories.

3 km/2 miles: *Caxias*, at the mouth of the Tagus, here 2 km/1¼ miles wide, with a number of old 17th c. fortifications projecting into the sea; Forte de São Bruno youth hostel.

2 km/1¼ miles: off the road to the right the seaside resort of **Paço de Arcos**; to the left, above the beach, a terrace from which there are magnificent views of the entrance to the Tagus estuary, divided into two by the *Cachopo Pequeno* reef (lighthouse), and to the rear, the banks of the Tagus as far as the Tower of Belém.

2·5 km/1½ miles: **Oeiras** (pop. 14,000), a popular resort, with the summer residence of the Marquês de Pombal, a handsome

18th c. villa set in beautiful gardens (statues, fountains and cascades). The building now belongs to the Gulbenkian Foundation.

The road now runs directly above the sea, passing the beaches of *Santo Amaro*, *Nova Oeiras* and *Carcavelos*, with superb views.

8 km/5 miles: *Estoril** (see p. 111).

3 km/2 miles: *Cascais** (see p. 94).

From Cascais continue on Road 247 (preferable to the shorter inland route on Road 9/1), which skirts the beautiful cliff-fringed coast to the Cabo Raso and then turns N.

2 km/1¼ miles: car park and lookout point at the *Boca do Inferno** (see under Cascais).

2 km/1¼ miles: *Farol da Guia* (lighthouse, 1761).

4 km/2½ miles: **Cabo Raso** (lighthouse), with a fine view northward to the Cabo da Roca.

2 km/1¼ miles: *Porto de Santa Maria*, with a beautiful sandy beach.

1 km/¾ mile: *Praia do Guincho**, a magnificent dune-fringed beach, sheltered by pinewoods.

7 km/4¼ miles: the road on the left leads to the imposing *Cabo da Roca**, the most westerly point in Europe, rising to a height of 144 m/472 ft above the Atlantic. Visitors can obtain a certificate confirming that they have been here. The headland, known to the Romans as *Promontorium Magnum*, is a granite outlier of the *Serra de Sintra* (see under Sintra). The ascent of the lighthouse should not be missed.

Costa Dourada

Historical province: Baixo Alentejo.
Districts: Setúbal and Beja.

ⓘ **Turismo Setúbal,**
Largo do Corpo Santo,
P-2900 Setúbal;
tel. (0 65) 2 42 84.

Still relatively undeveloped for tourism, Portugal's "Golden Coast",

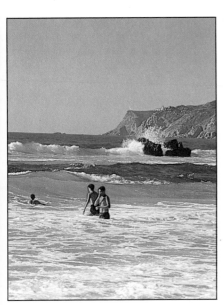
Praia do Guincho

the **Costa Dourada**, extends along the open Atlantic between the Ponta da Arrifana and the mouth of the Rio Sado.

This very beautiful stretch of coast, with its picturesque cliffs and its seemingly endless beaches, is less than ideal for a sun and sea holiday because of its fairly raw climate and the wind which blows in continually from the sea. Only in a few sheltered coves are there bathing beaches with modest facilities, and the accommodation available for visitors is correspondingly sparse.

RESORTS. – **Aljezur** (pop. 4000), with the ruins of a Moorish castle.
Roads run down from Aljezur to the pleasant beaches of *Praia de Arrifana* (SW) and *Praia de Monte Clérico* (NW).

Vila Nova de Milfontes, a fishing village and now a developing seaside resort, picturesquely situated above the mouth of the Rio Mira, it has a castle built by João IV.
There is a bridge over the river to the large dune-fringed beaches to the S.

Porto Covo, an attractive little fishing port which is also a rising holiday resort. There are numerous picturesque and sheltered little coves with good beaches.

Sines: see p. 195.

Costa Verde

Historical provinces: Douro Litoral and Minho.
Districts: Porto (Oporto), Braga and Viana do Castelo.
ⓘ **Turismo Porto**,
Praça do General Humberto Delgado,
P-4000 Porot;
tel. (02) 31 27 40.
Turismo Barcelos,
Rua dos Duques de Bragança,
Esplanada de Turismo,
P-4750 Barcelos;
tel. (00 53) 8 28 82.
Turismo Vila do Conde,
Rua do 25 de Abril 103,
P-4480 Vila do Conde;
tel. (00 52) 6 34 72.
Turismo Póvoa de Varzim,
Avenida de Mouzinho de Albuquerque 166,
P-4490 Póvoa de Varzim;
tel. (00 52) 6 46 09.
Turismo Viana do Castelo,
Avenida Cândido dos Reis,

P-4900 Viana do Castelo;
tel. (00 58) 2 26 20.
Turismo Caminha,
Rua Ricardo Joaquim de Sousa,
P-4910 Caminha;
tel. (0 58) 92 19 52.

ACCOMMODATION. – IN OPORTO, VILA DO CONDE, PÓVOA DE VARZIM, BARCELOS, VIANA DO CASTELO AND CAMINHA: see the entries for these places.

RECREATION and SPORT. – Wind-surfing, sailing, fishing; riding; golf-courses at Espinho and Praia de Miramar, near Oporto.

The Costa Verde ("Green Coast"), the stretch of the northern Portuguese Atlantic coast between the mouths of the Douro and the Minho, is a region of great scenic attraction, with its long beaches of fine sand fringed by dunes or sheltered by cliffs and its backdrop of green hills. Together with the Costa de Prata to the S it has long been a favourite Portuguese holiday area.

With its relatively cold water and its frequent winds blowing off the sea this is not the place for purely swimming and sunbathing holidays. It does, however, offer a variety of rewarding excursions into the hinterland – for example to *Braga, *Guimarães or the *Peneda-Gerês National Park (see the entries for these places).
*Oporto, **Vila do Conde** and **Póvoa de Varzim**: see the entries for these places.

Ofir and **Esposende**: see under Barcelos.

Viana do Castelo: see p. 203.

A seemingly endless expanse of dunes extends northwards to the Spanish frontier. The only resorts in this area are **Vila Praia de Âncora** and **Moledo do Minho** (see under Caminha).

Seaweed drying on Esposende beach

Covilhã

Historical province: Beira Baixa.
District: Castelo Branco.
Altitude: 700 m/2300 ft.
Population: 25,000.
Post code: P-6200.
Telephone code: 0 75.

ⓘ **Turismo,**
Praça do Município;
tel. 2 21 70.

ACCOMMODATION. – *Solneve*, P II, 24 r., *Neve*, P II, 18 r.; *Costa*, P II, 9 r.; *A Regional*, P II, 18 r.; *São Francisco*, P III, 13 r.; *Avenida*, P IV, 10 r. – OUTSIDE THE TOWN: *Estalagem Varanda dos Carqueijais*, I, 49 r., SP.

YOUTH HOSTEL. – *Pousada de Juventude*, Penhas da Saúde (11 km/7 miles NW of Covilhã), 144 b.

A local gastronomic speciality is *queijo da serra*, a soft ewe's-milk cheese.

RECREATION and SPORT. – Walking; winter sports in the Serra da Estrêla.

Finely situated on the SE slopes of the Serra da Estrêla, the hill town of Covilhã attracts many visitors as a pleasant summer resort in a beautiful wooded *setting and as a base for exploring the Serra da Estrêla.

Covilhã is a major location of the Portuguese textile industry, producing woollen goods under British licence for sale on the international market.

SIGHTS. – Covilhã is a picturesque old town of steep and winding streets. The town's life is focused on the Praça do Município, in which is the *Town Hall* (Câmara Municipal).
Above the square rises the 15th c. **church of Santa Maria**, its façade decorated with azulejos depicting scenes from the life of the Virgin.

Also of interest are the Romanesque *chapel of São Martinho* and the 16th c. *chapel of Santa Cruz*, with pictures and woodcarving.
Within the walls which formerly enclosed a Franciscan convent is the Municipal Park, from which there are fine views. – Another excellent lookout point is the **monument of Nossa Senhora da Conceição**.

SURROUNDINGS. – To the S of the town, between the Serra da Estrêla and the Serra da Guardunha, is the *Cova da Beira*, the wide and fertile valley of the Zêzere. The evident prosperity of this area is based on the extensive forests, the growing of corn, fruit and vegetables, the production of wine and, above all, on the woollen industry,

Covilhã is a good base from which to explore the *Serra da Estrêla (see p. 189).

Curia

Historical province: Beira Litoral.
District: Aveiro.
Altitude: 40 m/130 ft.
Post code: P-3780.
Telephone code: 0 31.

ⓘ **Turismo,**
Largo da Rotunda;
tel. 5 22 48.
Sociedade das Águas da Curia,
tel. 5 21 85.

ACCOMMODATION. – *Palace Hotel da Curia*, II, 122 r., SP; *Termas*, II, 39 r., SP; *Curia*, IV, 91 r.; *Boavista*, IV, 38 r.; *Santos*, P II, 40 r.; *Lourenço*, P II, 42 r.; *Imperial*, P II, 37 r.; *Natividade*, P II, 15 r.; *Avenida*, P II, 10 r.; *Portugal*, P III, 25 r.; *Santa Cruz*, P III, 25 r.; *Curia*, P III, 22 r.; *Bandeira*, P III, 11 r.; *Casa Silva*, P III, 9 r.; *Alves*, P III, 8 r.

RECREATION and SPORT. – Swimming; tennis; roller-skating rink. – Water sports in the Atlantic, within easy reach.

The spa of Curia, with hot springs containing calcium sulphate (season June to mid October), lies only 20 km/12 miles from the Atlantic in the Bairrada region of central Portugal, well known for its wine, both still and sparkling.

Curia has modern treatment facilities, a variety of sports and recreational facilities and an attractive park attached to the spa establishment.

Local culinary specialties are *chanfana* (pig's head) and *leitão assado* (roast sucking pig).

SURROUNDINGS. – Excursions can be made from Curia to the ****Buçaco National Park** (see p. 90) and ****Coimbra** (p. 99).

Douro Valley

The Douro (Spanish Duero), known to the Romans as the Durius, one of the great waterways of the Iberian peninsula, rises on the Pico de Urbión (2252 m/7389 ft) in the Spanish province of Soria and flows into the Atlantic after a total course of 925 km/575 miles through Spain and Portugal. In its upper reaches it traverses the plateau of Old Castile and León; it then forms the frontier between Spain and Portugal for a distance of 122 km/76 miles, flowing through a gorge up to 400 m/1300 ft

Valley of the Douro near Oporto

deep; and finally cuts through the Portuguese highlands between Trás-os-Montes and Beira in a wild and picturesque valley, to reach the Atlantic at Oporto.

Along the stretch of the river between Spain and Portugal there are a series of impressive dams providing hydroelectric power, built under an agreement between the two countries. Above Oporto the river is suitable only for specially designed

A *rabelo* carrying wine down the Douro

boats with a shallow draught (*rabelos*), owing to the extreme seasonal variations in water level (highest levels in autumn and spring, lowest usually in summer); the area around the mouth, below Oporto, is navigable by seagoing ships.

The vineyards of the upper Douro valley (the **"Pais do Vinho"**, "Land of Wine"), on the elaborately terraced slopes of slaty soil flanking the river, produce the excellent, rather heavy, wine used in the making of Portugal's most famous product, *port*.

Elvas

Historical province: Alto Alentejo.
District: Portalegre.
Altitude: 300 m/985 ft.
Population: 15,000.
Post code: P-7350.
Telephone code: 0 68.
ⓘ **Turismo,**
Praça da República;
tel. 6 22 36.

ACCOMMODATION. – *Estalagem de Dom Sancho II,* I, 50 r.; *Pousada de Santa Luzia,* 11 r.; *Dom Luis,* II, 50 r., SP; *O Lidador,* P II, 19 r.; *Quinta das Águias,* P II, 5 r.; *Central,* P IV, 21 r.; *Elvense,* P IV, 12 r. – OUTSIDE THE TOWN: *Estalagem Dom Quixote,* 5 r.

EVENTS. – *Festas do Senhor Jesús da Piedade* and *Feira de São Mateus* (end September), a popular and church festival typical of Alentejo.

*Elvas, on a hillside amid rich fruit orchards and olive groves, is an old frontier fortress town which has preserved much of its original

Moorish character. **Built to counter its Spanish opposite number, Badajoz, the town was ever more strongly fortified from the late medieval period onwards, and in the 17th and 18th c. was still further reinforced by powerful forts, which are among the best preserved and most impressive strongholds of their period in Portugal.**

Elvas is now a market and shopping area for the fertile agricultural country around the town. It is widely known for its candied plums.

SIGHTS. – The central feature of the town is the Praça da República.
On the S side of the square stands the old *Town Hall* (Câmara Municipal), on the N side the **Cathedral** (*Sé*), originally Late Gothic but rebuilt in Manueline style in the 16th c. (the façade is 17th c.); it has a beautiful three-aisled interior with polychrome azulejo decoration.

Above the Cathedral the **church of Nossa Senhora da Consolação**, belongs to a Dominican monastery founded in the mid 16th c. It is an unusual octagonal structure; the dome, borne on columns, is entirely covered with azulejos.

Adjoining the church is the picturesque triangular *Largo Santa Clara*, surrounded by handsome houses with elegant iron window grilles. In the middle of the square is a fine 16th c. *pelourinho* (pillory column).

*FORTIFICATIONS. – Above the town is the **Castle** (*Castelo*), built by the Moors in the 13th c. on the site of an earlier Roman fortress and enlarged in the 15th c., with a 15th c. keep. Fine views from the bastions.
To the N of the town rises the 18th c. **Fort of Nossa Senhora da Graça** (alt. 388 m/1273 ft), also known as *Forte Lippa* after Count Wilhelm von Schaumburg-Lippe, who commanded the Portuguese army in 1762–64.
To the S of the town in **Fort Santa Luzia** (alt. 366 m/1201 ft), an excellent example, excellently preserved, of 17th c. Portuguese military engineering.
A tour of the town's fortifications provides a pleasant walk (5 km/3 miles).

In the former Jesuit convent is the interesting **Museu de António Tomás Pires**, with a collection of religious art, archaeology (Roman mosaics), coins, pictures and sculpture of the 13th–16th c. and folk art.

SURROUNDINGS. – To the SW of the town is the *Aqueduto da Amoreira, an aqueduct more than 7 km/4½ miles long, built between 1498 and 1622 on the foundations of a Roman aqueduct, which still supplies water to the 17th c. Misericórdia fountain. The aqueduct, supported by over 800 arches (sometimes built up in four tiers) reaches a height of 31 m/100 ft at its highest point.

20 km/12½ miles NE of Elvas is **Campo Maior** (alt. 277 m/909 ft); pop. 9000), still enclosed within a complete circuit of walls (17th–18th c.), with a 14th c. castle built by King Dinis and a Gothic parish church (charnel-house).

Estoril

Historical province: Estremadura.
District: Lisboa (Lisbon).
Altitude: sea level.
Population: 16,000.
Post code: P-2765.
Telephone code: 01.
ⓘ **Turismo da Costa do Sol,**
Arcadas do Parque;
tel. 2 68 01 13.

ACCOMMODATION. – IN ESTORIL: *Palácio do Estoril, L, 168 r., SP; *Cibra, I, 85 r.; Casa Lennox, I, 17 r., SP; Belvedere, I, 14 r.; Fundador, I, 11 r.; Claridade, I, 10 r.; Paris, II, 100 r., SP; Lido, II, 55 r., SP; Arcadas, II, 46 r., SP; Alvorada, II, 33 r.; Inglaterra, III, 43 r., SP; São Mamede, II, 23 r.; Continental, P II, 14 r.; Lar de São Cristóvão, P II, 14 r.; Pica-Pau, P II, 8 r.; Chique do Estoril, P III, 16 r.; Marylus, P III, 9 r.; Costa, P III, 7 r. – Apartments: Vale do Sol, 300 r., SP.

IN MONTE ESTORIL: Atlântico, I, 175 r., SP; Grande Hotel, I, 72 r., SP; Zenith, II, 48 r., SP; Londres, III, 71 r., SP; Miramar, III, 39 r., SP; Real, P II, 11 r.; Casa Londres, P II, 9 r.

EVENTS. – Carnival; Sea Festival (July); Feira de Artesanato (Craft Fair, end July).

The beach, Estoril

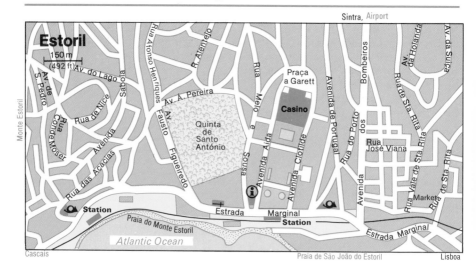

Sintra, Airport

Estoril

150 m
(492 ft)

Monte Estoril

Rua Afonso Henriques
R. Alentejo
Av. do Lago
Av. de S. Pedro
Rua Conde Moser
Rua de Nice
Av. A. Pereira
Av. Fausto
Rua das Acacias
Avenida
Rua das Acácias
Figueiredo

Quinta de Santo António

Praça a Garett

Casino

Avenida de Portugal
Rua do Porto
Bombeiros
Av. da Holanda
Av. da Suiça
Rua de Sta. Rita

Sousa
Avenida Aida
Avenida Clotilde

dos

Rua José Viana

Rua Vale de
Rua de Sta. Rita

Avenida

Market

Station

Estrada

Marginal
Station

Praia do Monte Estoril

Atlantic Ocean

Estrada Marginal

Cascais   Praia de São João do Estoril   Lisboa

Casino.

RECREATION and SPORT. – Water sports, sailing, fishing; riding. – Golf-course (18 holes) in Monte Estoril.

*Estoril, once a modest fishing village, began its rise into a fashionable summer and winter resort, frequented by an elegant international public, towards the end of the 19th c., thanks to its equable climate and beautiful subtropical gardens, and it is still the home of some illustrious figures, including a number of crowned heads. Its radioactive hot springs (33°C/91°F), containing carbonic acid, are recommended for the treatment of rheumatism and diseases of the joints.

SIGHTS. – Estoril itself has no particularly outstanding features of interest; it is visited primarily for its atmosphere of international elegance, its fine villas, the superb beaches in and around the town, for its magnificent park, where many species of tropical and exotic plants may be seen, and for its convenience as a base from which to visit Lisbon, to explore the Serra de Sintra, and to enjoy the beauties of the coast.

1·5 km/1 mile W of the Park is **Monte Estoril** (109 m/358 ft), around which a high-class residential district has grown up. Here, too, is a magnificent *golf-course (18 holes).

Beyond the MONTE ESTORIL district lies *Cascais (see p. 94), another elegant resort which with Estoril now forms a single built-up area.

Estremadura

Historical province: Estremadura.
Districts: Leiria, Lisboa (Lisbon) and Setúbal.
Area: 11,430 sq. km/4413 sq. miles.
Population: 3,000,000.

Chief town: Lisbon.
ⓘ **Turismo Lisboa,**
Rua Portas de Santo Antão,
P-1100 Lisboa;
tel. (01) 32 70 58.

The ancient province and region of Estremadura (from the Latin "Extrema Durii", "farthest land on the Douro"), consists of the three districts of Lisboa (Lisbon), Leiria and Setúbal together with the national capital, Lisbon. It comprises the area around the mouth of the Tagus, extending inland as far as the Ribatejo basin, northward by way of the Serra de Sintra and the southwesterly outliers of the Serra da Estrêla to just S of Coimbra, and southward by way of the Setúbal peninsula (Serra da Arrábida) to the mouth of the Rio Sado.

The intricate geological and topographical pattern of this region, affected in many places by tectonic action, is reflected in a degree of economic and cultural diversity scarcely to be found in any other Portuguese region.

The northern uplands, part of a massif of Mesozoic limestones, show typical features, with poljes and swallowholes, a sparse undergrowth in the depressions and a predominance of sheep and goat herding.

To the W of this area is a chain of hills of sandstones, a region of fertile soil which is the agricultural heartland of the province. Here, around Alcobaça, mixed farming of Mediterranean type predominates (wheat, maize, citrus fruits, vegetables, olives, vines).

To the S of this is the *Serra de Sintra*, a range of volcanic hills with fertile soils and a mild, wet oceanic climate which have produced a beautiful park-like landscape. This has become one of Portugal's leading holiday regions, with numerous thermal springs (Caldas da Rainha, Estoril, etc.) which provide an additional attraction.

The narrow coastal strip in the N and the areas around the mouths of the Tagus, the Sado, the Mondego and the Vouga – with areas of marshland, lagoons and long sand-spits – are chiefly orientated towards the sea. Here are the old-established fishing ports which are used by the deep-sea fishermen sailing to distant waters, particularly to Newfoundland, with their fish-canning and drying establishments and their extensive salt-pans. The marshy land in the valley basins also provides suitable conditions for the growing of rice.

Estremadura and Ribatejo between them have the largest single area of vineyards in Portugal.

Thanks to their fertility and their diversity of landscape pattern within a relatively small area, Estremadura and Ribatejo have since Roman times played a central part in the development of Lusitanian and later Portuguese culture. Here are to be found the country's principal intellectual areas, **Lisbon** and **Coimbra**, the great spiritual headquarters of *Alcobaça, *Batalha and Santarém and the former royal residences of *Queluz, Mafra and *Sintra (see the entries for these places).

Windmill, Estremadura

Cabo da Roca, the most westerly point in Europe

Estremoz

Historical province: Alto Alentejo.
District: Évora.
Altitude: 440 m/1445 ft.
Population: 9500.
Post code: P-7100.
Telephone code: 0 68.
(i) **Turismo,**
    Largo da República 26;
    tel. 2 25 38.

ACCOMMODATION. – *Pousada da Rainha Santa Isabel*, in Castelo, 23 r.; *Carvalho*, P III, 16 r.; *Mateus*, P III, 10 r.; *Estremoz*, P III, 8 r.; *Alentejano*, IV, 21 r.

RESTAURANT. – *Águias de Ouro*.

The little old-world town of Estremoz, built on a hill rising above the plain, has preserved much of its original Moorish character in the oldest part of the town with its picturesque narrow lanes and whitewashed houses, their windows kept small to afford protection from the fierce heat of summer.

Much use is made of the local white marble, which was widely renowned in

Estremoz

the Middle Ages. – Estremoz is also noted for its pottery.

SIGHTS. – The picturesque UPPER TOWN, enclosed within 17th c. Vauban-style fortifications with several massive towers, has some fine Gothic and Manueline burghers' houses.
On top of the hill stands the three-aisled **church of Santa Maria do Castelo** (1559), with two paintings of the Virgin by El Greco.

Above the town rears the well-preserved *Castle (Castelo), built in the first half of the 13th c. and altered in the 18th c., once the residence of King Dinis I and of his wife St Isabel, who died here in 1336.
The royal palace (14th c.; restored in 18th c.) is now a luxurious pousada (inn). From the imposing battlemented *keep*, 27 m/90 ft high, there are superb *views.

The central feature of the more modern LOWER TOWN is the *Praça do Marquês de Pombal* or Rossio, in which the weekly market is held.
In this spacious square stands the **Town Hall** (*Câmara Municipal*), originally built (1698) as a convent, which houses the *Municipal Museum* (pottery and azulejos, pictures, arms and armour, coins, archaeological material).

In the nearby Largo do General Graça are the 17th c. *Tocha Palace* (azulejo pictures) and the former *Franciscan convent*

(originally 13th c.; now a barracks) in which King Pedro I died in 1397; fine Gothic *church*.

SURROUNDINGS. – 10 km/6 miles E on the Borba road is the *Museu de Cristo*, with an interesting collection of crucifixes.

Sousel (pop. 2000) 16 km/10 miles N, founded by Nuna Álvares in 1387, has a 16th c, parish church and another 16th c. church, the Misericórdia, with 18th c. azulejo decoration.

25 km/16 miles S of Estremoz on a road which runs through the *Serra de Ossa* (649 m/2129 ft), passing the *Convento da Berra*, lies **Redondo** (alt. 305 m/ 1000 ft; pop. 7000), a pleasant little town with the ruins of a 14th c. castle built in the reign of King Dinis and the church of the Misericórdia, which has a Manueline choir.

Also within easy reach of Estremoz are *Evoramonte* (see under Évora), **Borba** (see p. 86) and **Vila Viçosa** (p. 206).

Évora

Historical province: Alto Alentejo.
District: Évora.
Altitude: 300 m/985 ft.
Population: 36,000.
Post code: P-7000.
Telephone code: 0 66.
ⓘ **Turismo,**
    Praça do Giraldo 71;
    tel. 2 26 71.

ACCOMMODATION. – *Pousada dos Lóios*, 32 r.; *Planície*, II, 33 r.; *Santa Clara*, III, 22 r.; *Giraldo*, P II, 23 r.; *Riviera*, P II, 22 r.; *Policarpo*, P III, 21 r.; *Os Manuéis*, P III, 18 r.; *O Alentejo*, P III, 17 r.

RESTAURANT. – *Portalegre*.

YOUTH HOSTEL. – *Pousada de Juventude*, Rua da Corredoura 32, 70 b.

CAMP SITE.

EVENT. – *Feira de São João* (end June), the largest fair in southern Portugal, with folk events.

*Évora, built on a low hill surrounded by rolling plains, was the old capital of the upland region of Alentejo and is now the chief town of a district and the see of an archbishop. With its walls of the Roman, Moorish and later periods, still largely preserved, and its narrow lanes, sometimes lined with arcades, it retains much of its Moorish and medieval character, and it has many individual buildings of great historical and artistic interest.

HISTORY. – Évora is believed to have been one of the oldest trading posts on the Iberian peninsula. In Roman times it was a place of some consequence, originally (in the praetorship of Sertorius) known as *Ebora* but renamed *Liberalitas Iulia* in the time of Caesar.

In 715 the town fell into the hands of the Moors and became known as *Yebora*. It was reconquered by Geraldo Sem-Pavor (Gerald the Fearless) in 1165 and reunited with the kingdom of Afonso Henriques. In the earlier part of the 14th c. it was for a time the residence of the Portuguese kings and became a focus of political and cultural life; but, with the transfer of the seat of government to Lisbon and later with the closing of its university, Évora's splendour and influence declined.

Évora is now the principal marketing town for the agricultural produce of Alentejo (wool, woollen cloths, cork).

A local culinary specialty is *porco à alentejana* (fried pork with clams).

Évora, looking towards the Cathedral

SIGHTS. – The central feature of the town is the elongated *Praça do Geraldo*, once a place of execution where many victims of the Inquisition went to the stake. In the square, which is partly surrounded by arcades, is a Renaissance *fountain* in Estremoz marble (by Afonso Álvares, 1571), on the site of a Roman triumphal arch which was pulled down in 1570 to make way for it.

On the N side of the square is the *collegiate church of Santo Antão*, built in 1557 by the archbishop who later became King Henrique II.

Above the Praça do Geraldo to the E stands the ***Cathedral** (*Sé*), a severe and fortress-like structure in Early Gothic style which was begun in 1186 and completed in the 13th and 14th c. The façade is dominated by the two asymmetrical towers flanking the massive doorway. Above the crossing is an octagonal tower with a helm roof of scale-like tiles.

The twelve *figures of apostles on the doorway are masterpieces of Portuguese Gothic sculpture.

From the roof of the Cathedral there are extensive panoramic *views.

The INTERIOR, notable for its regular masonry with white mortar joints, is of impressive simplicity and harmony.

The Baroque raised *Choir*, entered by a flight of steps in the S aisle, was remodelled in the 18th c. by Johann Friedrich Ludwig (architect of the convent of Mafra) and lavishly decorated with marble. The fine carved choir-stalls date from 1562.

In the *Sacristy* is the valuable ***Cathedral Treasury**, notable in particular for a 13th c. ivory triptych of the Virgin and Child. It also contains many outstanding examples of 16th and 17th c. gold and silver and enamel work.

Adjoining the Sacristy is the beautiful Gothic **Cloister** (14th c.).

The former *Archbishop's Palace*, on the N side of the Cathedral, now houses the well-stocked **Regional Museum** (*Museu de Évora*), with antiquities, Portuguese and Flemish pictures of the 16th–18th c., applied and decorative art, two cenotaphs by Nicolas Chanterene (Dom Álvares de Costa, 1535; Dom Afonso de Portugal, 1537) and much else of interest.

Beside the museum is the *Public Library* (Biblioteca Pública), with some 2000 incunabula and manuscripts.

Opposite the Archbishop's Palace is a ***Roman temple** of the 2nd or 3rd c. A.D., one of the best preserved Roman

Roman Temple, Évora

Opposite the temple, to the right, is the 15th c. **church of the Lóios** (azulejos), which belonged to the **Convent of São João Evangelista**, built in the 15th c., much altered in later periods and now converted into a pousada.

The beautiful *cloister* now serves as a charming garden for residents in the pousada. The former *chapterhouse* has Manueline stellar vaulting.

structures in Portugal, which is popularly but probably wrongly known as the Temple of Diana.

On the 3 m/10 ft high base, which is almost completely preserved, there still stand 14 of the original 18 Corinthian columns, with part of the architrave.

During the Middle Ages the temple was converted into a fortress, and later it was used for many years as a slaughterhouse – a use which at any rate saved it from demolition.

To the E of the convent are the extensive buildings of the **Old University** (*Antiga Universidade*), in Italian Renaissance style, founded in 1551 as a Jesuit college, raised to the status of a university in 1558 and closed in 1759, after the dissolution of the Jesuit order in Portugal. The *church*, dedicated to the Holy Ghost, was consecrated in 1574.

The university buildings, still containing some fine old furniture, are now occupied by a school, but can be visited during the school holidays.

To the S of the Cathedral, in the quaint and very picturesque *Largo das Portas de*

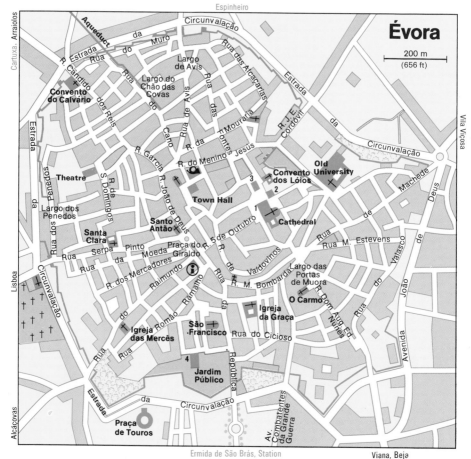

1 Regional Museum   2 Library   3 Roman temple   4 Palace of Manuel I

Moura, stands the **Casa Cordovil**, an elegant 16th c. palace in Moorish and Manueline style.
In the middle of the square is a handsome fountain (1556) with a marble basin containing a globe, symbolising the new age which had dawned.

In the southern part of the town, near the Praça do Geraldo, is the *church of São Francisco (second half of 15th c.), perhaps the finest example of Manueline architecture in southern Portugal.
The severe interior, with the same white mortar joints as the Cathedral, creates an effect of greater spaciousness than the Cathedral. Adjoining the S aisle is the *Casa dos Ossos*, a 17th c. charnel-house with a gruesome display of human bones.

Farther S is the Jardim Público (Municipal Park), with the *Palace of Manuel I* (15th c.), a mere fragment of the palace once occupied by Manuel's brilliant court. Near the W of the park, in Rua do Raimundo, can be found the *church of the Mercês*, which now houses the **Museum of Decorative Art** (arts and crafts, religious art).

Still farther S, on the road to the station, rises the fortress-like **Ermida de São Brás** (Hermitage of St Blaise), a rather gloomy building in a Late Gothic style showing Moorish influence which was erected in 1485 in thanksgiving for survival from the plague. The flat roof is crenellated and flanked by six conical pinnacles along each side.

SURROUNDINGS. – The **Aqueduct of Sertorius**, to the NW of the town, was constructed in 1552 and is said to be based on Roman foundations; it brings water from a spring 19 km/12 miles away.

3 km/2 miles NW of Évora is the **Convent of Nossa Senhora d'Espinheiro** (15th–16th c.), with a beautiful cloister.

The **Cartuxa** (Carthusian monastery), 3 km/2 miles N, has a classical-style church (17th c.) and a cloister decorated with azulejos.
2 km/1¼ miles beyond this, at the foot of Mt São Bento (364 m/1194 ft; fine views), stands the **Convent of São Bento de Castris** (founded 1274), with a church of the 14th–15th c., 18th c. azulejo decoration and a two-storey cloister (16th c.).

35 km/22 miles NE of Évora, prominently situated on a hill (474 m/1555 ft), are the massive ruins of **Evoramonte Castle** (14th c.), from which a magnificent *view of *Estremoz (p. 113) may be enjoyed.

11 km/7 miles SW of Évora is the **Quinta de Valverde**, once belonging to the Capuchins and now an agricultural college, with a round church (16th c.), a two-storey cloister and some fine outdoor sculpture.

22 km/14 miles farther SW, at the foot of the Serra de São João, lies **Alcáçovas** (pop. 2500), with a handsome 15th c. palace of the Counts of Alcáçovas and a notable parish church of the 15th and 16th c. The *chapel of Nossa Senhora da Esperança* (16th c.), above the village, 3 km/2 miles W, was once the church of a Dominican convent. From the hill on which it stands there are fine views.

30 km/19 mies S of Évora is **Viana do Alentejo** (pop. 3500), with an old castle and a handsome parish church (Manueline doorway, azulejo decoration).
10 km/6 miles farther SE stands the fine 16th c. mansion of *Água de Peixes*, in Hispano-Mauresque style.
11 km/7 miles S of Viana do Alentejo lies the little country town of **Alvito** (pop. 1500), with the characteristic white houses of the region, a beautiful parish chrch (magnificent 17th c. azulejo decoration) and a fine fortified castle (15th c.) built by the Marquês de Alvito.

41 km/25 miles SE of Évora is **Portel** (pop. 2500), with a 13th c. castle of the Bragança family which was rebuilt by Manuel I (view). The little chapel of Santo António is lavishly decorated with polychrome azulejos.

Faro

Historical province: Algarve.
District: Faro.
Altitude: sea level.
Population: 22,000.
Post code: P-8000.
Telephone code: 0 89.
ⓘ **Turismo,**
Rua Ataide de Oliveira 100;
tel. 2 40 67.
Rua da Misericórdia 8–12;
tel. 2 54 04.
ACP,
Praça de Dom Francisco Gomes;
tel. 2 47 53.

ACCOMMODATION. – *Eva*, I, 150 r., SP; *Faro*, II, 52 r.; *Albacor*, III, 38 r.; *Santa Maria*, III, 30 r.; *Condado*, P I, 17 r.; *Samé*, P II, 37 r.; *Marim*, P II, 29 r.; *O Faraó*, P II, 16 r.; *Oceano*, P II, 16 r.; *Algarve*, P II, 15 r.; *Iorque*, P II, 15 r.; *Solar do Alto*, P II, 13 r.; *Lumena*, P II, 11 r.; *Madalena*, P III, 16 r.; *Delfim*, P III, 14 r.; *Carminho*, P III, 11 r.; *Avenida*, P III, 10 r.; *Correia*, P III, 8 r.; *Dany*, P III, 8 r.; *Novo Lar*, P III, 8 r.; *Dina*, P III, 7 r.; *Tinita*, P III, 6 r.; *Tivoli*, P III, 6 r.; *Emília*, P III, 5 r.

RECREATION and SPORT. – Swimming, sailing, water-skiing; tennis; golf-courses at Vale do Lobo, Vilamoura, Quarteira and Quinta do Lago; sheltered yacht harbour.

EVENTS. – *Feira da Senhora do Carmo* (end July), display of folk arts and crafts; *Feira de Santa Iria* (end October).

The busy industrial town and port of Faro, chief town of its district, lies at the N end of a lagoon dotted with

islands (salt-pans). Its airport (7 km/ 4½ miles SW) has made it the focal point of the whole of the Algarve's tourist trade, and in consequence it has lost much of its original character.

The small, sheltered harbour handles the shipment of the local produce (wine, fruit, cork, fish).
The town, originally founded in the Moorish period, lost most of its major buildings in a devastating earthquake in 1755.

SIGHTS. – To the NE of the **harbour** is the palm-shaded Praça de Dom Francisco Gomes, with an *obelisk* 15 m/50 ft high commemorating the diplomat *Ferreira de Almeida*.

At the S end of the square stands the *Arco da Vila*, an arched gateway with a statue of St Thomas Aquinas which leads to the **Cathedral** (*Sé*). Originally Gothic, this suffered severe destruction in the 1755 earthquake. It has a plain Renaissance interior.

Faro Cathedral

In the square in front of the Cathedral, the Largo da Sé, is the **Town Hall** (*Câmara Municipal*), with the *Ferreira de Almeida Collection* of miscellaneous curios and arts and crafts.
Also in the square are the old and new *Bishop's Palaces*.

In the nearby Praça de Afonso III is the **Archaeological Museum** (*Museu Arqueológico Lapidar do Infante Dom*

Henriques), housed in the former Convent of Nossa Senhora da Assunção, a house of Poor Clares founded in 1518 (Renaissance cloister).

To the E of the Cathedral rises the *Arco do Repouso*, one of the old town gates, which gives access to the spacious Largo de São Francisco, with the 17th c. *church of São Francisco* (blue and white azulejo decoration in choir).

To the E of the Praça de Dom Francisco Gomes, the **Museum of the Sea** (*Museu Marítimo*), in the Harbourmaster's Office, gives a good general picture of seafaring and fishing in the Algarve.
Some 500 m/550 yd E of this museum is the *Museum of Regional Ethnography* (folk art and traditions of the region).

To the N of the harbour area is the twin-towered Baroque *church of the Carmo*, with an interesting charnel-house.

In the eastern part of the town, on a hill commanding far-ranging views, stands the little **church of Santo António do Alto** (1754), with a *museum* devoted to St Antony. From the top of the hill there is an extensive *panorama of the coastal lagoons.

SURROUNDINGS. – On an offshore island NW of the town, beyond the airport, is the extensive sandy beach of *Praia do Faro.

8 km/5 miles N of Faro, near the village of **Milreu**, are the remains of the Roman town of *Ossonoba*, where

1 Praça de Dom Francisco Gomes	8 Arco do Repouso
2 Church of Miseriocórdia	9 Church of São Francisco
3 Arco da Vila	10 Museum of the Sea
4 Town Hall	11 Museum of Ethnography
5 Cathedral	12 Church of Carmo
6 Archaeological Museum	13 Church of São Pedro
7 Arco da Porta Nova	

excavations carried out from 1876 onwards brought to light baths with mosaic pavements, a basilica and several houses.

1 km/¾ mile farther N, on higher ground, is **Estói**, with the palace of the Counts of Estói, set in beautiful gardens (private property).

Fátima

Historical province: Ribatejo.
District: Santarém.
Altitude: 800 m/2625 ft.
Population: 6500.
Post code: P-2495.
Telephone code: 0 49.

ⓘ **Turismo,**
Avenida Dom José,
Correira da Silva;
tel. 9 71 39.

ACCOMMODATION. – IN COVA DA IRIA: *Três Pastorinhos*, II, 92 r.; *De Fátima*, II, 76 r.; *Santa Maria*, II, 59 r.; *Cinquentenário*, III, 52 r.; *Pax*, III, 51 r.; *Regina*, IV, 30 r.; *Floresta*, P I, 32 r.; *Zeca*, P I, 12 r.; *Casa Beato Nuno*, P 11, 120 r.; *Casa Das Irmãs Dominicanas*, P II, 86 r.; *Exército Azul*, P II, 50 r.; *Estrêla de Fátima*, P II, 31 r.; *Avenida*, P II, 27 r.; *Casa Verbo Divino*, P II, 26 r.; *Catarino*, P II, 19 r.; *Fátima*, P II, 18 r.; *Santa Isabel*, P II, 16 r.; *Dávi*, P II, 11 r.; *Cruz Alta*, P II, 6 r.; *Coração de Fátima*, P III, 25 r.; *Católica*, P III, 21 r.; *Alecrim*, P III, 16 r.; *Santa Clara*, P III, 10 r.; *Avé Maria*, P III, 5 r.; *Santo António*, P IV, 6 r.

IN VILA NOVA DE OURÊM: *Ouriense*, P II, 25 r.; *Simões*, P IV, 10 r.

PILGRIMAGES from May to October on 12th–13th of month.

The famous pilgrimage town of *Fátima, where three peasant children (Lúcia de Jesús and Francisco and Jacinta Marto) claimed to have seen the "Virgin of the Rosary" on 13 May 1917 and again on the 13th of each subsequent month until October in that year, is 22 km/14 miles SE of Leiria on what was once the barren plateau of Cova da Iria.

Fátima now attracts hosts of believers from far and wide, particularly on the pilgrimage days, and the shrine has been developed on a correspondingly large scale. The large *torch-light processions in the evening are particularly impressive.

SIGHTS. – At the edge of the huge esplanade on which the pilgrims gather (area 150,000 sq. m/37 acres) is the little **chapel** built on the spot where the Virgin appeared to the children.

On the far side of the esplanade rises the gigantic **Basilica**, in neo-classical style, with a central tower 65 m/215 ft high, the construction of which was begun on 13 May 1928. It is flanked by colonnades linking it with the extensive *conventual* and *hospital buildings*. In the Basilica are the tombs of Francisco and Jacinta Marto,

Torch-light procession, Fátima

The three children of Fátima

who died in 1919 and 1920 respectively. – Around the esplanade are a considerable number of shops and stalls of all kinds.

SURROUNDINGS. – 11 km/7 miles NE, on an isolated hill rising out of the valley, is the little medieval walled town of *Ourém, a huddle of narrow lanes and picturesque nooks and corners with a ruined 15th c. castle looming over it.
The town has a fine collegiate church, originally Gothic but rebuilt in the 18th c. In the crypt is the magnificent tomb of Dom Afonso de Ourém, a descendant of João I who rebuilt and enlarged the original Moorish castle.
Ourém also has a beautiful Gothic fountain and a *pelourinho* (pillory column), both of the 15th c. – From the castle there is a fine panoramic * view.
Many of the inhabitants of Ourém have moved down to *Vila Nova de Ourém*, 2 km/1¼ miles to the E.

Figueira da Foz

Historical province: Beira Litoral.
District: Coimbra.
Altitude: sea level.
Population: 15,000.
Post code: P-3080.
Telephone code: 0 33.
ⓘ **Turismo,**
  Edificio Atlântico;
  tel. 2 29 35.
  Rua do 25 de Abril;
  tel. 2 26 10.

ACCOMMODATION. – *Grande Hotel da Figueira*, I, 91 r.; *Nicola*, I, 24 r.; *Piscina*, I, 20 r.; *Costa de Prata*, II, 66 r.; *Da Praia*, II, 61 r.; *Internacional*, II, 55 r.; *Wellington*, II, 34 r.; *Portugal*, III, 52 r.; *Hispânia*, III, 34 r.; *Universal*, IV, 19 r.; *Aliança*, P II, 31 r.; *Rio-Mar*, P II, 21 r.; *Esplanade*, P II, 19 r.; *Bela Vista*, P II, 18 r.; *Central*, P II, 15 r.; *Teimoso*, P II, 14 r.; *Jacques*, P II, 12 r.; *Paris*, P III, 21 r.; *Europe*, P III, 21 r.; *Peninsular*, P III, 21 r.; *Moderna*, P III, 14 r.; *Jomala*, P III, 10 r.; *Astória*, P III, 9 r.

CAMP SITE.

Casino and modern **yacht harbour.**

RECREATION and SPORT. – Swimming, sailing, rowing, scuba diving; tennis, riding; rental of bicycles.

EVENTS. – *Festas de São João* (end June), with midnight procession, dances and other folk events. – *Bullfights* in Praça de Touros.

The regularly laid out little port town of Figueira da Foz, at the mouth of the Mondego, is one of Portugal's most popular seaside resorts and one of the principal bases of the cod fisheries off the Portuguese Atlantic coast.

SIGHTS. – Almost the whole of the OLD TOWN dates from the 19th c.
The late 19th c. *Town Hall* (Câmara Municipal) contains the interesting **Museu Municipal do Dr Santos Rocha** (prehistoric and Roman material, applied and decorative art, pottery, furniture, religious art, ethnography of the Portuguese overseas territories).

Fish market, Figueira da Foz

Fishing harbour, Figueira da Foz

Also in the old town is the tile-clad **Paço da Figueira** (17th c.).

At the mouth of the river stands the old **Fort Santa Catarina** (observatory), beyond which extends a wide beach of fine sand 3 km/2 miles long.

Beyond the Municipal Park are the newer parts of the town, the BAIRRO NOVO.

SURROUNDINGS. – 3 km/2 miles NW lies the picturesque fishing village of **Buarcos**, with two 16th c. *pelourinhos* (pillory columns) and a beautiful beach.
3 km/2 miles farther on is **Cabo Mondego**, a rocky headland falling sheer down to the Atlantic in a mighty cliff. Adjoining the lighthouse is an observatory. – In the neighbourhood are abandoned lignite mines and limestone quarries.

10 km/6 miles N of Figueira da Foz is the **Serra de Boa Viagem** (258 m/846 ft), an area of scattered woodland which is excellent walking country.
From the summit of the *Alto da Vela* (209 m/686 ft) there are superb panoramic*views.

Figueira de Castelo Rodrigo

Historical province: Beira Alta.
District: Guarda.
Altitude: 627 m/2057 ft.
Population: 2000.
Post code: P-6440.
Telephone code: 071.
ⓘ **Turismo,**
Paços do Concelho.

ACCOMMODATION. – *Pensão-Restaurante Santos,* P III, 32 r.

The little frontier town of Figueira de Castelo Rodrigo lies 60 km/ 37 miles NE of Guarda in a beautiful setting on a plateau covered with fruit orchards. In the 19th c. the population of the nearby fortified town of Castelo Rodrigo, an important stronghold during the Middle Ages, began to move to Figueira, which soon overshadowed its older neighbour.

SIGHTS. – Figueira de Castelo Rodrigo has an 18th c. Baroque **church** with numerous carved and gilded altars.

SURROUNDINGS. – 2 km/1¼ miles SE is the former Cistercian **Convent of Santa Maria de Aguiar** (13th c.; private property), which has a three-aisled Gothic hall-church and a beautiful chapterhouse. Renaissance loggia with Tuscan columns.

On a hill 3 km/2 miles S of Figueira de Castelo Rodrigo is **Castelo Rodrigo**, now a decayed village but in the Middle Ages a fortified town of considerable importance, with a ruined 15th c. castle and keep, an old palace and a cistern. There are also a little Gothic church and a Manueline *pelourinho* (pillory column). There are fine panoramic views from the castle.
From Castelo Rodrigo a road runs S for 16 km/ 10 miles through the wild and rocky *Serra de Marofa*, with superb views, to the little town of **Almeida** (alt. 760 m/2495 ft; pop. 1500), still surrounded by Vauban-style fortifications.

6 km/4 miles W of Figueira de Castelo Rodrigo, the village of **Freixeda de Torrão** (pop. 6000) has an old castle and a church (Romanesque doorway).
The local wines are much esteemed.

28 km/17 miles SW of Figueira de Castelo Rodrigo is the little frontier town of **Pinhel** (alt. 600 m/1970 ft; pop. 3500), still enclosed within stout defensive walls with six towers.
Within the ruined castle, built by King Dinis, stands the 14th c. church of Santa Maria do Castelo, with a cycle of 14 paintings of scenes from the life of the Virgin (17th c.). – The town has numbers of typical old houses and a monolithic *pelourinho* (pillory column). Outside the walls are the ruins of the Romanesque church of the Trinidade.

45 km/28 miles NE of Figueira de Castelo Rodrigo, on the edge of a fertile valley basin, is the little town of **Freixo de Espada à Cintra**, birthplace of the navigator Jorge Álvares and of the poet Guerra Junqueiro (1850–1923; museum).

Above the town is the parish church, with a richly decorated interior (16th c.).

Guarda

Historical province: Beira Alta.
District: Guarda.
Altitude: 1057 m/3468 ft.
Population: 15,000.
Post code: P-6300.
Telephone code: 0 71.
ⓘ **Turismo,**
Praça de Luís de Camões;
tel. 2 22 51.

ACCOMMODATION. – IN GUARDA: *Turismo,* II, 102 r., SP; *Filipe,* P I, 32 r.; *Aliança,* P II, 29 r.; *Santos,* P III, 17 r.; *Guardense,* P III, 14 r.; *Belo Horizonte,* P III, 13 r.; *Gare,* P IV, 9 r.; *Gonçalves,* P IV, 7 r. – Numerous sanatoria. – CAMP SITE.

IN CELORICO DA BEIRA: *Parque,* P III, 27 r.; *Mondego,* P III, 9 r.

IN FORNOS DE ALGODRES: *Unidos,* P IV, 10 r.

IN MANGUALDE: *Cruz da Mata,* I, 10 r.; *Beira Alta,* P II, 27 r.

The old district capital of Guarda, the see of a bishop and once an important stronghold in the province of Beira Alta, lies on a plateau in the NE of the Serra da Estrêla. As Portugal's highest town,

Guarda

Rua M. Bombarda • São Vicente
Rua de Luís I
Praça Luís de Camões • Town Hall
Rua Vasco da Gama
Cathedral • Misericórdia
Torre de Menagem • Museu Regional
Largo do Marechal Carmona

Coimbra, Lisboa

1 Porta do Rei   2 Porta da Estrêla   3 Torre dos Ferreiros

with a healthy and very pleasant climate, it has become a popular health resort.

At first sight the town, built largely of granite, has a rather grey appearance, but a closer look will reveal numbers of finely decorated old burghers' houses, particularly in the Praça da Sé (the square with the Cathedral) and the Rua de Dom Luís I.

HISTORY. – There was already a strongly fortified town on this strategically important site in Roman times. In 80 B.C. it sided with Sertorius in his attempt to break away from Rome, and thereafter withstood many years of assaults and sieges by Caesar's forces. After the town was devastated by the Moors its inhabitants fled and the remaining buildings became derelict. Much later, in the 12th and 13th c., Guarda was rebuilt by Sancho I and Dinis I and strongly fortified against attack by the Moors or the Castilians.

SIGHTS. – In the middle of the town is the Praça de Luís de Camões or Praça da Sé. On the higher (S) side of the square stands the *Cathedral (Sé), a granite building of fortress-like appearance, with crenellated walls, which was begun in Gothic style in 1390 and completed in the 16th c. The Manueline additions – notably the W front and doorway – were built by Manuel I's great architect, Boytaca, on the model of Batalha Abbey.

The magnificent three-aisled INTERIOR achieves its effect by its harmonious proportions and simplicity of line. The stone **retable** (1550) was the work of John of Rouen (João de Ruão); the gilding was added in the 18th c.

It is well worth climbing up to the roof terrace of the Cathedral to see the method of construction of the roof, spanned by flying buttresses.

From the top there is a superb *view extending over the town to the Serra da Estrêla.

Outside the Cathedral is a modern *monument to Sancho I*, to whom the town owed its rebuilding in the medieval period and its economic and cultural rise.

The former *Bishop's Palace* (15th–16th c.) now houses the **Regional Museum** (pictures, old photographs, archaeological material).

Also worth seeing are two 18th c. Baroque **churches**, the **Misericórdia** and **São Vicente**. Though perhaps somewhat provincial in style, they are none the less attractive for that.

Of the town's 12th and 13th c. **fortifications** there remain the **keep** (*Torre de Menagem*), three town gates – the *Torre dos Ferreiros*, the *Porta da Estrêla* and the *Porta do Rei* – and some stretches of the town walls.

SURROUNDINGS. – 1 km/¾ mile from the town is the Romanesque **Ermida de Nossa Senhora da Póvoa de Mileu**, with finely carved capitals.

There is an attractive drive 85 km/53 miles NW to **Viseu**.
28 km/17 miles: **Celorico da Beira** (alt. 550 m/1805 ft), a little town with a ruined castle (*view).
17 km/11 miles: **Fornos de Algodres** (500 m/1640 ft; pop. 2500), in the upper Mondego valley. The road crosses the river here.
22 km/14 miles: **Mangualde** (545 m/1790 ft; pop. 7000), with the 17th c. palace of the Counts of Anadia (conducted tours), set in a beautiful park (*view).
1·5 km/1 mile N, on a hill commanding extensive views (628 m/2060 ft), is the *pilgrimage church of Nossa Senhora do Castelo*.
18 km/11 miles: **Viseu** (see p. 207).

Guarda is also a good base from which to explore the *Serra da Estrêla (see p. 189).

Guimarães

Historical province: Minho.
District: Braga.
Altitude: 200 m/655 ft.
Population: 25,000.
Post code: P-4800.
Telephone code: 0 53.
ⓘ **Turismo,**
Avenida da Resistência ao Fascismo 83;
tel. 41 24 50.

ACCOMMODATION. – IN GUIMARÃES: *Pousada de Santa Maria de Oliveira*, 16 r.; *Fundador Dom Pedro*, I, 63 r.; *Toural*, IV, 40 r. – CAMP SITE.

IN CALDAS DE VIZELA: *Sul Americano*, III, 64 r.; *Termas*, P III, 16 r.; *Nacional*, P IV, 6 r.

IN CALDAS DAS TAIPAS: *Vilas*, P IV, 11 r.

EVENTS. – *Festas das Cruzes* (beginning of May), popular festival, Guimarães; *International Folk Festival* (end July), Torcato; *Festas Gualterianas* (beginning of August), popular festival, with fireworks, Guimarães; *Festas de Vizela* (mid August), processions and folk events, Caldas de Vizela; *pilgrimage to Senhora da Penha*, Guimarães (beginning of September).

The historic old town of *Guimarães, known as the "cradle of the nation" (berço da nação), was the first capital of the newly established kingdom of Portugal and birthplace of its first king, Afonso Henriques, and of the celebrated poet and dramatist Gil Vicente. It lies in pleasant rolling country at the foot of the Serra de Santa Catarina.

Guimarães offers a great variety of attractions to the visitor – its well-preserved Old Town, with handsome burghers' houses notable for their wrought-iron balconies and profusion of flowers, its historic buildings and its treasures of art.

SIGHTS. – Above the town rears the grey bulk of the 10th c. *Castle (*Castelo*) with its high, slender battlements, one of the most complete and best preserved medieval strongholds in Portugal. As the birthplace on 24 June 1110 of the first Portuguese king, Afonso Henriques, it is also a national shrine.

In the middle of the oval courtyard rises the tall and massive keep, the *Torre de Menagem*, which could hold out on its own in case of need. This is believed to have housed in the 11th c. a Benedictine convent founded by the Galician Countess Mumadona.
From the curtain walls of the castle with their eight towers there are magnificent views.

Below the castle entrance stands the small **chapel of São Miguel** (1105), built of massive courses of dressed stone, in which Afonso Henriques was baptised. Mass is celebrated here annually on the king's birthday to commemorate the event.
Near the entrance to the chapel is the stone font.

At the foot of the castle hill is the large **Paço Ducal** (Ducal Palace), or *Palace of the Dukes of Bragança*, a magnificent residence originally built by Afonso, first

Duke of Bragança, in the French style fashionable in his day (completed 1442). After the seat of the Bragança family was transferred to Vila Viçosa the palace lost its earlier importance, and over the centuries fell into ruin. It was extensively restored and rebuilt in the 1930s, suffering considerable alteration (e.g. to the chapel) in the process. It has a fine interior, with 16th–18th c. furniture and furnishings.

Below the palace is a small *church*, in an unpretentious local version of Baroque; it originally belonged to a Carmelite convent.

In the picturesque *OLD TOWN the *Largo da Oliveira* has preserved its medieval aspect to a remarkable extent.
On the N side of the square is the **Paço do Concelho** (Old Town Hall), with Gothic arcades. Begun in the 14th c., during the reign of João I, it was radically altered in the 17th c.

On the S side of the Largo da Oliveira is the **collegiate church of Nossa Senhora da Oliveira**. The church, originally founded by Afonso Henriques in the 12th c., in thanksgiving for his victory in the battle of Ourique, stands on the site of an earlier convent founded by Countess Mumadona. It was considerably enlarged in 1387–1400 by João I to commemorate the battle of Aljubarrota, when most of the original Romanesque

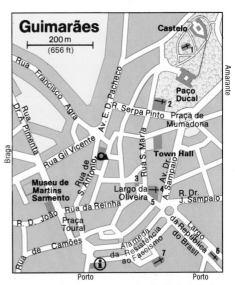

Guimarães
200 m
(656 ft)

1 Chapel of São Miguel do Castelo
2 Carmelite convent
3 Paços do Concelho
4 Church of N.S. da Oliveira
5 Museu de Alberto Sampaio
6 Church of Santos Passos
7 Church of São Francisco

cloister was demolished. The Manueline tower was added in 1505.

The adjoining cloister and part of the former Dominican convent now house the very fine *Museu de Alberto Sampaio, with pictures and sculpture, mainly by Portuguese artists of the 14th–16th c., goldsmiths' work and a valuable collection of historical costume and furniture.

Outstanding among the exhibits are the splendid sarcophagus of Constança de Noronhas, first Duchess of Bragança (in the cloister), a superb silver processional cross (16th c.) and the cloak which João wore over his armour at the battle of Aljubarrota.

In front of the church is a Gothic/Manueline **alpendre** (a canopy sheltering a crucifix) commemorating the battle of the Rio Salado (1340).

To the W of the Largo da Oliveira is the oldest and most picturesque part of the town. A particularly typical old street is *Rua de Santa Catarina*.

From the church of N.S. da Oliveira the long Praça do Brasil (formerly Campo da Feira) leads to the twin-towered Baroque **church of the Santos Passos**, with rich azulejo decoration and sculptural decoration showing Italian influence on the façade.

To the W stands the **church of São Francisco**, founded by João I about 1400 and remodelled in the Baroque period.

The spacious interior is entirely faced with azulejos. The sacristy has a massive coffered ceiling.

The town's busiest square is the Praça Toural, in a plain style of architecture. A little way NW of the square, in a former Dominican convent (13th c.), is an interesting archaeological museum, the **Museu de Martins Sarmento**, with material from the prehistoric settlements of Briteiros (see p. 90) and Sabroso.

SURROUNDINGS. – 6 km/4 miles SE is the **Penha** or *Serra de Santa Catarina* (617 m/2024 ft), a rocky height on which (reached by a beautiful little mountain road) stand a pilgrimage church (1898) and a statue of Pope Pius IX.

From the top there are superb *views, extending SE to the Serra de Marão (see under Amarante) and, in clear weather, northward to the Serra de Gerês (see under Peneda-Gerês National Park) and westward to the Atlantic.

10 km/6 miles SW of Guimarães, attractively situated on both banks of the Rio Vizela, is the spa of **Caldas de Vizela** (pop. 3000), with sulphurous springs which were already being frequented in Roman times. There are altogether 55 springs with an abundant flow of water at temperatures ranging from 16°C/61°F to 65·6°C/150°F.

There is an attractive park on the banks of the river (swimming, rowing), in which a "Spa Week" is held annually at the end of August, with folk events, competitions and contests, clay-pigeon shooting, etc.

Within easy reach of Caldas de Vizela are the late 17th c. *pilgrimage chapel of São Bento* (4 km/2½ miles) and the 12th c. Romanesque church of *São Miguel de Vilarinho* (3 km/2 miles), with a Gothic cloister adjoining the church.

Palace of the Dukes of Bragança, Guimarães

7 km/4½ miles NW of Guimarães is another spa which was also known to the Romans, **Caldas de Taipa**, with hot sulphurous springs (30°C/86°F). Here, too, there is an attractive park on the banks of the Rio Ave.

Lagos

Historical province: Algarve.
District: Faro.
Altitude: sea level.
Population: 10,000.
Post code: P-8600.
Telephone code: 0 82.

ⓘ **Turismo,**
   Largo Marquês de Pombal;
   tel. 6 30 31.

ACCOMMODATION. – IN LAGOS: *Lagos*, I, 287 r., SP; *Cidade Velha*, I, 17 r.; *Casa São Gonçalo*, I, 10 r.; *Motel do Parque de Turismo de Lagos*, II, 60 r., SP; *São Cristóvão*, II, 77 r.; *Riomar*, II, 40 r.; *Motel Marsol*, III, 20 r.; *Motel Torralta*, III, 6 r.; *Lagosmar*, P II, 21 r.; *Mar Azul*, P II, 17 r.; *Rubi Mar*, P II, 9 r.; *Caravela*, P III, 17 r.

ON THE MEIA PRAIA: *Meia Praia*, II, 65 r., SP.

ON THE PRAIA DA DONA ANA: *Golfinho*, I, 259 r., SP; *Sol e Praia*, P I, 43 r.; *Dona Ana*, P II, 11 r. – CAMP SITE.

RECREATION and SPORT. – Swimming, sailing, water-skiing, scuba diving. – Tidal yacht harbour.

The old fishing town of Lagos, the Roman Lacobriga, lies on the W side of a bay of the Rio Alvor, here fully 2 km/1¼ miles wide, which is sheltered on the E by the Ponta dos Três Irmãos and on the W by the Ponta da Piedade and the broad estuary of Ribeira de Bensafrim.

Once capital of the old province of the Algarve, Lagos was an important ship-building town and port, the starting-point of some of the great Portuguese voyages of discovery. It was the birthplace of Gil Eanes, the first navigator to round Cape Bojador in West Africa (1434).

SIGHTS. – The town's life revolves around the *Praça de Gil Eanes*, with the **Town Hall** (*Câmara Municipal*, 1798) and a modernistic *statue of King Sebastião*, who set out from Lagos with a 17,000-strong army to conquer North Africa for Christendom and never returned, and the *Praça Luís de Camões*.

Along the NE side of the town is a wide seafront promenade, the Avenida dos Descobrimentos ("Avenue of the Discoveries"), which follows the right bank of the river to the Praça da República

which is surrounded by handsome buildings and has a *statue of Henry the Navigator*, erected in 1960 to commemorate the 500th anniversary of his death.

On the S side of the Praça da República stands the **church of Santa Maria**, in which Henry the Navigator was originally buried; his remains were later transferred to Batalha Abbey.
Opposite the church is the *Custom House* (Delegação da Alfândega), under the arcades of which the slave market used to be held, the slaves being tied to the massive iron posts.

SW of the square is the Baroque *chapel of Santo António, built in 1769 on the site of an earlier church; it has talha dourada decoration.
Adjoining the chapel is the *Regional Museum*, with archaeological material, folk art, sacred art and a variety of relics and mementoes of the history of the town, including a remarkable collection of German emergency currency.

To the N of the Praça de Gil Eanes is the *church of São Sebastião*, with a fine Renaissance doorway.

On the SW side of the town are remains of the old **town walls**, enclosing the former *Governor's Palace* (restored) and ending at the **Fortaleza** which projects into the sea.

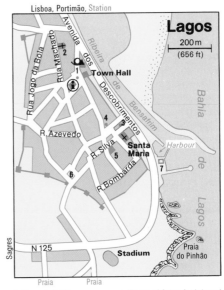

1 Praça de Gil Eanes
2 Church of São Sebastião
3 Praça da República
4 Slave market
5 Chapel of Santo António and Regional Museum
6 Praça de João de Deus
7 Fortaleza (Pau da Bandeira)

SURROUNDINGS. – 3 km/2 miles S is the *Ponta da Piedade (lighthouse), a rugged promontory with striking rock formations and numerous caves.

On either side of the estuary of the Ribeira de Bensafrim are sheltered beaches – to the E the *Meia Praia*, to the S the *Praia do Pinhão* and the *Praia da Dona Ana (hotel colony).

Lamego

Historical province: Beira Alta.
District: Viseu.
Altitude: 490 m/1610 ft.
Population: 10,000.
Post code: P-5100.
Telephone code: 0 54.

ⓘ **Turismo,**
Avenida do Visconde Guedes Teixeira,
tel. 6 20 05.

ACCOMMODATION. – IN LAMEGO: *Estalagem de Lamego*, I, 7 r.; *Do Parque*, IV, 32 r.; *Motel Turisserra*, III, 6 r.; *Solar*, P III, 25 r.; *Silva*, P IV, 14 r.

IN RESENDE: *Araújo*, P IV, 12 r.

IN CALDAS DE AREGOS: *Costa*, P III, 25 r.; *Central*, P IV, 20 r.; *Avenida*, P IV, 13 r.; *Comércio*, P IV, 11 r.

IN SOBRADA DE PAIVA: *Valonge*, P III, 7 r.

EVENTS. – *Pilgrimages to the church of Nossa Senhora dos Remédios* (first half of September), one of the best known and most popular festivals in northern Portugal, with processions and folk events.

The little episcopal town of Lamego, charmingly situated amid vineyards and fields on the slopes of Monte Penude, has been since medieval times an important market for the agricultural produce of the fertile surrounding countryside. Here the Portuguese Estates met for the first time in 1143 to proclaim Afonso Henriques king of the newly established state.

Lamego is famed for its dried ham and its sparkling wine (the wine-making establishments of Raposeira can be visited).

SIGHTS. – In the southern part of the town rises the massive Gothic **Cathedral** (*Sé*), rebuilt by Afonso Henriques in 1129 and much altered in the 16th and 17th c. Of the original building there survives only the sturdy square tower. The interior was completely remodelled in the 18th c. In the Renaissance cloisters are a number of fine chapels.

Near the Cathedral, in the Largo de Camões, is the former *Bishop's Palace* (18th c.), now housing the *Municipal Library* and the interesting **Regional Museum** (*Museu de Lamego*).

The museum contains fine 16th c. Flemish *tapestries from the original furnishings of the Bishop's Palace, Portuguese painting of the 16th–18th c., sculpture of the 13th–17th c., religious art and folk art.

Other features of interest in the town are the **church of the Desterro** (1640), richly decorated with 17th c. azulejos and talha dourada and with a fine painted coffered ceiling, and numerous handsome burghers' houses of the 16th–18th c.

On the hill above the town is the Romanesque *church of Santa Maria*, with fine carved capitals.

From here it is a short walk up to the **Castle** (*Castelo*, 11th–13th c.), originally a Moorish foundation, with a 13th c. keep and an underground water cistern.

SURROUNDINGS. – From the town a magnificent Baroque* staircase with 14 Stations of the Cross leads up to the *Calvário* and the conspicuous **pilgrimage church of Nossa Senhora dos Remédios,** a sumptuous 18th c. Baroque edifice on the summit of *Monte de Santo Estêvão* (also reached by road). Thousands of pilgrims gather here at the beginning of September every year to seek healing and consolation. From the terrace there is a beautiful *prospect of the town.

From Monte de Santo Estêvão a pleasant road passes through varied scenery, crossing the plateau of the **Serra de Montemuro** (1382 m/4534 ft) to reach *Castro Daire* (alt. 565 m/1854 ft), a distance of 33 km/ 21 miles, and from there it is another 37 km/23 miles to **Viseu** (see p. 207).

6 km/4 miles W of Lamego are the remains of the Lusitanian and Roman fort of **Castro de Penude** (alt. 900 m/2950 ft; *view).

3 km/2 miles NE of Lamego, in the valley of the Rio Balsemão, stands the *Visigothic church of São Pedro de Balsemão,** which is believed to be the oldest church in Portugal (7th c.).

Lamego

The church was restored in 1643 and given a coffered ceiling. It contains the sarcophagus of Afonso Pires, a 14th c. bishop of Oporto.

From Lamego to Sobrado de Paiva a beautiful road (No. 222) descends the **Douro valley** on the left bank of the river, taking in many places of interest on the way:

11 km/7 miles: **Barro**, charmingly situated above the valley, with a curious 12th c. Romanesque church.

5 km/3 miles: **São Martinho de Mouros**. At the far end of the village is a Romanesque church (9th–11th c.) with richly carved capitals. It contains a picture of St Martin which is ascribed to Vasco Fernandes.

17 km/11 miles: **Resende**, a trim little town, with the Romanesque church of São Salvador above the town (*view).

2 km/1¼ miles: *Anreade*, from which there is a cart-track (10 km/6 miles) to the Manueline church of Santa Maria de Cárquere, belonging to a convent founded in the 11th c.

5 km/3 miles: **Caldas de Aregos**, a little spa beautifully situated on a wooded hill above the Douro valley, with hot sulphur springs (50–61°C/122–142°F). It has a beautiful park. From the Penedo de São João, a crag above the town, there are fine views.

18 km/11 miles: **Cinfães**, a little country town famed for its *vinho verde*, with the *Quinta da Fervança*, an 18th c. country house.

4 km/2½ mies: *Nogueira*. Above the village is the church of *São Cristóvão de Nogueira*, Romanesque and much altered in later periods.

11 km/7 miles: **Tarouguela**, with the well-preserved Romanesque church of Santa Maria Maior, originally belonging to a 12th c. Benedictine convent, and the Romanesque and Gothic chapel of São João Baptista.

4 km/2½ miles: road to the simple Romanesque church of São Miguel, which has frescoes and azulejos of the 15th and 16th c. and a Romanesque font.

8 km/5 miles: **Sobrado de Paiva** (or *Castelo de Paiva*), a little town surrounded by hills which is renowned for its wine, with the finely situated *Quinta da Boa Vista*, an 18th c. country house. This is a good centre from which to explore the surrounding area.

15 km/9 miles N of Lamego, at the point where the little rivers *Corgo* (right bank) and *Baroso* (left bank) flow into the Douro, lies the pretty town of **Régua** or *Pêso da Régua* (pop. 6000), the focal point of the "Land of Wine" (País do Vinho: see under Douro Valley) and of the port trade.

The town is particularly lively during the vintage (end of September to end of October).

16 km/10 miles S of Lamego, off the road to Guarda, is the pretty village of **Tarouca**, in a beautiful setting at the head of a valley flanked by rugged walls of rock. In the church of the former Cistercian convent of São João de Tarouca, founded by Afonso I in 1171, is the imposing tomb of Conde Pedro de Barcelos (d. 1354), illegitimate son of King Dinis I and author of the "Livro das Linhagens", a register of the nobility. The sarcophagus of his wife, formerly in the church, is now in the museum in Lamego.

Leiria

Historical province: Beira Litoral.
District: Leiria.
Altitude: 30–113 m/100–370 ft.
Population: 9000.
Post code: P-2400.
Telephone code: 0 44.
ⓘ **Turismo,**
Jardim de Luis de Camões;
tel. 2 27 48.

ACCOMMODATION. – IN LEIRIA: *Euro-Sol*, II, 92 r., SP; *Lis*, III, 40 r.; *São Francisco*, P I, 18 r.; *Claras*, P I, 11 r.; *Ramalhete*, P II, 22 r.; *Leiriense*, P II, 17 r.; *Casa de Santo António*, P II, 13 r.; *Alcoa*, P III, 14 r.; *Piquenique*, P III, 7 r.

IN MARINHA GRANDS: *Albergaria Nobre*, I, 25 r.; *Paris*, P II, 30 r.

IN SÃO PEDRO DE MUEL: *São Pedro*, III, 60 r.; *Mar e Sol*, III, 33 r.; *Dom Dinis*, P II, 18 r.; *Miramar*, P II, 11 r.; *Rosa*, P III, 24 r. – YOUTH HOSTEL: *Pousada de Juventude*, 44 b. – CAMP SITE.

The busy district capital and market town of Leiria, the Roman Collipo, briefly a royal residence in the reign of Dinis I and since 1545 the see of a bishop, lies in an attractive setting on the left bank of the little River Liz, here joined by its tributary the Rio Lena.

The fertile farming area around Leiria has preserved many old crafts and customs (basketwork, pottery, woven blankets, glass-blowing; traditional costumes).

SIGHTS. – High above the town is the **Castelo de Leiria** (*view), with well-preserved walls and towers. It was built by Afonso Henriques in 1135 on the remains of a Moorish castle, which itself had succeeded an earlier Roman fortress.
Within the walls of the castle are the ruins of the Early Gothic **church of Nossa Senhora da Pena** (1314), in front of which are the well-preserved remains of the **Royal Palace**, once the residence of King Dinis and his queen, St Isabel. From the wide loggia there is a superb *view of the town.
An even more extensive view, extending as far as Batalha Abbey, can be had from the commanding *keep*, built by Dinis in 1324.
Below the castle is the 12th c. **church of São Pedro**, originally Romanesque but much altered in later centuries.
In the heart of the town is the Praça de Rodrigues Lobo, surrounded by handsome burghers' houses and noble

Castelo de Leiria

mansions. The arcades are the remains of the cloister of the former Convent of St Martin.

Other notable buldings in the old part of the town are the **Cathedral** (*Sé*), a plain Renaissance building (16th c.; restored in 18th c.), with an adjoining *museum* (pictures, furniture, pottery, glass), and the *church of the Misericórdia* (1544), on a site previously occupied by a synagogue.

Opposite the castle, on another hill, is the **Santuário de Nossa Senhora da Encarnação** (1588), reached by an 18th c. staircase. From the top there are panoramic *views.

SURROUNDINGS. – The most important sight in the immediate neighbourhood of Leiria is **Batalha Abbey** (see p. 81), 12 km/7½ miles S.

7 km/4½ miles N of Leiria is the pretty little town of **Milagres**, with handsome old houses and a much frequented 18th c. pilgrimage church.
15 km/9 miles farther N is the little spa of *Monte Real*.
13 km/8 miles farther W, at the mouth of the Rio Liz, is the little seaside resort of *Praia de Vieria*.

8 km/5 miles S of Leiria, at *Andreus*, are the remains of the Roman settlement of **Collipo**.

8 km/5 miles E of Leiria is an impressive gorge on the **Rio Caranguejeira**, with rock faces fully 100 m/330 ft high.

12 km/7½ miles W of Leiria is **Marinha Grande** (old glass-works), in the **Pinhal de Leiria** or **Pinhal Real**, the pinewoods originally planted by King Dinis with maritime pines from the S of France to provide protection against drifting sand. The trees yield resin and turpentine.
9 km/5½ miles farther W is the very charming little seaside resort of **São Pedro de Muel**.

Lisbon/Lisboa

Historical province: Estremadura.
District: Lisboa (Lisbon).
Altitude: 23–112 m/75–365 ft.
Population: 900,000.
Post code: P-1000-1900.
Telephone code: 01.

Direcção-Geral do Turismo
(*Directorate-General of Tourism*)
Information bureau:
Palácio Foz,
Praça dos Restauradores;
tel. 36 36 24.
Head office:
Avenida de António Augusto de Aguiar 86;
tel. 57 50 95.

Comissão Municipal de Turismo
(Municipal Tourist Board),
Rua das Portas de Santo Antão 141;
tel. 32 70 58.
Information bureaux:
Rua Jardim do Regedor,
Estufa Fria, Parque Eduardo VII,
Avenida Duarte Pacheco,
Auto Estrada do Norte.

Automóvel-Club de Portugal
(ACP: Automobile Club of Portugal),
Rua de Rosa Araújo 24–26;
tel. 56 39 31.

Air Portugal
(*Transportes Aéreos Portugueses*, TAP),
Praça do Marquês de Pombal 3;
tel. 53 88 52 and 57 50 20.

Shipping (Azores, Madeira)
Companhia Portuguesa de Transportes Marítimos (CTM),
Rua de São Julião 63;
tel. 87 89 81 and 87 75 61.

Motorail Services
Estação de Santa Apolónia;
tel. 86 46 75.

EMBASSIES. – *United States*: Avenida Duque de Loulé 39, tel. 57 01 02. – *United Kingdom*: Rua São Domingos à Lapa 35–37, tel. 66 11 91. – *Canada*: Rua Rosa Araújo 2, 6th floor, tel. 56 25 47.

HOTELS. –* *Lisboa-Sheraton*, Rua Latino Coelho 2, L, 400 r., SP; * *Tivoli*, Avenida da Liberdade 185, L, 350 r.; * *Ritz Intercontinental*, Rua Rodrigo da Fonseca 88, L, 300 r.; *Alfa Lisboa*, Avenida Columbano Bordalo Pinheiro, L, 275 r., SP; *Altis*, Rua Castilho 11, L, 230 r.; *Avenida Palace*, Rua 1 de Dezembro 123, L, 100 r.

Lisboa Penta, Avenida dos Combatentes, I, 590 r., SP; *Lutécia*, Avenida Frei Miguel Contreiras 52, I, 151 r.; *Mundial*, Rua D. Duarte 4, I, 146 r.; *Tivoli Jardim*, Rua Júlio César Machado 7, I, 119 r.; *Fénix*, Praça Marquês de Pombal 8, I, 114 r.; *Flórida*, Rua Duque de Palmela 32, I, 108 r.; *Embaixador*, Avenida Duque de

Loulé 73, I, 96 r.; *Lisboa Plaza*, Travessa do Salitre 7, I, 93 r.; *Diplomático*, Rua Castilho 74, I, 90 r.; *Dom Manuel I*, Avenida Duque de Ávila 187, I, 64 r.; *Insulana*, Rua da Assunção 52, I, 32 r.; *Pax*, Rua José Estevão 20, I, 30 r.; *Príncipe Real*, Rua da Alegria 53, I, 24 r.; *Do Cavalo Branco*, Avenida Almirante Gago Coutinho 146, I, 24 r.; *Terminus*, Avenida Almirante Gago Coutinho 153, I, 23 r., SP; *América*, Rua Tomás Ribeiro 47, P I, 56 r.; *York House*, Rua das Janelas Verdes 32, P I, 46 r.; *Imperador*, Avenida 5 de Outubro 55, P I, 45 r.; *Avenida Parque*, Avenida Sidónio Pais 6, P I, 39 r.; *Nazareth*, Avenida António Augusto de Aguiar 35, P I, 32 r.; *O Paradouro*, Avenida Almirante Reis 106, P I, 24 r.; *Roma*, Travessa da Glória, 22A, P I, 24 r.; *Mucaba*, Avenida de Liberdade 53, P I, 17 r.; *A Ponte*, Rua Pinheiro Chagas 1, P I, 12 r.

Roma, Avenida de Roma 33, II, 263 r.; *Miraparque*, Avenida Sidónio Pais 12, II, 94 r.; *Excelsior*, Rua Rodrigues Sampaio 172, II, 81 r.; *Dom Carlos*, Avenida Duque de Loulé 121, II, 73 r.; *Eduardo VII*, Avenida Fontes Pereira de Melo 5C, II, 68 r.; *Presidente*, Rua Alexandre Herculano 13, II, 59 r.; *Príncipe*, Avenida Duque de Ávila 199, II, 56 r.; *Torre*, Rua dos Jéronimos 8, II, 52 r.; *Capitol*, Rua Eça de Queiros 24, II, 50 r.; *Jorge V*, Rua Mouzinho da Silveira 3, II, 49 r.; *Do Reno*, Avenida Duque de Ávila 195, II, 46 r.; *Rex*, Rua Castilho 169, II, 41 r.; *Flamingo*, Rua Castilho 41, II, 35 r.; *Britânia*, Rua Rodrigues Sampaio 17, II, 30 r.; *Infante Santo*, Rua Tenente Valadim 14, II, 27 r. – Apartment hotels: *Impala*, Rua Filipe Folque 49, II, 26 r.; *Cidade Nova*, Avenida Gomes Pereira 29, II, 19 r.

Borges, Rua Garrett 108, III, 99 r.; *Suiço Atlântico*, Rua da Glória 13, III, 88 r.; *Duas Nações*, Rua da Vitória 41, III, 66 r.; *Lis*, Avenida da Liberdade 180, III, 62 r.; *Internacional*, Rua da Betesga 3, III, 54 r.; *Vip*, Rua Fernão Lopes 25, III, 54 r.; *Metrópole*, Praça de Dom Pedro IV 30, III, 48 r.; *Dom Afonso Henriques*, Rua Cristóvão Falcão 8, III, 33 r.

Americano, Rua 1 de Dezembro 73, IV, 49 r.; *Portugal*, Rua João das Regras 4, IV, 45 r.; *Bragança*, Rua do Alecrim 12, IV, 36 r.; *Universo*, Rua do Carmo 102, IV, 32 r.; etc.

Numerous PENSIONS (guest-houses).

YOUTH HOSTELS (*pousadas de juventude*). – Lisboa, Rua Andrade Corvo 46, 128 b.; São Bruno, Forte de São Bruno, Estrada Marginal, Caxias (15 km/ 9 miles W of Lisbon), 30 b.; Catalazete, Santo Amaro de Oeiras (20 km/12½ miles W of Lisbon), 80 b.

CAMP SITES in Parque Florestal de Monsanto (Monsanto Forest Park), on the S bank of the Tagus (Costa da Caparica), etc.

RESTAURANTS. – *Aviz*, Rua de Serpa Pinto 12B; *Tágide*, Largo da Biblioteca Pública 18; *Tavares*, Rua da Misericórdia 37; *Michel*, Largo de Santa Cruz do Castelo 5 (French); *Macau*, Rua Barata Salgueiro 37A (Chinese); *Gambrinus*, Rua das Portas de Santo Antão 25 (seafood a speciality); *Pabe*, Rua Duque de Palmela 27A; *Ibéria*, Rua Ivens 28; *Casa da Comida*, Travessa das Amoreiras 1; *O Paco*, Avenida de Berna 44B; *Escorial*, Rua das Portas de Santo Antão 47; *Dragão de Ouro*, Avenida Frei Miguel Contreiras 54B; *Noite e Dia*, Avenida Duque de Loulé 51A and B (always open; also self-service).

Lisbon: view over the Old Town towards the Tagus

CAFÉS and TEA-ROOMS in the large hotels; also *A Caravela*, Rua Paiva de Andrade 8; *Pastelaria Benard*, Rua Garrett 104–106; *Martinho da Arcada* (estab. 1782), corner of Rua de Prata and Praça do Comércio; *Montecarlo, Monumental*, Avenida Fontes Pereira de Melo 49 and 51B; *Nicola*, Praça de Dom Pedro IV 24; *Mexicana*, Avenida Guerra Junqueiro 30C; etc.

FADO CAFÉS AND RESTAURANTS. – *Taverna do Embuçado*, Beco dos Curtumes 10 (Alfama); *Parreirinha de Alfama*, Beco do Espírito Santo 1 (Alfama); *Tipóia*, Rua do Norte 102 (Bairro Alto); *A Severa, Lisboa à Noite*, Rua das Gáveas 51 and 69; *Luso*, Travessa da Queimada 10; *O Faia*, Rua da Barroca 56; *Adega Machado*, Rua do Norte 91; *O Forcado*, Rua da Rosa 221; *Painel do Fado*, Rua São Pedro de Alcântara 65–69; etc.

THEATRES and REVUES. – *Teatro de São Carlos*, Largo São Carlos; *ABC*, Parque Mayer; *Alberto*, Praça de Espanha; *Adoque*, Largo Martim Moniz; *Capitólio*, Parque Mayer; *Laura Alves*, Rua da Palma 261; *Maria Matos*, Avenida Frei Miguel Contreiras; *Maria Vitória*, Parque Mayer; *Monumental*, Praça Duque de Saldanha; *São Luis*, Rua António Maria Cardoso; *Trindade*, Rua Nova da Trindade; *Variedades*, Parque Mayer; *Vasco Santana*, Avenida da República; *Villaret*, Avenida Fontes Pereira de Melo 30A.

BULLRING: *Praça de Touros*, Campo Pequeno. – CIRCUS: *Coliseu dos Recreios*, Rua P. Santo Antão.

SPORT. – *Pavilhão dos Desportos*, Parque Eduardo VII; *Football Stadium*, Benfica.

EVENTS. – *Procissão do Senhor dos Passos da Graça* (beginning of March); *Festas dos Santos Populares* (end June).

SHOPPING. – Principal shopping districts are the **Chiado** in the newer part of the town around Rua Garrett, and the **Baixa**.

EMBROIDERY: *Casa Regional da Ilha Verde*, Rua Paiva de Andrada 4; *Madeira House*, Rua Augusta 131; *Eduardo Martins*, Rua Garrett 7.

PORTUGUESE ARTS AND CRAFTS: *Galeria Sesimbra*, Rua Castilho 77.

SILVER: *H. Stern*, in Ritz Hotel; *Joalharia Mergulhão*, Rua de São Paulo 162.

CARPETS (from Arraiolos): *Casa Quintão*, Rua Ivens 30; *Casa dos Tapetes de Arraiolos*, Rua da Imprensa Nacional 116E.

REGIONAL CRAFTS: *Caixote*, Rua do Carmo 110; *Casa Maciel*, Rua da Misericórdia 63–65; *Casa Penim*, Rua Augusta 184–186; *Madeira Supérbia*, Avenida Duque de Loulé 75A.

FLEA MARKETS: *Feira da Ladra* ("Thieves' Market": old coins) on Campo de Santa Clara and lower down at Santa Engrácia (Tues. and Sat. 10 a.m.–6 p.m.); *Feira da Luz*, at Benfica Stadium (27 June); on *Campo Santana*, behind São Vicente (Tues. and Sat.); junk stalls (*bricabraques*) at the corner of Rua da Veronica, above the gardens of the Military Court.

SIGHTSEEING TOURS (*Claras Tursimo*), Avenida Fontes Pereira de Melo 33; *Cityrama*, Avenida Praia da Vitória 12B):

City tours (3 hours; several times daily).

Lisbon by night (3–4 hours; daily, with or without dinner).

Historic Lisbon (3 hours; Tues., Thurs. and Sat.).

Art in Lisbon (3 hours; Wed., Fri. and Sun.).

Queluz, Mafra, Sintra and *Estoril* (5 hours; Wed. and Sat. in summer).

Serra da Arrábida (5 hours; Mon., Wed., Fri. and Sun. in summer).

Estoril Casino ($4\frac{1}{3}$ hours; Mon.–Sat., with or without dinner).

CAR HIRE. – *Avis*, Avenida Praia da Vitória 12C (tel. 56 11 77); *Hertz*, Avenida 5 de Outubro 10 (tel. 57 90 27); *Interrent*, Avenida Alvares Cabral 45B (tel. 36 67 51); *Iber Rent-a-Car*, Rua Ricardo Espírito Santo 4A (tel. 67 53 06); *Flamingo Rent-a-Car*, Rua Luciano Cordeiro 4A (tel. 54 91 82).

***Lisbon, in Portuguese Lisboa (pronounced "Lishbóa"), capital of Portugal and its principal port and commercial headquarters, the see of an archbishop and since 1911 a university town, lies some 17 km/ $10\frac{1}{2}$ miles from the Atlantic on the N bank of the Tagus, which here opens out into the Mar de Palha ("Sea of Straw"), 7 km/$4\frac{1}{2}$ miles wide. To the W of the city the estuary narrows again to 2–3 km/1–2 miles wide, forming a fine sheltered natural harbour.**

Thanks to its very fine ** setting Lisbon ranks among the most beautiful cities in the world. In recent years it has lost some of its former brilliance as a result of domestic political vicissitudes and the influx of large numbers of refugees, many of them destitute, from the former Portuguese colonies. Lisbon still preserves the treasures of art and architecture which bear witness to the city's glorious past and these, with the charm of the old town with its steep and narrow lanes, make a stay here a memorable experience for any visitor.

Lisbon's sea of whitish-grey houses extends over seven hills on the southern slopes of the Estremadura plateau, with considerable variations in height, the different parts of the city being linked by steep streets and by a number of elevators and funiculars.

The OLD TOWN is built on the slopes of the hill crowned by the castle and on the nearby hills to the NE.

The depression between the Old Town and the New Town is occupied by the LOWER TOWN built after the 1755 earthquake, with the principal shopping and commercial streets. The NEW TOWN lies on the hills to the W. Lisbon is impressively laid out with imposing squares and wide streets lined by massive office buildings and usually busy with city traffic.

Since the late 1930s a series of large housing developments, some ten in number, have been erected on the outskirts of the city. The largest of these publicly provided estates, the *bairros sociais*, is the suburb of Alvalade, on the N side of Lisbon, which has a population of 50,000. Extensive areas of makeshift housing in the outer districts accommodate the large population of refugees from the former overseas territories who have returned to Portugal, and particularly to Lisbon, in recent years. It will clearly take a considerable time to provide adequate housing for this large number of incomers.

HISTORY. – The Phoenicians were the first to take advantage of this excellent harbourage at the mouth of the Tagus, establishing a settlement which they called *Alis Ubbo*. Later the Lusitanian port of *Olisipo*, it was taken over by the Romans, surrounded by walls and, as *Felicitas Iulia*, became the administrative capital of the Roman province of Lusitania, the second most important town (after Mérida) in the Iberian peninsula.

In A.D. 407 the town was taken by the Alani; from 585 to 715 it was under Visigothic rule; and after the battle of Jerez it fell into the hands of the Moors, who called it *Al Oshbuna* or *Lishbuna*. Under the Moors (until 1147) it enjoyed economic prosperity and a great flowering of culture.

Lisbon became a town of major importance in 1260, when King Afonso Henriques made it his capital. The great discoveries of the late 16th c. and the conquest of the East Indies principally benefited the capital, which rapidly developed into one of the wealthiest cities in Europe.

On 1 November 1755 most of the town was laid in ruins by a devastating earthquake, but rebuilding soon began under the direction of the Marquês de Pombal. The new city was laid out on a magnificent scale to the plans of Manuel da Maira, incorporating such of the older Gothic and Manueline buildings as had survived.

The transfer of the capital to Rio de Janeiro from the French invasion (1807–08) until 1821, followed by the loss of Brazil as a colony, were considerable setbacks to Lisbon, from which it only gradually recovered in the second half of the 19th c.

Since then Lisbon has developed into a cosmopolitan modern city without losing its own very personal characteristics and attractions.

Museums, Galleries, etc.

American Library
(*Biblioteca Americana*),
Avenida do Duque de Loulé 22.
Mon.–Fri. 2–6 p.m.

Aquarium
(*Aquário de Vasco da Gama*),
Dafundo.
Mon.–Sat. noon–6 p.m., Sun. 10 a.m.–6 p.m.

Archaeological Museum of the Carmo
(*Museu Arqueológico do Carmo*),
Largo do Carmo.
A collection of pottery and coins of the prehistoric and historical period, housed in the Gothic church of a Carmelite convent.
Daily 10 a.m.–1 p.m. and 2–5 p.m.

Army Library
(*Biblioteca da Armada*),
Calçada do Combro.
In the headquarters of the Guarda Nacional Republicana.

Azulejo Museum
(*Museu do Azulejo*),
Rua da Madre de Deus 4B
(church of Madre de Deus).
A valuable collection of azulejos of the 16th–18th c.

Biblioteca da Ajuda,
Palácio da Ajuda,
Calçada da Ajuda.
Mon.–Fri. 10.30 a.m.–5 p.m.

Biblioteca Popular de Lisboa,
Rua da Academia das Ciências 19.
Mon.–Fri. noon–8.30 p.m.

Botanical Museum
(*Museu Botânico*),
Rua da Escola Politécnica.
Mon.–Fri. 9.30 a.m.–1.30 p.m. and 2–5.30 p.m., Sat. 9.30 a.m.–1.30 p.m.

Bullfighting Museum
(*Museu Tauromáquico*),
Praça de Touros do Campo Pequeno, Gate 20.

Carmo Museum
See Archaeological Museum of the Carmo.

Cathedral Treasury Museum
(*Museu do Tesouro da Sé Patriarcal*),
Praça da Sé.
Vestments, gold and silver.

Coach Museum
(*Museu Nacional dos Coches*),
Praça de Afonso de Albuquerque, Belém.
One of the world's largest collections of state coaches and carriages.
Daily 10 a.m.–5 p.m.

Customs Museum
(*Museu da Direcção-Geral das Alfândegas*),
Ministry of Finance,
Rua da Alfândega.

Fire Brigade Museum
(*Museu do Bombeiro*),
Avenida de Dom Carlos I.
Tues.–Fri. 3–5.30 p.m.

Folk Art Museum
(*Museu de Arte Popular*),
Avenida de Brasilia, Belém.

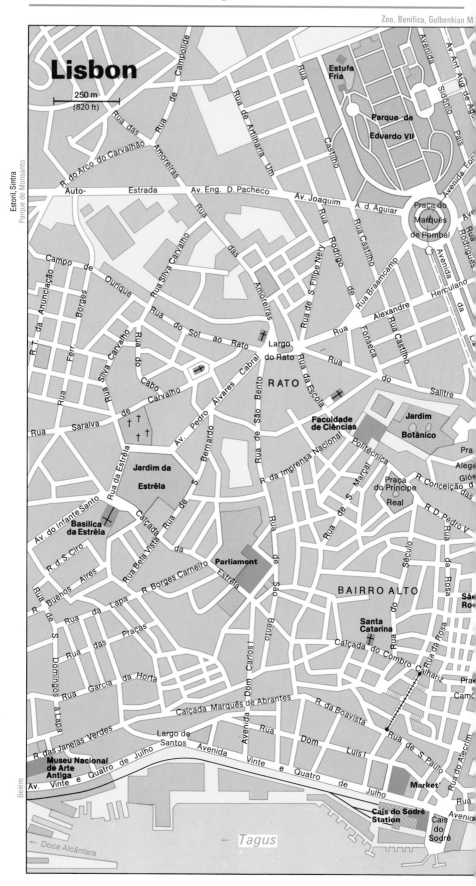

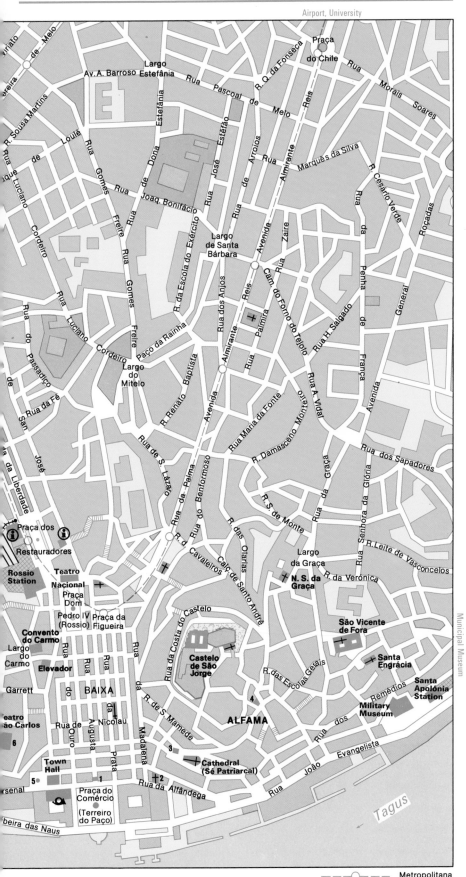

Airport, University

Municipal Museum

Tagus

corative Art   5 Praça do Município   6 Museum of Contemporary Art   7 Church of N.S. da Encarnação   8 Loreto church

Portuguese arts and crafts, porcelain, silver, pottery, blankets, etc.
Tues.–Sat. 10 a.m.–12.30 p.m. and 2–5 p.m.

Gulbenkian Museum
(*Museu da Fundação Calouste Gulbenkian*),
Avenida de Berna 45.
Pictures, porcelain, sculpture.
Daily 10 a.m.–5 p.m.

Gulbenkian Planetarium
(*Planetarium Calouste Gulbenkian*),
Praça do Império, Belém.
Presentations Mon. 3.30–4.45 p.m., Sat. and Sun.
4–5 p.m.

Instruments, Museum of,
(*Museu Instrumental*),
Biblioteca Nacional,
Campo Grande.
Mon.–Fri. 10 a.m.–1 p.m. and 2–5 p.m.

Library of the Academy of Sciences
(*Biblioteca da Academia das Ciências de Lisboa*),
Rua da Academia das Ciências 19.
Mon.–Wed. and Fri. 9.30 a.m.–noon and 2.15–5 p.m.,
Thurs. and Sat. 9.30 a.m.–noon.

Library of the Government Printing Office
(*Biblioteca da Imprensa Nacional*),
Rua da Escola Politécnica.
Mon.–Fri. 9–11.30 a.m. and 2–4.30 p.m., Sat. 9–
11.30 a.m.

Library of the Gulbenkian Foundation
(*Biblioteca da Fundação Calouste Gulbenkian*),
Avenida de Berna 56.
Mon.–Fri. 9 a.m.–1 p.m. and 3–6 p.m.

Military Archives
(*Arquivos Históricos Militares*),
Rua do Paraíso 8.
Mon.–Fri. 9.15 a.m.–1 p.m. and 2.45–6 p.m.

Military Museum
(*Museu Militar*),
Largo dos Caminhos de Ferro, Santa Apolónia.
Arms and armour from the 9th to the 20th c.
Tues.–Sat. 10 a.m.–4 p.m., Sun. 11 a.m.–5 p.m.

Mineralogical Museum
(*Museu de Mineralogia*),
Rua da Escola Politécnica.
Thurs. 10 a.m.–noon and 2–4 p.m.

Municipal Archives
(*Arquivos Históricos da Cidade*),
Praça do Municipio.
Mon.–Fri. 9 a.m.–noon and 2–5.30 p.m., Sat. 9 a.m.–
12.30 p.m.

Municipal Library
(*Biblioteca Municipal Central*),
Palácio Galveias,
Largo do Dr Alonso Pena.
Mon.–Fri. 9 a.m.–9 p.m., Sat. 9 a.m.–1 p.m.

Municipal Museum
(*Museu da Cidade*),
Palácio da Mitra,
Rua do Açúar 64.
Material illustrating the history of Lisbon.
Tues.–Sat. 11 a.m.–6 p.m.

Museu Antoniano,
Praça de Santo António da Sé.
A museum devoted to St Antony of Padua (a native of Lisbon).

Museum of Decorative Art
(*Museu de Artes Decorativas*),
Largo das Portas do Sol, Alfama.
Portuguese art of the 17th and 18th c., furniture, porcelain, silver, tapestries.
Tues.–Sat. 10 a.m.–1 p.m. and 2.30–5 p.m., Sun.
1–5 p.m.

Museum of the School of Decorative Art
(*Museu-Escola de Arte Decorativa da Fundação Ricardo Espírito Santo*),
Rua de São Tomé 90.
Tues.–Sat. 10 a.m.–5 p.m., Sun. 10 a.m.–noon.

Museum of Religious Art
(*Museu de Arte Sacra de São Roque*),
Praça de Trindade Coelho.
Tues.–Sat. 10 a.m.–5 p.m.

National Archives
(*Arquivos Nacionais da Torre do Tombo*),
Palácio da Assembleia Nacional,
Largo de São Bento.
Mon.–Sat. 11 a.m.–4 p.m.

National Library
(*Biblioteca Nacional*),
Campo Grande 83.
Mon.–Fri. 10 a.m.–9 p.m., Sat. 10 a.m.–1 p.m.

National Museum of Archaeology and Ethnology
(*Museu Nacional de Arqueologia e Etnologia*),
Praça do Império, Belém.
Tues.–Sun. 10 a.m.–12.30 p.m. and 2–5 p.m.

National Museum of Art
(*Museu Nacional de Arte Antiga*),
Rua das Janelas Verdes 9.
Painting, sculpture, ceramics, goldsmith's work, furniture, etc.
Tues., Wed., Fri. and Sat. 10 a.m.–5 p.m., Thurs. and Sun. 10 a.m.–7 p.m.

National Museum of Contemporary Art
(*Museu Nacional de Arte Contemporânea*),
Rua Serpa Pinto 6.
Tues.–Sat. 10 a.m.–noon and 2–5 p.m.

Naval Museum
(*Museu da Marinha*),
Praça do Império, Belém.
Ship models, uniforms.
Tues.–Sat. 10 a.m.–5 p.m.

Numismatic Museum
(*Museu Numismático Português*),
Avenida do Dr António José de Almeida.

Overseas Agriculture, Museum of
(*Museu e Jardim Agrícola do Antigo Ultramar Português*),
Calçada do Galvão 1, Belém.
Agriculture, forestry and fishing in the former overseas territories.
Daily 9 a.m.–5.30 p.m.

Overseas Archives
(*Arquivos Históricos do Antigo Ultramar Português*),
Calçada da Boa Hora 30.
Mon.–Fri. 1.30–6 p.m., Sat. 9.30 a.m.–noon.

Overseas Ethnography, Museum of
(*Museu Etnográfico do Antigo Ultramar Português*),
Rua das Portas de Santo Antão 100.
History and art of the peoples of the former overseas territories.
Tues.–Fri. 11 a.m.–1 p.m.

Pinheiro Museum
(*Museu Rafael Bordalo Pinheiro*),

Campo Grande 382.
Ceramics; drawings and caricatures.
Tues.–Sat. 10 a.m.–5.30 p.m.

Postal Museum
(*Museu dos CTT*),
Rua de Dona Estefânia 173–175.
History and development of the postal and telegraph systems.
Tues.–Sat. 10 a.m.–noon and 3–6 p.m.

São Roque Museum
See Museum of Religious Art.

Teatro Nacional de São Carlos,
Largo de São Carlos 21.
Archives, library and museum.
Seen by appointment (tel. 36 86 10).

Zoo
(*Jardim Zoológico*),
Parque das Laranjeiras,
Estrada de Benfica.
Daily 9 a.m.–6 p.m.

Sightseeing in Lisbon

Lower Town
(*Cidade Baixa*)

Lisbon's principal traffic artery is the *Avenida da Liberdade, a splendid thoroughfare 90 m/300 ft wide, with ten lines of trees and beautiful gardens, which traverses the Lower Town (Cidade Baixa) for a distance of 1·5 km/1 mile, rising slightly as it runs NW from the Praça dos Restauradores to the Praça do Marquês de Pombal.

In the busy **Praça dos Restauradores** stands the *Monumento dos Restauradores de Portugal*, an obelisk almost 30 m/100 ft high erected in 1882 to commemorate the rising of 1 December 1640 which put an end to sixty years of Spanish rule.

At the SW corner of the square is the **Rossio Station** (*Estação do Rossio*), terminus of the line to Sintra and Leiria, which leaves the city in a tunnel 2600 m/2850 yd long.

Just N of the station, in the steep Calçada da Glória, is a *funicular* running up to Rua de São Pedro de Alcântara, from which there are extensive views.

SE of the Praça dos Restauradores is another busy square, the **Praça de Dom Pedro IV**, usually known as the **Rossio**, with a *marble column* 23 m/75 ft high (erected 1870) topped by a bronze statue of King Pedro IV.

Above the SW corner of the square are the Convento do Carmo and an elevator (*elevador*).

On the N side of the square is the **Teatro Nacional de Dona Maria II**.

From the Rossio a number of parallel streets, laid out after the 1755 earthquake and originally intended for occupation by different trades and crafts, run S towards the Tagus. Among them are *Rua da Prata* ("Silver Street", for the silversmiths), *Rua Áurea* (for the goldsmiths) and *Rua Augusta* (for the cloth merchants). At the far end of these streets, looking on to the Tagus, is the *Praça do Comércio, also known as the **Terreiro do Paço** after the royal palace, the Paço da Ribeira, which was destroyed in the 1755 earthquake. Its traditional English name is Black Horse Square, after the bronze *equestrian statue of King José I* (erected 1775) in the middle of the square. The square is surrounded by arcades and by various public

Praça de Dom Pedro IV (Rossio)   Arco Monumental, Praça do Comércio

buildings (mainly government depart-
ments), most of which were built by
Santos de Carvalho after the earthquake.

On the N side of the square towers a
huge triumphal arch completed only in
1873, the **Arco Monumental da Rua
Augusta**, with statues of famous Portuguese figures.

On the W side of the square is the **Head
Post Office** (*Correio Geral*). – From the
Tagus embankment there is a view of the
river and the district of Almada on the S
bank, with the monument of Christ the
King rising above the houses.

Old Town
(*Alfama*)

A short distance along Rua da Alfândega
from the NE corner of the Praça do
Comércio is the **church of Nossa
Senhora da Conceição Velha**, rebuilt
after the earthquake but preserving a
richly decorated Manueline façade from
an earlier church.

From here it is a short distance farther NE,
up through the narrow lanes of the old
town, to the *Cathedral (*Sé Patriarcal*),
the oldest church in Lisbon.
The greater part of the Cathedral dates
from 1344 onwards, when it replaced an
earlier church which is believed to have
been converted from a mosque in 1150.
The fortress-like W front with its two
towers was built in 1380.

INTERIOR. – Immediately left of the entrance is the
font. In the first chapel on the left is a beautiful
terracotta *crib* (Nativity group) by Joaquin Machado
de Castro. In the Capela-mór are the *tombs of King
Afonso IV* and his queen, *Brites*. In St Vincent's
Chapel, at the near end of the ambulatory, is the silver
reliquary of St Vincent (d. 304).

In the Sacristy is the valuable *Cathedral Treasury*. –
There is also a fine two-storey 14th c. Cloister with a
superb Romanesque wrought-iron *screen*.

On the W side of the square, opposite the
Cathedral, is the *church of Santo António
da Sé* (rebuilt between 1757 and 1812),
said to mark the site of the house in which
St Antony of Padua was born.

Below the Cathedral, to the S, is the *Casa
dos Bicos*, built of ashlar blocks with
faceted surfaces.

To the E and NE of the Cathedral, on
the slopes of the hill, is the famous

*ALFAMA**, Lisbon's very picturesque old
town. This quarter of narrow stepped
lanes and romantic little squares attracts
large numbers of visitors, particularly in
the evening, when fado singers can be
heard in some of the cafés and restaurants.
The liveliest street in the Alfama is the
Rua de São Pedro, with its little shops,
tabernas and street vendors.

On the NW fringe of the Alfama, in Rua do
Limoeiro, is the *Miradouro de Santa
Luzia*, a terrace from which there is a fine
panoramic view of the city.
To the E of this, in Largo das Portas do Sol,
is the *Azurara Palace*, now housing the
Museum of Decorative Art (*Museu
das Artes Decorativas*), with a school and
workshops as well as a fine collection of
18th and 19th c. furniture, silver, carpets
and ceramics.
On top of the hill, once the middle of the
Moorish town, is the **Castelo de São**

Cathedral   Lisbon
Sé Patriarcal   Lisboa

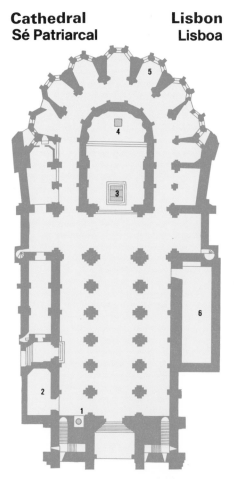

1 Font	4 Patriarchal throne
2 Crib (Nativity group)	5 Tomb of Afonso IV
3 High altar	6 Sacristy (Treasury)

A lane in the Alfama district

Jorge. Once a royal residence, converted from an earlier Moorish fortress, it was much altered in subsequent periods, and much of the present castle dates from the 19th c. It was restored in the style of a medieval fortresss in 1938–40.

From the tree-planted terrace on the S side of the castle and from the wall-walks and towers there are fine*views of the city and the Mar de Palha (orientation table). In one of the rooms of the castle is an excellent model of Lisbon before the 1755 earthquake.

Some 500 m/550 yd E of the Castle is the imposing **church of São Vicente de Fora** by the Italian architect Filippo Terzi; it was built between 1582 and 1627 and has a twin-towered façade and a richly decorated interior. In the adjoining convent, a former Augustinian house, are two *cloisters* with a profusion of 17th c. *azulejos.

In the former refectory is the **Panteão Real** (Royal Pantheon), installed here in 1855, with the tombs of members of the House of Bragança from João IV (d. 1656) to Queen Amalia (d. 1951).

To the SE of São Vicente is the **church of Santa Engrácia** (1530–1966), a Baroque church on a centralised plan with a finely decorated interior. It is now a pantheon with the tombs of famous Portuguese. The church, only recently completed, took more than four centuries

to build, so it is not surprising that the expression "obras de Santa Engrácia", meaning "a task in progress, long overdue", should have become part of the Portuguese language.

To the NW of São Vicente, also standing on high ground, is the former *Convento da Graça*, now a barracks, from which there are extensive*views to the W. In the S transept of the **church of Nossa Senhora da Graça** (built 1556, rebuilt after the 1755 earthquake) is an image of Nosso Senhor dos Passos which is revered as miraculous.

On a ridge of hill some 500 m/550 yd N of the Graça convent is the **Ermida de Nossa Senhora do Monte** (alt. 100 m/ 330 ft), built in 1243. From the terrace (orientation table) there are panoramic *views of Lisbon.

1·5 km/1 mile farther N is the *church of Nossa Senhora de Penha de França*, from which there are still more extensive *views.

From the Praça do Comércio the Rua da Alfândega and a succession of streets continuing the same line run NE to the former *Military Arsenal* (Arsenal do Exército), 1 km/¾ mile away near the banks of the Tagus, which now houses the **Military Museum** (*Museu Militar*), with a large collection of arms and armour and military trophies (including 14th c. cannon and Vasco da Gama's sword). Some of the rooms have rich Baroque decoration.

Beyond the Military Museum is the **Santa Apolónia Station** (*Estação de Santa Apolónia*), terminus of the northern line (Oporto, France; motorail).

500 m/550 yd NE of the station, situated on the banks of the Tagus in the XABREGAS district, is the *Convent of the Madre de Deus*, a former house of Poor Clares founded in 1509. Visitors can see the main part of the buildings, with two fine cloisters in Manueline style and the church. The convent now houses the *Azulejo Museum (Museu do Azulejo), with a large collection of Portuguese and foreign ceramic tiles. Some 2 km/ 1¼ miles farther on, in the MARVILA district, is the **Municipal Museum** (*Museu da Cidade*), which gives an excellent survey of the history and development of Lisbon.

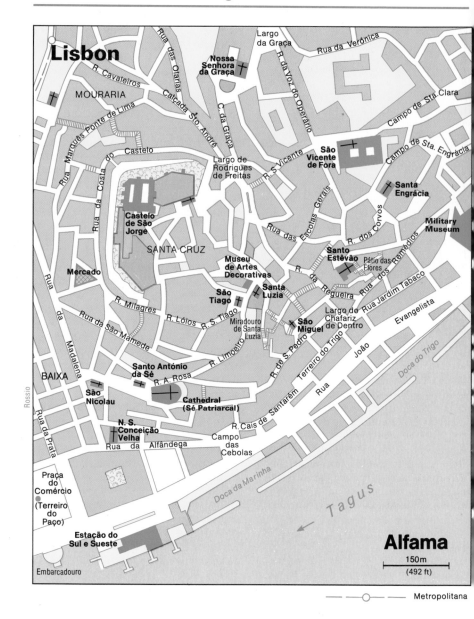

Upper Town
(*Bairro Alto*)

From the SW corner of the Rossio a busy shopping street, *Rua do Carmo*, runs S up the hill to the Upper Town (Bairro Alto). On the W side of Rua do Carmo is **Rua Garrett**, usually known as the **Chiado**, one of the busiest streets in the city, with many elegant shops and boutiques.

At the W end of Rua Garrett is the *Largo do Chiado* or Largo das duas Igrejas, with the *church of Nossa Senhora da Encarnação* (1784) on the S side and the *Loreto church* (1517) on the N side.
To the N of Rua Garrett is the Largo do Carmo, on the E side of which is the former

Convento do Carmo (1389–1423), most of which was destroyed in 1755. The nave of the church now houses an *Archaeological Museum* (medieval sculpture, tombs, etc.). From the Elevador (elevator) behind the choir there is a fine *view.

To the S of Rua Garrett are the* **Teatro de São Carlos**, Lisbon's famous opera-house (1792), and a former Franciscan convent which now houses the *Academy of Fine Art* (Academia de Belas Artes, founded 1836) and the *National **Museum of Contemporary Art** (*Museu Nacional de Arte Contemporânea*: entrance in Rua de Serpa Pinto), with works, mainly by Portuguese artists, from 1850 onwards.

Pictures by Tomás da Anunciação, Marques de Oliveira, Silva Porto, José Malhoa ("Outono"), Alfredo Keil, Columbano Bordalo Pinheiro ("A Chávena de Chá", "O Concerto de Amadores"), Henrique Pousão, Carlos Reis, Eduardo Viana ("A Viola"), Francisco Smith, Amadeu de Sousa-Cardoso, Abel Manta, Dórdio Gomes, António Soares, Carlos Botelho, Costa Pinto, Eduardo Malta, Mário Elói and Vieira da Silva.
Sculpture by Soares dos Reis, Teixeira Lopes ("A Viúva"), Francisco Franco, Diogo de Macedo, Canto da Maia ("Juventude") and Auguste Rodin.

The Largo do Chiado joins the tree-planted **Praça de Camões**, with a large *monument to Luís de Camões* (1524–80), Portugal's greatest poet, erected in 1867.
From the NE corner of the square Rua da Misericórdia climbs N to the Praça de Trindade Coelho, on the N side of which is the *church of São Roque, with a sumptuous interior. In the left-hand aisle is the * Capela de São João Baptista, built in Rome in 1740, using the most precious materials (marble, alabaster, semi-precious stones, gold and silver), and re-erected in Lisbon in 1747. Adjoining the church, in the former old people's home and foundling hospital of the *Misericórdia*, is the **Museum of Religious Art** (*Museu de Arte Sacre*), with a notable collection of goldsmith's work.

Rua de Misericórdia continues N to *Rua de São Pedro de Alcântara, with a terrace from which there are superb views of the city and the Tagus (orientation table).

From here Rua de Dom Pedro V runs NW to the *Praça do Príncipe Real*, on the highest point in the Upper Town. From the W end of the square there is a fine view.

From the Praça do Príncipe Real, Rua da Escola Politécnica continues NW to the *Faculty of Science* of Lisbon University, formerly a technical college, with a *Natural History Museum*.
Beyond this is the *Botanic Garden (*Jardim Botánico*), richly stocked with tropical and subtropical plants.

From the Praça de Camões a succession of streets, beginning with Rua do Loreto, lead NW, passing the Baroque *church of Santa Catarina* (Igreja dos Paulistas; *carved wood) to the Largo de Miguel Lupi.
In this square stands the **Parliament Building** (*Palácio da Assembléia Nacional*), converted from a 17th c. convent in 1834 and subsequently much

altered. Here are housed the valuable *National Archives* (founded in 1375).

From the Largo de Miguel Lupi the Calçada da Estrêla runs NW to the **Basilica da Estrêla** ("Basilica of the Star"), built 1779–90, with an imposing twin-towered façade and a high dome over the crossing. From here there is the finest *view of the whole city.
Opposite the church is the **Jardim da Estrêla**, a park with a profusion of flowers, ponds, fountains and grottoes.

Northern Districts

At the N end of the wide *Avenida da Liberdade* is the *Praça do Marquês de Pombal**, an important traffic intersection on the northern edge of the inner city, surrounded by hotels and restaurants. In the middle is a huge *monument to the Marquês de Pombal**, with numerous figures around the base.

Praça do Marquês de Pombal

Up the hill to the N extends the **Parque de Eduardo VII**, so named in honour of King Edward VII's visit to Lisbon in 1903. In the upper part of the park is the **Estufa Fria** (Cold House), an open-roofed greenhouse for tropical plants.
From the terrace there are extensive *views of the city and the Tagus estuary.

From the Parque de Eduardo VII it is 3 km/ 2 miles N by way of the Avenida de António Augusto de Aguiar and the Estrada de Benfica to the *Zoo (*Jardim Zoológico*), in the Parque das Laranjeiras (Park of the Orange-Trees).

1 km/¾ mile N of the Parque de Eduardo VII, in the angle between the Avenida de António Augusto de Aguiar and the Avenida de Berna (Praça de Espanha), lies a large **park** (17 acres) belonging to the **Gulbenkian Foundation** (*Fundação Calouste Gulbenkian*). The park contains a theatre, concert and conference halls, a library of some 400,000 volumes and the ** **Gulbenkian Museum** (*Museum da Fundação Calouste Gulbenkian*). It houses the extraordinarily rich collection assembled by the Armenian oil magnate Calouste Sarkis Gulbenkian (1869–1955), who lived in Lisbon from 1942 until his death 13 years later.

The BUILDINGS, a modern complex laid out on an open plan with a total area of 25,000 sq. m/ 30,000 sq. yd, were erected in 1964–69 to the design of Alberto Passoal, Pedro Cid and Ruy Athouguia. The *COLLECTION is particularly strong in Oriental art, in particular the art of Egypt, Mesopotamia, the Islamic countries and the Far East (China and Japan). There is also a very rich collection of * ceramics, as well as important Greek and Roman antiquities, including a fine collection of Greek coins.

The ** **picture gallery** has works by Flemish artists including *Rubens* ("Portrait of Hélène Fourment"), *Thierry Bouts* ("Annunciation"), *Van Dyck* ("Portrait of a Man") and *Gossaert*; the Dutch artists *Frans Hals* and *Rembrandt* ("Pallas Athene"); German masters, including a "Presentation in the Temple" (1445) by *Stefan Lochner*; French artists, including *Fragonard, Corot, Manet, Monet, Renoir* and *Degas* ("Self-Portrait"); English painters such as *Hoppner, Gainsborough, Romney, Lawrence* and *Edward Burne-Jones* ("Mirror of Venus"); the Venetian *Carpaccio* ("Virgin and Child with Donor"); and the Florentines *Ghirlandaio* and *Guardi* (ten pictures on Venetian themes).
There are also works of sculpture by *Houdon* ("Diana") and *Rodin* ("Burghers of Calais", in park), textiles, 18th c. French furniture and a large collection of *Art Nouveau work by Lalique.

In the park, with its luxuriant tropical and subtropical vegetation, is a seated bronze *figure*, 3 m/10 ft high, of *Calouste Gulbenkian* (by L. de Almeida) in front of a stone Horus falcon.

The Avenida de Berna leads E into the wide **Avenida da República**, which turns N, passing the **Bullring** (*Praça de Touros*), to the beautiful *Campo Grande* park, in which are the **National Library** (*Biblioteca Nacional*; over 1 million volumes) and the **University City** (*Cidade Universitária*).
To the E of the Avenida da República, in a part of the city which has been developed since 1940, are the monumental buildings of the **College of Technology** (*Instituto Superior Técnico*), the **National Statistical Office** (*Instituto Nacional de Estatística*) and the **Mint** (*Casa da Moeda*), with the *Numismatic Museum*.

From the College of Technology the *Alameda de Dom Afonso Henriques*, a wide avenue (120 m/395 ft) lined by modern blocks of flats, runs down to the E, crossing the *Avenida de Almirante Reis*, which extends for a distance of 3 km/ 2 miles from the Rossio to the north-eastern districts of the city, and ends at a large fountain, the **Fonte Monumental**.

4 km/2½ miles NE of the Alameda de Dom Afonso Henriques is **Lisbon Airport** (*Aeroporto Portela de Sacavém*).

Western Districts

To the W of the Praça do Comércio is the **Praça do Município** (Town Hall Square), also known as the Largo do Pelourinho from the 18th c. *pelourinho* (pillory column) with a twisted shaft which stands in the middle of the square. On the E side of the square is the **Town Hall** (*Município*, 1865–80).

A short distance W of the Praça do Município is the **Cais do Sodré Station** (*Estação do Cais do Sodré*: trains to Cascais), with the quay used by the Tagus ferry.

From here the Avenida do 24 de Julho runs W, passing the **Market** (*Mercado*) on the right, and 2 km/1¼ miles from the Town Hall reaches the ** **National Museum of Art** (*Museu Nacional de Arte Antiga*), popularly known as the "Casa das Janelas Verdes" ("House of the Green Windows"), which occupies a palace belonging to the Marquês de Pombal and a modern extension.

The greater part of the Museum is occupied by the large ** **Picture Gallery** on the upper floor, notable particularly for one of the great masterpieces of 15th c. Portuguese art, the famous ** **polyptych from St Vincent's altar**, formerly in the church of São Vicente de Fora, painted by Nuno Gonçalves between 1460 and 1470, with sixty portraits of leading figures in Portuguese history, including St Isabel (Isabel of Aragón, wife of King Dinis) and Henry the Navigator.

16th c. artists represented in the collection include *Vasco Fernandes* (Grão Vasco, a native of Viseu; "Adoration of the Virgin"), *Gregório Lopes, Cristóvão de Figueiredo* and *Frei Carlos*. The 17th c. is represented by *Josefa de Óbidos* and *Vieira Portuense* ("Dona Isabel de Moura") among others, the 18th and 19th c. by *Domingos António de Sequeira* ("Family of the first Viscount of Santarém" and "The Painter's Daughter playing the Piano").

Spanish artists include *Velázquez* ("Maria of Austria"), *Zurbarán* ("St Peter") and *Murillo*. Among outstanding works by Flemish artists are *Hieronymus Bosch*'s triptych, "The Temptation of St Antony", *Hans Memling*'s "Mother and Child" and *Pieter Coek*'s "Descent from the Cross".

German masters represented include *Albrecht Dürer* ("St Jerome"), *Lucas Cranach* ("Salome") and *Hans Holbein the Elder* ("Virgin and Child with Saints").

French painting is represented by *Fragonard* ("Two Cousins"), *Courbet, Poussin* and others; English painting by *Reynolds, Lawrence* and *Romney*; the Italian schools by *Piero della Francesca* ("St Augustine"), *Raphael* ("St Eusebius raising three men from the dead"), *Tintoretto* ("Descent from the Cross"), *Guardi* and others.

In addition to the picture gallery the Museum also has a collection of Egyptian, Greek and Roman *sculpture* (torso of an Apollo, 9th c. B.C.?), a notable collection

Polyptych "Veneração a São Vicente"   **Museo Nacional de Arte Antiga Lisbon**

Cistercian monks from Alcobaça | Nuno Gonçalves | Isabel of Aragón | Henry the Navigator | Infante João (João II) | Archbishop of Lisbon | Gomes Eanes de Azurara | Moorish knight | Beggar | Jew

Fishermen and pilots | Queen Isabel | St Vincent | King Afonso V | Infante Fernão | St Vincent | Knight | Fernão, 2nd Duke of Bragança | Cleric with St Vincent's skull

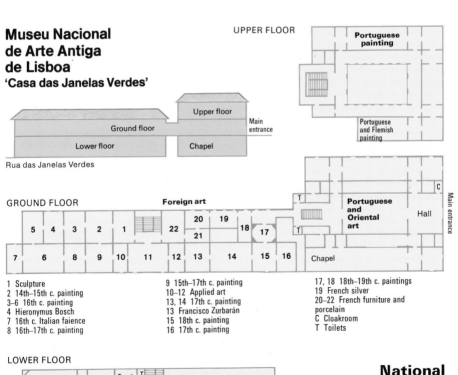

Museu Nacional de Arte Antiga de Lisboa
'Casa das Janelas Verdes'

UPPER FLOOR

Portuguese painting

Upper floor
Ground floor
Lower floor
Chapel
Main entrance

Portuguese and Flemish painting

Rua das Janelas Verdes

GROUND FLOOR   Foreign art

Portuguese and Oriental art   Hall

Chapel

20 19
21 18 17

5 4 3 2 1 22

7 6 8 9 10 11 12 13 14 15 16

1 Sculpture
2 14th–15th c. painting
3–6 16th c. painting
4 Hieronymus Bosch
7 16th c. Italian faience
8 16th–17th c. painting

9 15th–17th c. painting
10–12 Applied art
13, 14 17th c. painting
13 Francisco Zurbarán
15 18th c. painting
16 17th c. painting

17, 18 18th–19th c. paintings
19 French silver
20–22 French furniture and porcelain
C Cloakroom
T Toilets

LOWER FLOOR

Auditorium | Oriental art | Teach-ing | Administration
Graphic art | Library | Hall | Special exhibitions

National Museum of Art, Lisbon

The Ponte do 25 de Abril by night

of *pottery and porcelain* (including work by António Ferreira and Machado de Castro, 18th c.), magnificent examples of *goldsmith's and silversmith's work*, including a cross which belonged to Sancho I (13th c.) and *monstrances from Belém (16th c.) and Bemposta (18th c.), and a large collection of *French table silver*.

1 km/¾ mile NW of the National Museum of Art, on higher ground, is the **Palácio das Necessidades**, built in 1743–50 on the site of an earlier hermitage (Ermida N.S. da Necessidades), which was a royal palace until 1910 and is now occupied by the *Ministry of Foreign Affairs*.
The adjoining park, the *Tapada das Necessidades*, can be visited with permission from the Instituto Agronómico.

From the Cais do Sodré Station the *Avenida do 24 de Julho* runs W, keeping close to the Tagus. On the left is the *Alcântara Dock* (Doca de Alcântara). The Avenida da Índia then continues alongside the river, with the *Marine Station* (Estação de Alcântara), where the boats moor, to the left.
The Avenida da Índia now passes under the approach (945 m/1035 yd long, borne on massive piers) to the bridge over the Tagus, the ***Ponte Suspensa** or *Ponte do 25 de Abril*. This road bridge (in which it is planned to incorporate a rail crossing as well), was opened in 1966.

It is 2277 m/2471 yd long, with a span of 1013 m/1108 yd between the piers. The piers are 190·50 m/625 ft high; the carriageway is 70 m/230 ft above the water.

2 km/1¼ miles beyond the bridge the Avenida da Índia comes to the outlying district of Belém.

Belém

*Belém (=Bethlehem), a south-western suburb of Lisbon, lies on the right bank of the Tagus at the point where the river begins to open out again in its final approach to the sea. With its fine old buildings and very interesting museums, it makes a rewarding full-day trip from the capital.

Cloister, Convento de los Jerónimos, Belém

Convento dos Jerónimos de Belém (Lisboa)

Hieronymite Convent (Lisbon)

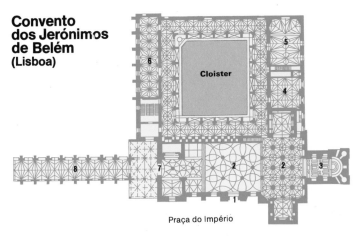

Cloister

Praça do Império

1 S doorway
2 Church of Santa Maria de Belém
3 Choir
4 Sacristy
5 Chapterhouse
6 Refectory
7 W doorway
8 National Museum of Archaeology (Dorter)

On the N side of the spacious Praça do Império, with its large illuminated fountain, the *Fonte Luminosa*, is the principal glory of Belém, the world-famous Hieronymite convent or **Convento dos Jerónimos de Belém**, the supreme achievement of Manueline architecture and the most impressive symbol of Portugal's power and wealth in the age of the great colonial conquests.

HISTORY. – The origins of the convent go back to a chapel for seamen built here by *Henry the Navigator*, within easy reach of the harbour at Restelo from which the voyages of discovery set out, and served by the Knights of Christ.
Tradition has it that *Vasco da Gama* spent the nights before sailing for India in 1497 praying in this chapel; and here, too, he was received by the king on his triumphant return.
To commemorate and give thanks for the voyage Manuel I built on the site of the little chapel one of the most splendid buildings in Portugal, and indeed in the whole of Christendom.

The building of the convent began in 1502 to the plans of *Boytaca* (probably a native of Languedoc), who was also concerned in the construction of Batalha Abbey. The detailed work was carried out in 1517–22 under the direction of *João de Castilho*, who also built the cloister.

After the dissolution of the convent in 1834 it was occupied by the Casa Pia, an orphanage.

At the SE corner of the complex is the three-aisled *church of Santa Maria, with a magnificent S front. The S doorway (by João de Castilho) and the W doorway (by Nicolas Chanterene) are particularly fine.
The choir, in High Renaissance style, was added in 1571–72.

The INTERIOR is 92 m/302 ft long, 22·6 m/74 ft wide and 25 m/82 ft high. The roof is supported on *octagonal piers* richly decorated with carving.
In the magnificent transepts and apse are the **tombs**, borne on elephants, of Manuel I and his successors

S front of Convento de los Jerónimos

and relatives – a total of five kings, seven queens and nineteen princes and princesses of the House of Avis. Under the organ-loft are the *sarcophaguses of Vasco da Gama and Luís de Camões* (who died of plague in 1580).
In the Coro Alto (access from cloister) are fine Renaissance *choir-stalls* (1560).

On the N side of the church is the splendid *Cloister (Claustro)*, 55 m/180 ft square, a master-work by João de Castilho, with two storeys of arcaded galleries.
In the NW corner is a *Lion Fountain*, which once stood in a basin in the middle of the cloister. Here, too, is the entrance to the former *Refectory* which has beautiful reticulated vaulting and rich azulejo decoration (17th c.) on the walls.

At the NE corner of the cloister is the former *Chapterhouse*, which contains the tombs of the writer and politician João Baptista da Silva Leitão de Almeida Garrett (1799–1854), the historian Alexandre Herculano (1810–77) and Oscar António de Fragoso Carmona (1869–1951), President of Portugal from 1928 until his death.

In the unfinished S wing of the cloister is the *Dorter* (Dormitory), which now houses the *National Museum of Archaeology and Ethnology (Museu Nacional de Arqueologia e Etnologia)*, with an extensive collection of prehistoric and early historical material and impressive works of art and other material of the Moorish and medieval periods.

To the W of the convent is the interesting *Naval Museum (Museu da Marinha)*. In a modern extension to the W the most notable exhibits are two 18th c. *ceremonial barges.

Between the two parts of the museum, set back a little, is the **Gulbenkian Planetarium** (1965).

To the E of the Convento dos Jerónimos is the Praça de Afonso de Albuquerque, with a *monument to Afonso de Albuquerque (c. 1450–1515)*, second Portuguese Viceroy of the East Indies. On the N side of the square stands the former royal palace, the **Paço de Belém**, built by the Conde de Aveiro in 1700, which is now the residence of the President of Portugal.

On the ground floor of the E wing the former Riding School (built 1726) now houses the *National Coach Museum (Museu Nacional dos Coches)*, one of the

Monument of the Discoveries, Belém

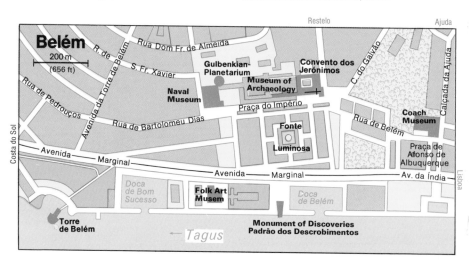

largest and most valuable collections of the kind in the world, with some 60 state and ceremonial coaches and carriages ranging in date from the 17th to the 19th c.

To the S of the Praça do Império, on the banks of the Tagus, towers the 54 m/175 ft high *Monument of the Discoveries (Padrão dos Descobrimentos), in the form of a ship's prow, erected in 1960, the 500th anniversary of the death of Henry the Navigator. It commemorates the Portuguese seamen who set out from here in the 15th c. on their voyages of discovery. The monument contains a small museum.

To the W of the Monument of the Discoveries the Museum of Folk Art (Museu de Arte Popular) houses a large collection of Portuguese folk art (costumes, tools and implements, furniture, pottery, etc.), arranged according to provinces.

Some 500 m/550 yd farther W, on the Tagus, is the **Tower of Belém (Torre de Belém), in the purest Manueline style, built in 1512–21 to protect the harbour of Restelo at the entrance to the Tagus. The tower was long used as a state prison.
From the platform of the tower there are fine *views.

To the E of the Paço de Belém the Calçada da Ajuda leads 1 km/¾ mile upstream to the Palácio Nacional da Ajuda, a former royal palace (begun in 1802 but never completed), finely situated above Belém, and which is now a modern Convention Complex. On the way there the road passes the subtropical park of the Museum of Overseas Agriculture (Museu Agrícola do Ultramar: on right) and the Adjuda Botanic Garden (on left: view), with a dragon tree planted in 1598.

To the N of the Ajuda Palace the Calçada do Mirante and its continuations run E to a large park, the Tapada da Ajuda, with an Observatory (view).

Farther N is the extensive Monsanto Forest Park (Parque Florestal de Monsanto: camp sites), which is traversed by the western motorway.
In the northern half of the park is an old fortress, the Forte de Monsanto.
Along the NW edge of the park runs the Aqueduto das Águas Livres (1728–48), an aqueduct 18 km/11 miles long which supplies Lisbon with drinking water.

Benfica

The elegant suburb of Benfica with its villas and handsome mansions, set in luxuriant gardens and parks, lies on the north-western outskirts of Lisbon.

Benfica is internationally famed as the home of the well-known and successful Sport Lisboa e Benfica football club, whose large stadium (built in 1854) in the Avenida do Marechal Carmona can accommodate 60,000 spectators.

In the Largo de São Domingos stands the church of São Domingos, belonging to a Dominican convent which was founded in 1399 and rebuilt after the 1755 earthquake. It contains azulejo pictures by António de Oliveira.

Near the church is the Casa do Marqueses de Fronteira, a palatial 17th c. mansion. In the beautiful gardens is a pool surrounded by blind arcades containing *azulejo pictures. The palace is private property, but the public are admitted to the gardens.

SURROUNDINGS of Lisbon

The* Ponte do 25 de Abril, an imposing suspension bridge, crosses the Tagus, here 2 km/1¼ miles wide, on the W side of Lisbon. On the far side of the river (also reached by car-ferry) is the little port of Cacilhas (fish restaurants), on a promontory below the town of Almada (pop. 40,000). From Cacilhas there is a fine view of Lisbon.

There is a still better *view from the Monument of Christ the King, erected on the hill above Almada in

Tower of Belém

1959. On a base 82 m/270 ft high (which contains a chapel) stands a 28 m/90 ft high reinforced concrete *figure of Christ* (elevator).

From Cacilhas a road runs along the Tagus and then a little way inland to the bathing resort of *Costa da Caparica*, on the **Costa de Lisboa** (see p. 104).

12 km/7½ miles N of Lisbon, at **Odivelas**, is the Cistercian *Convento de São Dinis e São Bernardo* (1295–1305), which was partly destroyed in the 1755 earthquake and rebuilt in Baroque style from 1757 onwards. In the church is the tomb of King Dinis, founder of the convent.

15 km/9 miles N of Lisbon, on the Rio Trançăo, is the little town of **Loures**, with a fine parish church (Igreja Matriz: rich talha dourada decoration in the Capela-mór). The nearby *Quinta do Correio-Mór*, a country house with a Baroque main block and two wings, contains azulejos, stucco decoration and paintings by José da Costa Negreiro; the kitchen (18th c.) has azulejo pictures.

10 km/6 miles farther NE is **Lousă**. The church of São Pedro has a fine Manueline doorway and azulejo decoration; in front of the church is a large fountain. Near the church of São Miguel is the Manueline doorway of a demolished church, now incorporated in a house.

*Estoril, Cascais and *Costa do Sol: see the entries for these places.

*Sintra: see p. 196.

Macao/Macau/ An Men

Territory under Portuguese administration (Território).
Area: 15·7 sq. km/6 sq. miles.
Altitude: 0–174 m/0–571 ft.
Population: 500,000.
Telephone code: 0 08 53.
(i) **Department of Tourism,**
　　Travessa do Paiva 1,
　　Macao;
　　tel. 7 72 18.

The former Portuguese overseas province of Macao (Portuguese Macau, Chinese An Men), now a territory under Portuguese administration, lies some 70 km/ 45 miles SW of the British colony of Hong Kong on the W side of the wide estuary of the Pearl River (Canton River).

The territory consists of the **Macao peninsula** (area 5·4 sq. km/2 sq. miles), with the capital, *Macao* (originally Cidade do Santo Nome de Deus de Macau), and two islands to the S, **Taipa** (3·6 sq. km/ 1½ sq. miles) and **Coloane** (6·7 sq. km/

2½ sq. miles), which are linked to the mainland by bridges and causeways.

HISTORY. – The first Portuguese trading post and fort was established in Macao in 1516, and in 1557 the Chinese granted Portugal a lease of the territory, in gratitude for Portuguese assistance in combating piracy. Macao thus became the first European colony in China.
The most celebrated Portuguese poet, Luís de Camões, lived in Macao from 1556 to 1558 as a financial and property executor, and completed the first six cantos of his "Lusiads" here.
The settlement soon developed into an important entrepôt in the East Indian trade, a focal point of political and diplomatic activity and a base for Catholic missionary work in the Far East.
From the middle of the 19th c. Macao's importance declined as a result of the economic rise of Hong Kong. A treaty with China in 1887 confirmed the status of Macao as a Portuguese colony.

From 1951 to 1976 Macao was a Portuguese overseas province with its own governor and full financial and administrative autonomy (currency unit the *pataca*). The political influences from the Chinese People's Republic, which increased in force from 1968 onwards, and the impossibility of suppressing such influences by a Portuguese military presence have demonstrated, however, that Macao still retains its age-old links with the culture and economy of China. The realisation of this, combined with financial considerations, led in 1974 to the withdrawal of all Portuguese troops and in 1976 to the grant of full autonomy in domestic affairs to the territory, Portugal remaining responsible only for its external relations. However, the Governor, traditionally a Portuguese army officer, is still appointed by the Lisbon government.

Some 98% of the population of 500,000 are Chinese; the rest are mostly Macao-born Portuguese (12,000) or of mixed race. The territory's flourishing economy is based on the production and export of textiles (particularly embroidery), matches, fireworks, small boats and, increasingly, electronic and optical apparatus. For a variety of historical as well as current political reasons the fruits of this activity are very unevenly distributed.

Macao attracts many day trippers and weekend visitors from Hong Kong, who come for its beautiful scenery, its five gambling houses (including a floating casino, the Macau Palace) and its reputation as a shoppers' paradise, offering goods of every conceivable kind, particularly antiques in great quantity and variety.

Madeira/ Archipélago da Madeira

Autonomous Region of Madeira (Região Autónoma da Madeira).
Area of islands: 796 sq. km/307 sq. miles.
Population: 270,000.

ⓘ **Turismo Funchal,**
Avenida de Arriaga 18,
P-5000 Funchal;
tel. (091) 2 56 58.

The archipelago of ****Madeira** lies in the Atlantic some **535 nautical miles SW of Lisbon and 240 miles N of Tenerife** in the Canaries, between lat. **33° 7' 34"** and **30° 1' 38" N** and between long. **15° 51' 11"** and **17° 15' 52" W.**

The group consists of the main island of **Madeira**, rising from a depth of 4000–5000 m/13,000–16,500 ft below sea level to an average height of something over 800m/2600 ft, with an area of 739 sq. km/285 sq. miles (length 58 km/36 miles, width 23 km/14 miles), together with the island of **Porto Santo** (highest point 507 m/1663 ft), 23 miles NE, and the three

almost uninhabited islets of *Ilhéu Chão, Deserta Grande* and *Ilhéu do Bugio,* 11 miles SW.

Also belonging to the group are the five uninhabited *Ilhas Selvagens* ("Wild Islands"; area 4 sq. km/1½ sq. miles) which lie some 170 miles S on the northern fringe of the Canaries.

HISTORY. – Legend has it that Madeira was part of the lost kingdom of Atlantis. The islands were known to the Phoenicians, and in the time of King Juba II of Mauretania (1st c. B.C.) they were called the *Insulae Purpuriae,* after the purple dye produced there.
When they were rediscovered by the Portuguese navigator João Gonçalves Zarco in 1419 they were uninhabited and covered with dense forest: hence the name **Ilha da Madeira** ("Island of Timber").

After the Portuguese colonisation Madeira prospered by the growing of sugar-cane and later also by the production of wine. Together with mainland Portugal and the Azores it was under Spanish rule from 1580 to 1640. Between 1807 and 1814 it was occupied by Britain.

The influx of tourists (at first mainly British) began in the middle of the 19th c. and has grown steadily since then.

There has for some time been a movement in Madeira, the Frente de Liberação da Madeira (FLAMA), which seeks to break away from Portugal. – Since 1980 the autonomous region of Madeira has had the right to issue its own stamps.

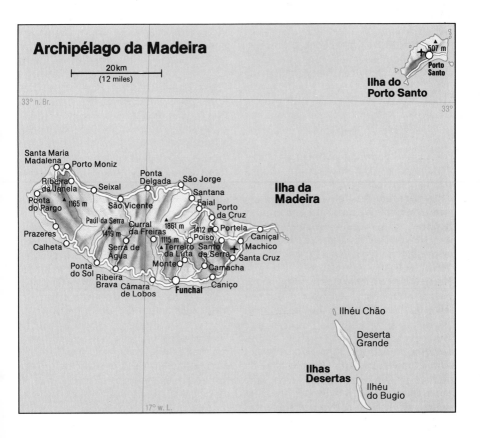

> **Wine-production** was introduced to Madeira soon after the discovery of the island and developed on a flourishing scale from the 17th c. onwards. Later, however, it suffered setbacks as a result of the ravages of a vine disease (*Oidium tuckeri*, from 1852) and phylloxera (1878–88) and competition from the port produced on the mainland.
>
> The main wine-producing area lies W of Funchal, around Câmara de Lobos, Estreito and Campanário.
>
> The most popular kinds of **madeira** are *Malmsey* (Malvasia), a sweet dessert wine; *Bual* or *Boal*; and the dry *Sercial*, which requires a long period of maturation. In order to speed up the process of maturation madeira is regularly stored for some months in hot houses (*estufas de calor*) at temperatures of between 40° and 60°C/104° and 140°F.
>
> Madeira has long had an international reputation as a wine for drinking before, after or between meals, but it also finds a use in the kitchen as a means of adding flavour to a sauce.

All the islands in the archipelago are hilly and, like the Spanish-owned Canaries, of volcanic origin. The oldest diabase formations have thus been overlaid since the Miocene period by many volcanic craters, now extinct. The later upthrust of the underlying rocks to some 400 m/1300 ft above their original level parallels the similar development in the Canaries.

The backbone of Madeira is a range of mountains with jagged ridges reminiscent of the Dolomites which runs in an E–W direction, reaching its highest point in the *Pico Ruivo* ("Red Peak") *de Santana* (1861 m/6106 ft). In the W of the island is the *Paúl de Serra* plateau, in the E the smaller plateau of *Santo António da Serra*.

On the southern and northern slopes of the range are the magnificent rugged valleys, enclosed within high cliffs, known as *currais* (singular *curral*), which make their way down to the sea in deep eroded gorges, patterned with alternating layers of volcanic ash and lava. The gorges on the N coast are particularly impressive.

The coasts of Madeira are steep and rocky, with narrow strips of coastal plain only here and there as the lava flows reach the sea.

Madeira owes its mild and equable climate to its southern latitude and its location in the open Atlantic. The daily and annual ranges of temperature on the sunny and sheltered S coast are lower than in any Mediterranean resort. The average January temperature in Funchal is 16·2°C/61·2°F, the average for July 29·8°C/85·6°F.

The average annual *rainfall* is 590 mm/ 23 in. Most of the rain falls between October and January or March in the form of cloudbursts. The number of hours of sunshine in the year averages 2124 (minimum of 97 hours in January, maximum of 251 hours in August). In spite of the nearness of the sea the relative humidity of the air is low (68%).

Water temperature average 17·4°C/ 63·6°F in February, 22·4°C/72·3°F in September.

From time to time there is a hot E wind, the *leste*, coming from Africa and bringing dust with it; but here it remains within tolerable limits, and drives away the banks of cloud which regularly form in the middle of the day at a height of 1200–1500 m/4000–5000 ft.

The *vegetation* of Madeira – the "Flor do Oceano" ("Flower of the Ocean") – is of almost tropical luxuriance, thanks to the mildness of the climate, the abundant winter rains and the system of irrigation which carries water from the hills to the fields and gardens along the coast through countless canals (*levadas*) and underground tunnels (*furados*).

The trees which grow here include not only pines and European deciduous species but also a great range of evergreen trees and shrubs of subtropical and tropical origin – palms, araucarias, hickory, cork-oaks, camphor trees and fig-trees, yuccas, medlars, mimosa, eucalyptus, bamboos, papyrus, tree ferns, agaves, etc. There are also small numbers of dragon trees, wild laurels and *Oreodaphne foetens* (Portuguese *tília*, a handsome tree of the laurel family, also known as Madeira ebony, which is found only on Madeira) – relics of the primeval forest which once covered the island and gave it its name but are now found only in the gorges on the N coast.

The gardens of Funchal – usually surrounded by high walls – are filled in winter and particularly in spring with a glorious profusion of flowers of every hue – roses, camellias, rhododendrons, azaleas, pelargoniums, begonias, bignonias (including *Jacaranda cuspidifolia*), daturas, bougainvilleas, wisterias and many more.

Only about a third of the island's area can be cultivated. Soon after the rediscovery of Madeira in the 16th c. deforestation by burning was begun and this led to the almost total destruction of the natural forest. Thereafter centuries of effort went into building up thousands of terraces (*poios*) on the hillsides which now constitute the major part of the cultivable land and give the island its characteristic appearance from the sea.

Since 1452 sugar-cane – grown on the N coast and, to an even greater extent, along the S coast – has been one of Madeira's most important products. Other crops include bananas, sweet potatoes, grain and early vegetables of all kinds. Much fruit is also grown, including in addition to melons and grapefruit such less usual species as the sugar apple or sweet-sop (*anona*), passion fruit (*maracujá*) and loquat.

A contribution is also made to the economy by cattle-farming and the associated manufacture of dairy products.

A subsidiary source of income since the mid 19th c. has been the making of *embroidery*, a craft introduced by an Englishwoman named Miss Phelps and which now provides employment for some 30,000 women, mostly working at home.

Much employment is also provided by the *tourist trade*, which has developed considerably in recent years.

Along the coasts *fishing* (tunny, mackerel, etc.) is an important source of revenue.

The *population*, originally purely Portuguese and still exclusively Portuguese-speaking, has in the course of the centuries received an admixture of Moorish, Jewish, Italian and African blood, particularly on the S coast.
The high population density (370 to the sq. km, or 958 to the sq. mile) and the predominance of large landholdings have long been reflected in a high emigration rate, particularly to South America (Brazil).

Funchal

Altitude: 0–111 m/0–365 ft.
Population: 100,000.
Post code: P-5000.
Telephone code: 091.
ⓘ **Turismo,**
Avenida de Arriaga 18;
tel. 2 56 58.

CONSULATE. – *United Kingdom:* c/o Agêncian Passos Freitas, Rua da Sé, tel. 2 74 69.

ACCOMMODATION on Madeira. – IN FUNCHAL: *Casino Parque*, L, 422 r., SP; *Savoy*, L, 359 r., SP; *Madeira Sheraton*, L, 311 r., SP; *Madeira Palácio*, L, 278 r., SP; *Reid's*, L, 180 r., SP.

Raga (apartments), I, 159 r., SP; *Duas Torres* (apartments), I, 118 r., SP; *Girassol*, I, 132 r., SP; *São João*, I, 208 r., SP; *Quinta do Sol*, I, 116 r., SP; *Vila Ramos*, I, 110 r., SP; *Bela-Vista* (apartments), I, 100 r., SP; *Santa Isabel*, I, 78 r., SP; *Nova Avenida*, I, 40 r.; *A Torre* (apartments), I, 39 r.

Monte Rosa, P I, 36 r.; *Greco*, P I, 28 r.; *Catedral*, P I, 24 r.; *Quinta da Penha da França*, P I, 16 r., SP; *Quinta Elisabete*, P I, 15 r., SP.

Do Mar (apartments), II, 260 r., SP; *Flora* (apartments), II, 170 r., SP; *Gorgulho* (apartments), II, 120 r., SP; *Estrelicia* (apartments), II, 148 r., SP; *Buganvilia* (apartments), II, 106 r., SP; *Mimosa* (apartments), II, 100 r., SP; *do Carmo*, II, 80 r., SP; *Santa Maria*, II, 75 r., SP; *Orquidea*, II, 70 r.; *Lido-Sol* (apartments), II, 60 r., SP; *Reno* (apartments), II, 47 r.; *Monte Carlo*, II, 40 r., SP; *Golden Gate*, II, 30 r., SP; *Casa Branca* (apartments), II, 30 r., SP; *Madeira*, II, 22 r., SP; *Santa Luzia* (apartments), II, 20 r., SP; *Miramar*, III, 32 r.

IN TERREIRO DA LUTA: *Pensão Windsor*, P III, 6 r.

IN SERRA DE ÁGUA: *Pousada dos Vinháticos*, 10 r.

IN CALHETA: *Porto Santo*, I, 120 r.

IN PORTO MONIZ: *Pensão Fernandes*, P III, 10 r.; *Lar da Baia*, P III, 10 r.

Reid's Hotel, Funchal

IN SANTANA: *Pensão Figueira*, P III, 8 r.

IN FAIAL: *Casa de Chá do Faial*, P III, 3 r.

IN SANTO DA SERRA: *Santo da Serra*, P III, 16 r.

IN MACHICO/ÁGUA DE PENA: *Atlántis Madeira*, L, 290 r., SP; *Dom Pedro da Madeira*, I, 218 r., SP; *Conjunto Turístico Matur* (holiday village), 521 r., SP.

IN SANTA CRUZ: *Pensão Matos*, P III, 5 r.

IN CANIÇO: *Galomar*, P II, 22 r., SP; *Inter-Atlis* (apartments), III, 133 r., SP; *Conjunto Turístico Caniço de Baixo* (holiday village), 4 r.

CAMP SITES. – None.

ACCOMMODATION on Porto Santo. – *Porto Santo*, II, 93 r.; *Pensão Residencial Sol*, P I, 20 r.; *Cristóvão Colombo*, P I, 8 r.; *Central*, P II, 12 r.; *Palmeira*, P IV, 12 r.; *Casa Fisherman*. – CAMP SITES. – None.

RECREATION and SPORT. – Swimming (only good beach on Porto Santo), water-skiing, scuba diving (Paúl do Mar, Ponta da Oliveira, Porto Cruz, Ponta Delgada, Porto Moniz); deep-sea fishing; walking; golf-course (9 holes) in Santo da Serra.

EVENTS. – *Festa da Senhora do Monte* (mid August), religious ceremonies and procession, traditional costumes, folk events; *Festas de São Silvestre*, New Year's Eve celebrations, with fireworks; Madeira Bach Festival, concerts of classical music.

Casino in Parque de Santa Catarina, Funchal.

*Funchal (from funcho, "fennel"), capital of the archipelago and the see of a bishop, is picturesquely situated (particularly when seen from the sea) amid rich subtropical vegetation on the S coast of Madeira. As the only port of any size on the island – though often exposed**

Wickerwork toboggan, Funchal

to heavy surf – it is an important port of call on the transatlantic shipping routes.

The town's steep streets, like most streets in the hilly parts of the island, are paved with smooth round basalt cobbles which make stout footwear very desirable.

Two characteristic local forms of transport are the *carros de bois*, sleds drawn by oxen, and the *carros de cesta*, toboggans with a basketwork frame which depend for their motive power on the force of gravity and are controlled by ropes held by two men running alongside.

SIGHTS. – On the seafront promenade, the Avenida do Mar, is the **Palácio de São Lourenço** (16th c.; much altered in later periods), the first fort built on Madeira, now the Governor's Palace. A little way E is the *Old Custom House* (Antiga Alfândega), also dating from the 16th c.

In front of the Governor's Palace, reaching out into the sea, is the *Cais* (landing-stage), from which there is a fine *view of the town.

From the N side of the palace the wide Avenida do Dr Manuel de Arriaga leads E to the **Cathedral** (*Sé*), in Manueline style, built between 1485 and 1514 – the first Portuguese cathedral in the country's overseas possessions. The most notable feature of the interior is the ceiling, of juniper-wood with ivory inlays.

To the W of the Governor's Palace, on the far side of the Avenida do Dr Manuel de Arriaga, is the *Jardim de São Francisco, luxuriantly planted with palms and other tropical species. On the S side of the park is the **Theatre** (*Teatro*).

Farther W the Avenida do Dr Manuel de Arriaga runs into the Praça do Infante. Above this square, to the SW, is the little *chapel of Santa Catarina* (15th c.), one of the oldest churches on the island, and beyond it is the **Parque de Santa Catarina**, on the site of an old cemetery, the Cemitério das Augustas. At the W end of the park, in the former *Quinta da Vigia* (once the residence of the Empress Elizabeth of Austria), is the **Casino**. From the terrace there is a magnificent *view of the town.

From the W end of the Avenida do Mar the Estrada da Pontinha continues SW along the seafront, passing below the Parque de Santa Catarina and the Casino, to the old **Molhe da Pontinha**, a breakwater begun in the 18th c. and several times extended, below the *Fort of Nossa Senhora da Conceição*. From the end of the breakwater there is a fine general view of the town.

On the E side of the Jardim de São Francisco the Rua de São Francisco runs N into Rua da Carreira, which leads E to the Praça do Município.
On the E side of this square stands the **Town Hall** (*Câmara Municipal*), on the W side the 17th c. **collegiate church of São João Evangelista**.
On the S side of the square (entrance at Rua do Bispo 21) is the former *Bishop's Palace*, now housing a **Museum of Sacred Art**.

From the N side of the Jardim de São Francisco a street leads up past the church of São Pedro (on right) and the **Municipal Museum** (opposite São Pedro, on left) to the **church of Santa Clara**, in the steep Calçada de Santa Clara. In this church, originally belonging to a convent, is the tomb of the navigator João Gonçalves Zarco, who rediscovered Madeira in 1419.
NW of the church is the former residence of the Zarco family, the *Quinta das Cruzes* (now a museum of art), set in beautiful gardens.

Continuing NW up the Calçada do Pico and turning left along Rua do Castelo, we come to the **Forte de São João do Pico** (1632), famed for its view.

Beyond the *Ribeira de João Gomes*, on the seafront is the *Campo Dom Carlos I*, the former drill ground.
Farther E, also on the seafront, is the **Forte de São Tiago** (1614), named after St James the Less, patron saint of Funchal.
Close by is the *church of Nossa Senhora do Socorro*, where a great procession is held annually on 1 May in memory of the plague which ravaged the town in 1538.

Also near here is the **Market** (*Mercado*), a lively and colourful spectacle which should not be missed.

Funchal harbour

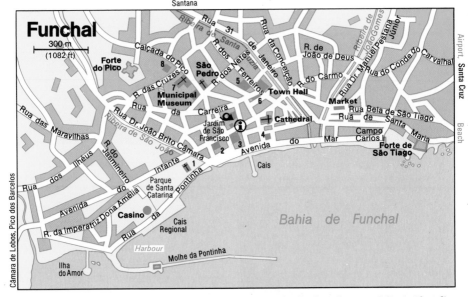

1 Chapel of Santa Catarina	3 Palácio de São Lourenço	5 Church of São João Evangelista	7 Church of Santa Clara
2 Theatre	4 Old Custom House	6 Museum of Sacred Art	8 Quinta das Cruzes

EXCURSIONS on Madeira

4 km/2½ miles from Funchal, on the old estate of *Quinta do Bom Sucesso*, is the very fine *Botanic Garden (*Jardim Botánico*), with a rich and varied collection of plants and flowers. From the terraces there are delightful views.

From Funchal an excellent road winds its way up between handsome villas and beautiful gardens to the little town of **Monte** (alt. 600 m/1970 ft; pop. 8000), 8 km/5 miles N. Set amid magnificent plane and oak forests, this was once a popular health resort.

On a spur of hill near the old cableway station is the *pilgrimage church of Nossa Senhora do Monte* (founded 1470, completely rebuilt in the 18th c.), with the tomb of the last Austrian Emperor, Karl I, who died in the nearby Quinta do Monte in 1922.

From the terrace in front of the church (68 steps) there is a superb *view of Funchal and the sea, extending SW as far as Cabo Girão. At the foot of the flight of steps is the neo-Baroque *chapel of Nossa Senhora da Conceição* (1906).

From here it is possible either to return direct to Funchal – perhaps in one of the local wickerwork toboggans – or to walk down by a longer route (3 hours) on beautiful (though inadequately way-marked) footpaths.

An attractive alternative is to continue 3 km/2 miles N (either by road or on footpaths) to **Terreiro da Luta** (876 m/2874 ft), with a *statue of Nossa Senhora da Paz* (Our Lady of Peace, commemorating the end of the First World War) and even more extensive *views than from the church at Monte.

From Terreiro da Luta the road continues up through the hills and comes in another 6 km/4 miles to the pass on *Pico Poiso* (1412 m/4633 ft). From here a good road (7 km/4¼ miles) goes off on the left to viewpoints on the *Pico de Juncal* (1800 m/5905 ft) and the *Pico de Arieiro* (1810 m/5940 ft), the second highest summit on the island. From both of these viewpoints there are magnificent panoramas of the central mountain range.

From the Poiso pass it is another 20 km/12½ miles through wild mountain scenery to the little town of **Faial**.

From Funchal to the Pico dos Barcelos and the Curral das Freiras (14 km/9 miles). – The road runs

NW from Funchal, at first through hilly country, well wooded and gay with flowers.

6 km/4 miles: **Pico dos Barcelos** (355 m/1165 ft). From the viewpoint terrace, with its profusion of flowers, there is a magnificent prospect of the S coast of Madeira.

The road continues uphill, with many bends, through a forest of eucalyptus trees, passing a number of superb viewpoints.

8 km/5 miles: *Eira de Serrato* (1026 m/3366 ft), a saddle on the NE slopes of the Pico Serrato.

From the saddle, or preferably from the nearby summit of the **Pico Serrato** ("Sawn-off Peak", 1115 m/3658 ft), there is perhaps the grandest **view on the island of the central mountain range of Madeira, extending from the Pico Ruivo (1861 m/6106 ft) and Pico Arieiro (1810 m/5939 ft) in the E to the Pico Grande (1607 m/5273 ft) and Pico do Jorge (1692 m/5515 ft) in the W.

From the saddle it is possible either to drive down on the modern road or to walk down the old bridle-path, endlessly twisting and turning, into the *Curral das Freiras ("Nuns' Valley") or *Gran Curral*, the crater of an extinct volcano, enclosed within high rock walls.

Far below, above the rock-strewn bed of the *Ribeira dos Socorridos*, can be seen the village of *Curral das Freiras* (690 m/2265 ft), an oasis in a waste of stone. The village was founded in the middle of the 16th c. by nuns from the convent of Santa Clara in Funchal who sought safety from pirate raids in the seclusion of the mountains and in later centuries pastured their cattle here.

From the Curral das Freiras a very attractive footpath descends through the valley of the Ribeira dos Socorridos to the N coast of the island.

AROUND THE ISLAND

From Funchal to Câmara de Lobos and São Vicente (55 km/34 miles). – The road runs W from Funchal on the *Estrada Monumental* (magnificent views), at some distance from the sea, and then circles the S side of the *Pico da Ponta da Cruz* (263 m/863 ft; *view), an old volcanic crater near the headland of the same name.

6 km/4 miles: road on right to *São Martinho* (250 m/820 ft; pop. 14,000) and the Pico dos Barcelos.

3 km/2 miles: **Câmara de Lobos** ("Wolves' Gorge"), a little fishing port picturesquely situated under the E side of **Cabo Girão** (589 m/1933 ft), a rugged headland falling almost vertically down to the sea. The village has long been a favourite with painters (among them Sir Winston Churchill).

The village owes its name to the wolf-fish which were once found here in large numbers. The grapes grown on the terraces around the village provide some of the finest wine on the island.

Beyond Câmara de Lobos the road climbs away from the coast, with numerous turns, to make its way around the N side of Cabo Girão.

6 km/4 miles: *Estreito de Câmara de Lobos* (500 m/1640 ft), a village renowned for its wine.

From here a minor road runs 4 km/2½ miles N to the *Jardim da Serra* (750 m/2460 ft), from which there are beautiful views.

Curral das Freiras

4 km/2½ miles: road on left (2 km/1¼ miles) to a *viewpoint above Cabo Girão.

6 km/4 miles: *Campanário* (300 m/985 ft), a village perched attractively on the hillside, with a 17th c. church.

6 km/4 miles: **Ribeira Brava** (pop. 7500), a little fishing town beautifully situated at the mouth of the stream of the same name. In the main square, which is paved with pebble mosaic, is a charming 16th c. church. Standing above the stream is a small 17th c. fort.

The picturesque Festas de São Pedro, with a procession and various folk events, take place annually here at the end of June.

The São Vicente road running N from Ribeira Brava, climbs inland, mostly on the W side of the river, through magnificent scenery.

12 km/7½ miles: *Pousada dos Vinháticos* (660 m/ 2165 ft), a good climbing base (Pico Grande, Pico do Jorge, Pico Ruivo, etc.) in a beautiful setting.

2 km/1¼ miles beyond this the road reaches the pass, the **Boca da Encumeada** (1007 m/3304 ft), with superb views of the Serra de Águia (1405 m/4610 ft) to the left and the Pico Grande to the right.
From the pass a path runs W to the Paúl da Serra plateau and the Rabaçal mountain hut.

The road now descends via *Rosário* to the coast.

10 km/6 miles: **São Vicente** (pop. 5000), a straggling settlement in wild mountain scenery on the N coast of the island. It was partly buried by a landslide in 1928.
São Vicente is a good base for the ascent of the *Pico dos Tanquinhos* (1524 m/5000 ft) and the *Pico Ruivo do Paúl* (1642 m/5387 ft), both offering magnificent views of mountain scenery, as well as opportunities for exploring the beautiful Paúl da Serra area.

From Ribeira Brava to Calheta, Porto Moniz and São Vicente (92 km/57 miles). Leave Ribeira on the coast road, going NW.

11 km/7 miles: **Ponta do Sol** (pop. 6000), a picturesque little place lying astride the stream of the same name. The church of Nossa Senhora da Luz

Câmara de Lobos

(15th c.) has a painted wooden ceiling and some fine examples of silversmith's work.
2 km/1¼ miles NE of Ponta do Sol, surrounded by extensive banana plantations, is the *Capela do Santo Espírito*, founded in the 16th c. by João Esmeraldo, one of Columbus's companions, who possessed large sugar-cane plantations in this area. The chapel was rebuilt in the 18th c.

5 km/3 miles: road on right (12 km/7½ miles N) to the plateau, often shrouded in mist, of **Paúl da Serra** (1419 m/4656 ft). Mainly a sheep-grazing area, this is also good country for mountain walkers.

5 km/3 miles: *chapel of Nossa Senhora de Loreto*, in Mozarabic and Manueline style.

9 km/5½ miles: **Calheta** (pop. 4000), a little port lying below the coast road amidst banana plantations and vineyards. The choir of the parish church (1639) has a carved wooden ceiling in Mudéjar style.
From Calheta a minor road runs 10 km/6 miles N to the *Rabaçal* hut (1143 m/3750 ft). From the "Balcão" (Balcony), a short distance NE of the hut, there are superb views of the *Risco Falls* and the green gorge known as *Vinte e Cinco Fontes* ("Twenty-five Springs").

Beyond the turning for Calheta the coast road continues to climb, with many bends.

4 km/2½ miles: road on left to **Estreito da Calheta** (339 m/1112 ft). The 16th c. Capela dos Reis Magos (Chapel of the Three Kings) has fine painted woodwork, a carved wooden ceiling and a triptych depicting the Three Kings.
From here a side road runs down to *Jardim do Mar*, in a beautiful setting.

5 km/3 miles: **Prazeres** (621 m/2038 ft), finely situated on a wooded plateau, with magnificent views.

6 km/4 miles: road on left to the village of *Fajã da Ovelha*, which lies in a forest setting at the foot of a massive crag, and to the little fishing settlement of *Paúl do Mar* (canning factory).

8 km/5 miles: **Ponta do Pargo** (473 m/1552 ft), near the western tip of the island (lighthouse, 375 m/ 1230 ft), in an area which has preserved many old traditions and customs. The beautiful old local costumes are still worn on feast-days and festivals. From the village a footpath leads down to the *Praia do Pesqueiro* ("Fisherman's Beach"), enclosed by cliffs.

10 km/6 miles: *Achadas da Cruz* (673 m/2208 ft).

6 km/4 miles: *Santa Maria Madalena* (500 m/1640 ft; pop. 800), with an unusual church.
The road now descends to the coast, with numerous sharp turns.

6 km/4 miles: **Porto Moniz** (pop. 2500), a little fishing port at the NW corner of the island. Protected by a rocky headland and the offshore islet of *Ilhéu Mole* with its fishermen's houses, this is the most sheltered harbour and the principal port on the N coast of Madeira.
2 km/1¼ miles SE of the village, on the rugged and much indented coast, are numerous natural pools (bathing).

3 km/2 miles: **Ribeira da Janela**, at the mouth of the little river of that name. Just off the mouth of the river

are three stacks (high, detached rocks), one of which, the *Ilhéu da Ribeira da Janela*, has the natural opening in the rock (*janela*, "window") from which the village gets its name.

7 km/4⅓ miles: *Seixal* (pop. 900), beautifully situated amid vineyards on the slopes of a projecting spur of hill.

Beyond Seixal begins the most impressive section of the *road along the N coast and one of the finest stretches of scenery in the whole of Madeira.
The magnificently engineered road, hewn out of the almost vertical cliffs, with numerous tunnels and projecting sections, runs high above the thundering sea and under the shadow of mighty rock faces, as if suspended between the sky and the ocean.

2 km/1¼ miles: viewpoint, with a famous*view of the gorge at the mouth of the *Ribeira do Inferno*.
The road continues, passing through tunnels and under the foaming waters of the stream.

5 km/3 miles: **São Vicente**.

From São Vicente to Machico and Funchal (90 km/56 miles). – The coast road continues E from São Vicente along the steep rock face.

8 km/5 miles: **Ponta Delgada** (pop. 2000), delightfully perched on a promontory amid orange-groves and sugar-cane plantations, with a simple little white church and a sea-water swimming pool.
Romaria festival on the first Sunday in September.

The road now leaves the coast and describes a wide bend inland before returning to the coast.

2 km/1¼ miles: **Boaventura** (pop. 3000), in a beautiful setting amid fruit orchards and plantations of willows (which supply the raw material for the local craft of wickerwork). There are many attractive walks from here, notably to the Curral das Freiras (p. 152).

7 km/4½ miles: *Arco de São Jorge*, beyond which is a viewpoint with a famous*prospect of the N coast.

9 km/5½ miles: **São Jorge** (pop. 3000), with a 17th c. Baroque church (fine altarpieces). From the nearby *Ponta de São Jorge* there are extensive*views of the N coast, extending to Porto Moniz in the W and Porto da Cruz in the E.

9 km/5½ miles: *Santana* (420 m/1380 ft; pop. 4500), chief town of the *Comarca de Santana*, the most fertile district on Madeira, and one of the most picturesque places on the island, with its thatched houses nestling in a profusion of flowers.
From Santana an attractive excursion can be made on a poor road (5 km/3 miles) to the mountain hut of *Casa das Queimadas* (883 m/2987 ft), continuing S on foot to the *Parque das Queimadas*, on the slopes of the **Pico Ruivo** (1861 m/6106 ft), which can be climbed from here. From the summit, in good visibility (which is exceptional), there are magnificent panoramic*views of the mountains of Madeira.

Beyond Santana the road again runs close to the sea, affording constantly changing views.

7 km/4½ miles: *Faial* (150 m/490 ft; pop. 1500), a modest little village surrounded by terraced vineyards, sugar-cane plantations and fields of vegetables. From the terrace in front of the church there is a fine view.

Penha de Águia

3 km/2 miles: road on right (EN103) over the Polso pass to Funchal.
The coast road then continues around the mighty crag known as the***Penha de Águia** ("Eagle Rock", 594 m/1949 ft).

3 km/2 miles: **Porto da Cruz** (pop. 4000), a little port situated at the foot of high rock walls (beach of volcanic ash).
Beyond Porto da Cruz the road turns away from the sea and climbs.

6 km/4 miles: **Portela pass** (662 m/2172 ft), with a *view of Porto da Cruz and Machico Bay. From here Road EN102 (30 km/19 miles) runs direct to Funchal, through beautiful forest scenery, via the health resort of **Santo (António) da Serra** (800 m/2625 ft; pop. 2000; golf-course), set on a plateau with great expanses of pastureland, and **Camacha** (715 m/2345 ft; pop. 6500), a little town notable for its preservation of old customs and traditions and for its thriving wickerwork industry.

3 km/2 miles before Funchal, to the left of the road, is the *Quinta do Palheiro Ferreiro*, a beautiful private park to which the public are admitted.

Beyond the Portela pass the main road descends the Machico valley to the coast.

9 km/5½ miles: **Machico** (pop. 11,000), an important fishing port (boatyard) at the mouth of the Rio Machico, with a State-run embroidery school. This was the landing place of the first settlers. The town is said to be named after an Englishman called Machin who was shipwrecked here about 1344 while eloping with his bride and who has been claimed as the discoverer of Madeira.
The Capela dos Milagres (1420; rebuilt in the 19th c.) is said to have been erected over the graves of the two lovers. The late 15th c. parish church (originally Manueline but later much altered) has a painted wooden ceiling. In the Capela de São Roque are fine azulejo paintings. Above the northern entrance to the bay stands a small 17th c. fort.
On the evening of 8–9 October the feast of the Senhor dos Milagres is celebrated by the lighting of bonfires on the surrounding hills.

From Machico Road EN101–3 runs 13 km/8 miles E via the little whaling station of **Caniçal** (8 km/5 miles) to the bathing beach of *Prainha*, on the S side

The rugged cliffs of Cabo Girão

of the narrow peninsula of Ponta de São Lourenço, the most easterly tip of Madeira. There are numerous fossils in this area.

The coast road continues SE from Machico, running close to the sea.

1 km/¾ mile: road on right (1 km/¾ mile) to the *Miradouro Francisco Álvares Nóbrega*, with a beautiful view of Machico Bay and the São Lourenço peninsula.
The main road continues along the coast, passing the new holiday village of *Água de Pena* and the *Santa Catarina* airport.

6 km/4 miles: **Santa Cruz**, lying below the road, with a 16th c. church and town hall. Around the village are extensive banana and sugar-cane plantations and terraced vineyards. A subsidiary source of revenue is the catching of ornamental fish.

11 km/7 miles: *Caniço* (229 m/751 ft; pop. 7500), at the mouth of the Rio Caniço, has an 18th c. parish church and the Manueline chapel of the Madre de Deus (16th c.).
There is an attractive walk from Caniço to *Cabo Garajau*.

4 km/2½ miles: *Miradouro do Pináculo*, from which there is a magnificent * view.

5 km/3 miles: **Funchal**.

EXCURSIONS by Sea

Some 23 nautical miles NE of Madeira (by boat, several times weekly, 3 hours; by air, twice weekly,

Columbus's house, Porto Santo

Porto Santo

20 minutes) is the table-shaped island of **Porto Santo** (pop. 3000; highest point Pico do Facho, 517 m/1696 ft), surrounded by five small rocky islets. Porto Santo, 12 km/7½ miles long by 6 km/4 miles wide, is very different in character from the main island of Madeira. With its expanses of sandy plateau and its arid climate it can be developed for agriculture only at great expense. In the little port of Porto Santo or Vila Baleira on the SE coast, the chief settlement on the island, is a house in which Columbus (whose father-in-law was the first governor) lived about 1479.
Porto Santo has the only * beach of fine sand in the whole of the Madeira archipelago, extending for several kilometres along the full length of the S coast. The facilities for visitors, however, are still very modest. The island is good walking country, with fine viewpoints which can be reached only on foot.

Some 11 miles SE of Madeira are the **Ilhas Desertas**, three waterless and uninhabited rocky islets: *Deserta Grande* (491 m/1611 ft), *Ilhéu de Bugio* (411 m/1348 ft) and the flat *Ilhéu Chão* (104 m/341 ft). Landing is possible only when the sea is calm. The islands have many features of geological interest, and are the home of the wolf spider (*Geolycosa ingens*), one of the largest European spiders. The sea-caves on Deserta Grande are the haunt of seals.

Mafra

Historical province: Estremadura.
District: Lisboa (Lisbon).
Altitude: 237 m/778 ft.
Population: 7000.
Post code: P-2640.
Telephone code: 061.
ⓘ **Turismo,**
　Avenida do 25 de Abril;
　tel. 5 20 23.

ACCOMMODATION. – *Albergaría Castelão*, II, 20 r.

CAMP SITE on road to Ericeira.

The modest little town of Mafra, 50 km/30 miles NW of Lisbon, is widely famed for its gigantic * palace-monastery, the largest complex of the kind in the Iberian peninsula.

Here King João V founded the "Mafra school" of sculpture, at which such leading artists as José Almeida and Joaquim Machado de Castro taught.

The ***Palácio Nacional de Mafra** was founded in 1717 by João V and his queen, Maria Ana of Austria, in fulfilment of a vow made in 1711 and in thanksgiving for the birth of an heir (later José I). It was built by a force of almost 50,000 workmen under the direction of the Italian-trained German architect Johann Friedrich Ludwig and his son Johann Peter Ludwig and completed in 1730.

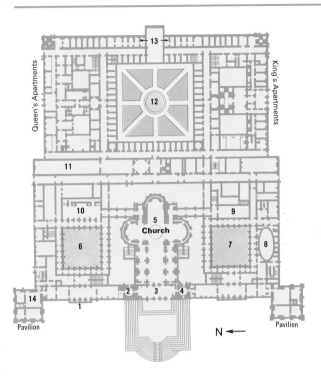

Palácio Nacional de Mafra

1 Entrance

2 Tower

3 Vestibule (statues of saints)

4 Tower

5 Dome

6 Cloister

7 Cloister

8 Chapterhouse

9 Sacristy

10 Campo Santo Chapel

11 Refectory

12 Cloister garth (gardens)

13 Library (upper floor)

14 Museum of Sculpture

This huge building, emulating the Escorial, Philip II's palace-monastery near Madrid, but intended by its founder to surpass even the Escorial in size and splendour, is the supreme exemplification in Portugal of cool Baroque magnificence, lavish extravagance and absolute royal power.

Built on an almost square plan and designed with the strictest regard for symmetry, the palace is 251 m/825 ft long by 221 m/725 ft wide and covers a total area of 40,000 sq. m/48,000 sq. yd. It has 900 rooms, 2500 windows and 5200 doors.

The convent buildings were originally occupied by Franciscans but in the late 18th c. were transferred to the Augustinians. The royal apartments were hardly ever occupied.

SIGHTS. – In the middle of the main front, which is precisely articulated and almost without decoration, is the **church**, flanked by twin towers 68 m/223 ft high (the N tower can be climbed: recommended). The carillon of 114 bells was made by an Antwerp bell-founder named Lavache.
In the vestibule of the church are 14 large marble statues of saints by the Italian sculptor Alessandro Giusti. – The aisleless interior is faced with white marble and has a coffered barrel-vaulted ceiling. Above the crossing is a mighty dome 70 m/230 ft high.

Visitors are shown the *Sacristy* and various convent buildings, including the *Pharmacy*, the *Hospital* (with its original 18th c. decoration and fittings), the *Kitchen*, faced with blue azulejos, the oval *Chapterhouse* and the cells occupied by the monks (who once numbered some 300).

The royal apartments contain valuable 18th c. furniture.

Of particular interest is the *Library, 88 m/290 ft long, with 30,000 volumes, including many incunabula and manuscripts, first editions of Camões' "Lusiads" and the plays of Gil Vicente, a trilingual Bible of 1514 and the earliest edition of Homer in Greek.

In the pavilion at the N end of the main front is the *Museum of Comparative Sculpture* (Museu de Escultura Comparada), with casts of famous works by Portuguese, Italian and French sculptors of the 12th–16th c.

To the rear of the palace extends the *Tapada de Mafra*, the royal deer-park, enclosed by a wall 20 km/12½ miles long, in which the royal family still hunted at the beginning of the 20th c.

The little town of **Mafra** has a fine Gothic church of the 13th–14th c., carefully restored, the *church of Santo André*, with the tombs of Dom Diogo de Sousa and his wife.

SURROUNDINGS. – 11 km/7 miles W of Mafra is the little fishing port of **Ericeira** (pop. 3000), with a good beach which attracts many bathers.

Marvão

Historical province: Alto Alentjo.
District: Portalegre.
Altitude: 862 m/2828 ft.
Population: 1000.
Post code: P-7330.
Telephone code: 0 45.
ⓘ **Turismo Portalegre,**
   Rua do Dr. Matos,
   Magalhães;
   tel. 9 32 26.

ACCOMMODATION. – *Pousada de Santa Maria*, 8 r.

The little market town of Marvão, the Roman Herminio Minor, lies near the Spanish frontier on a steep-sided hill in the Serra de São Mamede. Its great attractions are its unspoiled medieval atmosphere and the castle which rears up above the town.

This strategically situated little town was strongly fortified by King Dinis in the 13th c. In 1833, during the Miguelist wars, it was a stronghold of the Liberals.

SIGHTS. – The town is still completely surrounded by its medieval **walls**. The steep and narrow streets are paved with stone slabs, spanned by flying buttresses and lined with flower-decked houses, many of them with fine 17th c. wrought-iron window grilles.

Above the town stands the **Castle** (*Castelo*), built in the 13th c. and enlarged in the 15th and 17th c.
From the *keep*, enclosed within several rings of walls, there are panoramic *views, extending northward to Castelo Branco and the Serra da Estrêla, southward and westward to the Serra da São Mamede and eastward to Spain.

Outside the town is the former *Convento de Nossa Senhora da Estrêla* (originally

15th c.), now a hospital. The church has a fine Gothic doorway.

SURROUNDINGS. – 12 km/7½ miles NW is **Castelo de Vide** (see p. 97); 12 km/7½ miles SW is **Portalegre** (p. 180).

Matosinhos

Historical province: Douro Litoral.
District: Porto (Oporto).
Altitude: sea level.
Population: 25,000.
Post code: P-4450.
Telephone code: 0 2.
ⓘ **Turismo,**
   at the Market;
   tel. 93 44 14.

ACCOMMODATION. – IN MATOSINHOS: *Porto Mar*, III, 32 r.; *Central*, P III, 8 r. – CAMP SITE.

IN LEÇA DA PALMEIRA: *São Brás*, P III, 14 r.

IN LEÇA DE BALIO: *Estalagem Via Norte*, L, 12 r.

EVENT. – *Festas do Senhor de Matosinhos* (Whitsun), a popular festival with bull-running and fireworks.

The industrial town and port of Matosinhos, 9 km/5½ miles N of Oporto at the mouth of the little Rio Leça, is also a popular resort, with an excellent beach. The town has large fish-canning factories.

SIGHTS. – The **church of Bom Jesús de Bouças**, originally built in the 16th c., was enlarged in the 18th c.
Notable features of the interior are the carved and gilded decoration of the choir, the fine coffered ceiling and a very ancient and much revered crucifix (pilgrimage at Whitsun).

There is a fine municipal park, the **Quinta da Conceição**, on the site of a convent now represented only by the 18th c. *chapel of São Francisco* and a 15th c. *cloister*.

At the mouth of the river is the modern port of **Leixões**, its harbour protected by two breakwaters reaching out pincer-like into the sea, respectively 1597 m/1750 yd and 1145 m/1250 yd long. Leixões acts as an outer harbour for Oporto.

SURROUNDINGS. – Opposite Matosinhos on the right bank of the Leça (bascule bridge) is the little fishing town of **Leça da Palmeira** (oil refinery), with many handsome old houses and a popular beach. Farther N is the beach of *Boa Nova*, at the foot of a high cliff (lighthouse; wide* views), on top of which is the pilgrimage chapel of São João.

Farther NE, in **Leça do Balio**, is a Romanesque and Gothic fortified church (1336) which belonged to a convent of the Knights Hospitallers of St John of Jerusalem.
The church has richly carved capitals, 16th c. tombs and a beautiful Manueline font (16th c.). Adjoining the church is a Manueline *Calvário* (1514).

There is an attractive drive along the Leça valley. At *Santa Cruz de Bispo* the river is spanned by two Roman bridges, the Ponte de Guifões and the Ponte do Caro.

Mértola

Historical province: Baixo Alentjo.
District: Beja.
Altitude: 85 m/280 ft.
Population: 7000.
Post code: P-7750.
Telephone code: 0 86.

ⓘ **Turismo Beja,**
Rua do Capitão João Francisco de Sousa 25,
P-7800 Beja;
tel. (0 84) 2 36 93.

ACCOMMODATION. – None in the town. See under
BEJA.

The ancient little town of Mértola, still retaining a very Moorish appearance with its narrow and twisting lanes, is picturesquely set on the slopes above the left bank of the Guadiana, which is joined here by its tributary the Oreias.

The site was occupied in Roman times by the town of *Mirtilis*, mentioned by the Alexandrian geographer Ptolemy (2nd c. A.D.), and later was a Moorish stronghold.

SIGHTS. – Above the town are the ruins of the old **Moorish castle**, the *Castelo*

Mértola – view from the castle

dos Mouros, which was considerably enlarged in the late 13th c.
From the castle there is a magnificent *view of the town and the River Guadiana, which is navigable below this point.

Below the castle stands the fortified Romanesque **parish church** (*Igreja Matriz*), with crenellated walls and a handsome Renaissance doorway.
The church was converted in the 13th c. from an earlier mosque – an origin revealed by the square ground-plan, the arrangement of the clustered columns, the mihrab behind the high altar and the horseshoe arch above the sacristy door.

Another relic of the Moorish period is an old *tower* projecting into the river.

Minho

Historical province: Minho.
Districts: Braga and Viana do Castelo.
Area: 4838 sq. km/1868 sq. miles.
Population: 936,000.
Chief town: Braga.

ⓘ **Turismo Braga,**
Avenida da Liberdade 1,
P-4700 Braga;
tel. (053) 2 25 50.

The ancient province of Minho in the extreme NW of Portugal – formerly known, more accurately, as Entre Douro e Minho, the land between the rivers Douro and Minho – lies to the S of the river the name of which it bears. It is bounded on the S by the province of Douro Litoral and on the E by Spain and the province of Trás-os-Montes; on the W it lies open to the Atlantic on the "Costa Verde", a stretch of coast of almost northern aspect.

Formerly part of Castile the Minho region has, ethnically and culturally, a unity with Galicia – an affinity which is reflected also in certain linguistic features which the two provinces have in common.

The people of the Minho (*Minhotos*) are particularly attached to tradition and to the Catholic faith. In this region the numerous church festivals and *romarias* are celebrated with great enthusiasm, to the accompaniment of music and dancing.

The Minho region is occupied by an ancient mountain massif of granites, gneisses, argillaceous schists and quartzes which increases in height towards the E, reaching almost 2000 m/ 6560 ft in the **Serra do Gerês**, and is traversed from NE to SW by the three wide parallel valleys of the **Minho**, the *Lima* and the *Cávado*. These valleys allow moisture-bearing winds from the Atlantic to penetrate far inland, making this the rainiest part of the whole Iberian peninsula (1000–3000 mm/40–120 in. a year). Numerous recent fault lines allow the water to sink deep underground, where it is heated and re-emerges in many places as thermal springs.

Espigueiros – the typical Minho storehouses

The economy of the province is based on *agriculture*. In the fertile, well-watered depressions and valleys the land yields two harvests a year (wheat followed by maize), supplying not only food for human consumption but also fodder for livestock, the rearing of which is a thriving occupation.

Another major source of revenue is the production of *wine*. The vines, trained in the ancient Roman fashion on young trees (mainly eucalyptus) or on trellises, produce the much esteemed *vinho verde* ("green wine") or *vinho não murado* ("unripened wine"). Since autumn comes early here, the grapes are harvested early, yielding a wine which is characterised by youthful freshness, a slightly sharp taste and a natural effervescence.

The higher ground, deforested in ancient times, now provides pasturage for sheep.

In addition to agriculture the region has old-established *small-scale industries* – textiles (originally linen-weaving, now also cotton), the manufacture of cutting instruments and blades, leather-working, pottery and crafts such as embroidery and lace-making. There is no heavy industry. In recent years hydroelectric power stations have been established on the rivers in the mountains.

With its highly fertile soil, the Minho region has always been densely populated; but as a result of the small size of most of the farm holdings and the uneconomic working which this involves, it has never been able to provide adequate subsistence for its population. In consequence many of the men, particularly the younger ones, have taken up seasonal employment in South America (particularly Brazil) or, in recent years, have found work in Germany and other European countries. This male emigration has had the result that far more women than men are now employed in agriculture.

The scenery of the Minho is more reminiscent of northern Europe than of the south. The abundant supplies of granite have led to the development of a characteristic local style of building in stone, giving the towns and villages an appearance of greyness. All over the region can be seen the typical Minho *espigueiros* – small granaries or storehouses built on a high stone base for protection from vermin.

Miranda do Douro

Historical province: Trás-os-Montes.
District: Bragança.
Altitude: 690 m/2264 ft.
Population: 6000.
Post code: P-5210.
Telephone code: 073.

(i) **Turismo Bragança,**
    Avenida do 25 de Abril,
    P-5300 Bragança;
    tel. (092) 2 22 72.

ACCOMMODATION. – *Pousada de Santa Catarina*, 12 r.; *Planalto*, P II, 8 r.

EVENT. – *Festas de Santa Bárbara* (mid August), a popular festival with folk dances by men.

The grey old episcopal city of Miranda do Douro lies on a rocky hill above the deep valley of the Douro (Spanish Duero), dammed

just below the town, which here marks the frontier with Spain (no frontier crossing).

The remoteness of this region, one of the most thinly populated parts of Portugal, has acted as a brake on its cultural and linguistic development, so that it has preserved not only many old customs and traditions but also a local dialect close to Vulgar Latin, the *lingua charra* or *mirandês*.

Traditional crafts such as weaving and pottery are still widely practised.

Every year on the third Sunday in August (the feast of St Barbara) the old dance of the *pauliteiros* (wooden staves) is danced – a dance for men only which is reminiscent of the sword dances of the Romans.

SIGHTS. – The 12th c. castle which once dominated the town was destroyed by an explosion in 1760, leaving only a *watch-tower*.

On a projecting spur of rock above the Douro stands the **Cathedral** (*Sé*), a 16th c. building with a wide W front flanked by towers.

The spacious interior is notable for its massive piers. The high altar depicts scenes from the life of the Virgin and the Crucifixion. A quaint feature is the "Infant Jesus in an Opera-Hat", a naive ex-voto of the mid 19th c.

From the terrace in front of the Cathedral there is an impressive *view of the grey rocky valley of the Douro.

Near the Cathedral is the Baroque arcaded courtyard of the Archbishop's Palace, burned down in 1706.

In the town, particularly around the market square, there are a number of handsome old *burghers' houses* with coats of arms.

SURROUNDINGS. – 17 km/11 miles W, at the village of *Caçarelhos*, are large marble and alabaster quarries and beautiful stalactitic caves.

5 km/3 miles farther W is the village of **Vimioso**, with the ruins of a castle of King Dinis which was destroyed in the 18th c.

3 km/2 miles E of Miranda do Douro is the **Barragem de Miranda do Douro**, the first of a series of five dams on the Douro built and operated jointly by Spain and Portugal.

Some 25 km/15 miles downstream the *Barragem do Picote* is followed by the *Barragem da Bemposta*, the *Barragem de Aldeladávila* and the *Barragem de Saucelne*.

Mirandela

Historical province: Trás-os-Montes.
District: Bragança.
Altitude: 250 m/820 ft.
Population: 6000.
Post code: P-5370.
Telephone code: 078.

ⓘ **Turismo Bragança,**
Avenida do 25 de Abril,
P-5300 Bragança;
tel. (092) 22 27 2.

ACCOMMODATION. – *Mira-Tua*, III, 32 r.; *Flórida*, P III, 10 r.; *Praia*, P IV, 12 r.

EVENTS. – *Festas do Senhor do Amparo* and *Deira de Santiago* (end of July–beginning of August), religious and folk festivals with sporting contests.

The attractive little town of Mirandela lies on the left bank of the Rio Tua in one of the most isolated areas in Portugal.

SIGHTS. – On an eminence in the heart of the town stands the 18th c. **Paço dos Távoras**, with a granite Baroque façade, now the Town Hall.

There was a crossing of the Rio Tua here in Roman times, and the position of the Roman bridge is now occupied by a **medieval bridge** of 18 arches, 232 m/254 yd long. Beside it is a modern bridge.

SURROUNDINGS. – 33 km/20 miles SW is **Murça**, which was granted a municipal charter by King Sancho II in 1224. It is famous for the granite figure of a *wild boar, the subject of many legends, which was originally thought to date from the Iron Age but is now assigned to the 7th c.

Other features of interest are the 17th c. church of the Misericórdia and a Manueline *pelourinho* (pillory column, the symbol of municipal authority) in the pretty market square.

28 km/17 miles S of Mirandela is the little country town of **Vila Flor** (alt. 565 m/1855 ft; pop. 2000), with a handsome 18th c. palace, an old town hall, an azulejo-clad parish church and remains of the town walls.

Monção

Historical province: Minho.
District: Viana do Castelo.
Altitude: 98 m/322 ft.
Population: 2500.
Post code: P-4950.
Telephone code: 0 51.

ⓘ **Turismo,**
Largo Loreto;
tel. 5 27 57.

ACCOMMODATION. – *Albergaria Atlântico*, I, 24 r.; *Internacional*, P II, 16 r.; *Mané*, P II, 8 r.; *Chave d'Ouro*, P II, 8 r.; *Central*, P III, 21 r.; *Vaticano*, P III, 15 r.

IN PESO DE MELGAÇO: *Pensão Boavista*, P II, 25 r.; *Águias de Melgaço*, IV, 48 r.; *Rocha*, IV, 32 r.

EVENTS. – *Festa do Corpo de Deus*, Corpus Christi celebrations, with historical pageant play, "St George and the Dragon"; *Festas da Virgem das Dores* (end August), church festival with display of handicrafts and fireworks.

The old fortified frontier town of Monçâo, situated on the left bank of the River Minho (Spanish Miño) opposite the Spanish town of Salvatierra de Miño, is now a spa, with hot springs.

Local gastronomic specialities are sea-trout and lampreys (*lampreias*).

SIGHTS. – The Romanesque **parish church** of Santa Maria dos Anjos ("of the Angels"), dating from the 12th c. but later rebuilt, has a beautiful Manueline main doorway. The church contains a number of old tombs, including that of Deuladeu Martins, who defended the town against the Spaniards in 1368, a Manueline chapel (1521), rich talha dourada decoration and azulejos in the choir.

The town, still surrounded by its 17th c. walls, has many attractive balconied houses. Above the town are the ruins of a medieval castle.

SURROUNDINGS. – 3 km/2 miles S is the imposing early 19th c. *Brejoeira Palace*, set in beautiful gardens.

24 km/15 miles E is the health resort of **Peso de Melgaço** (alt. 180 m/590 ft), with mineral springs. The neighbouring village of *Melgaço* has a Romanesque parish church (12th c.), and, above the village, a 12th c. castle.

Montemor-o-Velho

Historical province: Beira Litoral.
District: Coimbra.
Altitude: 51 m/167 ft.
Population: 3000.
Post code: P-3140.
Telephone code: 039.
ⓘ **Turismo Coimbra,**
Largo da Portagem,
P-3000 Coimbra;
tel. (0 39) 2 55 76.

ACCOMMODATION. – None in the town. See under COIMBRA and FIGUEIRA DA FOZ.

The little town of Montemor-o-Velho, situated on a hill above the right bank of the Mondego a few kilometres E of its mouth, was of importance during the Middle Ages as an outpost defending the approach to Coimbra against the Moors advancing from Estremadura.

Montemor-o-Velho was the birthplace of the navigator Cavaleiro Diogo de Azambuja (1432–1518), the writer and world traveller Fernão Mendes Pinto (*c.* 1510–83) and the poet Jorge de Montemor (1520–61).

SIGHTS. – Above the town are the forbidding ruins of the 11th c. **Castle** (*Castelo*; *view), enclosed within a double circuit of walls, oval in plan, with imposing towers and battlements.
Within the walls is the Manueline *church of Santa Maria de Alcáçova* (16th c.) designed by the famous architect Boytaca, with a beautiful wooden ceiling, azulejo decoration in Moorish style (16th c.) and a double font.

In the romantic little town itself is the Manueline **church of Nossa Senhora dos Anjos** (Our Lady of the Angels), originally a monastic church. In the spacious interior are some notable works of Renaissance sculpture of the Coimbra school, including the magnificent sarcophagus of Diogo de Azambuja, carved during his lifetime by Diogo Pires-o-Moço.

SURROUNDINGS. – 11 km/7 miles NE is the little town of **Tentúgal**, with the church of Nossa Senhora do Mourão, belonging to the former Carmelite convent (15th c.), the church of the Misericórdia (16th c.) and a number of handsome burghers' houses.
3 km/2 miles farther NE the **church** of the *Hieronymite convent of São Marcos* (burned down in 1860) was a dependency of the convent at Belém; it was founded in 1452 by Dona Brites de Meneses, later Afonso V's wife, and subsequently became the burial-place of the Silva Meneses family. The decoration of the church, with its clearly articulated structure, betrays the hand of the architect of the convents of Belém and Santa Cruz (Coimbra).

Moura

Historical province: Baixo Alentjo.
District: Beja.
Altitude: 185 m/605 ft.
Population: 12,000.
Post code: P-7860.
Telephone code: 0 85.
ⓘ **Turismo,**
Praça de Sacadura Cabral;
tel. 5 22 29.

ACCOMMODATION. – *Moura*, III, 37 r.; *Alentejana*, P III, 8 r.

EVENT. – *Festa da Senhora do Monte do Carmo* (beginning of October), a church festival with a series of folk events.

The little spa of Moura (originally Vila da Moura, "town of the Moorish girl"), the Roman Nova Civitas Arruccitana, situated on the left bank of the Guadiana, has preserved many features which betray its Moorish past, in particular the charming old quarter called the Mouraria with its low white houses, often faced with azulejos, and characteristic openwork chimneys.

The name of the town is explained by a romantic legend. It is said that a young Moorish girl named Salúquia, daughter of the principal civic dignitary, threw herself from the battlements of the castle when her betrothed husband fell into a Christian ambush and was killed on the eve of their marriage; after which the Christian army, wearing the garments of the defeated enemy forces, tricked the guards and captured the castle. The event is commemorated in the town's coat of arms, which shows the Moorish girl at the foot of the castle walls. – Almotadide, Emir of Seville, wrote many of his poems in Moura, as an inscription on the Moorish fountain recalls.

SIGHTS. – Within the walls of the **Castle** (*Castelo*; *view), originally Moorish but rebuilt by King Dinis at the end of the 13th c., is the *church of Nossa Senhora da Assunção*, with the *Capela dos Rolins*, which contains the tombs of Álvaro and Pedro Rodrigues.

In the park of the spa establishment, below the castle, are the alkaline **mineral springs** which are used in the treatment of rheumatism.

In the town's main square, the Praça de Sacadura Cabral, stands the Gothic and Manueline **church of São João Baptista**, with a purely Manueline doorway. In the right-hand side chapel are azulejo pictures depicting the Cardinal Virtues.

Opposite the church is the **Town Hall** (*Município*), with arcades, and in front of it the *Três Bicas fountain* (with three jets).

Also of interest is the **church of the Carmo**, belonging to the oldest Carmelite convent in Portugal; it has an elegant 16th–17th c. cloister.

SURROUNDINGS. – 3 km/2 miles SE are the mineral springs of *Pisões-Moura*, which yield a table water (Água Castelo) much esteemed in Portugal.

Nazaré

Historical province: Estremadura.
District: Leiria.
Altitude: 0–110 m/0–360 ft.
Population: 9000.
Post code: P-2450.
Telephone code: 0 62.

ⓘ **Turismo,**
   Rua de Mouzinho de Albuquerque 72;
   tel. 4 61 20.

ACCOMMODATION. – IN NAZARÉ: *Da Nazaré*, II, 52 r.; *Praia*, II, 40 r.; *Madeira*, P II, 33 r.; *Central*, P II, 19 r.; *Dom Fuas*, III, 40 r.; *Ribamar*, P III, 22 r.; *Beira-Mar*, P III, 18 r.; *Europa*, P III, 16 r.; *Leonardo*, P III, 14 r.; *Nazarense*, P III, 10 r.; *Rocha*, P IV, 10 r.; *Ideal*, P IV, 8 r.

IN SÃO MARTINHO DO PORTO: *Concha*, I, 27 r.; *Americana*, P II, 26 r.; *Carvalho*, P II, 34 r.; *Parque*, III, 36 r.; *Luz*, P III, 8 r.

EVENTS. – *Carnival* (days before Ash Wednesday); *Romaria da Senhora de Nazaré* (beginning of September), church festival with folk events, bullfights, etc.

The very picturesque little fishing town of *Nazaré has drawn increasing numbers of visitors in recent years owing to its excellent beaches and the colourful life and activity of the port, still largely unspoiled. It is now one of the most popular resorts on the Portuguese Atlantic coast.

Women's costumes, Nazaré

Nazaré – a bird's eye view of the town and the beach

1 Pilgrimage Chapel of   2 Chapel of Memória
  Nossa Senhora de Nazaré   3 Church of Misericórdia

The people of Nazaré have preserved their old traditional costumes. The fishermen wear checkered shirts, trousers checkered in a different pattern and black stocking caps, in which they keep money and a variety of odds and ends. The younger women wear wide skirts reinforced by numerous petticoats (up to seven in number) and richly decorated with lace.

Visitors should not miss the performances of folk dancing and singing arranged by the local tourist office, which in spite of increasing commercialisation are still entirely authentic.

Nazaré is believed to have been founded by the Phoenicians, and in ancient times was situated in a bay sheltered on the N by the *Monte Sítio*, but which was later silted up. Although until quite recently Nazaré had no real harbour, it is nevertheless one of the principal fishing towns on the Portuguese Atlantic coast, its population depending almost exclusively on fishing for their subsistence. The man-made harbour which has quite recently been constructed, is to come into use in 1985.

In the absence of any quays or harbour facilities the brightly painted local boats with their high pointed prows were launched from the beach by being pushed into the water. On their return they were pulled up on shore by oxen (now increasingly by tractors) to be unloaded by the fishermen and the women who had been waiting for them.

The hauling in of the nets (*arte xávega*) was also interesting to watch. After the new harbour has been fitted out, these curious but laborious tasks will no longer be in evidence; however, visitors will still be able to watch the traditional fish auctions which are held towards evening in the covered fish-market.

SIGHTS. – Nazaré has no historic buildings, and the attraction of the town lies solely in the lively, colourful activity of its inhabitants and the atmosphere of tradition which the little town so attractively preserves.

In the lower part of the town are the districts of PEDERNEIRA, with the 16th c. *church of the Misericórdia* (from the square in front of the church there is a fine view over the beach towards Monte Sítio) and PRAIA.

In the district of SÍTIO, on the small promontory of Monte Sítio (110 m/360 ft; reached by funicular or a stepped lane, the Ladeira de Sítio), is the **pilgrimage chapel of Nossa Senhora de Nazaré** (built 1182, rebuilt in 17th c.), with an image of the Virgin which is revered as miraculous (pilgrimages on 15 August and in the second week in September) and 18th c. azulejos.

According to legend the chapel was founded by a local dignitary named Dom Fuas Roupinho in 1182. While he was out hunting one day the stag he was pursuing (who was the devil in disguise) leapt off the cliff here and his horse was about to follow suit when the Virgin appeared in response to his urgent prayer and halted it on the brink of the precipice where the hoofprint is said to be still visible. In thanksgiving for this miraculous aid Dom Fuas Roupinho built the *Capela da Memória* on the commanding terrace where it still stands. The **view is one of the finest on the Atlantic coast of Portugal.

Among the countless pilgrims who have visited the chapel over the centuries was Vasco da Gama, who came here after his voyage to India to give thanks for his safe return.

Some 500 m/550 yd W is the old *Fort of São Miguel*, now a lighthouse.

SURROUNDINGS. – 12 km/7½ miles S of Nazaré, on the NE side of a narrow sheltered bay and on the slopes of a high dune, is the little seaside resort of **São Martinho do Porto**, much favoured by families with small children.

Óbidos

Historical province: Estremadura.
District: Leiria.
Altitude: 70 m/230 ft.
Population: 5000.
Post code: P-2510.
Telephone code: 0 62.
ⓘ **Turismo,**
Rua Direita;
tel. 9 52 31.

ACCOMMODATION. – *Pousada do Castelo, 6 r.; Convento, I, 13 r.; Mansão da Torre, I, 6 r.

Commandingly set on a hill at the western edge of the coastal plain of the Lagoa de Óbidos, above the Rio da Vargem, the attractive little town of *Óbidos has been declared a national monument. Occupying an important strategic situation, the town was strongly fortified in Moorish times, and after its capture by Afonso Henriques its defences were further extended and strengthened.

Already a place of great attraction in medieval times, Óbidos was frequently chosen as the queen's dowry, and it was a favourite residence of St Isabel and other queens and kings of Portugal. Queen Leonor lived here for several years, mourning her only son who had been killed in a riding accident.

Óbidos is now the haunt of tourists and artists, but in spite of the influx of visitors it contrives to preserve its atmosphere and its charm, with its little narrow streets and its flower-decked houses.

The town has large numbers of antique dealers, shops selling handicrafts (in particular the local woven carpets) and many commercial art galleries.

SIGHTS. – The whole town is surrounded by **walls** 13 m/45 ft high, battlemented and reinforced by towers, in the form of an acute-angled triangle.

The very picturesque *OLD TOWN has many handsome patrician houses of the Renaissance and Baroque periods and numerous attractive little nooks and corners.

Pelourinho, Óbidos

From the town gate the main street (*Rua Direita*) leads to the market square, in which is the **parish church of Santa Maria** (originally Gothic but later re-modelled in Renaissance style), its interior entirely faced with 17th c. azulejos.

The church contains the tomb of João de Noronha, by João de Ruão (John of Rouen), and a painting by Josefa de Ayala Figueira (17th c.), the "Mystic Marriage of St Catherine".

In the square in front of the church are a beautiful *fountain* and a *pelourinho* (pillory column) with the emblem of Queen Leonor, a fisherman's net.

Other features of interest are the *church of the Misericórdia* (Baroque doorway), the Gothic *chapel of São Martinho* (14th c.) and the **Museu de Óbidos** (pictures, archaeological material) in the old town hall.

Above the town rises the imposing, many-towered **Castle** (*Castelo*), approached by a narrow lane. The old baronial residence is now the Pousada do Castelo. On the highest point is the *keep*, from which there are fine views of the town and surrounding area.

At the foot of the hill is the Baroque **church of the Senhor da Pedra** (1740–47), on a hexagonal plan, with an Early Christian cross on the altar.

To the S of the town is a 15th c. *aqueduct*.

SURROUNDINGS. – 7 km/4¼ miles W is the **Serra de El Rei** (141 m/463 ft), with the ruins of a 14th c. castle built by King Pedro I and a magnificent *view of **Peniche** (see p. 177).

Caldas da Rainha: see p. 93.

Olhão

Historical province: Algarve.
District: Faro.
Altitude: sea level.
Population: 17,000.
Post code: P-8700.
Telephone code: 0 89.

ⓘ **Turismo,**
Largo do Lagoa;
tel. 7 39 36.

ACCOMMODATION. – *Helena*, P II, 11 r.; *Bela Vista*, P III, 9 r.; *Caique* IV, 37 r.; *Torres*. P IV, 7 r.

The picturesque little fishing town of Olhão has a very Moorish air with its white cube-shaped *houses, two or three storeys high, their flat roofs used as terraces (*açoteias*), with openwork chimneys and rooftop look-out rooms.

This style of building was not in fact a Moorish inheritance but was taken over from neighbouring villages, as being particularly suitable for the hot, dry climate, when large numbers of fishermen from Aveiro settled here in the late 18th c.

The town's main source of revenue is fishing (sardines, tunny), and it has a fish canning factory. The port has the second largest turnover in the Faro district (after Portimão).

The inhabitants of Olhão are proverbial in Portugal for their cunning.

SIGHTS. – In the Praça da Restauração is the **parish church of Nossa Senhora do Rosário**, built by the local fishermen between 1681 and 1698. From the tower there is a fine *view of the town.

Nearby is the *chapel of Nossa Senhora dos Aflitos*, where the wives of Olhão pray

Rooftop view of the white houses of Olhão

for the safe return of their husbands from the sea.

An attractive promenade extends along the **harbour**.

There is a good bathing beach on the offshore island of **Armona**.

Oporto/Porto

Historical province: Douro Litoral.
District: Porto (Oporto).
Altitude: 0–140 m/0–460 ft.
Population: 350,000.
Post code: P-4000-4300.
Telephone code: 02.

ⓘ **Turismo,**
Rua do Clube Fenianos 25;
tel. 31 07 40.
ACP,
Rua de Gonçalo Cristóvão 2;
tel. 2 92 71.

CONSULATES. – *United Kingdom:* Avenida da Boavista 3072, tel. 68 47 89. – *United States:* Apartado No. 88, Rua Júlio Dinis 826–30, tel. 6 30 94.

ACCOMMODATION. – *Infante de Sagres*, Praça Dona Filipa de Lencastre 62, L, 84 r.; *Porto Atlântico*, Rua Afonso Lopes Vieira 66, L, 60 r., SP. *Da Batalha*, Praça da Batalha 116, I, 145 r.; *Dom Henrique*, Rua Guedes de Azevedo 179, I, 102 r.; *Castor*, Rua das Doze Casas 17, I, 63 r.; *Inca*, Praça Coronel Pacheco 52, I, 62 r., *São José*, Rua da Alegria 172–174, I, 45 r.; *Vice-Rei*, Rua Júlio Dinis 779, I, 45 r.; *Solar de São Gabriel*, Rua da Alegria 98, I, 30 r.; *Miradouro*, Rua da Alegria 598, I, 28 r.; *Jorge*, Rua do Bolhão 85, I, 20 r.; *Girassol*, Rua Sá da Bandeira 131–133, I, 18 r.

Porto, Rua de Santa Catarina 197, II, 100 r.; *Império*, Praça da Batalha 127–130, II, 95 r.; *Avis*, Avenida Rodrigues de Freitas 451, II, 89 r.; *Corcel*, Rua de Camões 135–137, II, 60 r.; *Pão de Açúcar*, Rua do Almada 262, II, 50 r.; *Universal*, Avenida dos Aliados 38, II, 43 r.; *Aliados*, Rua Elísio de Melo 27, II, 39 r.; *Pinto Bessa*, Rua da Estaçao 52–56, II, 28 r.; *Chique*, Avenida dos Aliados 206, II, 22 r.; *Paulista*, Avenida dos Aliados 214, II, 22 r.; *Escondidinho*, Rua Passo Manuel 135, II, 20 r.; *Vera Cruz*, Rua Ramalho Ortigão 14, II, 19 r.; *Lis*, Rua Antero de Quental 659, II, 14 r.; *São João*, Rua do Bonjardim 120, II, 14 r.; *Santa Luzia*, Rua da Alegria 147, II, 13 r.; *Constituição*, Rua da Constituição 1045 and 1051, II, 10 r.; *Brasil*, Rua Formosa 178, II, 9 r.
Peninsular, Rua Sá da Bandeira 21, III, 49 r.; *Nave*, Avenida Fernão de Magalhães 247, III, 48 r.; *Tuela*, Rua do Arquitécto Marquês da Silva 180, III, 43 r.; *Malaposta*, Rua da Conceição 80, III, 37 r.
Paris, Rua da Fábrica 27–29, IV, 41 r.; *Internacional*, Rua do Almada 131, IV, 35 r.; *Boa Vista*, Esplanada do Castelo, IV, 18 r.; etc.

CAMP SITE. In the Parque da Prelada.

IN SÃO DA FOZ: *Mary Castro*, P II, 12 r.

IN VALONGO: *Ventura Santos*, P III, 12 r.

RESTAURANTS. – *Portucale*, Rua da Alegria 598; *Orfeu*, Rua Júlio Dinis 928; *Escondidinho*, Rua de Passos Manuel 142; *Tripeiro*, Rua de Passos Manuel 195; *Aquário Marisqueiro*, Rua Rodrigues Sampaio 165; etc.
The local culinary speciality is *tripas à moda do Porto*, tripe prepared with haricot beans and curry powder and served in pottery bowls: a favourite dish which has earned the people of Oporto the name of *tripeiros*, "tripe-eaters". They are proud of the name because it is a reminder of the city's stubborn resistance to the French in the Napoleonic wars: the dish was invented when food was running short during a prolonged siege.

EVENTS. – IN OPORTO: *Festas de São João* (end of June).

Oporto – panorama of the city with the Douro

IN VILA NOVA DE GAIA: *Festas de São Gonçalo e São Cristóvão* (mid January).

IN SÃO JOÃO DA FOZ: *Festa de São Bartolomeu* (end of August), with parade of paper figures.

IN PAREDES: *Festas do Divino Salvador* (mid July), religious festival with animal contests.

IN PENAFIEL: *Festa do Corpo de Deus* (mid June), religious festival with traditional costumes; *Feira da São Martinho* (mid November), fair.

IN GULPILHARES: *International Folk Festival* (end of July).

SHOPPING. – *Port* and *vinho verde*, sold in many establishments in Oporto and Vila Nova de Gaia; *gold* and *silver* articles, particularly in Rua das Flores; *textiles*, *embroidery*, *wickerwork* (particularly in the Mercado do Bolhão); *pottery*.

FLEA MARKETS. – *Feira da Ladra* ("Thieves' Market"), in the hall of the new Cedofeita church, first Saturday and Sunday in month, 10 a.m.–1 p.m. and 3–7.30 p.m.; *Feira de Vendôme*. below the Cathedral, Saturdays.

CAR RENTAL. – *Avis*, Rua Guedes de Azevedo 125 (tel. 31 59 47); *Hertz*, Rua de Santa Catarina 899 (tel. 31 23 87); *Contauto-Europcar*, Rua de Santa Catarina 1158–1164 (tel. 31 83 98).

The lively port, industrial and commercial city of Oporto (known in Portugal as Porto: the traditional English name preserves the older form, from "o porto", the harbour), a university town and the see of a bishop, is Portugal's second largest town but also its most untypical, with a matter-of-fact and business-like approach to life which perhaps owes something to its British connections. Its enchanting *location alone makes it one of the most beautiful towns in the Iberian peninsula.

Here, barely 6 km/4 miles above its mouth, the Douro cuts a narrow passage through granite rocks, with Oporto on the N side and the suburb of Vila Nova de Gaia on the S side. Farther W the banks of the river become lower, finally ending at the cliffs of São João da Foz.

Oporto's fame and prosperity are based on **port**, made from the wine of the upper Douro valley (see p. 109) by a process which is practised here and nowhere else. Some 15–20% of brandy is added to the wine must, interrupting the natural fermentation and giving increased sweetness to the wine. The wine was formerly brought down the Douro from the "País do Vinho" ("Land of Wine") in the traditional *barcos rabelos* (shallow-bottomed boats), only a few of which are now left. The heavy ox-carts which used to convey the wine to the upper town have now also largely been replaced by trucks.

The wine is kept for many years at relatively high temperatures in huge vats in the wine lodges of the upper town and Vila Nova de Gaia (see below, p. 173).

The houses of the town are packed closely together against the steep rock faces, forming terraces of picturesque effect. Oporto resembles Lisbon in having the old town on a hill to the E and the newer districts on another hill to the W. Large-scale replanning in recent years has given the heart of the city attractive new streets and squares, with parks and gardens mingling northern and southern flora.

Oporto is the economic hub of the best cultivated and most thickly populated region in northern Portugal, the incoming and outgoing trade of which is mainly handled by its port and its outer harbour at Leixões (see under Matosinhos).

HISTORY. – In the Hellenistic period there was a trading post here, in Roman times the settlement of *Portus Cale*. Later the Suevi had a stronghold on this site, followed by the Visigoths. The town became the see of a bishop, but was taken by the Arabs in 716 and destroyed in 825.

After the Christian reconquest in the 10th c. the territory between the rivers Minho and Douro, with the rebuilt town of Oporto as its capital, became the County of *Portucalia*, the nucleus of the later kingdom of Portugal.

Oporto has traditionally been, and still is, a town of cosmopolitan and liberal attitudes. It was the birthplace of Henry the Navigator, who opened up the way to Portugal's conquest of the world. Over the centuries the people of Oporto repeatedly opposed arbitrary and dictatorial rule in bloody risings, as in 1628, 1661, 1757 and 1927. Here in 1808 French troops under Junot suffered their first defeat. The Liberals' fight against absolutism also began in Oporto, and as a result the town was besieged and partly destroyed by Dom Miguel's forces in 1832–33.

Museums, Libraries, etc.

American Library
(*Biblioteca Americana*),
Rua da Firmeza 521.
Mon.–Fri. 9 a.m.–noon and 2–6 p.m.

Casa do Infante,
Rua da Alfândega.
Mon.–Sat. 2–7 p.m.

District Archives
(*Arquivo Distrital*),
Praça da República 38.
Mon.–Sat. 11 a.m.–5 p.m.

Guerra Junqueiro House and Museum
(*Casa-Museu Guerra Junqueiro*),
Rua de Dom Hugo 32.
Ceramics, silver, furniture, textiles, carpets.
Mon.–Sat. 11 a.m.–5 p.m.

Library of the Faculty of Medicine
(*Biblioteca da Faculdade de Medicina*),
Hospital de São João,
Estrada da Circunvalação.
Mon.–Fri. 9 a.m.–noon and 2–5 p.m.

Library of the Faculty of Science
(*Biblioteca da Faculdade das Ciências*),
Praça Gomes Teixeira.
Mon.–Fri. 9 a.m.–7 p.m., Sat. 9 a.m.–noon and 2–5 p.m.

Municipal Archives
(*Arquivos da Cidade*),
Terreiro de Dom Afonso Henriques.

Municipal Library
(*Biblioteca Pública Municipal*),
Largo de São Lázaro.

Municipal Museum
(*Gabinete de História da Cidade*),
Rua da Alfândega.
Mon.–Fri. 9 a.m.–noon and 2–5.30 p.m., Sat. 9 a.m.–12.30 p.m.

Museum of Ethnography and History of Douro Litoral
(*Museu de Etnografia e História do Douro Litoral*),
Largo de São João Novo 11.
Mon.–Sat. 10 a.m.–noon and 2–5 p.m.

Soares dos Reis National Museum
(*Museu Nacional de Soares dos Reis*),
Rua de Dom Manuel II 56
(in Palácio dos Carrancas).
Painting, sculpture, ceramics, goldsmith's work, coins, archaeology.
Mon.–Sat. 10 a.m.–5 p.m.

Teixeira Lopes House and Museum
(*Casa-Museu Teixeira Lopes*),
Rua Teixeira Lopes 16,
Vila Nova de Gaia.

Avenida dos Aliados and Town Hall, Oporto

Sightseeing in Oporto

The busiest traffic intersection in Oporto is the spacious **Praça da Liberdade**, in the middle of which is an *equestrian statue of King Pedro IV* (d. 1834), who was also Emperor Pedro I of Brazil from 1822 to 1831.

Off the N side of the square opens the *Avenida dos Aliados*, a broad avenue laid out in 1923–29 after the demolition of an old quarter of the town and now linked by banks and imposing office blocks. At the far end is the new **Town Hall** (*Município*) with its tall central tower.

A short distance NE of the Praça da Liberdade is the *Praça de Dom João I*, another busy square created by the demolition of older property, with more large office blocks and an underground garage.

From the SW corner of the Praça da Liberdade the busy Rua dos Clérigos runs up to the **Igreja dos Clérigos**, built by the Italian architect Nicolò Nasoni in 1732–48; it has an oval interior and a beautiful Capela-mór.

Beyond the church is the 75 m/245 ft high **Torre dos Clérigos**, built in 1755–63 at the expense of the Oporto clergy. This is the highest point in the city, with a panoramic *view over the Douro valley to the Atlantic coast.

To the W of the Clérigos church is a large square, the **Campo dos Mártires da Pátria**, with the beautiful **Jardim de João Chagas** (*Jardim da Cordoaria*).

On the S side of the square stands the old *Prison* (18th c.), at the NW corner the *Hospital de Santo António* (begun 1769), designed by the English architect John Carr of York.

On the N side of the square is the **University** (founded in 1911: previously

1 Praça de Dom João I
2 Soares dos Reis Museum
3 Hospital de Santo António
4 Churches of Carmo and Carmelites
5 Jardim de João Chagas
6 Church and Tower of Clérigos
7 Church of Santo Ildefonso
8 Church of São Bento da Vitória
9 Stock Exchange
10 Church of São Francisco
11 Jardim do Infante Dom Henrique
12 Igreja dos Grilos
13 Guerra Junqueiro Museum

a technical college), with its main entrance in the Praça da Universidade. It contains a small *Natural History Museum*.

Across the Praça da Universidade from the University, at the NW corner of the square, are two adjoining churches. To the right is the *church of the Carmo* (1756), the E end of which is covered with blue azulejos (19th c.); to the left is the *church of the Carmelites* (1619–28). Both churches have richly gilded altars.

Some 500 m/550 yd NW of the Campo dos Mártires, in Rua de Dom Manuel II, the *Palácio dos Carrancas*, built in 1795 as a royal palace, now houses the **Soares dos Reis National Museum** (*Museu Nacional de Soares dos Reis*), with prehistoric and Roman antiquities, medieval and modern sculpture, pictures, pottery and porcelain, goldsmith's work, furniture and textiles.

The rich *ART COLLECTION contains *sculpture* by the Oporto sculptor **Soares dos Reis** (1847–99; "O Desterrado", "Inglesa", "Flor Agreste"), *Teixeira Lopes* ("Infância de Caim") and *Diogo de Macedo*. In the field of *painting* the 16th c. Portuguese school is represented by *Vasco Fernandes* and *Frei Carlos*, the 19th and 20th c. by *Henriques Pousão* (collection of his principal works), *Columbano Bordalo Pinheiro*, *António Carneiro*, *Antonio Cavalho da Silve Porto*, *Marques de Oliveira*, *Aurélia de Sousa* ("Self-Portrait"), *Eduardo Viana* and *Dórdio Gomes* ("Casas de Malakoff"). Works by non-Portuguese artists include pictures by *Jean Clouet* and *Jean-Baptiste Pillement*.

A little way S of the Soares dos Reis Museum is the beautiful park of a 19th c. "Crystal Palace" (Palácio de Cristal) which was replaced in 1952 by the circular **Sports Hall** (*Pavilhão dos Desportos*), with seating for 10,000 spectators, which is also used for concerts, exhibitions, etc.

From the S side of the park, with a *chapel* commemorating King Charles Albert of Sardinia (d. in Oporto 1849), there are superb * views of the city, the river and the sea.

SW of the Campo dos Mártires da Pátria is the Passeio das Virtudes, with a terrace which also affords extensive views of the Douro valley. Below the terrace, to the E, are the narrow lanes (*travessas*) of the old town, lined by old houses with balconies and curious skylights (*claraboias*).

At the higher N end of this part of the town is the twin-towered **church of São Bento da Vitória**, with a richly furnished interior.

From the terrace in front of the church steps lead down E to the Largo de São Domingos, on the N side of which is the end of *Rua das Flores*, once the street of the goldsmiths and cloth merchants.

From the E end of the Largo de São Domingos, *Rua de São João*, one of the busiest streets in Oporto, runs S, providing the main link between the upper town and the Ribeira ("Riverside") quarter. Off this street opens (on right) *Rua do Infante Dom Henrique*, a headquarters of the wholesale trade, with imposing office buildings. At the near end of this street, formerly known as the Rua dos Ingleses, is the **British Factory House** (*Feitoria Inglesa*), a handsome late 18th c. building erected as the headquarters of the association of British port firms.

Half-way along Rua do Infante Dom Henrique, on right, is the **Jardim do Infante Dom Henrique**, with a *monument* to Henry the Navigator. Here, too, is the *Instituto do Vinho de Portugal*, which supervises and controls the Portuguese wine trade.

On the W side of the park is the **church of São Francisco** (originally Gothic, but remodelled in Baroque style), with a large rose window. The interior has sumptuous talha dourada decoration (17th–18th c.). In the church is the elegant Renaissance tomb of the merchant Francisco Brandão Pereira (d. 1528).

On the N side of the church, occupying the site of the original Franciscan convent which was destroyed by fire, stands the

Monument of Henry the Navigator, Oporto

Cathedral
Sé

Oporto
Porto

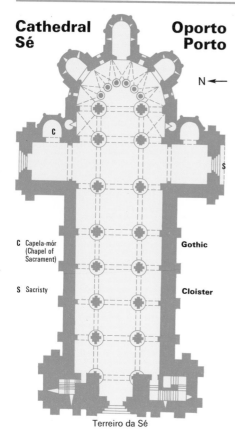

C   Capela-mór
(Chapel of
Sacrament)

S   Sacristy

Gothic

Cloister

Terreiro da Sé

on the highest point of the eastern hill, once the site of a Suevic stronghold.

In this square stands the twin-towered **Cathedral** (*Sé*), originally a Romanesque church built in the 12th c. but later altered in Gothic style and almost completely rebuilt in the 17th and 18th c. – From the terrace on the N side of the Cathedral there is an extensive view of the city's sea of houses.

The interior is predominantly Romanesque. There are several richly decorated altars, including the magnificent silver Altar of the Sacrament (to the left of the high altar, in the Capela-mór; 1632–1732).

In the S aisle is a doorway into the Gothic *Cloister* (1385). Adjoining this are remains of the Romanesque cloister.

To the S of the Cathedral is the former *Bishop's Palace* (begun 1771), an imposing building with an elegant staircase hall which is now occupied by municipal offices.

To the E, beyond the Avenida de Carvalho, the Gothic **church of Santa Clara** has an interior which is rather overloaded with talha dourada decoration.

Below the Cathedral, to the W, is the *Igreja dos Grilos* (by Baltazar Álvares, 1614), now occupied by a seminary and the *Museum of Sacred Art*.

To the E of the Cathedral the Avenida de Saraiva de Carvalho descends to the massive *Ponte de Dom Luís I* (1881–85), built by the Belgian Willebroeck Company, an iron bridge spanning the Douro in a single arch 172 m/565 ft

19th c. **Stock Exchange** (*Palácio da Bolsa*, 1842), with a sumptuously ornate Moorish Hall. Adjoining the Exchange is the charnel-house of a former Minorite convent.

Lower down, in a Renaissance building in Rua da Alfândega which is believed to occupy the site of the house in which Henry the Navigator was born, is the **Municipal Museum** (*Gabinete de História da Cidade*), with material illustrating the history of the city and mementoes of Henry the Navigator.

Rua de São João continues down to the Praça da Ribeira, a busy square on the banks of the Douro, with old-world gabled houses. From here it is possible to reach the Ponte Dom Luís I, to the E, either by the Cais da Ribeira or by Rua Cima do Muro, higher up.

Immediately S of the Praça da Liberdade is the busy *Praça de Almeida Garrett*, with the main railway station, the **Estação de São Bento**.

From here, going S along a new street and then bearing right up Rua Chã, we come to the *Terreiro de Dom Afonso Henriques*,

Ponte de Dom Luís I, with a boat carrying port

wide. There are two roads, the lower one 10 m/33 ft, the upper one 68 m/223 ft above the water. From the upper road, particularly from the S end, there are fine *views of the river with its steeply scarped banks and also of the city.

Just beyond the bridge, on the hill to the left, is the former Augustinian **convent of Serra do Pilar** (17th c.).
Adjoining the round *church* with its splendid dome is a *cloister*, also circular, with its barrel vaulting borne on 36 Ionic columns. From the terrace there is the finest *view of Oporto and the Douro valley with its bridges.

Farther to the SW is the suburb of VILA NOVA DE GAIA, the name of which recalls the ancient *Portus Cale*.
Here the wine-dealers of Oporto have their "lodges" (Portuguese *armazéns*) – the long, low rooms, often tunnelling deep into the granite, in which the port is stored before shipment. Many of the firms are of British origin. See plan below.

From the SE corner of the Praça da Liberdade Rua de Santo António leads up (with a fine view to the rear) past the Baroque *church of Santo Ildefonso*, which has a blue azulejo façade, to the busy Praça da Batalha.
On the S side of the square is the *Teatro de São João* (1920).

From here Rua de Alexandre Herculano goes SE to the *Alameda das Fontainhas*, a beautiful promenade high above the Douro, with superb *views.
To the right is the **Ponte de Dona Maria Pia**, a railway bridge (1877–78) designed by Gustave Eiffel, better known for the Eiffel Tower in Paris.

In the NW of the town, a little way S of the Avenida da Boavista, is the little Romanesque *church of São Martinho de Cedofeita* (12th c.).

At the W end of the Avenida da Boavista is the circular Praça de Mousinho de Albuquerque, or Rotunda da Boavista, in the middle of which is a massive *monument* (erected 1923–29) commemorating the war with France in 1808–09. On the N side of the square is the *Boavista Station*.

In the N of the town, in the Praça do Marquês de Pombal, is the *Church of the Immaculate Conception* (Imaculada Conceição), a good example of modern Portuguese church architecture (1939–47).

SURROUNDINGS of Oporto

5 km/3 miles downstream, on a road which runs immediately above the steep bank of the Douro, with fine *views of the city to the rear, and past the huge high bridge, the *Ponte da Arrábida* (1962), lies **São João da Foz** (or *Foz do Douro*), a suburb of Oporto, beautifully situated at the mouth (*foz*, from Latin *fauces*) of the Douro, and which is a very popular bathing resort. The *Douro Litoral* beach is fringed by palms.
From the breakwater with the harbour light there is an impressive view of the mouth of the river, commanded by the Castelo da Foz (1570), and the coast.

4 km/2½ miles NW of São João da Foz is the port and industrial town of **Matosinhos** (see p. 158).

14 km/9 miles S of Oporto is **Grijó**, with a former convent (founded in the 12th c., rebuilt in the 16th c.). The cloister has beautiful azulejo decoration and contains the tomb of Rodrigo Sancho (d. 1245), son of Sancho I. The church has a fine altar with talha dourada decoration.

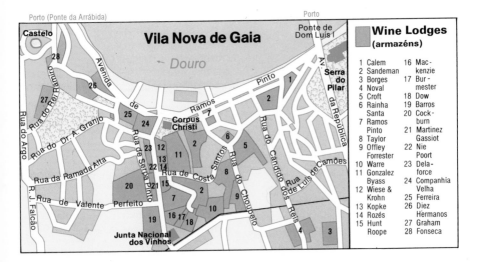

Porto (Ponte da Arrábida)   Porto

Vila Nova de Gaia

← Douro

Ponte de Dom Luis I

Serra do Pilar

Corpus Christi

Junta Nacional dos Vinhos

Wine Lodges (armazéns)

1	Calem	16	Mackenzie
2	Sandeman	17	Burmester
3	Borges		
4	Noval	18	Dow
5	Croft	19	Barros
6	Rainha Santa	20	Cockburn
7	Ramos Pinto	21	Martinez Gassiot
9	Offley Forrester	22	Nie Poort
10	Warre Byass	23	Delaforce
11	Gonzalez	24	Companhia Velha
12	Wiese & Krohn	25	Ferreira
13	Kopke	26	Diez Hermanos
14	Rozés	27	Graham
15	Hunt Roope	28	Fonseca

Near Paredes de Coura

12 km/7½ miles NE of Oporto **Valongo** (pop. 7000) has antimony mines and coal-mines.

23 km/14 miles E of Valongo by way of *Paredes de Coura* is **Penafiel** (alt. 500 m/1640 ft; pop. 6000), a long straggling little town attractively situated on high ground between the Rio Sousa and the Rio Tâmega; it was known until the late 18th c. as Arrifana de Sousa. It has a 14th c. castle and the Renaissance-style church of the Misericórdia (16th c.), originally the church of a Franciscan convent.

11 km/7 miles NE of Penafiel, in a valley on one side of Road EN15, stands a fortified church belonging to the former Benedictine convent of **Travança**. The church (three-aisled), originally founded in 970, was rebuilt in Romanesque style in the 12th c. and has remained substantially unchanged since then apart from the apse added in the 16th c. It has preserved very fine 12th c. * sculpture.

Some 10 km/6 miles SW of Penafiel is the important Romanesque monastic church of **Paço de Sousa** (12th c.), with rich * carved decoration in the interior. The column bases are hewn from millstones.
At the far end of the church is the sarcophagus (12th c.) of Egaz Moniz (1050–1140), tutor and confidant of Afonso Henriques, who played a major part in the history of his time. He is particularly remembered for an occasion in 1130 when, after Afonso Henriques had broken his word to Alfonso VII of León, he made his way to Alfonso's court with a rope around his neck, accompanied by his wife and children, in order to do penance on behalf of his master: whereupon Alfonso, impressed by his honesty and nobility, forgave the offence and allowed him to return to Portugal.
The relief decoration (much damaged) on the sarcophagus, which is supported on lions, depicts scenes from the dead man's life.
Of the convent buildings there survives only part of the cloister.
In the neighbourhood are two country houses, the *Quinta de Paço de Sous* and the *Paço de Franco*.

Palmela

Historical province: Estremadura.
District: Setúbal.
Altitude: 238 m/781 ft.
Population: 3000.
Post code: P-2950.
Telephone code: 01.
ⓘ **Turismo,**
   Largo do Chafariz;
   tel. 2 35 00 89.

ACCOMMODATION. – *Pousada do Castelo de Palmela*, 27 r., SP.

EVENT. – *Festa das Vindimas* (beginning of September), vintage festival, with bullfights.

The little hill town of Palmela, in the Serra de São Luís, an eastern outlier of the Serra da Arrábida, is worth a visit if only for the sake of its imposing castle.

During the Moorish period Palmela had the most powerful stronghold in southern Portugal, and after its final conquest by King Afonso Henriques in 1147 it was still further enlarged and strengthened. In 1168 it became the headquarters of the knightly Order of Santiago. In the 18th c. the castle was again strengthened to give it increased protection against artillery attack.

In 1484 the bishop of Évora, Garcia de Meneses, was imprisoned in a cistern in the castle, where he probably died by poison, for his involvement in a conspiracy.

SIGHTS. – Within the precincts of the **Castle** (*Fortaleza*) are the ruins of a *church*, built on the site of an earlier Moorish mosque, which collapsed during the 1755 earthquake.

From the late 14th c. **Keep**, below which is the bishop's prison, there is a good view of the whole castle complex. From the *castle esplanade* there is a magnificent * prospect extending to Lisbon and Sintra.

The western end of the castle precinct is occupied by the 15th c. *Convent of Santiago*.

The **church**, in a style transitional between Romanesque and Gothic, has beautiful azulejo decoration (16th and 18th c.) in the interior, and contains the tomb of Jorge de Lencastre (1481–1550), a natural son of King João II.

Below the castle is the 18th c. **church of São Pedro**, which contains fine *azulejo pictures of scenes from the life of St Peter.

Peneda-Gerês National Park/ Parque Nacional de Peneda-Gerês

Historical provinces: Minho and Trás-os-Montes.
Districts: Viana do Castelo, Braga and Vila Real.
Area: 193 sq. miles.
Altitude: up to 1545 m/5070 ft.

Turismo Braga,
Avenida da Liberdade I,
P-4700 Braga;
tel. (053) 2 25 50.

ACCOMMODATION. – IN CALDAS DO GERÊS: *Geresiana*, P II, 48 r.; *Casa da Ponte*, P II, 20 r.; *Baltazar*, P II, 15 r.; *Parque*, III, 60 r., SP; *Ponte*, P III, 48 r.; *Termas*, III, 32 r.; *Central Jardim*, P III, 26 r.; *Príncipe*, P III, 17 r.; *Universal*, IV, 70 r.; *Ribeira*, IV, 45 r.; *Maia*, IV, 42 r.

IN CANIÇADA: *Pousada de São Bento*, 10 r., SP.

IN CASTRO LABOREIRO: *Abrigo de Castro Laboreiro*, P II, 10 r.

CAMP SITE at Albergaria.

EVENT. – *Festas de São Brás* (beginning of August), a popular festival, with colourful processions and bull-running, in Terras do Bouro and other villages.

The *Peneda-Gerês National Park, Portugal's first national park, extends along the Spanish frontier from the Castro Laboreiro plateau by way of the Peneda, Soajo, Amarela and Gerês mountains to the Mourela plateau in the S.**

The park includes expanses of completely unspoiled country with magnificent forest and mountain scenery and beautiful artificial lakes (reservoirs: Barragems de Vilarinho, de Caniçada, da Salamonde, de Paradela). The highest peaks are in the Serra do Gerês, which rises within Portuguese territory to 1545 m/5069 ft in the Nevosa and 1538 m/5046 ft in the Altar de Cabrões.
The very varied pattern of relief gives rise to widely different micro-climates, and in consequence the plant life of the park shows unusual variety. Moreover, the remoteness of this region has protected many endemic species from destruction by man, so that plants are found here which have disappeared from the rest of Europe. In addition to great tracts of coniferous forest there are stands of centuries-old oaks (particularly at Pincães and São Lourenço), cork-oaks (at Ermida) and eucalyptus, and expanses of rocky country covered with heather.

The wildlife includes deer, wild pigs, hares, partridges, wild horses, lizards, snakes and even wolves and golden eagles.

Large areas within the park are a *nature reserve* in which the wildlife can be pursued only with a camera; but there is scope for fishing and shooting outside the park boundaries. Many of the roads are closed to cars, and others are unsuitable for motor traffic. The best way of seeing the unspoiled natural scenery of the park is on foot, on horseback or in one of the horse-drawn carriages which can be hired at many places within the park.

The archaeological remains found in and around the park show that this was a region of ancient human settlement. The *megalithic chamber tombs* (dolmens) of Mezio, Paradela, Cambezes, Pitões and Tourém date from the 3rd millennium B.C. Pre-Roman (presumably Celtic) *castros* have been excavated at Pitões, Tourém and Cidadelhe, and there are believed to be other prehistoric settlements still buried in the soil.
The first roads in this region were built by the Romans, and there is a famous stretch of *Roman road*, constructed and

Pousada de São Bento, Peneda-Gerês National Park

developed between A.D. 79 and 353, running along the SE side of the Vilarinho reservoir and up to the Portela do Homem on the Spanish frontier, which preserves the largest number of Roman milestones in the Iberian peninsula.

ENTRANCES to the National Park and SIGHTS. – **Lamas de Mouro** entrance (10 km/6 miles SE of Melgaço), at the N end of the park.

8 km/5 miles SE of the entrance is **Castro Laboreiro**, a castle (probably occupying the site of a Roman fortress) built by Afonso Henriques and strengthened by King Dinis. It was almost completely destroyed by an explosion when the powder tower was struck by lightning.

9 km/5½ miles S of the entrance is the fine *pilgrimage church of Nossa Senhora da Peneda* (pilgrimages in first week in September).

Mezio entrance (18 km/11 miles NE of Arcos de Valdevez).

5 km/3 miles SE is the little hill village of **Soajo**, in which the houses are built of undressed granite blocks without the use of mortar. The *pelourinho* (pillory column), of the 10th c., is believed to be the oldest stone column in Portugal.

From the Mezio entrance there are attractive drives into the northern part of the park and NE to *Adrão*.

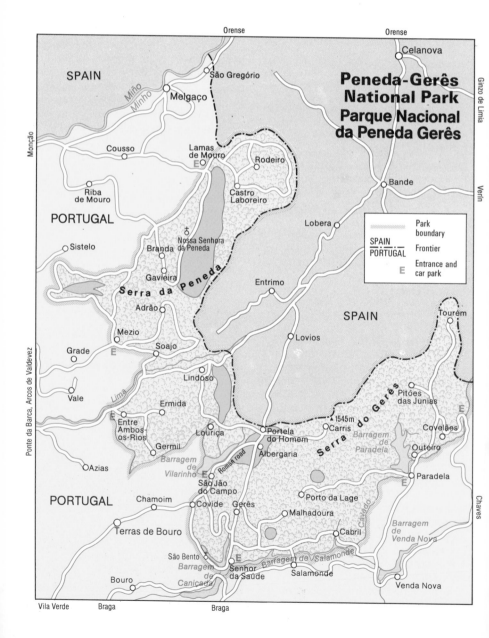

Entre-Ambos-os-Rios   entrance (13 km/8 miles NE of Ponte da Barca).
From here a road ascends the beautiful valley of the Rio Lima to the decaying village of **Lindoso** (alt. 468 m/1536 ft; pop. 1000), near the Spanish frontier, which is dominated by a magnificently situated castle built in 1287, in the reign of King Dinis. Around the village are many of the characteristic Minho granaries (*espigueiros*).
From Lindoso there are a variety of pleasant walks – e.g. to the artificial lake of *Vilarinho das Furnas*, to the *Miradouro Leira do Canto*, with a beautiful view of the Lima valley, to the pass of *Portela do Homem* (822 m/2697 ft) on the Spanish frontier, affording a magnificent prospect of the rocky valley of the Rio Homem, and S to *Cabril Forest*.

A dam in the Peneda-Gerês National Park

São João do Campo entrance (17 km/10 miles NE of the Terras de Bouro, 5 km/3 miles NE of Covide).
From here it is possible to go either NE to the Portela do Homem or SE to Caldas do Gerês.

Senhor da Saúde entrance (32 km/20 miles N of Braga, on the Barragem da Caniçada).
This is the principal means of access to the picturesque little spa of **Caldas do Gerês**, nestled in a narrow valley, it is a good base for walks and climbs in the Serra do Gerês.
From Caldas do Gerês a road runs N to the Portela do Homem; then E to *Carris*, at the foot of the **Altar de Cabrões** (a fine lookout point, easily climbed).

Paradela entrance (65 km/40 miles NE of Braga), at the dam forming the Barragem de Paradela.
25 km/16 miles W is *Porto da Lage*.

Covelães entrance (13 km/8 miles NW of Montalegre). This gives access to the eastern part of the National Park, notable features in which are the prehistoric sites of *Pitões* and *Tourém*.

Peniche

Historical province: Estremadura.
District: Leiria. Altitude: 0–15 m/0–50 ft.
Population: 13,000. Post code: P-2520.
Telephone code: 0 62.
ⓘTurismo,
  Rua de Alexandre Herculano; tel. 7 22 71.

ACCOMMODATION. – *Félita*, P II, 9 r.; *Avis*, P IV, 10 r.

YOUTH HOSTEL. – *Pousada de Juventude*, Praia da Arcia Branca (15 km/9 miles S of Peniche), 70 b.

RECREATION and SPORT. – Bathing (beaches on both sides of the isthmus), fishing, scuba diving.

EVENT. – *Festas da Senhora da Boa Viagem* (beginning of August), a traditional fishermen's festival with a procession of boats.

The busy and picturesque little fishing town of Peniche is one of the main places of the Portuguese crayfish, sardine and tunny fisheries (canning factories). It lies on a rocky peninsula on the Portuguese Atlantic coast, almost 3 km/2 miles long and just over 2 km/1¼ miles wide, edged by rugged cliffs, which is linked to the mainland by a narrow spit of sand.

Peniche has a State-run school of pillow-lace making, an old established local craft. In recent years it has also developed into a popular seaside resort, thanks to the excellent beaches on either side of the isthmus linking it with the mainland.
SIGHTS. – The town, and indeed the whole peninsula, is dominated by the well-preserved **Castle** (*Fortaleza*) built by Filippo Terzi in the 16th c. and considerably enlarged in the 17th c., with Vauban-style fortifications.
Other features of interest in the town are the Baroque *church of the Misericórdia* (wooden ceiling with New Testament scenes), the 17th c. **church of São Pedro**, also Baroque (18th c. talha dourada decoration in choir) and the

Ajuda church, with rich azulejo decoration and ceiling paintings in the choir.

To the SE of the town, the **harbour**, protected by two breakwaters, is the scene of lively activity when the fishing boats return to port and their perishable cargoes are quickly unloaded by a swarm of harbour workers, appraised by the fish dealers and taken away for processing.

Rock formations on Cabo Carvoeiro

SURROUNDINGS. – 2 km/1¼ miles W, reached either by road or by an attractive footpath, is *Cabo Carvoeiro (lighthouse), a rocky headland which has been eroded into bizarrely shaped pinnacles and sea-caves. There are good catches of fish and crayfish to be had in the offshore waters.
There are a number of good lookout points affording beautiful *prospects of coastal scenery, the *Nau dos Corvos* (the "Ravens' Ship") and the **Berlenga Islands** (see p. 85).

Pombal

Historical province: Beira Litoral.
District: Leiria. Altitude: 221 m/725 ft.
Population: 11,000. Post code: P-3100.
Telephone code: 0 36.
ⓘ **Turismo,**
Largo Cardal;
tel. 2 32 30.

ACCOMMODATION. – *Terrabela*, P III, 32 r.; *Verdegaio*, P IV, 15 r.

The pretty little town of Pombal, in the valley of the Rio Soura, owes its fame to José I's powerful minister Sebastião José de Carvalho e Mello, Marquês de Pombal (1699–1782), who retired to Pombal after his fall and died there.

As the great apostle of enlightened absolutism in Portugal the Marquês de

Monument to the Marquês de Pombal, Lisbon

Pombal left a powerful imprint on the history of the country. The scion of a family of the minor nobility of Lisbon, he gained his first experience of public life as Portuguese ambassador in London and Vienna, where he also concerned himself with economic affairs. In 1750 King José I appointed him foreign minister and in 1756 prime minister.

Pombal carried out the duties of his various offices with skill and independence, showing little scruple in the means he adopted for realising his ambitious aims. He saw his main tasks as the reorganisation of the national finances, the reform of the educational system, the promotion of trade and industry, the shaking off of Britain's economic hegemony and the abolition of slavery.

One of his greatest achievements was the rebuilding of Lisbon after the devastating earthquake in 1755.

He was a resolute opponent of the Jesuits and the lesser nobility, whose privileges stood in the way of his reforms.

After José I's death Pombal fell into disgrace, was banished to Pombal and died there a year later.

SIGHTS. – In the main square are the church of São Martinho (founded 1323, rebuilt 1520) and a **monument** to the Marquês de Pombal.

Arcos de Valdevez, on the Rio Vaz

ACCOMMODATION. – IN PONTE DA BARCA: Carvalho, P II, 18 r.; Freitas, P III, 16 r.

IN ARCOS DE VALDEVEZ: Ribeira, P II, 12 r.; Telheiro, P III, 15 r.

EVENT. – Festas de São Bartolomeu (end of August), a religious festival.

Ponte da Barca

Historical province: Minho.
District: Viana do Castelo.
Altitude: 178 m/584 ft.
Population: 1500.
Post code: P-4980.
Telephone code: 058.
ⓘ **Turismo Viana do Castelo,**
    Palácio dos Távoras,
    Avenida de Cândido dos Reis,
    P-4900 Viana do Castelo;
    tel. (058) 2 26 20.

The quiet little market town of Ponte de Barca, on the left bank of the Rio Lima, is a popular base for excursions into the Peneda-Gerês National Park.

SIGHTS. – The most notable feature is the handsome **parish church** (Igreja Matriz, 15th c.), with a beautiful coffered ceiling. It has a fine silver crucifix presented by King Manuel I.

The old bridge over the Rio Lima at Ponte da Barca

In the market square, in the lower part of the town, is a 16th c. *pelourinho* (pillory column).

The Rio Lima is spanned by a 15th–16th c. **bridge** (with later rebuilding and alteration), from which there are fine *views of the town and the surrounding hills.

SURROUNDINGS. – 5 km/3 miles SW is **Bravães**, on the outskirts of which is the little Romanesque *church of São Salvador (12th c.), with elaborately sculpted doorways (figures of animals, etc.). The aisleless interior also has rich relief decoration and carved friezes and contains the remains of 14th c. frescoes, the best of which are displayed in the Soares dos Reis Museum in Oporto.

5 km/3 miles N of Ponte da Barca, straddling the Rio Vez, is the picturesque little market town of **Arcos de Valdevez** (pop. 3000), with a 14th c. parish church (remodelled in the 17th c.). In front of the church is a particularly fine Manueline *pelourinho* (pillory column); behind it, in the Praça do Terreiro, stands the 16th c. Casa do Terreiro.
Other features of interest in the town are the Baroque façade of the church of Nossa Senhora da Lapa and a monolithic column in front of the Espírito Santo church in the upper town, commemorating the town's support of Afonso Henriques in his conflict with the Spaniards.

* **Peneda-Gerês National Park**: see p. 175.

Portalegre

Historical province: Alto Alentejo.
District: Portalegre.
Altitude: 477 m/1565 ft.
Population: 13,000.
Post code: P-7300.
Telephone code: 045.
ⓘ **Turismo,**
    Rua do 19 de Junho 40–42;
    tel. 2 18 15.

ACCOMMODATION. – *Dom João III*, II, 54 r., SP; *Plátano*, P II, 23 r.; *Nova*, P II, 12 r.; *Quinta da Saúde*, P II, 10 r.; *São Pedro*, P II, 8 r.; *Alto Alentejo*, P III, 14 r.; *Pires da Costa*, P III, 10 r.

CAMP SITE. – *Quinta da Saúde*.

The district capital of Portalegre, the Roman Amoea, lies near the Spanish frontier at the foot of the Serra de Portalegre, a westerly outlier of the Serra de São Mamede. With its trim white houses reaching up the steep slopes of the hill and its numerous handsome old palaces it is the great showcase of Portuguese Baroque architecture.

This old episcopal city rose to prosperity in the 16th c. through its woollen industry, in particular the production of tapestries, but its real heyday came in the late 17th c. with the rise of the silk-weaving industry. It is still important for the woollen industry, and also for woodworking and cork-processing.

SIGHTS. – The great charm of Portalegre lies in its many handsome *burghers' houses* of the Baroque period with their richly decorated façades.

In the Largo da Sé at the W end of the old town, which is still surrounded by its medieval **walls**, is the 16th c. **Cathedral** (*Sé*), with an 18th c. façade flanked by towers.
The three-aisled Renaissance interior has been preserved in its 16th c. form. In the second chapel on the right is an altarpiece with scenes from the life of the Virgin; the sacristy has an azulejo picture of the Flight into Egypt. The *cloister* is 18th c. From the nearby terrace there are fine views.

Opposite the Cathedral, to the NE, is the **Municipal Museum**, which has an outstanding collection of ceramics and tiles from Portugal (17th–18th c.), Spain (Moorish), Italy, Flanders and Holland (particularly 18th c. Delft ware), together with archaeological material, arms and armour and religious art.

Also in the Largo da Sé is the 18th c. **Town Hall** (*Município*).
SE of the Town Hall, in Rua Santa Clara, is a 14th c. *Convent of Poor Clares*, with a fine cloister.

To the N of the Cathedral is the **Palácio Amarelo** ("Yellow Palace"), properly known as the *Palácio dos Albrançalhas*, with 17th c. *ironwork which is among the finest of its kind in Portugal.

From the Cathedral *Rua do 19 de Junho*, lined by handsome burghers' houses of the 17th and 18th c., leads SE to the Praça da República, with many handsome mansions, some of them faced with azulejos, including the *Palácio dos Condes de Avilés* (now occupied by the Civil Governor) and the *Palácio dos Fonseca Acciolo* (now a school).
Also in the Praça da República is a former **Franciscan convent**, founded in the 13th c. and largely rebuilt in the 18th c.

To the NE, outside the old town, is the Parque de Miguel Bombarda, on the W side of which is a former **Jesuit convent**

(17th c.), now occupied by the silk-weaving and tapestry workshops, which can be visited and which were founded by the Marquês de Pombal.

A short distance N is the **church** of the *Convent of São Bernardo* (now a barracks; seen on application), which was founded in 1518 and later remodelled in Baroque style. The church contains the splendid marble *tomb of the bishop of Guarda, Dom Jorge de Melo, founder of the convent, which is ascribed to the 16th c. French sculptor Nicolas de Chanterene.
The convent has two fine *cloisters*, one Manueline and the other Renaissance; in the larger of the two is a beautiful marble fountain. The chapterhouse has fine groined vaulting.

To the W of the Parque Bombarda, in the town's busy main square, the Rossio, stands the *Hospital of the Misericórdia*, with an 18th c. façade and a beautiful patio.

On the NE side of Portalegre, above the old town, are the ruins of the massive medieval **Castle** (*Castelo*, 1290).

In Rua de José Régio is the **Casa de José Régio**, once the home of the poet José de Régio (1901–69), containing the remarkable collection of figures of Christ and other religious statuettes which he assembled.

SURROUNDINGS. – 2 km/1¼ miles NW is the **Penha de São Tomé**, a magnificent viewpoint. There are also panoramic views from the summit of the *Serra de São Mamede (1025 m/3363 ft), which can be climbed without difficulty.

12 km/7½ miles N of Portalegre, near the village of *Aramenha*, are the remains of the Roman settlement of **Medobriga**. Material from the site can be seen in the Museum of Archaeology in Belém.

20 km/12½ miles N of Portalegre is **Castelo de Vide** (see p. 97); 12 km/7½ miles NE is **Marvão** (p. 158).

Portimão

Historical province: Algarve.
District: Faro.
Altitude: 0–35 m/0–115 ft.
Population: 18,000.
Post code: P-8500.
Telephone code: 0 82.
(i) **Turismo,**
    Largo do 1 de Dezembro;
    tel. 2 36 95 and 2 20 65.

CONSULATE. – *United Kingdom:* Rua de Santa Isabel 21/I, tel. 2 30 71.

ACCOMMODATION. – *Nelinanda*, P I, 32 r.; *Mira-Fóia*, P I, 25 r.; *Miradoiro*, P I, 26 r.; *Globo*, II, 68 r.; *Pimenta*, P II, 30 r.; *Afonso III*, P II, 30 r.; *Grade*, P II, 28 r.; *Central*, P II, 20 r.; *São Roque*, P II, 12 r.; *do Rio*, P II, 12 r.; *Caracol*, P II, 10 r.; *Denis*, P II, 7 r.; *Baltazar*, P III, 22 r.; *Roma*, P III, 16 r.; *Dom Carlos I*, P III, 14 r.; *O Pátio*, P III, 14 r.; *Santa Isabel*, P III, 10 r.; *Lúcio*, P III, 8 r.; *Brasilia*, P III, 8 r.; *Esplanada*, P IV, 35 r.

CAMP SITE at Ferragudo.

Penina Golf, 5 km/3 miles W, L, 213 r., SP; golf-course.

RECREATION and SPORT. – See under **Praia da Rocha**.

Algarve sightseeing flights. – Information from Turismo office.

Fishing boats in Portimão harbour

The busy industrial town and port (canning factory, shipyard) of Portimão, which is believed to occupy the site of a Carthaginian settlement known to the Romans as Portus Hannibalis, lies on the W side of the wide estuary of the Rio Arade.

It offers a lively spectacle when the sardine boats return to harbour with their catch.

SIGHTS. – Portimão has no major tourist sights: what draws visitors to this increasingly popular resort is the busy life and activity of its harbour and the beautiful beaches within easy reach of the town.
On a low hill is the **parish church** (*Igreja Matriz*), which was rebuilt after its destruction in the 1755 earthquake. Of the original Gothic structure only the doorway survives.
The beautiful azulejo decoration dates from the 17th and 18th c.

SURROUNDINGS. – 3 km/2 miles S of the harbour is the outlying district of *Praia da Rocha (see p. 182).

On the E side of the Rio Arade, which is spanned by a bridge 337 m/370 yd long, lies the village of *Ferragudo*, with a 16th c. castle and a good bathing beach.

5 km/3 miles W of Portimão and 1 km/¾ mile inland is the modest village of *Alvor*, where King João II died in 1495 after seeking a cure at Caldas de Monchique (see under Algarve). The church (*Matriz*) has a Manueline doorway.

Póvoa de Varzim

Historical province: Douro Litoral.
District: Porto (Oporto).
Altitude: sea level.
Population: 17,000.
Post code: P-4490.
Telephone code: 052.
ⓘ **Turismo,**
Avenida de Monzinho de Albuquerque 160;
tel. 62 46 09.

ACCOMMODATION. – *Vermar Dom Pedro*, I, 208 r., SP; *Póvoa*, II, 105 r.; *Costa Verde*, P I, 49 r.; *Gett*, P II, 20 r.; *Luso-Brasileira*, P II, 11 r.

RECREATION and SPORT. – Swimming, fishing, sailing; bullfights; horse-races; casino. – Yacht harbour under construction.

EVENTS. – *Festas de Semana Santa*, Holy Week celebrations; *Festas de São Pedro* (end of June), popular festival with folk dancing; *Festas da Senhora da Assunção* (mid August), fishermen's festival with parade of boats, bullfights and fireworks; *Festas da Senhora das Dores* (mid September), religious festival.

The lively little fishing town of Póvoa de Varzim, straggling along the Atlantic coast N of Oporto, is a popular seaside resort, much frequented by the Portuguese themselves, with a broad beach some 2 km/1¼ miles long.

The beach, Póvoa de Varzim

Póvoa de Varzim was the birthplace of the great Portuguese novelist Eça de Queirós (1845–1900), who is commemorated by a monument outside the Town Hall.
A local gastronomic speciality is *caldeirada à Póvoa*, a fish stew.

SIGHTS. – The old *fishermen's quarter* is very picturesque. – The **Municipal Museum** (*Museu Municipal de Etnografia e História*) contains interesting material on local history and folk traditions.

SURROUNDINGS. – On the nearby *Monte São Félix* (*view) is an old windmill which features in a local folk song.

From Póvoa de Varzim an 18th c. **aqueduct** of 999 arches, 7 km/4½ miles long, runs S to the former Convent of Santa Clara in **Vila do Conde** (see p. 204).

Praia da Rocha

Historical province: Algarve.
District: Faro.
Altitude: 20 m/65 ft.
Population: 2000.
Post code: P-8500.
Telephone code: 0 82.
ⓘ **Turismo,**
Rua Tomás Cabreira;
tel. 2 22 90.

ACCOMMODATION. – IN PRAIA DA ROCHA: *Algarve, L, 213 r., SP, boutiques; *Júpiter*, I, 144 r., SP; *Mir-Sol*,

Praia da Rocha from the sea

I, 38 r.; *São João*, I, 25 r.; *Alcalá*, I, 22 r.; *3 Castelos*, I, 10 r.; *Rocha*, II, 77 r.; *Sol*, P II, 32 r.; *Bela Vista* (in an old villa immediately above the beach), II, 27 r.; *Solar do Pinguim*, P II, 13 r.; *Oceano*, P III, 10 r. – *Tarik* (apartments), 296 r., SP.

ON PRAIA DOS TRÊS IRMÃOS AND PRAIA DE ALVOR: *Alvor Praia*, L, 201 r., SP; *Aldeamento Turístico da Prainha*, 63 r., SP.

IN PORTIMÃO: see p. 181.

Hotel Algarve, Praia da Rocha

RECREATION and SPORT. – Swimming, deep-sea fishing; bullfights. – Golf-courses (18 and 9 holes) at Penina Golf Hotel (10 km/6 miles NW: see under Algarve).

EVENT. – *Carnival* (1–3 August).

The seaside resort of * **Praia da Rocha (administratively part of the town of Portimão, 3 km/2 miles N), situated in one of the most beautiful parts of the Algarve, has long attracted visitors with its extraordinarily mild climate and its beautiful beaches of golden yellow sand edged by rugged cliffs.**

Originally a favourite residential area with well-to-do citizens of Portimão, who built their elegant villas here, Praia da Rocha began around the turn of the 19th c. to become increasingly popular with visitors not only from other parts of Portugal but also from abroad (particularly from Britain).

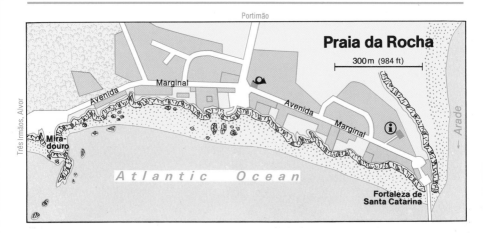

The principal ***beach**, almost 2 km/ 1¼ miles long and 100 m/110 yd wide, lies below the town at the foot of the cliffs and is equipped with the most modern facilities.

The tree-shaded *seafront promenade*, a little way in from the edge of the cliffs, extends from the **Fortaleza de Santa Catarina** (*view; restaurant; landing-stage below the fort), above the W bank of the Rio Arade, to the *Miradouro above the W end of the beach, from which there is a superb view of the very picturesque coastal scenery.

SURROUNDINGS. – To the W of Praia da Rocha are a succession of idyllic sandy *bays separated from one another by projecting crags and reefs, around which there have developed in recent years several very large holiday colonies including *Prainha*, **Praia dos Três Irmãos** ("Beach of the Three Brothers") and **Praia de Alvor** (see *Alvor*, under Portimão).

Portimão: see p. 181.

Queluz

Historical province: Estremadura.
District: Lisboa (Lisbon).
Altitude: 125 m/410 ft.
Population: 48,000.
Post code: P-2475.
Telephone code: 01.
ⓘ **Comissão Municipal de Turismo de Lisboa,**
Rua das Portas de Santo Antão 141,
P-1000 Lisboa;
tel. (01) 36 66 24 and 32 70 58.

ACCOMMODATION. – None in the town. See under LISBON.

The modest little market town of Queluz, a few kilometres NW of Lisbon, owes its importance and its fame to the charming Rococo palace of *Queluz, once a summer residence

of the Bragança kings, which is still used for official government receptions.

The palace, consisting of a central block and two lower wings, was built between 1747 and 1794 for Pedro III and his wife, later Queen Maria I, to the design of the Portuguese architect Mateus Vicente de Oliveira, a pupil of the German architect Johann Friedrich Ludwig who built the Convent-Palace of Mafra. In contrast to the cold magnificence of Mafra, however, the ***Palácio Nacional de Queluz** is a gay and friendly building which has sometimes been compared with Frederick the Great's palace of Sanssouci near Berlin.

The rich interior decoration is notable for the high quality of the craftsmanship and the sure taste with which the details are contrived and related to one another. Outstanding among the many rooms in the palace are the *Throne Room*, the *Queen's Dressing-Room* (beautiful azulejo pictures) and the *Hunting Room*

Palácio Nacional de Queluz

Azulejo-decorated fountain in the gardens of Queluz

(ceiling paintings of hunting scenes).
The *Kitchens*, also decorated with azulejos, are now occupied by a luxury restaurant, the Cozinha Velha.

In front of the palace is the spacious Largo do Palácio, with the **Royal Chapel**, in the purest Rococo style.
Also in the square is a *statue of Queen Maria I*. Here the changing of the guard takes place.

Behind the palace are the Rococo-style **Gardens* (*Jardins do Palácio*), laid out from 1755 onwards by the French architect Jean-Baptiste Robillon, with fountains, grottoes and sculpture (including some lead statues cast in Britain). In the lower part of the gardens is the *Ribeira de Jamor*, a basin beautifully faced with azulejos.

Ribatejo

Historical province: Ribatejo.
District: Santarém.
Area: 6600 sq. km/2550 sq. miles.
Population: 460,000.
Chief town: Santarém.
ⓘ **Turismo Santarém,**
Rua de Capelo Ivens 63,
P-2000 Santarém;
tel. (0 43) 2 31 40.

Taken in the narrowest sense, the Ribatejo region, roughly corresponding to the present district of Santarém, comprises only the alluvial basin of the lower Tagus valley, in the E of the province of Estremadura. This is a highly fertile area of some 600 sq. km/230 sq. miles which is still in process of sinking as a result of tectonic movements.

The historical province of Ribatejo, however, with its capital at Santarém, also includes the fertile upland regions to the N and S and the plateau to the E – all relics of the Tertiary and Quaternary tableland through which the Tagus has carved its course.

The drier upland region to the N is densely populated and intensively farmed, mainly by small holdings practising mixed farming (wheat, olives, wine, citrus fruits, figs).
The area to the S, on the other hand, is sparsely populated. Here the large estates and the growing custom of single-crop farming (wheat, olives, cork-oaks) show the same agricultural structure as in the Alentejo region to the S.

The water meadows which form a strip some 50 km/30 miles wide along the

A Ribatejo cattle-herder

Bridge over the Tagus, Vila Franca de Xira

Tagus and are flooded every spring (January–April) provide ideal conditions for growing grain and rice.

Here, too, is the grazing land (frequently rather acidic) for the traditional horse and cattle rearing. Most of the Portuguese fighting bulls come from the Ribatejo, particularly from the area around **Vila Franca de Xira** (pop. 9000; Estalagem da Leziria, I, 30 r.; Gado Bravo, I, 16 r.), where the "Agrinxira" agricultural and livestock show is held annually in May and the popular and gay "Festival of the Red Waistcoat" (Festa do Colete Encarnado), with processions and bull-fights, is celebrated every July.

The mounted cattle-herder (*campinos*) with their picturesque costumes and their long lance-like poles are still a regular feature of the Ribatejo landscape.

Sagres

Historical province: Algarve.
District: Faro.
Altitude: 35 m/115 ft.
Population: 1500.
Post code: P-8650.
Telephone code: 0 82.
(i) **Turismo,**
   Município;
   tel. 6 41 25.

ACCOMMODATION. – *Pousada do Infante* (in the former residence of Henry the Navigator), 15 r.; *Baleeira*, II, 108 r., SP; *Dom Henrique*, P I, 13 r.; *Motel Gambozinos*, II, 17 r.; *Estrêla do Mar*, P IV, 7 r. *Casa de Chá da Fortaleza do Belixe*, 4 r.

YOUTH HOSTEL. – *Pousada de Juventude*, Promontório, in the former school of navigation, 70 b.

RECREATION and SPORT. – Swimming, scuba diving. – Bathing beaches: *Praia do Tonel* (to W); *Praia da Mareta* (to S); *Praia da Baleeira* and *Praia do Martinhal* (to E).

The modest little houses of the port of Sagres lie widely dispersed on the rocky plateau, swept bare by the wind, which forms the extreme SW corner of Portugal (and of the whole of Europe).

As a holiday area this is to be recommended only to those who enjoy the simple life and a harsh climate or are keen scuba divers or fishermen.

On the **Ponta de Sagres**, a narrow promontory projecting into the sea to the

S which was known to the Romans as the *Promontorium Sacrum*, are the ruins of the *School of Seamanship* founded by Henry the Navigator in 1421.

The Infante Dom Henrique (1394–1460), known as Henry the Navigator ("O Navigador"), fourth son of King João I, famed for his campaigns in Morocco and appointed Duke of Viseu and Governor of the kingdom of the Algarve, withdrew after the capture of Ceuta (1415) to the seclusion of this "Finis Terrae" ("End of the World"), accompanied by the most famous geographers, cartographers and astronomers in the country, in order to devote himself to developing new techniques of navigation and to training young seamen in the new methods in the school which he founded here.

Sagres – fishing-boats in the harbour

By evolving new navigation procedures, using the quadrant and the astrolabe, Henry laid the foundations for the great Portuguese voyages of discovery, many of which set out from the nearby port of Lagos; and the caravels which were built in his shipyards, incorporating the latest technical developments, were far superior in manoeuvrability and seaworthiness to the traditional types of sailing ships.

Of the 15th c. buildings there survives only the chapel. On the site of the former dwelling of the Infantas there is now a pousada.

In the paving of the parade ground is a large *compass face* which was used in the training of seamen.

SURROUNDINGS. – *Cape St Vincent* and **Algarve coast**: see under Algarve.

Santarém

Historical province: Ribatejo.
District: Santarém.
Altitude: 108 m/354 ft.
Population: 18,000.
Post code: P-2000.
Telephone code: 0 43.

ⓘ **Turismo**,
Rua de Capelo Ivens 63;
tel. 2 31 40.

ACCOMMODATION. – *Abidis*, III, 28 r.; *Muralha*, P II, 10 r.; *Central*, IV, 25 r.

EVENTS. – *Agricultural Show* (beginning of June) in Santarém; *Festas da Senhora do Castelo* (mid August), a typical Ribatejo festival, with bullfights, in Coruche.

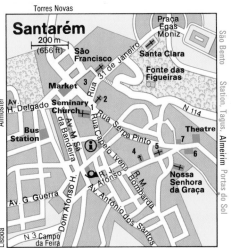

1 Praça Sá da Bandeira
2 Church of N.S. da Piedade
3 Jardim da República
4 Church of Misericórdia
5 Marvila church
6 Church of São João de Alporão (Archaeological Museum)
7 Torre das Cabeças

Santarém, capital of the old province of Ribatejo, is a town of low whitewashed houses built above the right bank of the Tagus, occupying a position of great strategic importance.

HISTORY. – In Roman times, under the name of *Iulianum Scalabitanum*, the town ranked with Braga and Beja as one of the main trading posts in Lusitania. During the Moorish period (8th–12th c.) a castle was built here. After its recapture by Afonso Henriques in 1147 Santarém became the residence of a number of Portuguese kings.
Here in 1319 King Dinis received the papal bull recognising the order of the Knights of Christ which he had founded.

SIGHTS. – The central feature of the town is the *Praça de Sá da Bandeira*, in which Álvaro Gonçales and Pedro Coelho, the murderers of Inês de Castro, were executed with refined cruelty in 1357.
On the W side of the square is the **Seminary Church** of the former Jesuit convent (by Baltazar Álvares, 1676),

Seminary Church, Santarém

which contains superb 17th c. azulejo pictures.
On the NE side of the square stands the *church of Nossa Senhora da Piedade*, founded by Afonso VI in 1665 in thanksgiving for his victory over Juan de Austria, commander of the Spanish army.

To the N, in the Praça da República, is a former **Franciscan convent** (now a barracks), with a 13th c. cloister.

From the Praça de Sá da Bandeira Rua Serpa Pinto runs SE to the *Marvila church* which has a fine Manueline doorway (16th c.) and polychrome azulejo decoration (17th c.).

To the SE is the **Convento da Nossa Senhora da Graça**, with a notable Late Gothic *church* which may have been built by the architects of Batalha Abbey.
The church was the burial-place of the Meneses family. The founders of the family, João Afonso Teles de Meneses and his wife Dona Guimar de Vila Lobos, lie under grave-slabs bearing their coats of arms in the choir, their daughter's tomb adjoining. To the right of the choir is the tomb of Pedro Álvares Cabral (1467/68–1526), discoverer of Brazil, and his wife.

Obliquely across from the Graça church stands the Romanesque and Gothic **church of São João de Alporão**, with fine stellar vaulting in the choir, which now houses the *Archaeological Museum* (Lapidarium).
The church contains the Gothic cenotaph

of Duarte, son of Pedro I, who fell in the battle of Alcácer-Kibir (Morocco) in 1458, only one of his teeth being brought back to Portugal.

To the N is the great landmark of Santarém, the *Torres das Cabeças*, which is believed to have originally been a minaret, with an unusual clock; around the bell are sound-boxes to give it increased resonance.

Farther SE, on the rocky plateau towards the river which was once occupied by the Moorish castle, is the magnificent *lookout point of *Portas do Sol*.

To the N, outside the old town, stands the severely Gothic **church of Santa Clara** (13th c.), belonging to a convent founded by Queen Leonor. Her simple tomb is in the church.
A short distance away, lower down, is a Gothic fountain, the *Fonte das Figueiras*.

Parish church, Santiago do Cacém

SURROUNDINGS. – 10 km/6 miles E, beyond the Tagus, is **Alpiarça**, with the Casa dos Patudos, a country house which belonged to the politician and art lover José Relvas (d. 1929) and is now a museum housing his very fine collection.
The collection includes notable works by many European painters, tapestries (17th–19th c.), porcelain and faience.

6 km/4 miles SE of Santarém is *Almeirim*, where the Infante Afonso, son of João II and Queen Leonor, was killed in a riding accident in 1491.

Santiago do Cacém

Historical province: Estremadura.
District: Setúbal.
Altitude: 210–254 m/689–833 ft.
Population: 7000.
Post code: P-7540.
Telephone code: 0 69.
ⓘ **Turismo Setúbal,**
 Rua do Corpo Santo,
 P-2901 Setúbal;
 tel. (0 65) 2 42 04.

ACCOMMODATION. – *Pousada de São Tiago*, 7 r., SP; *Gabriel*, III 23 r.

The little country town of Santiago do Cacém occupies a commanding spot on a hill crowned by a castle in the southern part of the Serra de Grândola, 20 km/12½ miles NW of the port of Sines.

SIGHTS. – The town is dominated by the old Templar **Castle** (*Castelo*, 254 m/

833 ft), which can be reached by road. There is a pleasant walk with beautiful *views round the outside of the walls.

Below the castle is the imposing **parish church** (*Igreja Matriz*; 13th c., with later alterations), which has a fine Romanesque and Gothic doorway.
The church contains a 14th c. relief of St Tiago, who was killed during a Moorish attack on the town.

The **Municipal Museum** contains archaeological material from the area and a collection of coins.

SURROUNDINGS. – Rather more than 1 km/¾ mile W of the town, approached along a stretch of Roman road, are the remains of the Roman settlement of **Mirobriga**.

Santo Tirso

Historical province: Douro Litoral.
District: Porto (Oporto).
Altitude: 75 m/245 ft.
Population: 10,000.
Post code: P-4780.
Telephone code: 052.
ⓘ **Turismo,**
 Praça do Município;
 tel. 5 10 91.

ACCOMMODATION. – *Caroço*, P IV, 13 r.

EVENTS. – *Pilgrimages* and *fair* in honour of São Bento (St Benedict; 10–11 July), with exhibition of pottery and folk events.

The little town of Santo Tirso, situated in pleasant wooded country on the left bank of the Rio Ave, attracts many visitors who come to explore the surrounding area. The town's main source of income is the textile industry, supplemented by various handicrafts, including the making of pottery.

SIGHTS. – The town's most important building is the **Convent of São Bento** (now an agricultural college), which has a fine Baroque façade.
The *church* is richly decorated with talha dourada and sculpture. There is a beautiful two-storey *cloister* (14th–17th c.).
In front of the church is a *Calvário* of reddish granite.

The little *Museu do Abade Pedrosa* contains prehistoric and medieval material.

SURROUNDINGS. – 10 km/6 miles E stands the fine Romanesque church (12th c.) of the former Benedictine convent of **Roriz**, richly decorated with 12th c. sculpture.

14 km/9 miles E lies the village of **Paços de Ferreira**, which has an unusual Romanesque church with a separate tower.

São Pedro do Sul

Historical province: Beira Alta.
District: Viseu.
Altitude: 168 m/551 ft.
Population: 3500.
Post code: P-3660.
Telephone code: 032.
ⓘ **Turismo,**
    on Road EN16 (E51);
    tel. 7 13 20.

ACCOMMODATION. – IN TERMAS DE SÃO PEDRO DO SUL: *Lisboa*, III, 53 r.; *Ultramarina*, P III, 30 r.; *Avenida*, P III, 21 r.; *David*, P III, 17 r.; *Miradouro*, P III, 7 r.; *Vouga*, IV, 20 r.

In the northern foothills of the Serra do Caramulo at the junction of the Rio Vouga and the Rio Sul, the attractive little town of São Pedro do Sul is a popular base for exploring the beautiful wooded hills in the immediate surroundings, particularly the Serra da Gralheira and the Serra do Caramulo.

SURROUNDINGS. – 3 km/2 miles S is the little spa of **Termas de São Pedro do Sul**, with hot sulphur and sodium springs (68°C/154°F) which were already being frequented in Roman times (remains of Roman baths) and are still used.

King Afonso Henriques spent some time here receiving treatment after his leg was broken in the battle of Badajoz in 1169.

7 km/4½ miles SW of São Pedro do Sul is the ancient little town of **Vouzela** (pop. 1500), with a Romanesque and Gothic parish church (12th c.; fine sculptural decoration) standing above the town. In the market square is the Rococo chapel of São Gil (18th c.).
3 km/2 miles farther S, on a hill, is the *pilgrimage church of the Castelo* (*view; pilgrimage on the Sunday after 5 August).
6 km/4 miles beyond this is the village of *Cambra*, with a ruined castle. The Celtiberian site of **Cova de Lobishomem** (Werewolf's Cave) lies a short distance S of the village.

Serra da Estrela

Historical province: Beira Alta.
Districts: Viseu, Guarda, Coimbra and Castelo Branco.
ⓘ **Turismo Covilhã,**
    Praça do Município,
    P-6200 Covilhã;
    tel. (0 75) 2 21 70.

ACCOMMODATION. – IN SEIA: *Estalagem de Seia*, I, 15 r., SP; *Camelo* (with annexe), P II, 13 r.; *Serra da Estrela*, P II, 20 r.

IN GOUVEIA: *Estrela*, P III, 20 r.

IN MANTEIGAS: *Serradalto*, P II, 18 r.; *Pousada de São Lourenço* (6 km/4 miles NW), 10 r.

IN PENHAS DA SAÚDE: *O Pastor*, I, 8 r.; *Serra da Estrela*, II, 35 r.

EVENT. – *Festas do Senhor do Calvário* (mid August), religious celebrations, dog races and folk festival in Gouveia.

The *Serra da Estrela, renowned for the beauty of its scenery, is a mighty granite ridge which extends for some 100 km/60 miles, with a breadth of 30 km/20 miles, from Guarda to S of Coimbra. It is Portugal's main watershed range, formerly the southern frontier of the country and still the boundary between northern and southern Portugal. With its bizarrely shaped crags and gorges, its mountain streams and lakes, its beautiful forests and magnificent views, it ranks among Portugal's outstanding scenic attractions.

The range contains the highest peak in Portugal, the **Malhão da Estrela** or *Torre* (1991 m/6532 ft). It has a healthy and bracing climate, with February temperatures falling as low as −10°C/14°F, and thus offers reasonably good skiing conditions.

The bare hills provide grazing for sheep and goats; the valleys have an old-established woollen industry.

*Tour of the Serra da Estrela, from Covilhã to Belmonte** (150 km/ 95 miles, partly on unmade roads). – The route suggested takes in the principal beauty-spots and features of interest in the range, starting from **Covilhã** (see p. 109) and going SW on Road N230.

7 km/4½ miles: *Tortosendo* (alt. 500 m/ 1640 ft; pop. 5000), a small textile town. The undulating road continues W and crosses a tributary of the Rio Zêzere.

16 km/10 miles: **Unhais da Serra** (675 m/2215 ft), beautifully located in the valley of the Rio Alfora.
The road then winds its way uphill, with fine views, and crosses the boundary between the districts of Castelo Branco and Guarda in the *Pedras Lavradas* defile.

26 km/16 miles: *Loriga* (740 m/2430 ft). The road now climbs steeply, then descends to *Valezim* (sharp bends) and crosses the Rio Alva on the *Ponte da Jugais* (fine view).

15 km/9 miles: *São Romão* (590 m/ 1935 ft). From here a road runs 12 km/ 7½ miles SE to the *hermitage of the Senhora do Desterro* (790 m/2590 ft), built in 1650, near which is a hydroelectric power station (*view).

Shorter alternative route from Covilhã to São Romão: take the road which runs NW from Covilhã past the large *sanatorium* (6 km/4 miles) to the mountain and winter sports resort of **Penhas da Saúde** (10 km/6 miles; 1453 m/4767 ft), magnificently situated below the E side of the **Malhão da Estrela** (1991 m/6532 ft); then down to São Romão (23 km/ 14 miles).

4 km/2½ miles: **Seia** (532 m/1745 ft; pop. 3500), with the parish church situated on higher ground above the town (view).

·1 km/¾ mile beyond Seia to the NE the road joins Road N17 (on left), coming from Coimbra. Bear right into this road, going NE.

13 km/8 miles: road junction. Turn right off the main road into Road N232, going SE.

3 km/2 miles: **Gouveia** (650 m/2135 ft), a little town on the Rio Mondego, a popular base for exploring the Serra da Estrela.

The road then winds its way up the rocky hillside, with ever more extensive views of beautiful mountain scenery.

21 km/13 miles: **Penhas Douradas** (formerly *Poio Negro*, 1496 m/4908 ft), a group of houses and holiday villas (viewpoint), a good walking and climbing base (e.g. to the mighty rock faces from which the place takes its name).

The road now descends through the forest to the *Pousada de São Lourenço* (1450 m/4755 ft), with a superb view of Manteigas and the Zêzere valley, to which the road winds its way down, with many sharp bends.

15 km/9 miles: **Manteigas** (720 m/ 2360 ft; pop. 2000), a pretty little market town.

2 km/1¼ miles S, in the upper Zêzere valley, is the spa of *Caldas de Manteigas* (775 m/ 2545 ft), with hot carbonic acid and sulphur springs (43°C/109°F). 3 km/ 2 miles farther up the valley is the *Poço do Inferno* ("Well of Hell", 1066 m/3498 ft), a waterfall tumbling down into a cavern.

Beyond Manteigas the road goes down the Zêzere valley, past wooded slopes and cultivated fields and gardens. Beyond *Valhelhas* (520 m/1705 ft) the river is crossed on a narrow bridge.

23 km/14 miles: the road joins Road N18 (on right), coming from Covilhã. Turn left into this road.

3 km/2 miles: **Belmonte** (see p. 85).

Serra de Lousã

Historical province: Beira Litoral.
Districts: Coímbra, Leiria, Castelo Branco and Santarém.
ⓘ **Turismo Coimbra,**
Largo da Portagem,
P-3000 Coimbra;
tel. (0 39) 2 55 76.

ACCOMMODATION. – IN LOUSÃ: *Bem-Estar*, P III, 18 r.; *Avenida*, P III, 10 r. – *Quinta da Alfocheira* (3 km/ 2 miles SE, with fine view), P III, 14 r.

The Serra de Lousã, a quartz and schist massif eroded into picturesque rock formations, extends SW from the mighty granite ridge of the Serra da Estrela to the SE of Coimbra. Reaching a height of 1204 m/3950 ft in the Alto do Trevim, it falls sharply down to the Lousã basin in the N and is bounded on the S by the Zêzere valley.

The main crop grown in this area is corn (maize), which is cultivated on terraces in the valleys, many of which are very narrow. There is also a fair amount of sheep and goat herding.

SIGHTS. – The best base from which to explore the Serra de Lousã is the little town of **Lousã** (alt. 172 m/564 ft; pop. 7500) which lies below the N side of the range and which has some handsome 18th c. burghers' houses. High above the town (3 km/2 miles by road) is the *Miradouro de Nossa Senhora da Piedade*, from which there are panoramic views.

An attractive trip from Lousã is up the narrow valley of the *Rio Aronce*, past numerous little white chapels, to the *Penhasco dos Eremitas* (fine view).

2 km/1¼ miles NE of Lousã is *Figueiró dos Vinhos* (pop. 5000), which is famed for its pottery. The choir of the church is covered with 18th c. azulejo pictures.

Serra de Monchique

Historical province: Algarve.
District: Faro.
ⓘ **Turismo Monchique,**
Município,
P-8550 Monchique.

ACCOMMODATION. – IN MONCHIQUE: *Estalagem Abrigo da Montanha* (on road to Fóia), I, 6 r.; *O Planalto*, P III, 5 r.

IN CALDAS DE MONCHIQUE: *Central*, P III, 25 r.; *Internacional*, P IV, 18 r.

The Serra de Monchique extends from E to W along the N side of the coastal plateau of the western Algarve, forming a protective barrier against cold air from the Atlantic and thus helping to give this area its almost North African climate.

Geologically the range is a much broken-up mass of volcanic rock overlying the basement schists of the region and cut into a western and eastern half by the Ribeira de Odelouca. As a result of the impermeable character of the ground the abundant rainfall is channelled down in numerous rivers and streams (some of them dammed to form artificial lakes) to the coastal plain, which is thus well watered and suitable even for the cultivation of rice. The volcanic nature of the region is also reflected in the emergence of a number of hot springs.

The fertile volcanic soil and the abundance of water have clothed the hillsides and valleys with dense subtropical woodland in an unusually wide range of species, with spruce, arbutus, eucalyptus and mimosa predominating in the valleys and holm oaks and pines at the higher levels. The high ground over 800 m/ 2625 ft is covered with sparse grass and stony soil.

The climate is always mild and equable, though usually cooler than on the coast.

The main occupation is agriculture (cotton and sugar-cane, often grown on terraces), and the favourable climate makes it possible to take two or three crops off the land every year.

The chief place in the Serra de Monchique is the little hill town of **Monchique** (458 m/1503 ft; pop. 10,000). Much of the town's income comes from the sale of handicrafts and local products (needlework, basketwork, pottery; *medronho*, a brandy made from the fruit of the arbutus, with or without honey).

Features of interest in the town are the parish church, with a Manueline doorway – unexpected in this remote rural area – and the highly picturesque ruins, gay with flowers, of the convent of Nossa Senhora do Desterro.

From Monchique a road (6 km/4 miles) winds its way up past the beautiful *Estalagem Abrigo da Montanha* (* view from terrace) to the bare summit of **Fóia** (902 m/2959 ft), the highest point in the range, from which, in clear weather, there are superb panoramic* views.

Another attractive trip from Monchique is the climb to the summit of *Picota* (774 m/ 2539 ft), also affording extensive views.

Below Monchique, idyllically situated in a cool wooded valley, lies the old-established little spa of **Caldas de Monchique** (250 m/820 ft).

Sesimbra

Historical province: Estremadura.
District: Setúbal.
Altitude: 0–249 m/0–817 ft.
Population: 7000.
Post code: P-2970.
Telephone code: 01.

ⓘ **Turismo,**
   Largo do Município;
   tel. 2 23 33 04.

Hotel do Mar, Sesimbra

ACCOMMODATION. – *Do Mar*, I, 119 r., SP; *Náutico*, P II, 15 r.; *Espadarte*, III, 80 r.; *Casa Mateus*, P III, 6 r.

CAMP SITE.

EVENT. – *Festa do Senhor das Chagas* (beginning of May), with a fishermen's procession.

RECREATION and SPORT. – Swimming, sailing, fishing. – Good scuba diving.

The pleasant little fishing town of Sesimbra, below rugged red cliffs on the southern slopes of the Serra da Arrábida, is also a popular seaside resort.

A lively and gay spectacle is provided by the fish auctions when the fishing fleet returns to port.

SIGHTS. – Above the town stands the **Castle** (*Castelo*), built at the beginning of the 17th c. for King João IV by the

Sesimbra – general view, with the beach and the castle

Flemish Jesuit and architect Cosmander (wide *view).

Near the lighthouse are the old *Fort São Teodósio* (17th c.) and the *beach*.

SURROUNDINGS. – Sesimbra is a good base for exploring the **Costa de Lisboa** (see p. 104) and the **Serra da Arrábida** (p. 105).

Setúbal

Historical province: Estremadura.
District: Setúbal.
Altitude: sea level.
Population: 98,000.
Post code: P-2900.
Telephone code: 0 65.

ⓘ **Turismo,**
Rua do Corpo Santo;
tel. 2 42 84 and 2 42 04.

ACCOMMODATION. – *Esperança*, II, 76 r.; *Casa de São João*, P I, 8 r.; *Naval Setubalense*, P II, 16 r.; *Avenida*, P III, 13 r.; *Setubalense*, P IV, 11 r.; *Regional*, P IV, 8 r. – *Pousada de São Filipe* (in Castle), 15 r.

CAMP SITE.

RESTAURANT. – *O Beco*, Rua da Misericórdia 24.

EVENT. – *Feira de Santiago* (end of July and beginning of August), a regional agricultural, industrial and craft show.

The industrial town and district capital of Setúbal, situated on the N side of the wide estuary of the Rio Sado, is Portugal's fourth largest town and third largest port, with large fish canneries, a car assembly plant, shipyards and salt-pans. The Roman town which occupied this site was founded to replace the Celtic settlement of Cetobriga on the Tróia peninsula to the SE, which was destroyed by a tidal wave. Its remains have been excavated.

For a time during the 15th c. Setúbal was a royal residence. It was the birthplace of the poet and satirical writer Manuel Maria de Barbosa du Bocage (1765–1805; small museum in the house in which he was born in Rua de São Domingos) and the opera-singer Luisa Todi (1754–1833).

SIGHTS. – To the N of the Avenida de Luisa Todi is the crowded and picturesque old town, with the few historic old buildings which were spared by the 1755 earthquake.

To the NW stands the Gothic and Manueline **Igreja de Jesús** (1490–91), the first major work by the celebrated architect Boytaca.
The monastic buildings and the cloister of

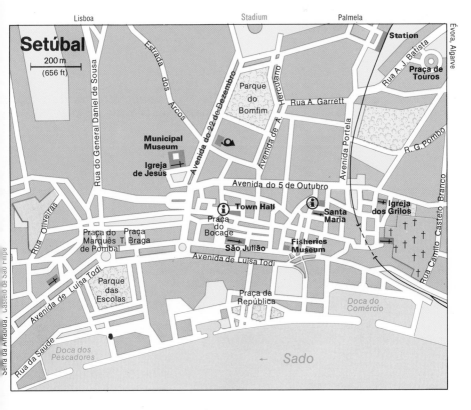

Setúbal – view over the harbour towards the town

Arrábida marble (17th c.) of the Convento de Jesús now house the *Municipal Museum*, with pictures by Portuguese, Flemish and Catalan artists and archaeological material.

At the E end of the old town is the 16th c. **church of Santa Maria da Graça**, with 17th c. pictures.

Also worth seeing are the *church of São Julião* (16th and 18th c.) and the *Convento dos Grilos*, with an elegant Rococo interior (fine azulejos).

To the N of the **Harbour** (*Porto*) is the Praça da República, with beautiful gardens, and close by the **yacht harbour**.

There is also an interesting **Museum of Oceanography and Fisheries** (*Museu Oceanográfico e de Pesca*), which has a large collection of rare species of sponge.

Above the town to the W, the 16th c. **Forte de São Filipe**, built by the Italian military engineer Filippo Terzi, is now a pousada, from which there is an extensive view over the town.

SURROUNDINGS. – 5 km/3 miles SW, at the mouth of the Rio Sado, is the *Torre do Outão*, originally a Roman temple of Neptune (far-ranging *views).

15 km/9 miles W lies the village of *Vila Fresca de Azeitão*, with the church of São Simão (17th c. azulejo decoration).
Nearby is the 16th c. **Palácio da Bacalhoa**, with three Moorish-style domed towers, set in a beautiful park (private property); in the Casa de Prazer is an early azulejo picture of Susanna and the Elders (mid 16th c.). Here, too, is the *Quinta das Torres*, now a hotel, surrounded by gardens.
Somewhat farther away is the palace of the Dukes of Aveiro at *Vila Nogueira de Azeitão*, built by Jorge de Lencastre in 1530. There are interesting wine cellars in the village.

There are attractive trips from Setúbal into the *Serra da Arrábida** and to the *Tróia peninsula* (ferry service). See under Costa de Lisboa.

Palmela: see p. 174.

Silves

Historical province: Algarve.
District: Faro.
Altitude: 85 m/280 ft.
Population: 10,000.
Post code: P-8300.
Telephone code: 082.
ⓘ **Turismo,**
    Rua 25 de Abril,
    P-8300 Silves;
    tel. 4 22 55.

ACCOMMODATION. – *Pensão Central*, P IV, 12 r.

The little country town of Silves, situated on the Rio Arade (Rio de

Silves with its mighty Moorish castle

Silves) and surrounded by forests of cork-oak, was once the Moorish city of Xelb. This was the capital of the province of Al-Gharb and a focal point of intellectual and cultural pursuits, which in its day rivalled Granada in splendour and influence.

The town is believed to have been founded by the Phoenicians. After its recapture from the Moors by Afonso III in 1242 it became the see of a bishop, but after the transfer of the see in 1580 to the new capital, Faro, and the destruction caused by the 1755 earthquake it sank into complete insignificance. It is now an attractive old-world little town with some handsome old burghers' houses.

SIGHTS. – Above the town rears the massive **Moorish Castle** (*Castelo dos Mouros*) with its imposing battlemented walls of red sandstone (restored 1940). A walk round the walls is an experience not to be missed, affording excellent views.
In the courtyard are imposing vaulted cisterns and ventilation shafts.

In the town itself is the 13th c. **Cathedral** (*Sé*), also built of red sandstone. It contains the tombs of a number of crusaders.

Opposite the Cathedral stands the *church of the Misericórdia*, with Manueline windows.

In the lower town is the Manueline *chapel of Nossa Senhora dos Mártires*, with battlemented walls.

At the E end of the town a Manueline wayside cross 3 m/10 ft high, the **Cruz de Portugal** (16th c.), has figures of Christ on the front and the Virgin on the back.

Sines

Historical province: Baixo Alentejo.
District: Setúbal.
Altitude: sea level.
Population: 10,000.
Post code: P-7520.
Telephone code: 069.
ⓘ **Turismo,**
  Avenida do General Humberto Delgado,
  Mercado Municipal, loja 4;
  tel. 63 29 52.

ACCOMMODATION. – *Malhada* (with annexe), P II, 33 r.; *Búzio* (with annexe), P II, 40 r.; *Clemente*, P II,

30 r.; *Habimar*, P II, 17 r.; *Carvalho*, P III, 16 r.; *Beira-Mar*, P III, 16 r.; *Avenida*, P III, 7 r.

CAMP SITE.

The little fishing town of Sines, in a rocky bay on a dune-fringed stretch of the southern Atlantic coast of Portugal, is now in process of development into one of the largest ports and industrial complexes ("industry park", with oil refinery) in the country – a change which quite overshadows its earlier role as a modest seaside resort.

Sines was the birthplace of Vasco da Gama (1469–1524), who discovered the sea route to India in 1497–98.

SIGHTS. – The rebuilt Birthplace of Vasco da Gama now houses a small museum.

Above the **Harbour** is the fishermen's **chapel of Nossa Senhora das Salas** (1335; altered in 16th c.), with a Manueline doorway. In front of the chapel is a terrace with good views.

In the **parish church** (*Igreja Matriz*) are the relics of St Torpes, said to have been found on an abandoned ship which ran aground here in A.D. 45.
From the ruined *castle* there are fine views.

To the W of the town the **Cabo de Sines** (alt. 56 m/184 ft; lighthouse) projects into the Atlantic.

SURROUNDINGS. – 17 km/10½ miles NE is **Santiago do Cacém** (see p. 188).

The beach, near Sines

Sintra

Historical province: Estremadura.
District: Leiria.
Altitude: 225 m/740 ft.
Population: 21,000.
Post code: P-2710.
Telephone code: 01.

ⓘ **Turismo,**
Praça da República 3; tel. 9 23 11 57.
Cabo da Roca; tel. 9 29 09 81.

ACCOMMODATION. – IN SINTRA: *Pacácio dos Seteais* (an 18th c. palace), L, 18 r., with an excellent *restaurant; Estalagem da Raposa*, I, 9 r.; *Sintra*, P II, 10 r., SP; *Bristol*, P III, 12 r.; *Central*, P III, 10 r.; *Nova Sintra*, P III, 10 r.; *Casa Adelaide*, P III, 8 r.: *Solar de São Pedro*, P IV, 8 r. – CAMP SITE.

IN COLARES: *Estalagem do Conde*, I, 10 r.; *Miramonte*, III, 89 r.; *Camarão*, P II, 13 r.; *Recreio da Várzea*, P II, 13 r. – IN PRAIA DAS MAÇÃS: *Real*, P III, 18 r.; *Praiamar*, P III, 6 r.

EVENTS. – *Car races* (varying dates); *Feira Grande de São Pedro* (end of June), an agricultural show; *Feira da Sintra* (second and fourth Sundays in month), a junk market in São Pedro de Sintra.

The little town of Sintra (perhaps better known in English in the older spelling Cintra) lies between Lisbon and the Atlantic on a promontory of land between two gorges below the N side of the well-wooded * Serra de Sintra. With its beautiful setting and its equable climate it became

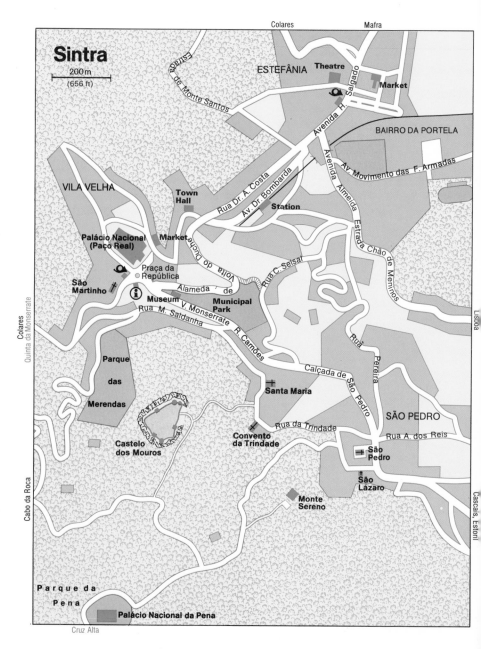

from an early period the summer residence of the Portuguese royal family.

Immediately above the town, on a steep-sided crag, stands the **Moorish castle** which Afonso Henriques captured from the Arabs in 1147, and above this again is the **Pena**, with the Palácio da Pena.
The beauty of the **scenery, combined with the magnificent subtropical vegetation and the nearness of the sea, make Sintra one of the most enchanting spots in the whole Iberian peninsula, well meriting Byron's phrase of "glorious Eden".

SIGHTS. – In the middle of the town is the Praça da República, with a Late Gothic *pelourinho* (pillory column) which has been converted into a fountain.
On the NE side of the square is the imposing *Palácio Nacional de Sintra or *Paço Real*, the ancestral seat of the House of Avis.

Palácio Nacional de Sintra

(Paço Real)

1 Entrance	10 Hall of Stags (Armorial
2 Guard-Room	Hall)
3 Hall of Swans	11 Chapel
4 Hall of Magpies	12 Kitchen
5 Hall of Sirens	13 Central Court
6 Hall of Lions	14 Court of the Lion
7 Hall of Arabs	15 Court of Diana
8 Hall of Chinese	16 Lindaraya Garden
9 Afonso VI's Room	17 Garden of the Negress

The palace was built in the 14th c., partly in Moorish and partly in Late Gothic style, on the foundations of an earlier Moorish castle. Its most characteristic features are the two tall conical chimneys (18th c.).
Remodelled in the reign of Maria II, the palace was the favourite residence of Luís I and became the dower house of his widow Maria Pia. Its richly decorated and furnished interior make it one of the great tourist attractions of Sintra.

The *INTERIOR of the palace offers a survey of Portuguese art and architecture of many different periods, with its shady patios and their refreshing

fountains, its carpeted halls, its coffered ceilings and its azulejo-faced walls. Particularly notable are the *Hall of the Magpies*, the *Hall of the Swans* and the **Hall of the Stags** or *Armorial Hall* (1508), resembling a Persian mosque with its octagonal dome and 72 stags' heads. The Mudéjar influence is particularly striking.

Other features of interest in the town of Sintra are the *churches* of *Santa Maria* and *São Martinho* (12th c.; both much altered) and the **Municipal Museum** in the *Palácio Valenças* (pictures, prints, etc., on the history of the town).

From the S side of the town a beautiful *road branches off on the right and, passing first between magnificent gardens and then through park-like woodland, winds its way steeply uphill, with a number of sharp bends. In some 2·5 km/1½ miles a side road on the left leads to the *Moorish Castle (*Castelo dos Mouros*, 8th–10th c.; alt. 429 m/1408 m). From the gateway we continue on foot, climbing the northern hill and then following the wall-walk around the double outer wall to the southern hill, on which is the Torre Real (Royal Tower). From the wall-walk there is an extensive prospect of the surrounding country, with a particularly fine *view from the tower.

Some 500 m/550 yd farther up a side road on the right leads to the Convento dos Capuchos. From here it is another 1 km/¾ mile to the car park at the entrance to the grounds of another royal summer residence, the *Palácio Nacional da Pena or *Castelo da Pena* (528 m/1732 ft), perched on the summit of a steep rocky crag.

This extraordinary structure was built for Ferdinand of Saxe-Coburg-Koháry,

Palácio Nacional de Sintra

Palácio Nacional de Sintra

consort of Queen Maria II, by Col. von Eschwege in the 1840s, incorporating parts of an old 16th c. convent; the principal tower was modelled on the Tower of Belém near Lisbon. There are conducted tours of the interior (valuable furniture, china, weapons, etc.). From the wall-walk around the castle (the Galeria) and from the dome (access by an external staircase) there is a superb *view (the finest in the Serra de Sintra) over the Estremadura countryside to the Atlantic.

The extensive *Parque da Pena surrounding the castle (closed at night; cars admitted on payment of charge; no charge for car park at entrance to castle) contains over 400 species of trees (including tree ferns) and shrubs; it is particularly beautiful in spring, when the camellias, rhododendrons and azaleas are in bloom.

Some 500 m/550 yd S of the Pena are a rocky pinnacle crowned by a statue of Vasco da Gama and, behind this, the *Cruz Alta (540 m/1772 ft), the highest point in the Serra de Sintra (good views).

SURROUNDINGS. – A very rewarding trip from Sintra is to the **Cabo da Roca** (20 km/12½ miles or 24 km/15 miles). This can be reached either by taking the main road via Colares (N247), which runs NW from Sintra, or by following the narrower but more attractive Caminho de Colares (N375), 4 km/2½ miles shorter, which climbs into the hills to the W, through beautiful forests, passing the 18th c. **Palácio de Seteais** (now a luxury hotel with an excellent restaurant) and the historic old *Quinta da Penha

Verde, set in a beautiful park, which was built in the first half of the 16th c. by João de Castro, fourth Viceroy of India.

3 km/2 miles: entrance to the *Quinta de Monserrate, a Moorish-style villa built in the mid 19th c. for an Englishman, Sir Francis Cook and which now belongs to the State. The beautiful hilly park is notable for its abundance of subtropical plants, including tall tree ferns.
The road now runs sharply downhill between beautiful gardens.

1 km/¾ mile: *Eugaria*.

1 km/¾ mile: Road N375 joins the main road from Sintra to Colares (N247).

1 km/¾ mile: **Colares** (39 m/128 ft), a village famous for its wine and which is also a summer holiday resort.

1 km/¾ mile beyond Colares a road goes off on the right and descends (5 km/3 miles) through the valley of the little Rio Colares to the two small resorts of *Praia das Maçãs* and *Azenhas do Mar*, on a rugged coast much eroded by the pounding of the waves.
The main road, from which there are glimpses of the sea, now winds its way uphill between beautiful gardens. To the left can be seen the Pena, crowned by its castle.

3·5 km/2 miles: *Pé da Serra*. From here an attractive detour can be made on Road N247/3 to the **Convento dos Capuchos** (1560), a former Capuchin house situated 3 km/2 miles E at the foot of the *Monge* (491 m/1611 ft).

3 km/2 miles: a very beautiful forest road (3 km/2 miles; unmade; toll) goes off on the left to the *Peninha (489 m/1604 ft), with a student hostel and an azulejo-decorated chapel of 1711; good views of the Serra de Sintra and the sea.

6·5 km/4 miles: road on right to the *Cabo da Roca (see p. 107). For the continuation of the coast road to Lisbon see under **Costa do Sol**.

Tavira – a view from the Ribeira da Asseca

Tavira

Historical province: Algarve.
District: Faro.
Altitude: sea level.
Population: 12,000.
Post code: P-8800.
Telephone code: 0 81.

ⓘ **Turismo,**
in Town Hall, Praça da República;
tel. 2 25 11.

ACCOMMODATION. – *Eurotel*, II, 80 r., SP; *Arcada*, P III, 20 r.; *Lagoas*, P III, 16 r.; *Mirante*, P III, 7 r.; *Avenida*, P IV, 5 r. – Conjunto Turístico *Pedras d'el Rei I*, at Santa Luzia beach, 1000 r., SP; Conjunto Turístico *Pedras d'el Rei II*, at Cabanas (to NE), 1200 r., SP; Conjunto Turístico *Quinta das Oliveiras*, 145 r., SP.

EVENTS. – Tunny fishing in July and August.

RECREATION and SPORT. – Swimming and water sports on the Ilha de Tavira.

The little town and seaside resort of Tavira, straddling the mouth of the Ribeira da Asseca, has preserved a very Moorish aspect. Once flatteringly known as the "Venice of the Algarve" because of its numerous canals, it dates in its present form from the latter part of the 18th c., when it was almost completely rebuilt after the devastating 1755 earthquake.

Tavira is important for tunny-fishing and has extensive salt-pans around the mouth of the river. It is also noted for a local type of caramel.

SIGHTS. – In the upper part of the town are the remains of an old Moorish castle, the **Castro dos Mouros** (private property; *view). Nearby is the Gothic church of *Santa Maria do Castelo*, converted from a mosque, with a fine Renaissance doorway.

Of the old Arab town walls there remains only the *Arco da Misericórdia*.

The little Renaissance-style *church of the Misericórdia* (1541) has an 18th c. doorway and azulejos.

The round arches of the *bridge* over the Ribeira da Asseca date from the Roman period.

Tomar

Historical province: Ribatejo.
District: Santarém.
Altitude: 122 m/400 ft.
Population: 15,000.
Post code: P-2300.
Telephone code: 0 49.

ⓘ **Turismo,**
Avenida do Dr Cândido Madureira;
tel. 3 30 95.

ACCOMMODATION. – *Templários*, I, 84 r.,SP; *Santa Iria*, I, 10 r.; *União*, P II, 17 r.; *Luanda*, P II, 14 r.; *Nuno Álvares*, P III, 26 r.; *Bonjardim*, P III, 14 r.; *Tomarense*, P III, 12 r.

CAMP SITE.

EVENT. – *Festa dos Tabuleiros* (July in even-numbered years), a procession of girls·carrying elaborately built-up cane structures containing loaves.

Festa dos Tabuleiros, Tomar

The little town of Tomar, beautifully situated on the Rio Nabão, a N bank tributary of the lower Tagus, in the fertile region of Ribatejo in central Portugal, is dominated by the mighty ****Convent-Castle of the Knights of Christ.**

The Order of the Knights of Christ (Ordem de Cavalharia de Nosso Senhor Jesús Cristo) was founded by King Dinis in 1317 for the purpose of "defending the faith, fighting the Moors and enlarging the Portuguese monarchy", following the dissolution in 1314 of the order of Templars which had been established at Tomar since 1159. The new order flourished particularly under its famous Grand Master Henry the Navigator (1418–60).

The Order financed voyages of discovery to the W coast of Africa and thus began the process of colonial expansion of the European nations. In the reign of King Manuel I (Grand Master from 1484) its possessions in Africa and the East Indies made it the wealthiest order in Christendom. In 1523 the knightly order became a monastic order. It was secularised in 1789 and dissolved in 1910.

SIGHTS. – The central feature of the town is the Praça da República, with the **church of São João Baptista** (*c.* 1490), which has an elegant Manueline doorway and contains six pictures by 16th c. Portuguese artists.

To the N is the octagonal *chapel of São Gregório* (originally Manueline, later remodelled in Baroque style), with a tiled

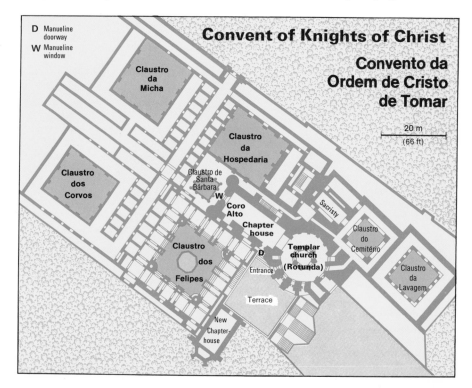

D Manueline doorway
W Manueline window

Convent of Knights of Christ

Convento da Ordem de Cristo de Tomar

20 m
(66 ft)

Claustro da Micha

Claustro da Hospedaria

Claustro dos Corvos

Claustro de Santa Bárbara

W

Coro Alto

Chapter house

Claustro do Cemitério

Sacristy

Claustro dos Felipes

D

Templar church (Rotunda)

Entrance

Claustro da Lavagem

Terrace

New Chapter-house

porch. Beyond this, reached by a flight of 286 steps flanked by gardens, is the *pilgrimage chapel of Nossa Senhora da Piedade* (1613), from which there are extensive views.

Beyond the old bridge, on the far side of the Rio Nabão, is the *Capela de Santa Iria*, with a fine Renaissance doorway (1536).

To the right, below the cemetery, is the old Templar *church of Santa Maria do Olival*, with a mainly Renaissance interior. This was long the seat of the Grand Chapter of the Templars and later the Knights of Christ, the mother church of all the Order's churches in the colonies and the burial-place of leading members of the Order.

From the Praça da República we go SW, passing close to the elegant Renaissance *church of Nossa Senhora da Conceição* (16th c.) and continuing on a road which winds its way up to the **Convent-Castle of the Knights of Christ** (*Convento da Ordem de Cristo*), an extensive complex of imposing buildings ranging in date from the 12th to the 17th c.

TOUR of the Convent (1–2 hours). – Passing through two outer gates of the first *Templar castle* (Castelo), now in ruins, visitors come to a terrace on the left of which is the unfinished *New Chapterhouse*. They then continue past the crenellated Templar church to the magnificent *doorway* of the *Church of the Knights of Christ*, one of the finest achievements of the Manueline style (by João de Castilho, begun 1515).

The exterior of the church is overloaded with decoration, particularly the W front with the extravagantly ornate *window* of the Old Chapterhouse, which shows the Manueline style at its most sumptuous (best view from the terrace of the Claustro de Santa Bárbara).
Almost three-quarters of the interior of the church is occupied by the Coro Alto which was reserved for the monks.

At the SE end of the church a massive pointed arch gives access to the immediately adjoining *Templar church or Rotunda* (begun 1162), modelled on the Church of the Holy Sepulchre in Jerusalem: a 16-sided structure with a central octagon (*charola*) containing the high altar. When the Manueline church was built this became the choir (Capela-mór).

On the NE side of the Templar church is the Gothic **Claustro do Cemitério** (Cemetery Cloister), the only part of the whole complex which dates from the time of Henry the Navigator (azulejos in Mudéjar style).
From the E side of this cloister there is an attractive view of the ruins of the Gothic *Claustro da Lavagem* (15th c.).
From the church of the Knights of Christ a richly ornamented doorway leads into the upper gallery of the *Claustro dos Felipes, a beautiful Late Renaissance structure (1557–62) from the roof of which there is an excellent view of the whole convent.
On the NE side of this cloister (elegant 17th c. *fountain*) a doorway (originally a window) leads into the **Chapterhouse**, now housing a museum, with magnificent vaulting and richly ornamented Manueline windows.

At the NW end of the Knights' church is the little Early Renaissance **Claustro de Santa Bárbara** (St Barbara's Cloister).
To the N and W are three other cloisters, the *Claustro da Hospedaria, Claustro da Micha* and *Claustro dos Corvos*, surrounded by 16th and 17th c. monastic buildings which are now occupied by a missionary school and a military hospital.

Torre de Moncorvo

Historical province: Trás-os-Montes.
District: Bragança.
Altitude: 380 m/1280 ft.
Population: 3000.
Post code: P-5160.
Telephone code: 094.
(i) **Turismo,**
    Edifício da Câmara;
    tel. 2 22 88/9.

ACCOMMODATION. – *Passarinho*, P III, 10 r.; *Campos Monteiros*, P III, 9 r.; *Torre*, P IV, 8 r.

The ancient little town of Torre de Moncorvo, also known simply as Moncorvo, lies in a great tract of arid country given up to the growing of fruit and vegetables on the N side of the Serra do Roboredo (800 m/ 2625 ft; iron-mining), roughly half-way between Bragança and Guarda.

A local sweet is *cobertas* (sugar-coated almonds).

SIGHTS. – The 19th c. *Town Hall* occupies the site of a castle built by King Dinis.

The **parish church** (*Igreja Matriz*), a three-aisled Renaissance building (16th c.), has beautiful talha dourada decoration and contains a fine Gothic triptych of carved wood with scenes from the life of St Anne and St Joachim, the Virgin's parents. The choir has a coffered ceiling.

The *church of the Misericórdia* has a beautifully carved Gothic pulpit of granite.

In the town are a number of handsome old *houses bearing coats of arms*.

SURROUNDINGS. – 16 km/10 miles SW the village of **Vila Nova de Foz Côa** (alt. 439 m/1440 ft; pop.

2500) has a Manueline church (remodelled in the 18th c.) and a fine pelourinho.
18 km/11 miles farther W is *Freixo de Numão*, with a Romanesque church and a ruined castle.

Torres Vedras

Historical province: Estremadura.
District: Lisboa (Lisbon).
Altitude: 66 m/217 ft.
Population: 10,000.
Post code: P-2560.
Telephone code: 0 61.
ⓘ **Turismo,**
　　Rua do 9 de Abril;
　　tel. 2 30 94.

ACCOMMODATION. – IN TORRES VEDRAS: *Moderna*, P II, 28 r.; *Avenida*, P III, 25 r.

IN TERMAS DOS CUCOS: *Termas dos Cucos*, IV, 30 r.

EVENT. – *Carnival* (four days before Ash Wednesday), with processions.

The ancient town of Torres Vedras lies some 60 km/37 miles N of Lisbon on the left bank of the Rio Sizandro, in a region long famed for its wine. The town features in British military history as the headquarters of Wellington's Lines of Torres Vedras, fortified to defend Lisbon during the Peninsular War.

SIGHTS. – Above the town are the ruins of an old Moorish castle, the **Castelo dos Mouros** (*view), to which King Manuel added a handsome battlemented gateway after the reconquest of the town

Other features of interest are the *church of São Pedro* and the conventual *church of São Gonçalvo* (late 16th c.).

SURROUNDINGS. – 2 km/1¼ miles E is the little spa of **Termas dos Cucos.**

Trás-os-Montes

Historical province: Trás-os-Montes.
Districts: Bragança, Vila Real, Viseu and Guarda.
Area: 10,784 sq. km/4164 sq. miles.
Population: 500,000.
Chief town: Bragança.
ⓘ **Turismo Bragança,**
　　Avenida do 25 de Abril,
　　P-5300 Bragança;
　　tel. (073) 2 22 72.

In the extreme NE corner of Portugal lies the rugged mountain province of **Trás-os-Montes** (="beyond the mountains"), **bounded on the N and E by Spain, on the W and SW by the Minho and Douro Litoral regions and on the S by Beira Alta.**

Geologically Trás-os-Montes is part of the Spanish Meseta, which here reaches heights of between 1300 m/4250 ft and 1500 m/4900 ft (Serra do Mogadouro) and is slashed by broad tectonic collapse zones.

The province's relative distance from the Atlantic reduces the moderating oceanic influence on the climate. This is a region of raw winds and considerable temperature fluctuations, with precipitation (in winter frequently in the form of snow) decreasing from W to E.

The archaeological evidence shows that Trás-os-Montes, like the Minho province, was a region of ancient human settlement. Now as in the past the population is concentrated in the fertile valleys (particularly the upper Douro valley: see p. 109), where the soil is suitable for vines and fruit. The bare and arid plateaux provide pasture for sheep and goats.

In addition to agriculture the region has a long tradition of craft production (cloth, lace, pottery). – Small quantities of gold and wolfram (ore yielding tungsten) are also extracted.

In this remote region many old customs and traditions have been preserved. The *romarias* (pilgrimages) celebrated in many places with processions in traditional costume are a major tourist attraction.

Valença do Minho

Historical province: Minho.
District: Viana do Castelo.
Altitude: 72 m/236 ft.
Population: 3000.
Post code: P-4930.
Telephone code: 0 51.
ⓘ **Turismo,**
　　tel. 2 21 82.
　　ACP,
　　on Road N13;
　　tel. 2 24 68.

ACCOMMODATION. – *Pousada de São Teotónio* (in Fortaleza), 10 r.; *Ponte Seca*, III, 10 r.; *Valenciana*, P II, 20 r.; *Rio Minho*, P II, 16 r.

The ancient little town of Valença do Minho lies on a commanding hill above the left bank of the River Minho (Spanish Miño), which here forms the frontier between Portugal and Spain (frontier crossing).

Valença do Minho

1 Capela de São Sebastião
2 Baluarte do Faro (bastion)
3 Igreja Matriz
4 Church of Santa Maria dos Anjos (St Mary of the Angels)
5 Pousada

A local gastronomic speciality is *caldo verde*, a highly seasoned vegetable soup.

SIGHTS. – Above the town rises the massive *Fortaleza, a 17th c. fortress in the manner of Vauban.

At various points on the walls of the fortress there are superb *views of the town, the Minho valley and the mountains of Galicia.

The **Railway Station** (*Estação*) is the terminus of an old-time railway, the "19th c. Train", with a steam locomotive and carriages from various European countries dating from between 1875 and 1891, which runs regular services between Valença do Minho and Oporto.

SURROUNDINGS. – 7 km/4½ miles SE, on the left bank of the Minho, is the **Monte do Faro** (566 m/1857 ft; chapel), from the summit of which there are panoramic *views of the Minho valley, extending eastward to the Peneda-Gerês National Park (see p. 175) and westward to the Atlantic coast.

Viana do Castelo

Historical province: Minho.
District: Viana do Castelo.
Altitude: 20 m/65 ft.
Population: 15,000.
Post code: P-4900.
Telephone code: 0 58.
ⓘ **Turismo,**
  Palácio dos Távoras,
  Avenida de Cândido dos Reis;
  tel. 2 26 20.

ACCOMMODATION. – *Parque*, I, 123 r., SP; *Afonso III*, I, 89 r., SP; *Viana-Mar* (with annexe), P II, 35 r.; *Laranjeira*, P II, 27 r.; *Terra Linda*, P II, 20 r.; *Matriz*, P II, 13 r.; *Rali*, III, 37 r.; *Guerreiro*, P III, 18 r.; *Bela Terra*, P III, 5 r.; *Aliança*, IV, 29 r.; *Magelhães*, P IV, 8 r.; *Vianense*, P IV, 6 r.; *Arezes*, P IV, 5 r. – *Santa Luzia* (on Monte de Santa Luzia), I, 46 r.

CAMP SITE.

EVENTS. – *Festa da Senhora das Rosas* (mid May); *Romaria de Nossa Senhora da Agonia* (third week in August), with procession in traditional costume, and fireworks.
There is a well-known *market* on Fridays.

RECREATION and SPORT. – Water sports; bullfights.

The district capital of Viana do Castelo, charmingly situated at the mouth of the Rio Lima below Monte de Santa Luzia, is an attractive little town which attracts many visitors both on its own account and for its excellent beaches.

HISTORY. – The site was originally occupied by a Greek trading post. During the Middle Ages it remained a modest little coastal village and port, but during the period of the great voyages of discovery in the reign of Manuel I it rose to prosperity and importance, primarily as a result of the very profitable cod fisheries off the coast of Newfoundland. These great days are recalled by the numerous handsome burghers' houses and mansions, many of them with decorated granite façades in Manueline or Renaissance style, still to be seen in the town.
The castle, on a pentagonal plan, which stands above the town and the mouth of the river was built by Philip II of Spain. During the conflict between the Liberals and the monarchy in the 19th c. it became a stronghold of the royalists.

SIGHTS. – In the middle of the town is the Praça da República, with the **Paços do Concelho** (16th c.), the former Town Hall, and in the square a Renaissance *fountain*.
On the N side of the square is the

Viana do Castelo and the Rio Lima

Viana do Castelo

400 m
(1312 ft)

Santa Luzia

Ponte da Barca

Porto

Avenida do 25 de Abril

Avenida Dom Afonso III

Estrada do Papanata

Navarro

Av. Rocha Paris

R. d. Aveiro

Avenida do 25 de Abril

Station

Town Hall

Market

Rua da Bandeira

Av. da Carreira

C. d. Reis

3

Igreja das Almas

N.S. da Agonia

Av. dos Combatentes da G. G.

2

1

4

Avenida de Luis de Camões

Valença

Rua de Monserrate

Rua S. Tiago

Rua Gen. L. do Rego

4

Avenida Marginal

Beach

Praça do Gen. Barbosa

Rua Gen.

Municipal Museum

Rua Man. Espregueira

Lima

Rua de Altamira

Campo do Castelo

S. Domingos

Rua do Loureiro

Harbour Office

Castelo

Doca

1 Praça da República   2 Paços do Conselho   3 Church of Misericórdia   4 Parish church

Renaissance *church of the Misericórdia* (1589), with beautiful 17th c. azulejos. Adjoining the church is the *Hospice* (Hospital), in Flemish Renaissance style. SE of the Praça da República is the Romanesque and Gothic **parish church** (*Igreja Matriz*; 15th c.), which contains fine polychrome wood sculpture, mainly 17th c.
Close by is the 15th c. *Casa de João Lopes*, with armorial bearings.

The interesting **Municipal Museum**, housed in the 18th c. mansion of the Barbarosa Macieis family, contains furniture from Portuguese India (17th c.) and Moorish Spain and a large collection of Portuguese ceramics of the 16th–19th c.

Above the town to the W, approached by a Baroque staircase, is the Baroque **pilgrimage church of Nossa Senhora da Agonia** (pilgrimage on 15 August).

SURROUNDINGS. – 5 km/3 miles NE (funicular near railway station; also reached by road) is *Monte de Santa Luzia (250 m/820 ft), with the 19th c. pilgrimage church of Santa Luzia in neo-Byzantine style. From the top of the hill there are magnificent distant *views.

From here it is 23 km/14 miles along the right bank of the Rio Lima to the old-world little town of **Ponte de Lima** (alt. 300 m/985 ft), where the river is spanned by a medieval bridge of 24 arches, and another 18 km/11 miles to **Ponte da Barca** (see p. 179), within easy reach of the *Peneda-Gerês National Park (p. 175).

Vila do Conde

Historical province: Douro Litoral.
District: Porto (Oporto).
Altitude: sea level.
Population: 15,000.
Post code: P-4480.
Telephone code: 052.
ⓘ **Turismo,**
Rua do 25 de Abril 103;
tel. 6 34 72.

ACCOMMODATION. – *Estalagem do Brasão*, I, 25 r.

CAMP SITE.

EVENTS. – *Midsummer Night* celebrations (23–24 June), with processions; *Feira de Artesanato* (end of July), craft fair.

RECREATION and SPORT. – Swimming, water sports.

Casino.

The industrial town and seaside resort of Vila do Conde (the "Count's Town") lies in a beautiful setting at the mouth of the Rio Ave.

The town's main sources of income are shipbuilding, textiles (cotton), the traditional craft of pillow-lace making and now increasingly the tourist and holiday trade.

SIGHTS. – The town is dominated by the imposing bulk of the **Convent of Santa Clara**, founded in 1318 and subsequently much enlarged; it now houses a school.

On the W front of the fortified *church* (originally Gothic) is a beautiful rose window.

Notable features of the interior (aisleless) are the splendid Renaissance tombs (16th c.) of the founders of the convent, Dom Afonso Sanches and Dona Tareja Martins, and their children. Note also the finely carved coffered ceiling and the choir screen.

From the square in front of the church there is a fine view of the town and the mouth of the river.

On the S side of the church in the *cloister* is a fountain which is supplied with water by an 18th c. aqueduct (7 km/4½ miles long; 999 arches) from Póvoa de Varzim (see p. 182).

In the old part of the town stands the fortified **parish church** (*Igreja Matriz*), with a fine Manueline doorway (16th c.) and a pulpit of gilded wood (17th–18th c.).

In front of the church is a *pelourinho* (pillory column), the symbol of municipal authority.

SURROUNDINGS. – 2·5 km/1½ miles N, on the right bank of the Rio Ave, lies the little fishing port of *Azurara*, with a fine fortified church in Manueline style (16th c.).

6 km/4 miles NE, near the junction of the Rio Este with the Rio Ave, are the remains of the Celtic settlement of **Cividade de Bagunte**, where excavation has recovered well-made objects of stone and bronze.

4 km/2½ miles farther up the valley of the Rio Ave (passing, on right, a handsome Roman bridge over the river) is the village of *Rio Mau*, with the Romanesque *church of São Cristóvão*, originally belonging to a convent founded in 1151.

2 km/1¼ miles N of Rio Mau at **Rates** stands the fine Romanesque church of São Pedro which was built by French architects for Henry of Burgundy at the beginning of the 12th c. It replaced an earlier church on the spot where St Pedro of Rates is believed to have been martyred by Roman soldiers in the 1st c. The church (which was altered in later periods) has rich 12th c. sculptural decoration.

Vila Real

Historical province: Trás-os-Montes.
District: Vila Real.
Altitude: 422 m/1385 ft.
Population: 14,000.
Post code: P-5000.
Telephone code: 0 59.
ⓘ **Turismo,**
　Avenida do 1° de Maio 70;
　tel. 2 28 19.

ACCOMMODATION. – *Cabanelas*, I, 24 r.; *Tocaio*, III, 48 r.; *Excelsior*, P III, 15 r.; *Mondego*, P III, 10 r.; *Coutinho*, P IV, 15 r.

EVENTS. – *Fair* on SS Peter and Paul (29 June); *car races* (varying dates).

Avenida de Carvalho Araújo

Convent of Santa Clara, Vila do Condo

The attractive old episcopal city and district capital of Vila Real, amid fruit orchards and vineyards at the junction of the Rio Corgo and Rio Cabril, on the N side of the Serra de Marão, preserves many handsome burghers' houses of the 15th to 18th c.

The district is famed for its pottery, particularly the ware made at Bisalhães.

SIGHTS. – The main commercial street and traffic artery of the town is the *Avenida de Carvalho Araújo*, in which the principal sights are to be found. At No. 11 is the *birthplace of the navigator Diogo Cão* (who discovered the mouth of the

Congo), a house in Italian Renaissance style.

The Gothic **Cathedral** (*Sé*; 14th c.) was originally the church of a Dominican convent. It preserves Romanesque capitals from the earliest church on the site.

The **church of São Pedro** (16th c.) is richly decorated with polychrome azulejos of the 17th c. The choir has a gilded coffered ceiling.

There are fine *views from the hill above the town, once occupied by a castle, and from the **Calvário** (460 m/1509 ft), with the 16th c. *church of Santo António*.

SURROUNDINGS. – 4 km/2½ miles E is **Mateus** (pop. 1500), with the Baroque country house of the Counts of Vila Real (fine wood ceilings and valuable furniture), surrounded by beautiful gardens (fountains).
The famous Mateus rosé wine is produced in the surrounding area.

7 km/4½ miles SE of Vila Real, at *Panóais*, are the remains of a Lusitanian/Roman temple of Serapis, with a number of rock inscriptions.

There is a beautiful drive of 50 km/30 miles westward from Vila Real through the wild and romantic **Serra do Marão** to **Amarante** (see p. 63).

Vila Real de Santo António

Historical province: Algarve.
District: Faro.
Altitude: sea level.
Population: 10,000.
Post code: P-8900.
Telephone code: 0 81.
ⓘ **Turismo,**
Praça do Marquês de Pombal;
tel. 4 44 95.

ACCOMMODATION. – *Apolo*, III, 32 r.
IN MONTE GORDO: see under Algarve.

CONSULATE. – *United Kingdom:* Rua do General Humberto Delgado 4, tel. 4 37 29.

The little frontier town of Vila Real de Santo António lies on the right bank of the Guadiana which is navigable as far up as Mértola; it was founded by the Marquês de Pombal in 1774 near the site of the earlier town of Santo António da Avenilha which had been destroyed by a tidal wave at the beginning of the 17th c.,

and peopled with fishermen from Aveiro. It is an important port for the shipment of copper and tin and is also engaged in processing the tunny which are caught between April and July.

There is a regular ferry service across the Guadiana between Vila Real de Santo António and the Spanish frontier town and port of *Ayamonte*.

SURROUNDINGS. – There are pleasant drives along the** **Algarve coast** to Cape St Vincent (see under Algarve).

4 km/2½ miles NW of Vila Real de Santo António, above the plain of the Guadiana, is **Castro Marim**, dominated by the huge 14th c. castle of the Knights of Christ, headquarters of the order until its move to Tomar in 1334.

A fishing boat on the Guadiana

Vila Viçosa

Historical province: Alto Alentejo.
District: Évora.
Altitude: 422 m/1385 ft.
Population: 4000.
Post code: P-7160.
Telephone code: 068.
ⓘ **Turismo,**
Praça da República;
tel. 4 23 05.

The little town of Vila Viçosa, built on the slopes of a hill covered with fruit orchards, was once the residence of the Dukes of Bragança and of several kings of the House of Bragança. After the abolition of the monarchy in 1910 the previously flourishing town reverted to provincial insignificance.

SIGHTS. – The principal sight is the **Palace** (*Solar*) **of the Dukes of**

Bragança, built in the 16th and 17th c. on the remains of Moorish, and perhaps even Roman, buildings, which was for many centuries the seat of a brilliant court and the hub of intellectual life. The marble façade, 100 m/330 ft long, has the strictly articulated architectural form of the Italian Renaissance.

The interior is richly decorated and furnished in styles ranging from the 16th to the 20th c., with fine ceiling paintings and family portraits, 17th c. azulejos, tapestries and porcelain, a well-stocked armoury and a collection of coaches. There is an attractive inner courtyard resembling a cloister, with a beautiful fountain.

Adjoining the palace is the *Tapada*, a deer-park of some 5000 acres, which until the beginning of the 20th c. was a royal hunting preserve.
In front of the palace is the spacious *Terreiro do Paço*, with an *equestrian statue* of King João IV.

On the E side of the square, opposite the palace, stands the church of a former *Augustinian convent* (17th–18th c.), with a richly decorated interior.
In this church are the tombs of the Dukes of Bragança. Their wives were buried in the *Convento das Chagas* on the S side of the square.
Just N of the square is a relic of the 16th c. town walls, the curious **Porta dos Nôs** ("Gate of Knots").

Looming above the town is the ruined **Castle** (*Castelo*), with imposing battlemented walls, founded by King Dinis in the 13th c. and enlarged and strengthened in the 17th c.
Within the walls are the Renaissance

church of the Conceição and an archaeological museum.

SURROUNDINGS. – 10 km/6 miles S is **Alandroal** (pop. 2000), with the ruins of a 13th c. castle built by King Dinis.

10 km/6 miles farther S, above *Terena*, are the ruins of another medieval castle, from which there are panoramic views.

Viseu

Historical provinces: Beira Alta.
District: Viseu. Altitude: 540 m/1770 ft.
Population: 20,000. Post code: P-3500.
Telephone code: 0 32.

ⓘ **Turismo,**
Avenida de Calouste Gulbenkian;
tel. 2 22 94.

ACCOMMODATION. – IN VISEU: *Grão Vasco*, I, 86 r., SP; *Viriato*, I, 10 r., SP; *Rossio Parque*, P II, 14 r.; *Avenida*, III, 40 r.; *Bocage* (with annexe), P III, 27 r. – CAMP SITE.

IN CARAMULO: *Pousada de São Jerónimo*, 6 r., SP; *São Cristóvâo*, P IV, 10 r.

The old district capital of Viseu lies on the left bank of the Rio Paiva in a wooded setting amidst the famous wine-producing region of Dão. It is a town of beguiling charm, with its handsome burghers' houses and palaces of the Renaissance and Baroque periods, its narrow granite-cobbled lanes, flights of steps and cosy little nooks and corners.

In the 16th c. Viseu was the headquarters of one of the great Portuguese schools of painting, the principal representatives of which were the landscape artist Gaspar Vaz (d. about 1568) and Vasco Fernandes, known as Grão-Vasco (c. 1480–1543), a native of the town.

Terreiro do Paço, Vila Viçosa

Viseu

Viseu is now an important agricultural town, noted also for its craft industries (carpets, lace, black pottery).

SIGHTS. – In the heart of the charming old part of the town lies the spacious and rather austere *Praça da Sé*.

On the E side of the square stands the Romanesque and Gothic **Cathedral** (*Sé*), originally built in the 12th c., remodelled in the 16th c. and enlarged in the 18th c.

The interior was rebuilt in the 16th c. in the form of a hall-church (i.e. with nave and aisles of equal height), and the Gothic piers now supporting Manueline vaulting. On the massive Baroque high altar is a 14th c. figure of the Virgin.

The *Chapterhouse* contains the valuable Cathedral Treasury. The lower part of the *Cloister* is Renaissance; the upper storey was added in the 17th c.

Built on to the NE side of the Cathedral is a Renaissance palace (remodelled in the 18th c.), the *Paço dos Três Escalões*, which now houses the *Museu de Grão Vasco**, with sculpture of the 13th–16th c., paintings of the Viseu school ("St Peter" and "Crucifixion" by Vasco Fernandes, etc.), works by modern Portuguese painters (19th and 20th c.) and by

Spanish, French, Flemish and Dutch masters, ceramics (16th–18th c.) and carpets and furniture of the 17th and 18th c.

In the *Casa-Museu de Almeida Moreira* (Largo do Major Teles), which is associated with the Grão Vasco Museum, is a further collection of pictures, ceramics, furniture and weapons.

From the Praça da Sé a broad flight of steps leads up to the **church of the Misericórdia**, in the purest Baroque style, its whitewashed walls contrasting with the granite framing of the doors and windows.

The hill is believed to have been occupied in prehistoric times by a Celtiberian settlement.

On the E side of the old town stands the Baroque *church of São Bento*, with 17th c. azulejos.

There are many handsome old houses of the 16th–18th c. (fine wrought-iron grilles), particularly in the town's main street, *Rua Direita*, and in Rua dos Andradas and Rua da Senhora da Piedade.

To the S, outside the old town, is the busy Praça da República, on the W side of which is the **Town Hall** (*Município*). Farther S again is the Baroque *church of São Francisco*, with rich azulejo and talha dourada decoration.

To the N of the town lies the **Cava de Viriato**, a park of roughly pentagonal form which occupies the site of a Lusitanian and Roman fortified camp associated (wrongly) with the last stand of the Lusitanian leader Viriathus.

Viseu

1 Praça da Sé   2 Praça da República   3 Praça de Dom Duarte

SURROUNDINGS. – There is an attractive road from Viseu (40 km/25 miles SW) through the beautiful rugged hills of the *Serra do Caramulo** (highest point 1071 m/3514 ft) to the health resort of **Caramulo** (800 m/2625 ft), set delightfully on the slopes of a hill.

The town's principal attraction is the *Museu do Caramulo*, with a varied collection which includes medieval art, furniture, tapestries, porcelain and ceramics. It is notable particularly, however, for a remarkable collection of pictures by Portuguese and other European artists, mainly of the 19th and 20th c., including works by such famous painters as Picasso, Dalí, Miró, Chagall, Léger, Dufy and Vlaminck.

On the ground floor is an exhibition illustrating the development of the automobile since 1902, with some 50 veteran and vintage cars.

A beautiful *panoramic road* descends the Vouga valley from Viseu to **Aveiro** (see p. 65).

Practical Information

On Albufeira beach (Algarve)

Safety on the Road. Some Reminders for the Holiday Traveller

When to Go

The best times to visit mainland Portugal are in spring and autumn, from mid March to the beginning of June and from the beginning of September to the beginning of November.

The Portuguese spring is at its finest in the W of the country and in the southern province of Algarve. In summer, when the heat is tempered by cool N winds, the seaside resorts attract large numbers of visitors.

In the extreme S of Portugal and on the Atlantic islands the winter is also delightful (with the almond-trees coming into blossom in January and February).

Weather

Under the moderating influence of the Atlantic Ocean the climate of Portugal is marked by comparatively mild winters and summers which are not unduly hot. With increasing distance from the coast, however, continental influences become stronger and the differences in temperature between summer and winter become greater.
Most of the country's rain falls during the winter. The summer rainfall decreases towards the S.
The N winds coming from the area of high pressure over the Azores help to cool the air in summer – an influence which is also reflected in water temperatures.

Maritime influences are of course predominant in the Azores and Madeira, which have more frequent and heavier rain than mainland Portugal.

For a more detailed account of climatic conditions in Portugal see pp. 13–14.

Time

Portugal observes **Western European Time**, i.e. **Greenwich Mean Time**. Portuguese Summer Time is in force from the end of March to the end of September. The time in Portugal is thus the same as in Britain, except to the extent that the dates for beginning and ending Summer Time may differ in the two countries.

Travel Documents

British, United States and Canadian citizens (and nationals of many other countries) require only a **passport** (or British Visitor's Passport) to enter Portugal. No visa is required for a stay of up to

Air and Water Temperatures in °C (°F)			
	Jan.–March	Apr.–June	July–Sept.	Oct.–Dec.
Lisbon	17·1/14·9 (62·8/58·8)	21·8/17·5 (71·2/63·5)	26·3/19·5 (79·3/67·1)	17·2/16·1 (63·0/61·0)
Algarve	17·0/15·9 (62·6/60·6)	22·4/19·4 (72·3/66·9)	27·3/22·6 (81·1/72·7)	17·7/17·0 (63·9/62·6)
Azores	17·0/17·2 (62·6/63·0)	19·7/18·8 (67·5/65·8)	23·9/22·2 (75·0/72·0)	19·4/20·5 (66·9/68·9)
Madeira	19·4/18·7 (66·9/65·7)	21·8/20·0 (71·2/68·0)	24·9/22·7 (76·8/72·9)	21·3/21·4 (70·3/70·5)

Frontier Crossings – Opening Times

Portuguese side	Spanish side	Apr.–Oct.	Nov.–Mar.
Caminha	La Guardia	9 a.m.–6.30 p.m.	9 a.m.–6.30 p.m.
Valença do Minho	Tuy	7 a.m.–1 a.m.	8 a.m.–midnight
Monção		7 a.m.–midnight	8 a.m.–9 p.m.
São Gregório	Puentes Barjas	7 a.m.–midnight	8 a.m.–9 p.m.
Portela do Homem	Lovios	7 a.m.–9 p.m.	closed
Vila Verde de Raia	Feces de Abajo	7 a.m.–midnight	8 a.m.–9 p.m.
Quintanilha	Alcãnices	7 a.m.–midnight	8 a.m.–9 p.m.
Miranda do Douro	Torre Jamones	7 a.m.–midnight	closed 16 Jan.–31 May
Barca d'Alva	La Fregeneda	7 a.m.–midnight	8 a.m.–9 p.m.
Vilar Formoso	Fuentes de Oñoro	7 a.m.–midnight	8 a.m.–9 p.m.
Segura	Piedras Albas	7 a.m.–midnight	8 a.m.–9 p.m.
Marvão (Galegos)	Valencia de Alcántara	7 a.m.–midnight	8 a.m.–9 p.m.
Caia	Caya	7 a.m.–midnight	8 a.m.–midnight
São Leonardo	Vila Nueva del Fresno	7 a.m.–midnight	8 a.m.–9 p.m.
Vila Verde Ficalho	Rosal de la Frontera	7 a.m.–midnight	8 a.m.–9 p.m.
Vila Verde de Santo António	Ayamonte	8 a.m.–midnight	8 a.m.–9 p.m.

60 days. This period can be extended by applying to the Foreigners Registration Service, Avenida António Augusto de Aguiar 18, Lisbon (tel. 55 40 47) or to one of its regional offices.

Visitors intending to take up employment in Portugal require a visa and a work permit.

Cars may enter Portugal for a period of up to 6 months on production of the **registration document** and an **international insurance certificate** ("green card"). A British **driving licence** is valid in Portugal.

Visitors driving a car which is not their own must be able to produce evidence that they have the owner's permission to drive it. Drivers who have held a full driving licence for less than 12 months are limited to a speed of 90 km p.h. (56 m.p.h.), and a disc, available at the border, must be displayed on the rear of the vehicle.

It is advisable to take out **medical insurance**. British visitors requiring emergency treatment can receive free treatment in a hospital outpatient department on production of their passport.

Customs Regulations

Visitors can take in personal effects and holiday equipment without payment of duty. There are also duty-free allowances of 200 cigarettes (or 50 cigars or 250 grams of tobacco), a bottle of wine and a half a litre of spirits.

Caravanners must produce an inventory of the contents of their caravan.
There are no special requirements for taking in boats provided that the usual international papers are available.
"Citizens' band" radios on the 27 MHz frequency can be operated only with a government permit, application for which must be made to the Direcção dos Serviços Radio-Eléctricos, Rua do Conde de Redondo, P-1100 Lisbon. Information from Portuguese National Tourist Office. Video apparatus must be declared on entry.

The **frontier crossings** between Spain and Portugal are closed at night.

Currency

The Portuguese unit of currency is the **escudo** (esc. or $) of 100 *centavos.*

There are banknotes for 50, 500, 1000 and 5000 escudos and coins in denominations of 10, 20 and 50 centavos and 1, $2\frac{1}{2}$, 5, 10, 20, 25 and 50 escudos.

Exchange Rates (subject to variation)	
100 esc.=0·65 US dollars	1 US dollar=153 esc.
100 esc.=£0·38 sterling	£1=262 esc.

There is no limit on the amount of foreign currency that may be taken into Portugal, but sums exceeding the equivalent of 30,000 esc. must be declared on entry. No

more than 30,000 esc., or the declared amount if higher, may be taken out.
No more than 50,000 esc. per head in Portuguese currency may be taken out of the country.

It is advisable to take money in the form of travellers' checks. International credit cards are widely accepted in Portugal, particularly in the larger resorts.

Postal Rates

Letters (up to 20 grams): abroad 40 esc.

Postcards: abroad 40 esc.

Getting to Portugal

By air. – There are direct scheduled services from London (Gatwick) to Lisbon (British Airways, British Caledonian), Oporto (British Airways) and Faro (British Airways); from London (Heathrow) to Lisbon (TAP-Air Portugal, Varig and other international airlines with stopover in Lisbon), Oporto (TAP) and Faro (TAP); and from Manchester to Lisbon (TAP). Seats are also available on many charter services.

By car. – There is a wide choice of cross-Channel car ferry services between Britain and France. From the French Channel ports it is approximately 1200 miles to Lisbon, 1100 miles to Oporto and 1400 miles to Faro.
There is also a motorail service from Paris to Lisbon. Information from French Railways, 179 Piccadilly, London W1 (tel. 01–499 9333).
An alternative route is by the car ferry from Plymouth to Santander in northern Spain. From Santander it is some 600 miles to Lisbon, 500 miles to Oporto and 800 miles to Faro. Information from Brittany Ferries, Millbay Docks, Plymouth PL1 3EF (tel. 0752–21321).

By rail. – There is a daily service between London (Victoria) and Lisbon via Paris and Irun/Hendaye. The journey from Paris to Lisbon takes about 25 hours. Information from British Rail Travel Centres.

Suggested Itineraries

The following routes are merely suggestions which can be varied in accordance with individual preferences.

Route 1
From Valença do Minho along the Atlantic coast to Oporto and Leiria

From **Valença do Minho**, on the Spanish-Portuguese frontier, the main road to Oporto, running close to the coast for most of the way, follows a fairly straight course through vineyards and tracts of heath with coniferous forests. The first stretch runs down the left bank of the Minho (here forming the frontier with Spain) at some distance from the river, which comes into sight only just before Vila Nova.

15 km/9 miles: *Vila Nova da Cerveira*. The road then continues along the Minho, with fine views of the river.
At *Lanhelas* (on right) is an old castle keep (15th c.).
Just before Caminha the road crosses the *Rio Coura*, which flows into the Minho here.

29 km/18 miles: **Caminha**. The road continues close to the coast, through pinewoods.

33 km/20 miles: *Moledo*. Soon afterwards the open sea comes into view some 200 m/220 yd away beyond the rugged coastal cliffs.
Beyond the little seaside resort of *Vila Praia de Âncora* the road again runs through coniferous forest, with the Serra de Santa Luzia to the left.

52 km/32 miles: **Viana do Castelo**, a finely situated district capital.
Beyond the town the road crosses the estuary of the *Rio Lima* (ahead, the *Fort of São Tiago*) on a two-level iron girder bridge (with the railway on the lower level), 560 m/610 yd long, built by Gustave Eiffel's firm in 1877. Beyond this is a beautiful stretch of road, bordered by flowers, running at some distance from the coast through a well-cultivated region in which orchards and vineyards alternate with fields of corn and forests of firs or cork-oaks.

69 km/43 miles: *Mar*, close to the sea. 750 m/½ mile off the road to the right, on a dune-fringed beach, is a small fishing settlement where visitors can observe the harvesting of seaweed for use as a fertiliser or for the manufacture of agar-agar, iodine, bromine, potash, alginic acid, etc. – Then on via *Marinhas*.

73 km/45 miles: *Esposende*. The road crosses the *Rio Cávado*.

77 km/48 miles: road on right (1 km/¾ mile) to the resort of *Ofir*, situated in a pinewood on a beautiful beach.
The main road continues through *Fão* and then runs at some distance from the sea between fields, pinewoods and vineyards.

92 km/57 miles: **Póvoa de Varzim**. – The road then continues close to the sea. To the left is the 7 km/4½ mile long aqueduct supplying the Convent of Santa Clara in Vila do Conde.

95 km/59 miles: **Vila do Conde**. The road crosses the Rio Ave on a narrow iron girder bridge.

98 km/61 miles: viewpoint on right, at the entrance to *Azurara*.
Beyond the village the road leads inland through wooded and park-like country and between beautiful gardens.

111 km/69 miles: *Moreira*. The road then continues on a fairly straight line through the suburbs of Oporto, with the expressway running parallel on the left; then along the Avenida da França to the Praça Mousinho de Albuquerque, and turn left along Rua da Boa Vista to reach the Praça da República in

123 km/76 miles: **Oporto**. – To continue to Leiria on the coast road the best plan is to leave Oporto on the highway which takes off on the W side of the city and crosses the *Douro* on the Ponte da Arrábida. Then, some 10 km/6 miles from the middle of the city, turn off the highway into the Espinho road, which approaches the coast beyond *Valadáres*. Off the road to the right is the resort of *Praia de Miramar*.

143 km/89 miles: *Praia da Granja*, a beautiful seaside resort, with many villas.

147 km/91 miles: **Espinho**. The road now runs a little way inland through a landscape of dunes, coniferous woodland and eucalyptus trees.

165 km/103 miles: road on right (1 km/¾ mile) to the little town of **Ovar** and, 4 km/2½ miles beyond this, *Praia do Furadouro*.

180 km/112 miles: *Estarreja*. Then over the *Rio Antuã* and on through a rice-growing area, with numerous canals.

190 km/118 miles: *Angeja*, where a road branches off on the left to Albergaria-a-Velha.
The road crosses the *Rio Vouga* on a concrete bridge.

201 km/125 miles: **Aveiro**. The road continues S, between 6 km/4 miles and 10 km/6 miles from the sea. Beyond *Ílhavo* it passes *Vista Alegre* (large porcelain manufactory) and then passes through the market village of *Vagos*.

228 km/142 miles: *Mira*. Then through areas of woodland, through *Tocha* and past the *Lagoa da Vela*.

265 km/166 miles: **Figueira da Foz**.
Just before Figueira the Leiria road goes off on the left and crosses the *Rio Mondego* and the island of *Morraceira* on a bridge of 17 arches, with a fine view of Figueira to the rear.

270 km/168 miles: *Gala*. The road turns inland over a fertile plain, with rice-fields and vineyards.
Some kilometres farther on, on the right, is the *Pinhal do Urso*, the second largest pine forest in Portugal, extending westward to the coastal dunes.

299 km/186 miles: *Monte Redondo*, where a road goes off on the right to the beach of Pedrógão, 10 km/6 miles away.

304 km/189 miles: road on right to the small health resort of *Monte Real*, on a hill 1·5 km/1 mile W. 12 km/7½ miles beyond this, at the mouth of the Rio Liz, is the tiny seaside resort of *Praia de Vieira*.
The main road continues to

318 km/198 miles: **Leiria**, chief town of the district of the same name.

Route 2
From Valença do Minho via Braga, Oporto and Coimbra to Leiria

From **Valença do Minho** the road runs up the beautiful *Minho* valley on the left bank of the river; the opposite bank is Spanish.
At *Lapela* is an old defensive tower (14th c.).

16 km/10 miles: **Monção**. Here the road turns S, away from the river, and runs through a well-cultivated upland region with many small villages and hamlets and isolated farmhouses.
Beyond *Barroças* the road winds its way up to the *Serra do Extremo*, with a chapel commanding extensive views.
After *Santo Estêvão de Aboim* the road descends again.

51 km/32 miles: *Arcos de Valdevez*. Then down the valley of the *Rio Vez* to its junction with the *Rio Lima*, which is crossed on an old bridge.

56 km/35 miles: **Ponte da Barca**, where the road down the Lima valley to Viana do Castelo goes off on the right, at first running along the left bank, then crossing to the right.
The Braga road leaves the Lima valley and climbs, with many bends, to the *Portela de Vade* (fine views). It then descends to the little market town of

75 km/47 miles: *Vila Verde*. The road now follows a fairly straight course, and in another 6 km/4 miles crosses the *Rio Cávado* and the *Rio Homem* (which join here) on a bridge of 12 arches.

88 km/55 miles: **Braga**. The road (now signposted to Oporto) leaves Braga by the old town gate, the Arco da Porta Nova, passes the station and continues SW through a fertile upland area, with a view of Braga, dominated by its Cathedral, to the rear.
Beyond Braga the *Serra de São Tiago da Cruz* is seen on the left. To the right is the village of the same name, with a 16th c. castle.

106 km/66 miles: **Vila Nova de Famalicão**.

121 km/75 miles: *São Cristóvão de Muro*. 9 km/5½ miles farther on is the *Estalagem do Galo*.
Then on an expressway through the suburbs of Oporto, along Rua de Antero de Quentel to the Praça da República, then along Rua do Almada to the Praça da Liberdade in

138 km/85 miles: **Oporto**. – Then over the Ponte de Dom Luís I, which crosses the deeply indented valley of the *Douro* in a single span of 172 m/188 yd. Above the river on the far side is the Convent of the Serra do Pilar.

141 km/88 miles: road fork, where it is possible either to bear left on the old main road, which climbs gradually (magnificent panoramic view of Oporto from beyond Carvalhos), or to keep straight ahead on the highway. The two roads join again at *Perozinho*, 7 km/ 4½ miles farther on.

148 km/92 miles: *Carvalhos*. The road continues through pleasant rolling country.

166 km/103 miles: crossroads. The left-hand road winds its way up to the spa of *Caldas de São Jorge*, 4 km/2½ miles NE; the right-hand road runs 4 km/2½ miles SW to the market town of **Vila da Feira**. The main road continues straight ahead through wooded country, and beyond *Arrifana* begins to climb slightly.

173 km/107 miles: *São João da Madeira*. Then on through a further stretch of forest (fine view to left).

181 km/112 miles: **Oliveira de Azeméis**, a busy little town situated above the beautiful valley of the *Antuã*. Then a gentle descent through wooded country, followed by a hilly region of vineyards and woodland.

200 km/124 miles: **Albergaria-a-Velha**, an ancient town at a road intersection: W to Aveiro, E to Viseu.
The Coimbra road continues S through wooded country.

205 km/127 miles: road on right to the attractive *Pousada de Santo António*.
The road continues downhill, crosses the *Rio Vouga* to the town of the same name and then climbs through the forest past *Mourisca*.

215 km/134 miles: *Águeda*, where a road goes off on the right to Aveiro.
The main road follows a dead straight course through the forest.

230 km/143 miles: road on right to the popular spa of **Curia**, 2 km/1¼ miles W.

238 km/148 miles: **Mealhada**, where a road goes off on the left to the spa of *Luso*, 9 km/5½ miles E, and the beautiful **Buçaco National Park**, one of Portugal's principal tourist attractions.
The main road continues through extensive plantations of olives, pines and cork-oaks, which provide the raw material for a considerable cork industry.

252 km/157 miles: road on right to Figueira da Foz. Soon afterwards the road begins to run downhill, with a view of the imposing Coimbra University.
Just beyond this the Coimbra bypass bears right over the Mondego. Bear left to enter the town.

257 km/160 miles: **Coimbra**.
The Leiria road leaves Coimbra by the bridge over the *Rio Mondego*, passing the old and new convents of Santa Clara and the miniature village of Portugal dos Pequenitos. It then winds its way uphill, with views of Coimbra to the rear, and continues over the plateau.

267 km/166 miles: *Cernache*, with a beautiful park and castle (to right).
The road runs between hedgerows of roses and olive-groves.

271/168 miles: *Condeixa*, a market village, with the 17th c. Palácio Lemos. 2 km/1¼ miles SE is the extensive Roman site of Conimbriga, and 14 km/9 miles farther SE the picturesque little town of Penela.
The main road runs to the W of the village of *Venda Nova* and then crosses the boundary between Beira Litoral and Estremadura. Shortly before reaching Pombal the road enters the valley of the *Rio de Soure*. The Pombal bypass bears right: bear left to enter the town.

300 km/186 miles: **Pombal**, where José I's all-powerful minister, the Marquês de Pombal, died in disgrace in 1782.
The road to Leiria affords an attractive backward view of Pombal and then continues in a long straight stretch through coniferous forest and olive plantations.

321 km/199 miles: *Boa Vista*. 5 km/ 3 miles farther on a road goes off on the left to **Fátima**.
The road runs downhill, with views of the sanctuary of Nossa Senhora da Encarnação on its hill, and, after a bend to the right, of the looming castle of Leiria.

328 km/204 miles: **Leiria**.

Route 3
From Leiria via Peniche and Sintra to Lisbon

From **Leiria** the coast road runs W.

12 km/7½ miles: *Marinha Grande*, in the *Pinhal de Leiria* (or *Pinhal Real*), the pine forest originally planted by King Dinis with maritime pines from the S of France in order to prevent the sand from drifting.
– 9 km/5½ miles farther W is the charming seaside resort of *São Pedro de Muel*.
From Marinha Grande the road continues SW through the Pinhal Real.

33 km/21 miles: **Nazaré**, a picturesque fishing town famed for its unusual costumes and its traditional customs.
Beyond the town the road keeps along the coast for a short distance and then turns inland, passing through *Famalicão*.

46 km/29 miles: **São Martinho do Porto**, a seaside resort surrounded by pinewoods.
From here the road runs inland again to *Alfeizerão*, and in another 5 km/3 miles runs into the main road from Leiria to Caldas da Rainha.

63 km/39 miles: **Caldas da Rainha**, a much frequented spa (sulphur springs).
Beyond Caldas da Rainha the main road continues SE towards Lisbon. In 2 km/1¼ miles turn off into a side road on the right.

68 km/42 miles: **Óbidos**, an old-world town high above the Rio da Vargem.
In another 1·5 km/1 mile turn right into a minor road, which runs up into the

81 km/50 miles: *Serra de El Rei*, from which there is a magnificent view of Peniche on its promontory.
The road then descends via *Atouguia* to the coast.

92 km/57 miles: **Peniche**, a fishing port on the rocky *Cabo Peniche*. From here there are boats to the *Berlenga Islands*, jutting out of the sea like teeth.
From Peniche return along the Óbidos road and in 3 km/2 miles turn right along the coast.

110 km/68 miles: *Lourinhã*. The road now turns inland again.

129 km/80 miles: **Torres Vedras**, an old town on the left bank of the *Sizandro*.
2 km/1¼ miles E is the spa of *Termas do Cucos*; 15 km/9 miles NW is the pretty little seaside resort of *Praia de Santa Cruz*.
From Torres Vedras it is possible to take the direct coast road to Ericeira (25 km/

15 miles; typical old windmills) or to continue S through the hills of inland Estremadura, via *Turcifal* and *Freixofeira*, to a

153 km/95 miles: road junction. Turn right off the direct road to Lisbon (42 km/26 miles) into a side road which follows a winding course SW via *Gradil* and *Murgeira* to another road junction (10·5 km/6½ miles). To the right is the direct road to Ericeira: take the other road, which comes in 1·5 km/1 mile to

165 km/103 miles: **Mafra**, famous for its huge 18th c. monastery-cum-palace.
From Mafra return to the junction and continue via the village of *Achada* towards the coast.

176 km/109 miles: **Ericeira**. – The road now runs inland to the SE.

181 km/112 miles: *Carvoeira*. Then up the valley of the *Rio Cheleiros* and continue via *Alvarinhos* and *Terrugem* to

198 km/123 miles: **Sintra**, in a setting which ranks among Portugal's principal beauty spots.
From here the coast road runs via *Cascais* and *Belém* to

258 km/160 miles: **Lisbon**.

Route 4

From Leiria via Batalha and Alcobaça to Lisbon

At **Leiria** the main road from Oporto to Lisbon crosses the *Rio Lena* and then runs uphill, with fine backward views of the town and the castle. It then continues through pleasant rolling country, with vineyards, olive-groves and pinewoods. The Pinhal Real can be seen in the distance on the right.

5 km/3 miles: *Azóia* (bypass), surrounded by fine oaks. The road continues between fields of grain and vineyards, interspersed with tracts of coniferous woodland.
The road then begins to descend, with a view straight ahead of Batalha Abbey. Bear left to reach

11 km/7 miles: **Batalha Abbey**, on the spot where the decisive battle for Portugal's independence began; the abbey was declared a national monument in 1840.

From here a road on the left runs 17 km/ 10½ miles E to the pilgrimage town of Fátima and, 29 km/18 miles beyond this, Tomar.

From Batalha we return to the main road and, turning left, cross a small tributary of the Rio Lena. The road leads uphill, with fine views to the rear of the abbey and the fertile Lena valley.

14 km/9 miles: *São Jorge* (bypass). 2 km/ 1¼ miles beyond this, leave the main road, which continues straight ahead via Rio Major, and turn right into the road for Alcobaça and Caldas da Rainha.

Passing a scattered hamlet (shops selling pottery) and plantations of pines, the road comes to the battlefield of *Aljubarrota*, where on 14 August 1385 the newly elected king of Portugal, João I, defeated Juan I of Castile. To the left is the Serra de Aire.

The road now runs down, with fine views, into a lush and fertile region. Then Alcobaça comes into view, and the road crosses the *Rio Alcoa* to enter the town.

32 km/20 miles: **Alcobaça**, with its magnificent 13th c. Cistercian abbey.

Beyond Alcobaça the road follows the Baça valley and then climbs to *São Martinho do Porto* (198 m/650 ft), with a view (on left) of the Serra dos Candieiros. It then runs down, with views of the sea on the right, to the

45 km/28 miles: *Pousada de São Martinho*, to the right of the road. The road continues downhill, with many bends. To the right can be seen the Concha de São Martinho.

47 km/29 miles: road on right to the little port of São Martinho do Porto.

The road then follows a fairly straight and level course, passing through the village of *Tornada*, surrounded by vineyards.

58 km/36 miles: **Caldas da Rainha**, a much frequented spa (sulphur springs).

59 km/37 miles: the very attractive road via Óbidos and Sintra (see Route 3) goes off on the right. Continue SE on the direct road to Vila Franca de Xira and Lisbon, which runs through hilly country, with fine views.

81 km/50 miles: *Cercal*.

83 km/52 miles: we rejoin the main road from Batalha to Lisbon, which climbs into the **Serra de Montejunto** and through an area of forest and heath, with Montejunto (666 m/2195 ft) to the right. It then descends gradually to the village of

95 km/59 miles: *Ota*. Beyond the village the road crosses the little Rio Ota. Some 6 km/4 miles farther on there is a picturesque view of the old town of Alenquer above the opposite bank of the river.

103 km/64 miles: road on right (2 km/ 1¼ miles) to **Alenquer**.

The main road continues between orchards and olive plantations.

107 km/66 miles: *Carregado*, where the road to Santarém goes off on the left.

A short distance farther on, to the right of the road, is the ancient little town of *Castanheira*.

113 km/70 miles: access road to motorway (toll), which runs parallel to the old road to 2 km/1¼ miles beyond Sacavém.

Soon afterwards, on left, a road goes off on the left to the *Ponte Marechal Carmona* (built 1949–51; 1·25 km/¾ mile long;), which leads over the Tagus to *Atalho*.

The road to Lisbon passes under the approach ramp.

115 km/71 miles: **Vila Franca de Xira**, in the middle of an area where fighting bulls are bred.

The road now runs alongside the *Tagus*, which gradually opens out into an estuary 30 km/19 miles long and up to 12 km/ 7½ miles wide.

135 km/84 miles: *Sacavém*, an industrial suburb of Lisbon on the navigable River *Ribeira*, which is now crossed by the road and by a high arched bridge carrying Lisbon's water supply.

2 km/1¼ miles beyond Sacavém, on right, is the highway exit.

The road then passes **Lisbon Airport**, on right, and continues straight ahead to enter.

146 km/91 miles: **Lisbon**.

Route 5

From Lisbon via Alcácer do Sal and Santiago do Cacém to Cape St Vincent

Leave **Lisbon** either by the huge

suspension bridge over the *Tagus*, here 2 km/1¼ miles wide, and then a 12 km/ 7½ mile stretch of motorway to the exit for Sesimbra (passing the Cacilhas exit), or by the car ferry (12 minutes) to the small port of

2 km/1¼ miles: **Cacilhas**, from which there is a fine view of Lisbon (there is an even better view from the *Monument of Christ the King* on the hill above Almada). From Cacilhas a good road, bearing left, runs alongside the Tagus, then in 2·5 km/ 1½ miles turns inland, passing the access road to the highway. Then either 9 km/ 5½ miles W to the seaside resort of *Costa de Caparica* or to

14 km/9 miles: a side road on the right (a detour of 30 km/19 miles, particularly attractive in spring), which runs through the *Pinhal de Aroeira* to the charmingly situated little fishing town of **Sesimbra**, 23 km/14 miles S.
Returning from Sesimbra, we come in 2 km/1¼ miles to a T junction where the left-hand road leads to *Cabo Espichel*, 7 km/4½ miles E. 5 km/3 miles along the road to the right turn right to reach the beautiful coast road, which comes in 3 km/2 miles by way of *Santa Margarida* (stalactitic cave, chapel) to the magnificent beach of *Portinho da Arrábida*.
Then, returning 3 km/2 miles to the main coast road, continue on this, at times high up on the slopes of the **Serra da Arrábida** (*Formosinho*, 499 m/1637 ft), with the Convento da Arrábida, to Setúbal (18 km/11 miles).

The main road from Cacilhas to Setúbal continues to

29 km/18 miles: *Vila Nogueira de Azeitão*, which is noted for its wine. Immediately before the town turn sharp left for *Vila Fresca de Azeitão*. – Beyond this, off the road to the left, is the Palácio de Bacalhoa (15th–16th c.). Then uphill and down again into the plain. Before Setúbal there is a view, to left, of the castle of Palmela.

43 km/27 miles: **Setúbal**, a port at the mouth of the Rio Sado.

65 km/40 miles: road junction (large gas (petrol) station). To the left is Mérida, to the right the road to Alcácer do Sal, which we now follow. This crosses the River

Marateca, passes through the village of that name and runs up to the Alentejo plateau.

79 km/49 miles: *Palma*. The road crosses the Rio de São Martinho, traverses a low-lying area of rice-fields, then climbs slightly and descends again.

96 km/60 miles: **Alcácer do Sal**. From here either take the direct road to Faro via Ferreira do Alentejo or, at the far end of the town, cross the *Rio Sado* on a bascule bridge 280 m/306 yd long and continue S to

119 km/74 miles: *Grândola*. From here the road runs over the *Serra da Grândola*, passing the *Pousada de São Tiago* 1 km/ ¾ mile before

144 km/89 miles: **Santiago do Cacém**. The road continues S through hilly country, with beautiful views.

175 km/109 miles: *Cercal do Alentejo*, under the E side of *Cercal* (346 m/ 1135 ft).

200 km/124 miles: **Odemira**. The road then crosses the *Rio Mira* and runs up to *São Teotónio*, where the sea comes into view on the right.

225 km/140 miles: *Odeceixe*, where the road leaves Alentejo and enters the **Algarve**, a region held by the Moors for 500 years. The road continues S at a distance of 3–5 km/2–3 miles from the sea, with the **Serra de Monchique** to the left.

243 km/151 miles: *Aljezur*, at the foot of a steep hill crowned by a tower belonging to a former Moorish stronghold.
The road continues between hedges of eucalyptus trees.

250 km/155 miles: *Alfambra*, where the road divides. The left-hand road leads direct to Lagos (24 km/15 miles) over the Serra de Espinhaço de Gão (250 m/ 820 ft); the road to Cape St Vincent bears right via Bordeira, running through a region of dunes.

274 km/170 miles: *Vila do Bispo*, where we join the road along the S coast of the Algarve (see under Algarve in the A to Z section), turning right (SW).

284 km/176 miles: **Sagres**. From here a road runs NW over a tract of heath to

290 km/180 miles: **Cape St Vincent** (*Cabo de São Vicente*), the rocky promontory at the south-western tip of Portugal.

Route 6

From Alcácer do Sal via Ferreira do Alentejo to Faro

1 km/¾ mile beyond **Alcácer do Sal** the road from Lisbon passes a side road on the left to the large artificial lake on the rivers Alcáçovas and Sitimos (12 km/7½ miles NE), crosses the *Ribeira de Sitimos* and continues up the right bank of the *Rio Sado* through a fertile agricultural region.

13 km/8 miles: *Porto do Rei*. Soon afterwards the road leaves the Sado valley and runs through plantations of eucalyptus, pines and cork-oaks just N of the beautiful *Xarrama reservoir*. In 10 km/6 miles a road goes off on the right to the dam (2 km/1¼ miles).
Then over the *Rio Xarrama* to

34 km/21 miles: *Torrão*. The road goes SE to *Odivelas*, where it crosses the river of that name.

64 km/40 miles: **Ferreira do Alentejo**, from which a road runs E via Beja and Serpa to *Vila Verde de Ficalho*, on the Spanish frontier.
The road continues S over the Alentejo plateau and beyond *Ervidel* crosses the *Ribana de Roxo*.

87 km/54 miles: **Aljustrel**, off the road to the right. Then through a featureless tract of country to

110 km/68 miles: **Castro Verde**. The road then climbs a little (beautiful views to the rear), passing *Monte Urza* (287 m/942 ft), and continues in long straight stretches through pastureland and woods of cork-oak.

131 km/81 miles: *Almodôvar*, with a 17th c. Franciscan convent. – 6 km/4 miles beyond this the road crosses the *Rio de Oeiras*.

143 km/89 miles: *A-do-Gueno*. Soon afterwards the road crosses from Alentejo into the Algarve and climbs into the **Serra**

do Caldeirão, with beautiful views of this hilly region (iron-mines).

154 km/96 miles: *Ameixial*. 8 km/5 miles beyond this, on right, is the *Observatório do Caldeirão*. The road reaches its highest point (545 m/1788 ft), with the *Miradouro do Caldeirão* (superb views), and then winds its way down to

175 km/109 miles: *Barranco do Velho*, from which a road runs W to Silves (52 km/32 miles). The main road continues S, winding its way up, via *Alportel*, to a

187 km/116 miles: road to the *Pousada de São Brás* (500 m/550 yd), from the terrace of which there is a beautiful view of Faro.

189 km/117 miles: *São Brás de Alportel*, a little market town in a charming setting at the intersection with the Loulé–Tavira road.
The Faro road continues straight ahead, winding down to the fertile coastal plain of the **Algarve**.

198 km/123 miles: *Estói* (off the road to the left). The road now follows a straight and level course through fruit orchards to

207 km/129 miles: **Faro**, capital of the old province of the Algarve.

Route 7

Lisbon via Évora or Arraiolos to Elvas

Leave **Lisbon** either by the Vila Franca de Xira road as far as Atalho (see Route 4) or, preferably, by the Tagus bridge (see Route 5) to **Setúbal** and on to

65 km/40 miles: a road junction beyond *Águas de Moura*. Turning left here, we continue through a sandy region, passing *Pegões station* (11·5 km/7 miles) and coming in another 2·5 km/1½ miles to

79 km/49 miles: *Atalho*, on the road from Lisbon via Vila Franca de Xira.
From here the road continues E in a dead straight line over the Alentejo tableland, here highly fertile (maize, vines, olives, etc.), with some stretches of woodland.

91 km/57 miles: *Vendas Novas*. The road follows a straight course through heath and pastureland (rearing of bulls).

In 15 km/9 miles the imposing ruined castle of Montemor comes into view. The road then gradually descends into the valley of the *Ribeira de Canha* and after crossing the river climbs again to

114 km/71 miles: **Montemor-o-Novo.** Beyond the town the road forks: to the left is the direct road (80 km/50 miles) via Arraiolos and Estremoz to Borba, to the right the 8 km/5 miles longer but more rewarding road via Évora, which we now follow. Beyond Montemor the road passes a spring and then a lake (on left). Before reaching Évora the road offers a beautiful view of the town.

144 km/89 miles: **Évora**, capital of Alentejo. The road, in excellent condition, continues NE, with a fine backward view of Évora, traversing a hilly plateau between grazing land (horses) and cultivated fields.
Beyond *São Miguel de Machede* the road crosses the watershed between the Guadiana and the Tagus.

178 km/111 miles: *Redondo*. The road continues between arable fields and olive-groves and along the foot of the *Serra de Ossa* (649 m/2129 ft) to *Bencatel*, beyond which Vila Viçosa comes into view.

197 km/122 miles: **Vila Viçosa**. Then 5 km/3 miles NW to

202 km/126 miles: **Borba**, where we join the direct road via Arraiolos and Estremoz.

220 km/137 miles: *Vila Boim*. Beyond this there are beautiful stretches of tree-lined road. In 7·5 km/4½ miles the castle of Elvas comes into sight, and 3 km/2 miles farther on the road runs past the *Aqueduto de Amoreira*, on left.

232 km/144 miles: **Elvas**. From here it is another 11 km/7 miles to *Punto de Caya*, on the Spanish frontier.

Route 8

From Lisbon via Castelo Branco to Guarda

Leave **Lisbon** on the Oporto road (or on highway as far as Vila Franca de Xira).

39 km/24 miles: *Carregado*. Turn right

into a road which runs NE over the fertile Ribatejo plain at some distance from the right bank of the *Tagus*.

51 km/32 miles: *Azambuja*, just to the W of the Azambuja Canal which was constructed to drain the flood plain on the right bank of the Tagus.

64 km/40 miles: *Cartaxo*, in a region famed for its wine.
Beyond the beautiful *Vale de Santarém* the road runs closer to the Tagus, offering a fine view of Santarém.

78 km/48 miles: **Santarém**. The road now runs steeply down in wide curves to *Portelas de Pareidas*, then continues through a fertile agricultural region at some distance from the Tagus. Beyond *Pernes* it crosses the *Rio Alviela*.

118 km/73 miles: **Torres Novas**, a small industrial town to the left of the road.

126 km/78 miles: *Entroncamento*, a railway and road junction, from which there is a rewarding alternative route to Castelo Branco via Tomar (detour of 29 km/18 miles).
The better and shorter road via Abrantes runs E to *Barquinha* on the right bank of the *Tagus*, which we now follow upstream.
Beyond *Tancos* a detour can be made to the banks of the Tagus to see the Templar castle of *Almourol*, on a rocky islet in the river.
The road then crosses the *Rio Zêzere*, which flows into the Tagus here and is dammed a few kilometres upstream to form the Castelo do Bode reservoir.

139 km/86 miles: *Constância*. The road continues above the right bank of the Tagus (fine views), passing the beautiful village of *Rio de Moinhos*.

151 km/94 miles: **Abrantes**, from which there is a road to Castelo Branco running NE through hilly country via *Chão de Codes*.

The preferable route (3 km/2 miles shorter) winds its way down from Abrantes to the Tagus and crosses the river on a 370 m/400 yd long bridge to *Rossio* (fine view of Abrantes to the rear). The road then continues up the left bank of the Tagus. Beyond *Alvega* a road runs

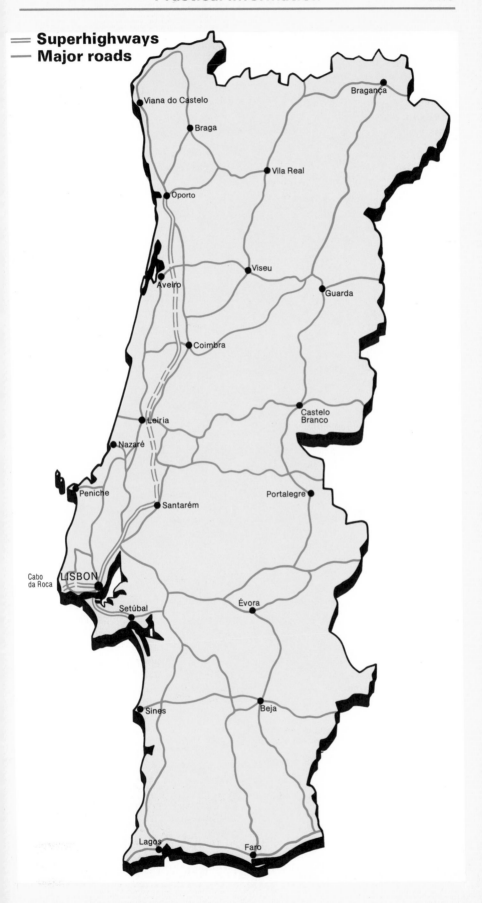

Superhighways
Major roads

Viana do Castelo
Bragança
Braga
Vila Real
Oporto
Viseu
Aveiro
Guarda
Coimbra
Castelo
Branco
Leiria
Nazaré
Portalegre
Peniche
Santarém
Cabo
da Roca
LISBON
Setúbal
Évora
Sines
Beja
Lagos
Faro

steeply down on the left to the Belver reservoir, formed by damming the Tagus. The road now leaves Ribatejo and enters the NE corner of Alentejo.

178 km/111 miles: **Gavião**. The road turns away from the Tagus, and the rice-fields, agaves and fig-trees gradually give place to a bare plateau.

196 km/122 miles: the main road continues E to Castelo de Vide and Cáceres (Spain). Turn left into a road which runs NE over the Alentejo plateau and crosses the *Ribeira de Figueiro*.

207 km/129 miles: **Nisa**. The road then descends again.

224 km/139 miles: *Portas de Ródão*, where the Tagus flows through a rocky defile only 45 m/150 ft wide. The road crosses the river, which here forms the boundary between the provinces of Alentejo and Beira, and then climbs, bearing right. A side road on the left leads to the little market town of *Vila Velha de Ródão*.
The road now crosses the sparsely populated plateau of Beira Baixa.

253 km/157 miles: **Castelo Branco**, capital of the district of Beira Baixa. The road to Guarda continues over the stony and monotonous steppe of the *Campos de Castelo Branco*, beyond

which is another region of vineyards and woodland.

284 km/176 miles: *Alpedrinha*, an ancient little town in a beautiful setting in the eastern foothills of the *Serra da Gardunha*, through which the road now pursues a winding course, with many ups and downs.

297 km/185 miles: **Fundão**. The road continues towards the Serra da Estrêla, crossing the

309 km/192 miles: *Rio Zêzere*, in a green valley, the *Cova da Beira*, which forms a striking contrast to the bare hills which rise above it.

315 km/196 miles: **Covilhã**, the starting-point of an attractive tour of the Serra da Estrêla (see A to Z, Serra da Estrêla).
From Covilhã the road continues NE through the foothills of the Serra de Estrêla, with the peak of Malhão to the left.

335 km/208 miles: road on right (2 km/ $1\frac{1}{4}$ miles) to the market town of **Belmonte**, on a commanding hill.
The main road continues along the foot of the hills, passing from Beira Baixa into Beira Alta.

360 km/224 miles: **Guarda**, chief town of the district of Beira Alta.

Travelling in Portugal
Driving

The **road system** is comparable in density with that of Spain. The only super-highways (*auto-estradas*), however, are short stretches around Lisbon, Coimbra and Oporto. Most long-distance traffic is carried by the numbered **national highways** (*estradas nacionais*), which are of good quality and sometimes provided with parking places and watering points. The *secondary roads* are often in course of (or in need of) improvement, but most of the roads leading to features of tourist interest are perfectly adequate.

Driving in Portugal. – As in the rest of continental Europe, vehicles are driven on

the right, with overtaking on the left. At junctions or intersections of roads of equal importance traffic coming from the right has priority. Although motor vehicles have, strictly, priority over other traffic, motorists should drive with caution at all times and take particular care to watch non-motorised vehicles.
Warning: Should you break down or need assistance on the Ponte 25 de Abril (on

An Air Portugal plane

the southern approach to Lisbon), keep the vehicle as near to the right-hand side of the bridge as possible, remain in the vehicle and hang a white handkerchief out of the window. You must wait inside the vehicle until assistance arrives. Vehicles must not be towed, except by purpose-built towing vehicles, or pushed by hand on the bridge. If you run out of petrol on the bridge you will be fined 600 esc. and have to buy 10 litres (2 gal 1½ pt) of petrol from the bridge authorities at the official price.

You must display an *international distinguishing sign* of the approved type and design. Failure to comply with this regulation is punishable by a fine.

The use of *full headlights* is prohibited in built-up areas. It is recommended that *children* do not travel in the front seats of a vehicle.

Seat-belts must be worn outside built-up areas.

Driving under the influence of alcohol is prohibited.

Road signs and markings are in line with international standards.

A *warning triangle* is compulsory equipment for all vehicles (excluding two-wheelers).

Speed limits: in built-up areas, cars and motorcycles **60 km p.h.** (37 m.p.h.), cars with trailers **50 km p.h.** (31 m.p.h.); on ordinary roads, cars and motorcycles **90 km p.h.** (56 m.p.h.), cars with trailers **70 km p.h.** (43 m.p.h.); on highways, cars and motorcycles **120 km p.h.** (74 m.p.h.), cars with trailers **80 km p.h.** (50 m.p.h.).

There is a minimum speed limit of **40 km p.h.** (24 m.p.h.) on highways except where otherwise stated.

Gas (petrol). Standard and premium petrol and diesel fuel are all available. It is *forbidden* to carry petrol in cars within Portugal.

Air Travel

In addition to its international services the Portuguese national airline **Air Portugal** (*Transportes Aéreos Portugueses*, TAP) also flies domestic services within Portugal and between mainland Portugal and the Atlantic islands. TAP *Regional* also serves smaller airports. Inland routes are served by *Transportes Aéreos Continentais* (TAC).

Air services within the Azores are flown by a local airline, SATA.

Rail Travel

The Portuguese railways are run by a partly State-controlled corporation, the

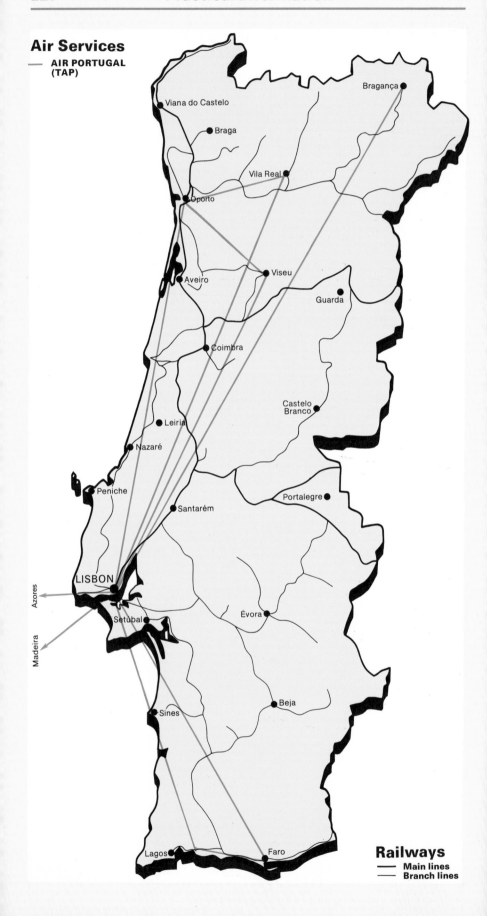

Air Services
— **AIR PORTUGAL (TAP)**

Bragança

Viana do Castelo

Braga

Vila Real

Oporto

Viseu

Aveiro

Guarda

Coimbra

Castelo Branco

Leiria

Nazaré

Peniche

Portalegre

Santarém

LISBON

Azores

Madeira

Setúbal

Évora

Sines

Beja

Lagos

Faro

Railways
— **Main lines**
— **Branch lines**

Companhia dos Caminhos de Ferro Portugueses (CP).

Except around Lisbon and Oporto the network is fairly thin on the ground. The frequency and punctuality of the services are broadly in line with European standards. The interiors of the coaches will often strike a nostalgic chord.

As in Spain, the main lines are broad-gauge (1674 mm/5 ft 6 in., compared with the normal European gauge of 1435 mm/4 ft $8\frac{1}{2}$ in.). Branch lines are often on a narrower gauge.

Fares are low, and various kinds of reduced fares are available in the form of *kilometric tickets* (allowing travel for a total distance of 3000 km/1864 miles and valid for 3 months), *tourist tickets* allowing unlimited travel for a period of 7, 14 or 21 days, family tickets, etc. Senior citizens, on production of their passports, can obtain a *cartão dourado* ("gold ticket"), which costs about 20 esc. and entitles them to a reduction of 50% of the fare for journeys over 100 km/63 miles. – Children under 4 travel free; from 4 to 12 they pay half fare.

There is a **motorail** service between Paris and Lisbon during the summer months.

Bus Services

The rail services are supplemented by more than 500 bus routes covering the whole country, run by a State corporation, the *Rodoviária Nacional*, and various private companies. Timetables are available from local tourist offices, travel agencies, etc.

Boat Services

There are a number of fast motor-launch services on the Tagus, based on Lisbon. Excursions are run in summer.

Old-time Railways

Portuguese Railways run old-time steam trains on two sections of line.

A *"Historic Railway"* (with a German steam locomotive of 1905, German and Belgian saloon cars, Portuguese passenger coaches and a French luggage van) runs on the *Tâmega line* between Livração and Arco de Baúlhe.

A *"19th c. Train"* (with a British steam locomotive of 1875, Portuguese and French saloon cars, French and Swiss passenger coaches and a French luggage van) runs on the *Minho line* between Valença do Minho and Oporto.

Language

Portuguese (*português*), a Romance language, is spoken in mainland Portugal, the Portuguese Atlantic islands (the Azores and Madeira) and the territory of Macao in southern China. It is also still used in the former Portuguese colonies in Africa, India and Indonesia.

Galician, spoken in NW Spain, is a dialect of Portuguese.

Portuguese, in a locally modified form, is also the official language of the 115 million inhabitants of Brazil.

Altogether between 125 and 135 million people in the world speak Portuguese, giving it seventh place (after Chinese, English, Spanish, Hindi, Russian and Arabic) among the world's most widely spoken languages.

The foreign languages most commonly spoken in Portugal are Spanish, English and French, and there are now also numbers of "guest workers" who have learned some German while working in Germany. It is a great help, however, to have at least a smattering of Portuguese when visiting the country.

On first hearing Portuguese spoken a visitor may not quite know what to make of it: it may sound at first rather like a Slav language. The written form of the language, however, can at once be recognised as a Romance language, and some knowledge of Latin or Spanish will be a great help in understanding it.

Portuguese is the direct descendant of the Lusitanian form of Vulgar Latin (the ordinary spoken Latin language). Among the Romance languages it is most closely related to Spanish, though it tends to be of more archaic form than Spanish.

The differences between the various dialects of Portuguese are less marked than dialectal differences in other western Romance languages.

The vocabulary of Portuguese is overwhelmingly Romance (i.e. Latin). There are only trifling Basque and Germanic elements, the latter mainly of Visigothic origin. Since Portugal was reconquered from the Moors considerably earlier than Spain there are fewer traces of Arabic influence in Portuguese than in Castilian. The Portuguese spoken in Brazil includes a significant vocabulary of words taken over from the indigenous Indian population or from Africa.

The Portuguese literary language and the received pronunciation – mainly influenced by the language of educated people in Lisbon and Coimbra – assimilated French, Italian and Spanish elements from an early stage.

Some peculiarities of Portuguese pronunciation:

a	unstressed, like a whispered *e*
à	long *ah*
c	*k* before *a*, *o* and *u*; *s* before *e* and *i*
ç	*s*
ch	*sh*
e	unstressed, like a whispered *i*; in initial position before *s*, practically disappears ("escudo" pron. *shkúsu*; Estoril pron. *Shturíl*)
ê	closed *e*
é	open *e*
g	hard *g* (as in "go") before *a*, *o* and *u*; *zh* (like *s* in "pleasure") before *e* and *i*
gu	hard *g*
h	mute
i	nasalised after *u* ("muito" pron. *muínto*)
j	*zh*
l	in final position as in English or, in Brazil, like a weak *u* ("animal" pron. *animáu*)
lh	*ly* (with consonantal *y*): cf. Spanish *ll*
m, n	in final position nasalise the preceding vowel
nh	*ny* (with consonantal *y*): cf. Spanish *ñ*
o	unstressed, like *u*
ô	closed *o*
ó	open *o*
qu	*k*
r	trilled
rr	strongly rolled
s	*s* before vowels; *z* between vowels; *sh* before hard consonants and in final position; *zh* before soft consonants
x	*sh*
z	in final position *sh*; otherwise *z*

The Brazilian pronunciation of Portuguese is markedly different from that of Portugal. In particular final *s* and *z* are pronounced *s* and not *sh*, and initial *r* sounds almost like *h*.

Portuguese grammar is notable for the rich tense system of the verbs, in particular for the preservation of the Latin pluperfect (e.g. *fôra*, "I had been"). A further peculiarity is the inflected personal infinitive ("Entramos na loja para *comprarmos* pão", "We go into the shop to buy bread").

The **plural** is formed by the addition of *s*, in some cases with modification of the preceding vowel or consonant:

Singular	Plural
o animal	os animais
o hotel	os hoteis
a região	as regiões

The **definite article** *is* o (masculine) or *a* (feminine) in the singular, *os* or *as* in the plural.

The **declension** of nouns and adjectives is simple. The nominative and accusative are the same; the genitive is indicated by *de* ("of"), the dative by *a* ("to").
The prepositions *de* and *a* combine with the definite article as follows:

de + o = do	de + a = da
de + os = dos	de + as = das
a + o = ao	a + os = aos
a + a = à	a + as = às

The Portuguese spoken in Portugal seems lacking in resonance, but soft and melodious, without the hard accumulations of consonants and the rough gutturals of Castilian Spanish. It is notable for its frequent sibilants and for the nasalisation of vowels, diphthongs and triphthongs. Unstressed vowels and intervocalic consonants are much attenuated or disappear altogether.

The stressed syllable of a word so dominates the whole word that the other syllables are radically altered in tone quality and not infrequently are reduced to a mere whisper.

In the spoken language the boundaries between words are so blurred (in the phenomenon known as *sandhi*) that the

Numbers

0	zero
1	um, uma
2	dois, duas
3	três
4	quatro
5	cinco
6	seis
7	sete
8	oito
9	nove
10	dez
11	onze
12	doze
13	treze
14	catorze
15	quinze
16	dezasseis
17	dezassete
18	dezoito
19	dezanove
20	vinte
21	vinte-e-um (uma)
22	vinte-e-dois (duas)
30	trinta
31	trinta-e-um (uma)
40	quarenta
41	quarenta-e-um (uma)
50	cinquenta
51	cinquenta-e-um (uma)
60	sessenta
70	setenta
80	oitenta
90	noventa
100	cem, cento
101	cento-e-um (uma)
200	duzentos, -as
300	trezentos, -as
400	quatrocentos, -as
500	quinhentos, -as
600	seiscentos, -as
700	setecentos, -as
800	oitocentos, -as
900	novecentos, -as
1000	mil
2000	dois (duas) mil
1,000,000	um milhão de

Ordinals

1st	primeiro, -a
2nd	segundo, -a
3rd	terceiro, -a
4th	quarto, -a
5th	quinto, -a
6th	sexto, -a
7th	sétimo, -a
8th	oitavo, -a
9th	nono, -a
10th	décimo, -a
11th	undécimo, -a
	décimo primeiro
12th	duodécimo, -a
	décimo segundo
13th	décimo terceiro
20th	vigésimo, -a
21st	vigésimo, primeiro
50th	quinquagésimo, -a
100th	centésimo

Fractions

$\frac{1}{2}$	meio, meia
$\frac{1}{3}$	um terço,
	uma terça parte
$\frac{1}{4}$	um quarto
$\frac{3}{4}$	três quartos,
	três quartas partes

individual word within a group largely loses its independence: thus the phrase "os outros amigos" ("the other friends") is run together into a single phonetic unit and pronounced something like *usótrushamígush*.

The nine vocalic phonemes used in Portuguese are represented by the five vowels *a, e, i, o* and *u* together with three diacritic signs or accents (´ ` ^), two of which (´ and ^) also indicate the stress. Nasalisation is indicated by the tilde (Portuguese *til*: ˜) or by the consonant *m* or *n*.

The stress is normally on the penultimate syllable of a word ending in a vowel or in *m* or *s* and on the last syllable of a word ending in a consonant other than *m* or *s*. Exceptions to this rule are marked by the use of an accent.

It should be noted that *ia, io* and *iu* are not treated as diphthongs as in Spanish but as combinations of separate vowels. Thus the word *agrário*, for example, with the stress on the second *a*, requires an accent to indicate this in Portuguese but not in Spanish (*agrario*).

Everyday expressions

Forms of address. – Men are usually addressed as *o Senhor*, women as *minha Senhora*. If you know a man's name you should address him by his name with the prefix *o Senhor*; younger women, particularly if they are unmarried, are addressed by their Christian name with the prefix *a Menina*, older ladies only with Senhora Dona and their Christian name. – "You" in direct address is *o Senhor*, *a Senhora* or *Vossê*, in the plural *os Senhores*, *as Senhoras* or *Vossês*. – In Portuguese names, which are frequently very long, the maternal surname usually comes first.

Good morning, good day	Bom dia
Good afternoon	Boa tarde
Good evening, good night	Boa noite
Goodbye	Adeus, Até à vista
Yes, no	Sim, não
Excuse me (apologising)	Desculpe, Perdão
Excuse me (e.g. when passing in front of someone)	Com licença
Please (asking for something)	Faz favor
Thank you (very much)	(Muito) obrigado
Not at all (You're welcome)	De nada, Não tem de quê
Do you speak English?	O senhor fala inglês?
A little, not much	Um pouco, não muito
I do not understand	Não compreendo
What is the Portuguese for . . . ?	Como se diz em português . . . ?
What is the name of this church?	Como se chama esta igreja?
Have you any rooms?	Tem um quarto livre?
I should like . . .	Queria . . .
A room with private bath	Um quarto com banho
With full board	Com pensão completa
What does it cost?	Quanto custa?
Everything included	Tudo incluido
That is very dear	É muito caro
Bill, please!	Faz favor, a conta!
Where is . . . Street?	Onde é a rua . . . ?
the road to . . . ?	a estrada para . . . ?
a doctor?	un médico?
a dentist?	um dentista?
Right, left	À direita, esquerda
Straight ahead	Sempre a direito
Above, below	Em cima, em baixo
When is it open?	A que horas está aberto?
How far?	Que distância?
Wake me at six	Chama-me às seis

Road signs

Alfândega	Customs
Alto!	Stop
Atenção	Caution
Auto-estrada	Highway
Bifurcação	Road fork
Cuidado!	Caution
Curva perigosa	Dangerous curve
Dê passagem!	Give way/yield
Desvio	Diversion
Devagar!	Slow
Direcção única, Sentido único	One-way street
Estacionamento proibido	No parking
Grua	Breakdown service
Ir a passo!	Dead slow
Ir pela direita, esquerda	Keep right, left
Nevoeiro	Mist, fog
Obras na estrada!	Road works
Parque de estacionamento	Car park, parking place
Passagem proibida	No entry
Peões	Pedestrians
Perigo!	Danger
Portagem	Toll
Praia	Bathing beach
Proibido ultrapassar	No passing
Rebanhos	Beware of livestock

Driving terms

accelerator	o acelerador
automobile	o auto, o carro
axle	o eixo
battery	a bateria
bearing	a chumaceira
bolt	o parafuso
bonnet/hood	o capot
brake	o travão
breakdown	a avaria
bulb	a lâmpada eléctrica
bumper	o pára-choque
bus	a camioneta (de passageiros)
car	o auto, o carro
carburettor/carburetor	o carburador
change (pol, tyre/tire, etc.)	mudar
charge (battery)	carregar
check	verificar
clutch	a embraiagem
contact	o contacto
cylinder	o cilindro
damaged	avariado, avariada
diesel engine	o motor Diesel
direction indicator	o indicador de direcção
distributor	o distribuidor
driver	o motorista, o condutor
driving licence	a carta de condutor
dynamo	o dínamo
engine	o motor
exhaust	o escape
fan belt	a correia da ventoinha
fault	a avaria
float	o flutuador
fuse	o fusível
garage	a garage, a garagem
gas/petrol	a gasolina
gas/petrol pump	a bomba de gasolina
gas/petrol station	o posto de gasoline
gas/petrol tank	o depósito de gasolina
gasket	o empanque
gear	a velocidade, a mudança
gearbox	a caixa de velocidades
grease (v.)	lubrificar
headlamp	o farol
hood:bonnet	o capot
horn	a buzina
ignition	a ignição
inflate	dar à bomba
inner tube	a câmara-de-ar
jack	o macaco
jet	o gicleur
lorry/truck	o camião
magneto	o magneto
make (of car)	a marca
maximum speed	a velocidade máxima
mixture	a mistura
motorcycle	a motocicleta
number-plate	a placa, a matrícula
nut	a porca
oil	o óleo
oil pump	a bomba de óleo
park (v.)	estacionar
parking place, car park	o estacionamento
petrol/gas	a gasolina

petrol/gas pump	a bomba de gasolina
petrol/gas station	o posto de gasolina
petrol/gas tank	o depósito de gasolina
piston	o postão
piston ring	o segmento de pistão
pump	a bomba
radiator	o radiador
rear light	a lâmpada de trás
repair	reparar
repair garage	a oficina de reparação
road map	o mapa das estradas
scooter	o scooter
shock absorber	o amortecedor
snow chain	a cadeia antideslizante
spanner	a chave inglesa
spare part	a peça de substituiação
sparking plug	a vela
speedometer	o velocimetro
spring	a mola
starter	p arranque
steering	a direcção
steering wheel	o volante
tow away	levar a reboque
transmiossion	a condução
truck/lorry	o camião
two-stroke engine	o motor a dois tempos
tyre/tire	o pneu
tyre/tire pressure	a pressão dos pneus
valve	a válvula
wash	lavar
water-pump	a bomba de água
wheel	a roda
windscreen/windshield	o párabrisas
windscreen/windshield wiper	o limpapárabrisas
wing	o guarda-lama

Travelling

aircraft	aeroplano, avião
airport	aeroporto
all aboard!	partida!
all change!	transbordo!
arrival	chegada
baggage	bagagem
baggage check	guia, senha
bus	autocarro, camioneta
conductor (ticket-collector)	revisor
couchette car	furgoneta
departure	partida
fare	preço
flight	voo
information	informação
line (railway)	via férrea
luggage	bagagem
luggage ticket	guia, senha
no smoking (carriage)	não fumadores
platform	plataforma, gare
porter	moço de fretes
restaurant car	carruagem-restaurante
railway station	estação
sleeping car	carruagem-cama
smoking (carriage)	fumadores
steward	comissário de bordo
stewardess	hospedeira (do ar)
stop	paragem
ticket	bilhete
ticket-collector (conductor)	revisor
ticket office	bilheteria, guichet
timetable	horário
toilet	toilette
train	comboio
waiting room	sala de espera

Months

January	Janeiro
February	Fevereiro
March	Março
April	Abril
May	Maio
June	Junho
July	Julho
August	Agosto
September	Setembro
October	Outubro
November	Novembro
December	Dezembro
month	mês
year	ano

Days of the week

Sunday	Domingo
Monday	Segunda-feira
Tuesday	Terça-Feira
Wednesday	Quarta-feira
Thursday	Quinta-feira
Friday	Sexta-feira
Saturday	Sábado
day	dia
holiday, feast-day	dia de festa, dia feriado

Feast-days

New Year's Day	Ano-Novo
Easter	Páscoa
Ascension	Ascensão
Whitsun	Espírito Santo, Pentecostes
Corpus Christi	Festa do Corpo de Deus
All Saints	Todos os Santos
Christmas	Natal
New Year's Eve	Véspera do Ano-Novo, Noite de São Silvestre

At the post office

address	endereço
air mail	correio aéreo
by air mail	por avião
express letter	carta urgente
letter	carta
letter-box, post-box	marco postal
packet	embrulho
parcel	pacote
postage	porte
postcard	bilhete postal
poste restante	poste restante
postman	carteiro
post office	correio
registered letter	carta registada
stamp	selo, estampilha
telegram	telegrama
telephone	telefone
telex	telex

Glossary (mainly of geographical and topographical terms)

abadia	abbey
água	water
alameda	avenue

albergaria, albergue	inn	herdade	farm
aldeia	small village, hamlet	hospital	hospital
altura	hill, eminence	hotel	hotel
ancoradouro	anchorage	igreja	church
anfiteatro	amphitheatre	ilha	island
angra	creek, bay	ilhéu	islet
aqueduto	aqueduct	janela	window
arco	arch	jardim	garden
arquipélago	archipelago	lago	lake
avenida	avenue	lagoa	small lake, lagoon
azulejos	glazed tiles (see p. 31)	largo	(small) square
baia	bay	leste	east
bairro	district of town	mar	sea
balneário	bath(s)	mata	wood, forest
barco	boat	miradouro	viewpoint
barragem	dam, reservoir	moinho	mill
beco	blind alley, cul-de-sac	molhe	pier, mole
biblioteca	library	montanha	mountain (range)
cabo	cape	monte	hill
cabril	gorge	mosteiro	monastery
cais	quay	muralha	(town) wall
calçada	street, road (with steep gradient)	museu	museum
		norte	north
caldas	hot springs, spa	oeste	west
câmara municipal	town hall	paço	palace
caminho	path, track, road	paços de concelho	town hall
caminho de ferro	railway	padrão	monument
campo	field, country	palácio	palace
capela	chapel	pântano	marsh, bog
capela-mór	principal chapel (containing the high altar)	panteâo	pantheon
		parque	park
		parque nacional	national park
casa	house	pátio	courtyard
casal	farm, hamlet	paul	marsh, bog
cascata	waterfall	pelourinho	pillory column
castelo	castle	penha	rock, cliff; rocky hill
cemitério	cemetery, churchyard	península	peninsula
cidade	town, city	pensão	pension, guest-house
citânia	prehistoric fortified settlement	pico	peak
		pinhal	pinewood
claustro	cloister	pintura	painting
colina	hill	planalto	plateau
convento	convent (in the most general sense of religious house)	planície	plain
		poço	well
		ponta	point
coro	choir	ponte	bridge
coro alto	raised choir (over W end of church)	porta	door, town gate
		portal	doorway
costa	coast	portão	gate
cova	cave, pit	portela	pass
cruzeiro	wayside cross	porto	harbour, port
cumeada	mountain ridge	pousada	(State-run) hotel, inn
cúpula	dome	póvoa	(small) village
desfiladeiro	pass, defile	povoação	village, small town
doca	dock	praça	square
encruzamento de ruas	street intersection	praça de touros	bullring
ermida	pilgrimage chapel, hermitage	praia	beach
		quinta	farm, manor-house
estabelecimento balnear	spa establishment	retábulo	retable, reredos
estação	(railway) station	ria	estuary, inlet
estádio	stadium	ribeira	river bank, (small) river
estalagem	inn, hotel	rio	river
estrada	road	roca, rocha	rock, crag
estreito	strait	rua	street
farol	lighthouse	sala	hall, room
floresta	forest, wood	sé	cathedral
fonte	spring, fountain	serra	mountain range, range of hills
fortaleza	fortress, castle		
forte	fort	solar	manor-house, mansion
foz	mouth of river	sul	south
fronteira	frontier	talha dourada	gilded woodwork (see p. 33)
funicular	funicular		
furna	cavern	tapada	park
garganta	gorge	tapeçaria	tapestry
gruta	cave	termas	hot springs, spa

terreiro	square, open space	(posto de) turismo	tourist information office
tesouro	treasury	vale	valley
torre	tower	vila	(small) town
travessa	lane, alley	vulcão	volcano

Manners and Customs

The relaxed manner of the educated Portuguese and the native courtesy of all classes of the population make it easy for visitors to feel at home in Portugal. They should, however, always take care to observe the customs of the country and behave with tact and discretion. It should be borne in mind that the Portuguese people have a strongly developed sense of equality and that even the humblest expects to be treated as a *cavalheiro* (gentleman). The national pride of the Portuguese is easily hurt: visitors should be careful about engaging in political discussion or criticising Portuguese manners and customs. And a display of impatience does not go down well with the Portuguese.

Considerable importance is still attached to neatness of **dress**. It is not considered quite the thing for men to go about in a town in shorts or shirt-sleeves; and ties are much more commonly worn even in summer than in some other European countries. In northern Portugal the attitude to dress and behaviour is stricter than in the more easy-going south. Although the police still keep a watch on bathing beaches, two-piece bathing suits are now very common in Portugal; but there is up to now no provision for nude bathing. – Women should not enter churches wearing sleeveless or low-necked dresses, unduly short skirts or shorts.

Guides (singular *o guia*) are to be found at the principal sights and in the larger hotels; their charges are often high. Interpreters (*o intérprete*) usually ask twice as much as guides; before engaging one, it is advisable to test his competence. Some of the guides are well informed and helpful, but visitors should beware of "guides" who are merely touts, anxious to entice customers into a particular shop or restaurant.

Tipping (*serviço*). – As in other countries, hotels and restaurants include a service charge in the bill, but it is usual to give a small tip (*gorjeta*) on top of this to waiters (*empregado*), chambermaids (*criada do quarto*), porters (*moço*: it is not usual to carry your own bags), lift-boys, etc. A tip is also expected by custodians at tourist sights and the attendants who show you to your seat in cinemas, theatres, bullrings, etc. It is advisable, therefore, to carry sufficient small change. The tactful offer of an appropriate sum can also sometimes help to solve some particular difficulty (if a hotel is full, an office is closed, tickets are sold out, etc.).

Accommodation

Hotels

In the larger towns and resorts and **hotels** in the higher categories are fully up to international standards of comfort and amenity. Off the main tourist routes, however, the standard is often lower than in some other European countries.

There are numerous **pensions** or guest-houses (*pensões*, singular *pensão*), which replace hotels in the smaller places and are often very similar to hotels.

Hotel Algarve, Praia da Rocha

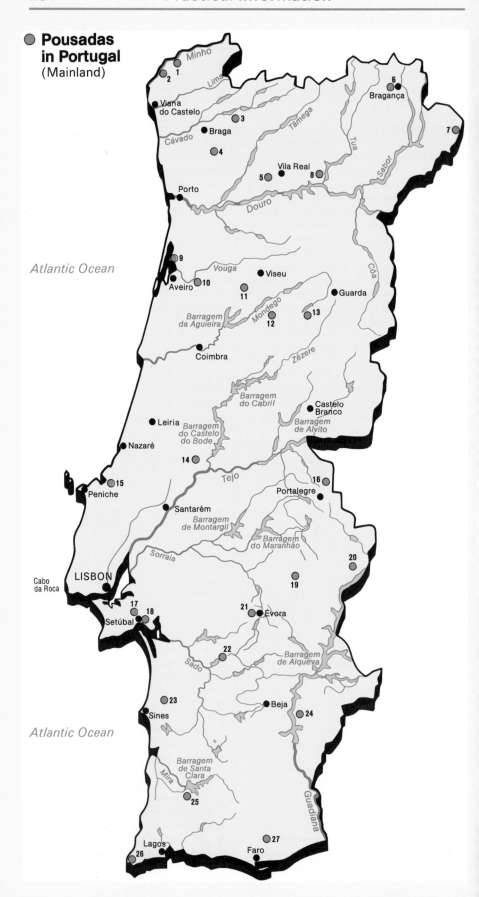

**Pousadas
in Portugal**
(Mainland)

Minho

2 1

Viana
do Castelo

Lima

Bragança

6

7

Cávado

3

Braga

Tâmega

4

Tua

Sabor

Vila Real

5   8

Porto

Douro

Côa

Atlantic Ocean

9

Vouga

Viseu

Aveiro 10

11

Guarda

Barragem
da Aguieira

Mondego

12

13

Coimbra

Zêzere

Barragem
do Cabril

Castelo
Branco

Leiria

Barragem
do Castelo
do Bode

Barragem
de Alvito

Nazaré

14

Tejo

16

Portalegre

Peniche

15

Santarém

Barragem
de Montargil

Sorraia

Barragem
do Maranhão

20

Cabo
da Roca

LISBON

19

17
18

21

Évora

Setúbal

22

Sado

Barragem
de Alqueva

23

Sines

Beja

24

Atlantic Ocean

Barragem
de Santa
Clara

Mira

Guadiana

25

Lagos

27

26

Faro

Hotel Tariffs (in Escudos)

official	Category in this Guide	Rooms for 2 persons	Breakfast per person
Hotels			
*****	L	12500–21500	350–700
****	I	8000–15500	300–600
***	II	5500–11500	250–400
**	III	4000–8500	200–350
*	IV	2500–4500	50–250
Pensions			
****	P I	3500–10000	200–400
***	P II	3000–7000	200–350
**	P III	2500–6000	150–300
*	P IV	1500–4000	100–200
Estalagens and Albergarias			
*****	L	7000–15500	300–600
****	I	6000–12500	300–550
***	II	5500–1000	250–300

The price for a single room is approximately 30% less. Prices given are approximate and not binding.

Motels and Apartments

		Rooms for 2 persons	Rooms for 3 persons	Rooms for 4 persons
****	I	4000–15500	5500–18000	6000–21500
***	II	3500–13000	4000–15500	5500–18000

Albergarias and hotels described as *residências* have no restaurants. The simplest form of accommodation is provided by **casas de hóspedes**.

The **pousadas** are State-owned hotels, mostly in the country, which are excellently equipped and managed; their prices compare favourably with those charged in privately run hotels of similar category. The maximum period of stay is 5 days (November to May 7 days; no restriction in pousadas with over 10 rooms). Similar to pousadas are the numerous privately run *estalagens* (singular *estalagem*), which are also found in towns.

Hotels and pensions are classified in categories designated by stars (from 1 to 5). Pousadas are indicated by a special symbol and are not classified in the normal categories.

Tariffs vary within each category according to the area and the situation of the hotel.

It is usual to take meals in your hotel; if you eat out the room charge may be increased by 20%.

Hotels are required to keep a complaints book.

● Pousadas

1 Valença do Minho
Pousada de São Teotónio
32 r. tel. (51) 2 22 52.

2 Vila Nova de Cerveira
Pousada de Dom Dinis
29 r. tel. (51) 9 56 01.

3 Viera do Minho Caniçada
Pousada de São Bento
10 r. tel. (53) 5 71 90/1.

4 Guimarães
Pousada de Santa Maria da Oliveira
16 r. tel. (53) 41 21 57.

5 Amarante/Serra do Marão
Pousada de São Gonçalo
15 r. tel. (55) 46 11 13.

6 Bragança
Pousada de São Bartolomeu
16 r. tel. (503) 2 24 93.

7 **Miranda do Douro**
Pousada de Santa Catarina
12 r. tel (92) 4 22 66.

8 **Alijó**
Pousada do Barão de Forrester
11 r. tel. (59) 9 54 67.

9 **Murtosa**
Pousada da Ria
10 r. tel. (34) 4 83 32.

10 **Serém**
Pousada de Santo António
13 r. tel. (34) 52 12 30.

11 **Caramulo**
Pousada de São Jerónimo
6 r. tel. (32) 8 62 91.

12 **Póvoa das Quartas**
Pousada de Santa Bárbara
16 r. tel. (38) 5 22 52.

13 **Manteigas**
Pousada de São Lourenço
12 r. tel. (75) 4 71 50.

14 **Castelo do Bode**
Pousada de São Pedro
15 r. tel. (41) 3 81 75.

15 **Óbidos**
Pousada do Castelo
6 r. tel. (62) 9 51 05.

16 **Marvão**
Pousada de Santa Maria
8 r. tel. (45) 9 32 01/2

17 **Palmela**
Pousada de Palmela
29 r. tel. (1) 235 0410.

18 **Setúbal**
Pousada de São Filipe
14 r. tel. (65) 2 38 44.

19 **Estremoz**
Pousada da Rainha
Santa Isabel
23 r. tel. (68) 2 26 18

20 **Elvas**
Pousada de Santa Luzia
11 r. tel. (18) 6 21 94.

21 **Évora**
Pousada dos Lóios
32 r. tel. (66) 2 40 51.

22 **Vale de Gaio**
Pousada do Vale de Gaio
6 r. tel. (65) 66100.

23 **Santiago do Cacém**
Pousada de São Tiago
7 r. tel. (69) 2 24 59.

24 **Serpa**
Pousada de São Gens
17 r. tel. (84) 9 03 27.

25 **Santa Clara a Velha**
Pousada de Santa Clara
6 r. tel. (83) 5 22 50.

26 **Sagres**
Pousada do Infante
21 r. tel. (82) 64222/3.

27 **São Brás de Alportel**
Pousada de São Brás
23 r. tel. (89) 4 23 05.

Youth Hostels

Youth hostels (*pousadas de juventude*) offer accommodation at reasonable prices, suitable particularly for young people (though there is no upper age limit for youth hostellers in Portugal). They are relatively few in number, and advance booking is therefore advisable, particularly in July and August. Parties of more than five must book through the head office.

Information: **Associaço Portuguesa de Pousadas de Juventude,**
Rua Andrade Corvo 46,
P-1000 **Lisboa** 1;
tel. (01) 57 10 54.

Camping and Caravanning

There are at present some 70 camp sites (*parques de campismo*) in Portugal, mostly on the coast. Many sites require the production of a camping carnet.

Free-lance camping is not permitted within built-up areas and protected water supply areas or within a kilometre of camping sites, bathing beaches, etc.

Information: **Federação Portuguesa de Campismo e Caravanismo,**
Rua da Voz do Operário 1,
P-1000 **Lisboa** 2;
tel. (00 19) 86 23 50.

● Camp Sites (selection)

1	Caminha
2	Vilar de Mouros
3	Chaves
4	Viana do Castelo
5	Cabedelo
6	Caldas das Taipas
7	Guimartães
8	Vila do Conde
9	Amarante
10	Matosinhos
11	Oporto
12–13	Vila Nova de Gaia
14	Lamego
15	Espinho
16	Esmoriz
17	Cortegaça
18	Oliveira de Azeméis
19	Termas de São Pedro do Sul
20	São Pedro do Sul
21	Murtosa
22	Aveiro
23	Viseu
24	Ílhavo
25	Guarda
26	Aguada de Baixo
27	Mira
28	Dunas de Mira

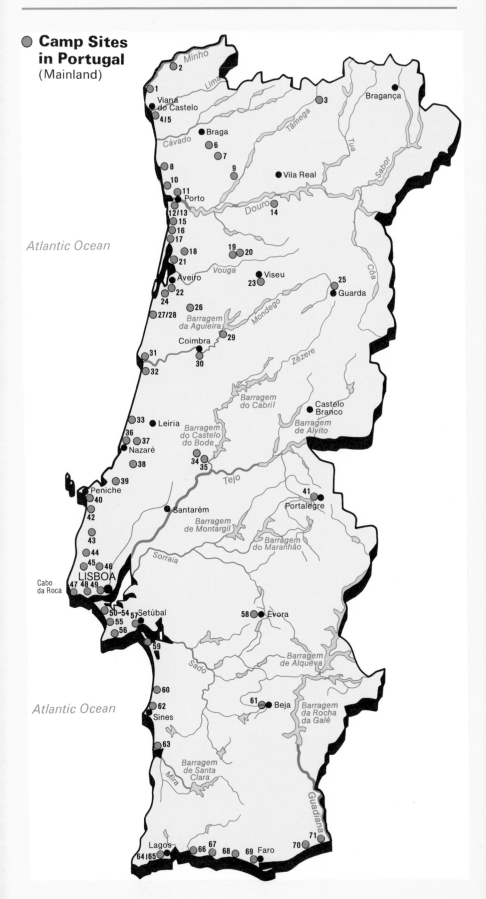

Camp Sites in Portugal
(Mainland)

Food and Drink

Portuguese cooking is solid and nourishing, making much use of olive oil and herbs such as thyme, rosemary, bay-leaves and coriander leaves; and Portuguese meals tend to be substantial, consisting of several courses.

There are numerous fish dishes, often based on stockfish (dried cod). Seafood, egg dishes and rice also feature prominently on the menu. Lamb and pork, too, are cooked in a variety of ways.

The Portuguese Menu
(*lista, ementa, carta*

MEALS. – Breakfast *pequeno almoço*; lunch *almoço*; dinner *jantar*; supper (late snack) *ceia*.
Menu *ementa*; dish of the day (plat du jour) *prato do dia*.
Bill *conta*.

TABLE SETTING. – Knife, fork and spoon *talher*; spoon *colher*; teaspoon *colher de chá*; knife *faca*; fork *garfo*; plate *prato*; glass *copo*; cup *chávena*; napkin *guardanapo*; corkscrew *saca-rolha(s)*.
Bread *pão*; roll *pãozinho*.

HORS D'ŒUVRE (*antepastos*). – *Azeitonas* olives.

"ONE-DISH MEALS" (substantial soups and stews which are a meal in themselves). – *Cozido à portuguesa* meat stew, with sausages, bacon, beef, chicken, vegetables, potatoes and rice; *caldo verde* cabbage soup, with potatoes and slices of sausage; *gaspacho* a cold soup made with tomatoes, paprika, cucumber and onions, seasoned with vinegar and pepper and sprinkled with croûtons; *caldeirada* fish soup.

SOUPS (*sopas*). – *Açorda* garlic soup containing slices of bread; *sopa de coentros* soup made with coriander leaves, garlic, olive oil, bread and a poached egg; *canja (de galinha)* chicken soup with rice; *sopa de coelho* rabbit soup; *sopa de grão de bico* chick-pea soup; *sopa de peixe* fish soup; *sopa de mariscos* seafood bisque.

EGG DISHES (*pratos de ovos*). – *Ovo* egg (*cru* raw, *fresco* fresh, *duro* hard-boiled, *quente* soft-boiled). – *Omeleta* omelette; *ovos mexidos* scrambled eggs; *ovos estrelados* fried eggs.

FISH DISHES (*pratos de peixe*). – *Peixe* fish (*frito* fried, *assado* roast, *grelhado* grilled, *cozido* boiled). – *Bacalhau* cod, stockfish; *sardinhas* sardines; *atum* tunny; *salmonete* red mullet; *espadarte* swordfish; *pescada* hake; *linguado* sole; *lampreia* lamprey; *salmão* salmon.

SEAFOOD. – *Amêijoas* cockles, clams; *mexilhões* mussels; *lagosta* Norway lobster; *lulas* cuttlefish, squid.

MEAT DISHES. – *Carne* meat (*bife* steak, *assado* roast, *costeleta* cutlet, *espetada* roasted on the spit, *grelhado* grilled). – *Porco* pork; *leitão* sucking pig; *cordeiro* lamb; *carneiro* mutton; *cabrito* kid; *vitela* veal; *vaca* beef; *coelho* rabbit.

COLD MEAT. – *Presunto* ham; *salame* salami; *enchido* smoked sausage; *carnes frias* cold meat.

POULTRY (*aves*). – *Frango* chicken; *ganso* goose; *pato* duck; *peru* turkey.

GAME (*caça*). – *Corça* roe-deer; *lebre* hare; *javali* wild pig; *perdiz* partridge.

VEGETABLES (*legumes, hortaliça*). – *Couve* cabbage; *repolho* white cabbage; *couve-flor* cauliflower; *couve de Bruxelas* Brussels sprouts; *tomates* tomatoes; *pimento* red or green pepper; *cebolas* onions; *espargos* asparagus; *espinafre* spinach; *ervilhas* peas; *grão-de-bico* chick-peas; *feijões* beans; *pepinos* cucumbers.

GARNISHINGS. – *Arroz* rice; *batatas* potatoes; *batatas frites* fried potatoes; *massa(s)* noodles, pasta.

SALADS, ETC. – *Salada* salad; *condimento* condiment; *sal* salt; *pimenta* pepper; *vinagre* vinegar; *azeite* olive oil; *óleo* groundnut oil; *mostarda* mustard; *alho* garlic; *manteiga* butter. – *Molho* sauce.

CHEESE (*queijo*). – *Queijo da serra* mountain cheese (ewe's-milk or goat's-milk); *alvorca* a rindless hard cheese (made from the milk of either cows, ewes or goats); *flamengo* similar to Edam; *queijo seco* a strong, salty dry cheese; *queijo fresco, requeijão* cream cheese.

National and Regional Specialities

Cozido à portuguesa
Meat and vegetable stew
(A national dish)

Caldo verde
Cabbage soup
(Minho)

Gaspacho
Cold vegetable soup, highly seasoned
(Southern Portugal)

Caldeirada
A substantial fish soup
(All along the coasts)

Sardinhas assadas
Grilled sardines
(A national dish. The streets are filled with the
smell of grilling sardines at mealtimes)

Bacalhau com todos
Stockfish with a variety of vegetables
(Found all over Portugal)

Arroz de lampreia
Lampreys on rice
(Minho)

Bife de atum
Tunny steak
(Algarve)

Amêijoas na cataplana
Cockles steamed in a copper pot with sausages
and herbs
(Algarve)

Lagosta suada
Steamed lobster
(Peniche)

Carne de porco à alentejana
Fried pork with clams
(Alentejo)

Leitão assado
Roast sucking pig
(All over Portugal)

Tripas à moda do Porto
Tripe with haricot beans
(Oporto)

Espetada da Madeira
Meat roasted on the spit
(Madeira)

Alcatra dos Açores
Roast beef
(Azores)

Presunto
Smoked ham
(Chaves)

Linguiças
Smoked tongue sausages
(Oporto)

Grilling sardines, Nazaré

Queijo da serra
Ewe's-milk cheese
(Serra da Estrêla)

Cabreiro
Salty goat's-milk cheese
(Many places)

Rabaçal
Goat's-milk cheese
(Round Pombal)

Queijo da ilha
A strong hard cheese
(Made only in the Azores, but served also in
mainland Portugal)

Queijinhos
Small cream cheeses
(Tomar)

Doces de ovos
A sweet egg dish
(Central Portugal)

Bolo de ovos e amêndoa
Marzipan cake
(Algarve)

Bolo de mel
Honey cake
(Madeira)

The best known **table waters** come from *Luso*
(still) and from *Castelo*, *Carvalhelhos*, *Vidago* and
Pedras Salgadas (containing carbonic acid).

Portuguese **spirits** include *bagaço* (distilled from
the pips and skins left from the making of wine),
medronho (made from the fruit of the arbutus),
cana (from sugar-cane), *grinjinha* (a cherry
liqueur) and aniseed brandy.

Wine: see page 240.

FRUIT (*fruta*). – *Laranja* orange; *maçã* apple; *pera* pear; *pêssego* peach; *figo* fig; *cerejas* cherries; *uva* grapes; *amêndoa* almond; *banana* banana.

DESSERTS (*sombremesas*). – *Doces* sweets (usually based on eggs); *bolo* cake; *pastéis* tarts; *pão-de-ló* sponge-cake; *pudim flan* caramel custard; *arroz doce* rice with sugar and cinnamon; *gelado* ice.

Drinks (*bebidas*)

Água water; *água mineral* mineral water; *água gasosa* aerated water; *sumo de fruta* fruit juice; *limonada* lemonade; *laranjada* orangeade.
Cerveja beer.
Vinho wine (*branco* white; *tinto* red; *verde* "green", i.e. young; *doce* sweet); *cidra* fruit wine.
Aguardente, *brandy* brandy, schnaps.
Café coffee; *café com leite*, *garoto* white coffee, coffee with milk; *chá* tea; *chocolate* chocolate; *leite* milk.

Wine

Wine-production in Portugal is concentrated almost entirely in the central and northern parts of the country. The area N and E of Oporto produces **vinho verde**, the best known Portuguese table wine. The name *verde*, "green", refers not to the colour of the wine – there is a red as well as a white vinho verde – but to the way it is made: it is "green" in the sense of being a young wine. The grapes are gathered relatively early and allowed to ferment for a very brief period, producing a light, rather sharp wine which continues to ferment for a time in the bottle. The result is a fresh, often slightly effervescent, wine which is pleasant to drink but does not keep well.

Both red and white wines are produced in the valley of the River *Dão*. The white wine is an excellent table wine, best drunk young. The red wine is dry and full-bodied, and after a sufficient period of maturation develops a marked bouquet, with some resemblance to claret.

The steep hillsides of the upper *Douro* valley produce the grapes used in the making of Portugal's most famous wine, **port**.

Port, which takes its name from the town of Oporto, is made from partly fermented red wine with an admixture of brandy. The high alcohol content inhibits the process of fermentation, producing a wine of considerable strength and high sugar content. Thereafter it is allowed to mature in store for periods ranging between two and fifty years. For this purpose the wine is taken down the river to Oporto, where it is bottled and marketed.

Grape harvest in the Douro valley

Where the wine produced in a particular year is of especially high quality it is declared a *vintage* year. In other years the wines are blended to produce port of standard quality which is matured in wooden casks; this non-vintage port is drier than vintage port.

The Language of the Wine Label

Vinha	Vineyard
Quinta	Estate, "château"
Adega	Wine-cellar, wine-making establishment
Colheita	Year, vintage
Região demarcada	Statutorily defined wine-producing region
Denominação de origem	"Appellation contrôlée"
Reserva	Reserve (wine of better quality)
Garrafeira	"Private cellar" (i.e. best quality)
Vinho verde	"Green" (i.e. young) wines: a regional designation for the very light red and white wines produced in the Minho province
Vinho de mesa	Table wine
Vinho de consumo	Ordinary drinking wine
Maduro	Old, matured wine
Engarrafado na origem	Bottled by the producer
Branco	White
Tinto	Red
Rosado	Rosé
Clarete	Light red or dark rosé
Seco	Dry
Doce, adamado	Sweet
Espumante	Sparkling

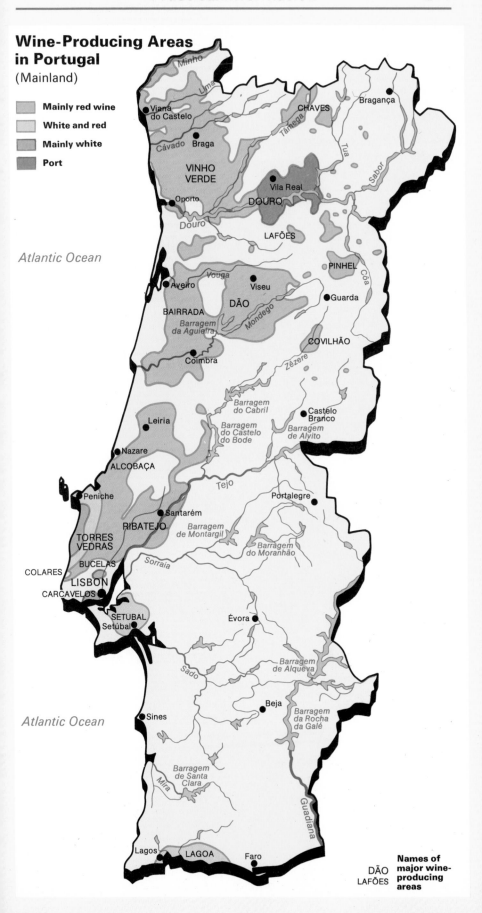

Wine-Producing Areas in Portugal

(Mainland)

- Mainly red wine
- White and red
- Mainly white
- Port

Atlantic Ocean

Minho

Lima

Viana do Castelo

CHAVES

Bragança

Cávado Braga

Tâmega

Tua

Sabor

VINHO VERDE

Vila Real

Oporto

DOURO

Douro

LAFÕES

PINHEL

Côa

Atlantic Ocean

Aveiro

Vouga

Viseu

DÃO

Guarda

BAIRRADA

Barragem da Aguieira

Mondego

COVILHÃO

Coimbra

Zêzere

Barragem do Cabril

Leiria

Castelo Branco

Barragem do Castelo do Bode

Barragem de Alvito

Nazaré

ALCOBAÇA

Tejo

Peniche

Portalegre

Santarém

Barragem de Montargil

RIBATEJO

TORRES VEDRAS

Barragem do Moranhão

BUCELAS

Sorraia

COLARES

LISBON

CARCAVELOS

SETUBAL

Setúbal

Évora

Sado

Barragem de Alqueva

Beja

Barragem da Rocha da Galé

Sines

Atlantic Ocean

Barragem de Santa Clara

Mira

Guadiana

Lagos

LAGOA

Faro

DÃO
LAFÕES

Names of major wine-producing areas

Portuguese Wines

Regions	Characteristics of wine

REGIÕS DEMARCADAS
(statutorily defined wine-growing regions)

Regions		Characteristics of wine
VINHOS VERDES	Throughout NW Portugal Monçao (Alvarinho: the best) Lima, Braga (Centro), Basto, Amarante, Penafiel, Oporto, Arouca	"Green" wines: white (very light in colour) and dark red; light, sharp, immature, slightly effervescent
VINHO DO PORTO	On the terraced slopes of the upper Douro valley Régua: the first wine-growing area to be officially defined (by the Marquês de Pombal in 1756)	Portugal's best wine, with an international reputation. Made from three parts partially fermented wine and one part brandy. Matured for 2–50 years: *vintage* port, unblended, in bottle; *tawny* and *ruby* port, blended, in large wooden casks. Vintage port (produced only in especially good years), after 20 years' maturation, is full and sweet, with a flowery bouquet; tawny is dry and lighter
DÃO	Valleys of the Dão and Mondego	The Portuguese equivalent of Rioja; ruby-red or light yellow
COLARES	NW of Lisbon, on the coast (with some vines growing on dunes)	Red wines (the best), deep red in colour, with low alcohol content; white wines, less good
BUCELAS	N of Lisbon	White wine only; fresh and aromatic
SETUBAL	Moscatel de Setúbal	Muscatel wine
CARCAVELOS	Immediately W of Lisbon. Area of vineyards, and quantity of wine produced, reduced by the growth of Estoril	Dry or sweet
MADEIRA	Malmsey, Bual, Verdelho, Sercial	Fortified wines produced by a unique process involving the heating of the must. Drunk before, during or after meals, and also used in cooking

OTHER REGIONS

Regions		Characteristics of wine
Lafões	To the S of the *vinho verde* region	White (light yellow) and red
Pinhel	S of the port region	White and red
Agueda, Barraida	W of the Dão region	Red (dark-coloured, full-bodied, with high alcohol content); white (lighter); also sparkling wine
Alcobaça		A pleasant wine, light red in colour
Caldas da Rainha		White
Óbidos		White
Oeste	Torres Vedras	Red (dark-coloured, with high tannic acid content)
	Alenquer, Cadaval	White (smooth, with high alcohol content)
Ribatejo	On both sides of the Tagus Cartaxo Almeirim	Red (dark-coloured, low alcohol content) White (low acidity, high alcohol content)
Alentejo	Borba, Redondo, Vidigueira, Cuba, Alvito	White and red; strong
Algarve	Lagoa (small quantities)	Light-coloured; high alcohol content

Britain has long been a major market for port. Considerable quantities are also exported to France.

To the E of Alcobaça, extending S towards Lisbon, is the old province of Estremadura, the two best known wine-producing regions in which, *Ribatejo* and *Torres Vedras*, provide mainly red wines. Farther S less wine is grown. Round Setúbal there are vineyards of muscatel grapes, mainly used to make dessert wines. In the extreme S, on the Algarve coast, there is another region of vineyards, producing mostly red wines.

Taking the Cure

● Spas

1 Caldas do Gerês
Recommended for liver complaints

2 Caldas de Chaves
Stomach and intestines, liver, rheumatism, metabolic disorders

3 Vidago
Stomach and intestines, liver, metabolic disorders

4 Pedras Salgadas
Stomach and intestines, liver

5 Caldelas
Stomach and liver, skin

6 Termas de São Vicente
Respiratory passages

7 Caldas de Vizela
Rheumatism, skin, respiratory passages, gynaecological conditions

8 Caldas de São Jorge
Rheumatism, skin, respiratory passages

9 Termas de São Pedro do Sul
Rheumatism, skin, respiratory passages, gynaecological conditions

10 Caldas de Felgueira
Skin, respiratory passages

11 Curia
Kidneys and urinary tract, rheumatism

12 Luso
Kidneys and urinary tract, rheumatism, skin, circulation

13 Termas de Monte Real
Stomach and intestines, liver

14 Fonte Santa de Monfortinho
Liver, kidneys and urinary tract, skin

15 Piedade
Stomach and intestines, liver, skin

16 Caldas da Rainha
Rheumatism, respiratory passages, gynaecological conditions

17 Águas Santas do Vimeiro
Stomach and intestines, liver, skin

18 Termas dos Cucos
Rheumatism

19 Caldas de Monchique
Stomach and intestines, liver, rheumatism, respiratory passages

Bathing Beaches

● Costa Verde

1 Moledo do Minho
Beach of fine sand, dunes; restaurant

2 Vila Praia de Âncora
Beach of fine sand, dunes; restaurant

3 Viana do Castelo
Gently sloping beaches of fine sand, dunes; several restaurants

4 Esposende
Lagoon, sandbanks; several restaurants

5 Ofir
Gently sloping beach of fine sand, woods; restaurant

6 Póvoa de Varzim
Sandy beach, parts not clean; several restaurants

7 Vila do Conde
Sandy beach, with some cliffs; restaurant

8 Miramar
Gently sloping sandy beach; several restaurants

9 Espinho
Flat sandy beach, sometimes with strong surf; several restaurants

● Costa de Prata

10 Praia de São Jacinto
Beach of fine sand, dunes, woods

11 Palheiros de Mira
Sandy beach, parts not clean

12 Figueira da Foz
Flat sandy beach with some rocks; strong surf; several restaurants

13 Pedrógão
Flat sandy beach with some rocks; strong surf; restaurant; fishing harbour

14 Vieira
Gently sloping beach of fine sand; surf; several restaurants

15 São Pedro de Muel
Gently sloping beach of fine sand, parts not clean; rocks; several restaurants

16 Nazaré
Sandy beach, water with some pollution; several restaurants

17 São Martinho do Porto
Gently sloping sandy beach, dunes; scuba diving; several restaurants

18 Peniche
Gently sloping sandy beach, rocks; scuba diving; several restaurants; fishing harbour

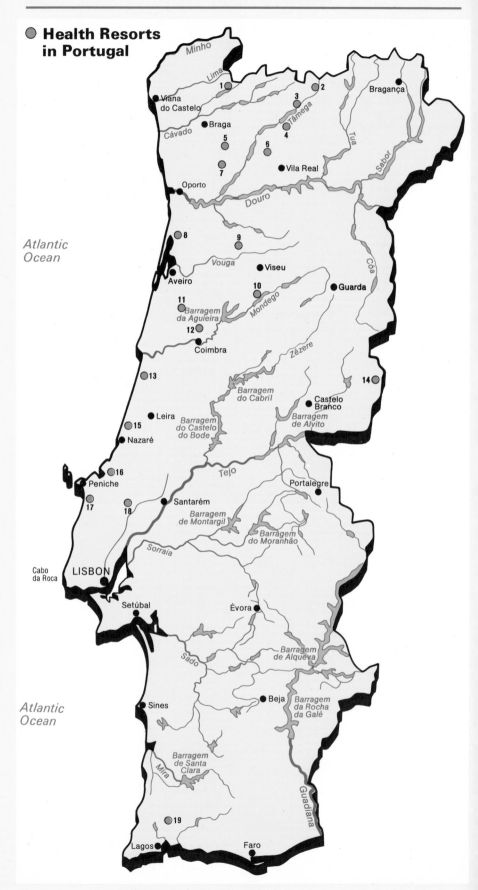

Health Resorts in Portugal

Minho

Lima

1

2

Bragança

Viana
do Castelo

3

Braga

Tâmega

Cávado

5

4

6

7

Vila Real

Oporto

Douro

Atlantic
Ocean

8

9

Vouga

Viseu

Aveiro

10

Mondego

Guarda

11

Barragem
da Aguieira

Côa

12

Coimbra

Zêzere

13

Barragem
do Cabril

14

Leira

Castelo
Branco

15

Barragem
do Castelo
do Bode

Barragem
de Alvito

Nazaré

16

Tejo

Peniche

Portalegre

17

18

Santarém

Barragem
de Montargil

Barragem
do Moranhão

Sorraia

Cabo
da Roca

LISBON

Setúbal

Évora

Barragem
de Alqueva

Sado

Atlantic
Ocean

Sines

Beja

Barragem
da Rocha
da Galé

Barragem
de Santa
Clara

Mira

Guadiana

19

Lagos

Faro

Fishing boats and bathers, Praia do Carvoeiro (Algarve)

19 **Praia de Santa Cruz**
Beach of fine sand, strong surf, dunes, cliffs; restaurant

20 **Ericeira**
Flat sandy beaches, rocks, cliffs; several restaurants; fishing harbour

21 **Praia Grande**
Flat sandy beach, cliffs; several restaurants

○ Costa do Sol

22 **Cascais**
Flat beach of fine sand, rocks; several restaurants; fishing harbour

23 **Estoril**
Flat beach of fine sand; several restaurants

● Costa de Lisboa

24 **Costa da Caparica**
Flat sandy beach, dunes, cliffs; restaurant

25 **Sesimbra**
Sandy beach, parts not clean; scuba diving; several restaurants; fishing harbour

26 **Portinho da Arrábida**
Flat sandy beach, some rocks; several restaurants; fishing harbour

27 **Tróia**
Wooded peninsula, beach of fine sand; scuba diving; several restaurants

● Costa Dourada

28 **Porto Covo**
Flat sandy beach, rocks; several restaurants; fishing harbour

29 **Vila Nova de Milfontes**
Sandy beach, dunes; several restaurants

● Costa do Algarve

30 **Aljezur**
Flat sandy beach, rocks, dunes, strong surf; restaurant

31 **Sagres**
Flat beaches of fine sand, rocks; scuba diving; restaurant

32 **Salema**
Flat sandy beach, cliffs; several restaurants

33 **Praia da Luz**
Sandy beach, rocks; scuba diving; several restaurants

34 **Lagos**
Sandy beaches, rocks; scuba diving; several restaurants; fishing harbour

35 **Alvor**
Flat sandy beach, rocks; several restaurants

36 **Praia da Rocha**
Sandy beach, rocks; scuba diving; several restaurants

37 **Carvoeiro**
Sandy bay, rocks; several restaurants

38 **Armação de Pêra**
Beach of fine sand, dunes; scuba diving; several restaurants

39 **Albufeira**
Beaches of fine sand, rocks, cliffs; scuba diving; several restaurants; fishing harbour

40 **Olhos de Água**
Flat beach of fine sand, rocks, cliffs; restaurant

41 **Vilamoura**
Sandy beach, with some cliffs; several restaurants; fishing harbour

42 **Quarteira**
Sandy beach; several restaurants

43 **Vale do Lobo**
Beach of fine sand, part of it flat; rocks, cliffs; several restaurants

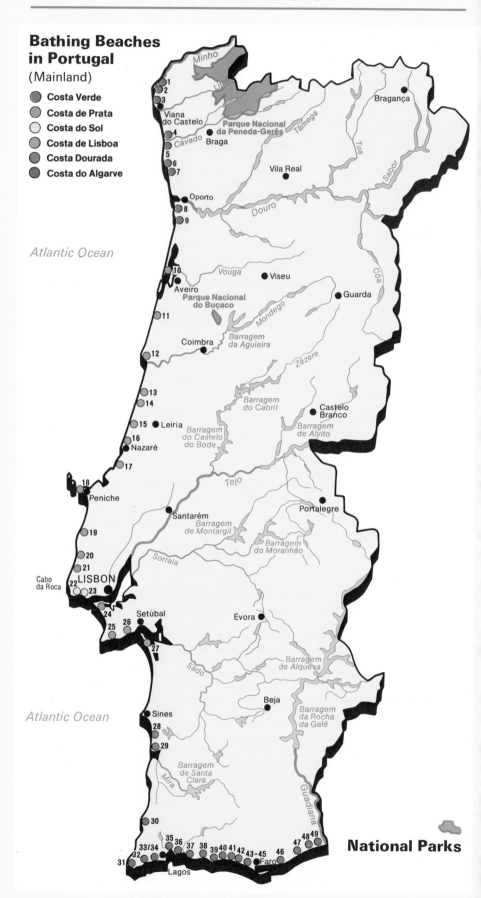

Bathing Beaches in Portugal
(Mainland)

- Costa Verde
- Costa de Prata
- Costa do Sol
- Costa de Lisboa
- Costa Dourada
- Costa do Algarve

Atlantic Ocean

Atlantic Ocean

National Parks

Minho
Lima
Bragança
Viana do Castelo
Parque Nacional da Peneda-Gerês
Cávado
Braga
Tâmega
Tua
Sabor
Vila Real
Oporto
Douro
Côa
Vouga
Viseu
Aveiro
Parque Nacional do Buçaco
Guarda
Mondego
Coimbra
Barragem da Aguieira
Zêzere
Barragem do Cabril
Castelo Branco
Leiria
Barragem do Castelo do Bode
Barragem de Alvito
Nazaré
Peniche
Tejo
Santarém
Portalegre
Barragem de Montargil
Barràgem do Moranhão
Sorraia
Cabo da Roca
LISBON
Setúbal
Évora
Sado
Barragem de Alqueva
Beja
Sines
Barragem da Rocha da Galé
Barragem de Santa Clara
Mira
Guadiana
Faro
Lagos

44 Quinta do Lago
Sandy beach, dunes, lagoon

45 Faro
Long flat beach of fine sand, lagoon; several restaurants

46 Ilha da Armona
Large flat sandy beach opposite the fishing port of Olhão

47 Ilha de Tavira
A wooded island with a flat sandy beach and dunes; several restaurants; fishing harbour at Tavira

48 Cabanas
Flat beach of fine sand; several restaurants

49 Monte Gordo
Flat beach of fine sand, dunes; several restaurants

Golf-Courses and Casinos (map, see p. 248)

● Golf-Courses

1 Vidago
9 holes

2 Praia de Miramar
9 holes

3 Espinho
18 holes

4 Vimeiro
9 holes

5 Estoril
18 holes

6 Linho
18 holes

7 Belas
18 holes

8 Aroeira
18 holes

9 Torralta Tróia
18 holes

10 Maia Praia
18 holes

11 Penina
18 holes

12 Vilamoura
18 holes

13 Almansil
18 holes

14 Almansil
27 holes

15 Vale do Lobo
Three 9-hole courses

On Madeira

Santo da Serra
9 holes

In the Azores

Lajes (*Terceira*)
18 holes

São Miguel
9 holes

● Casinos

16 Póvoa de Varzim

17 Espinho

18 Estoril

19 Alvor

20 Vilamoura

21 Monte Gordo

On Madeira

Funchal

Golf-course at Vilamoura (Algarve)

● Golf-Courses
● Casinos
in Portugal
(Mainland)

Atlantic Ocean

Minho

Lima

Cávado

Tâmega

Tua

Sabor

Viana
do Castelo

Braga

Bragança

1

16

2   Porto

Vila Real

Douro

Côa

3
17

Vouga

Viseu

Aveiro

Guarda

*Barragem
da Aguieira*

Mondego

Coimbra

Zêzere

*Barragem
do Cabril*

Castelo
Branco

Leira

*Barragem
do Castelo
do Bode*

*Barragem
de Alvito*

Nazaré

Tejo

Peniche

Santarém

Portalegre

*Barragem
de Montargil*

4

*Barragem
do Maranhão*

Sorraia

LISBON

Cabo
da Roca

5   6   7
18

8   Setúbal

9

Évora

Sado

*Barragem
de Alqueva*

Atlantic Ocean

Sines

Beja

*Barragem
da Rocha
da Galé*

*Barragem
de Santa
Clara*

Mira

Guadiana

19   11
10   20
12   13
  14   15

21

Lagos   Faro

Folk Traditions

As in other Romance countries, popular festivals with folk singing and dancing play an important part in the life of the people of Portugal. This may appear to run counter to the general reputation of the Portuguese for being melancholy and reserved by nature. It is true that at first sight they may appear shy and unforthcoming; but behind this external appearance there is a very real warmth and sincerity, and on better acquaintance visitors to Portugal will be charmed by the winning character of the people.

The deep longing, caused by death, separation, loss (*saudade*), which is a Portuguese characteristic, finds expression in the **fado** (see Introduction, Music), a melancholy folk-song, often of rather monotonous effect, which is accompanied by different types of guitars.

Of a very different character, however, are the numerous **folk dances** (*danças populares*), often very lively indeed, which are performed by groups of gaily costumed dancers.

Among the best known dances are the vigorous *gota* and the rhythmic *viras* of northern Portugal, the *fandango* of the Ribatejo, the *corridinho* of the Algarve and the *chulas* of Beira.

The dances are accompanied by guitars, percussion instruments, bagpipes and sometimes concertinas.

The old folk dances are mostly danced at the various popular festivals (*romarias*, *festas*) which are particularly numerous in spring and late summer. In country areas the harvest thanksgiving festival is an occasion for great celebration, based on a service giving thanks for a good harvest or on the blessing of the livestock and the fields.

In a profoundly Catholic country like Portugal the various **religious festivals** are naturally of prime importance. Particularly in the conservative North there are numerous *romarias* in honour of a particular saint or in commemoration of some miracle or apparition. The more important of these may last several days, with secular celebrations as well as religious ceremonies.

The **romaria** is basically a pilgrimage, with long processions of pilgrims, fes-tively dressed, and splendidly decorated floats. Sometimes a romaria is dedicated to a particular craft (in a fishing town, for example, to the fishermen); but this does not prevent large numbers of spectators and visitors from joining in and playing their part in the celebrations.

The central feature of the religious ritual is a solemn procession accompanying some sacred symbol, which in some cases may be merely a large candle (*cirio*), to the place of pilgrimage, usually a church. On arriving at the church the procession usually walks round it several times, to the accompaniment of music and a great deal of noise, before setting up the cross or candle or other symbol by the high altar. In order to obtain forgiveness for their sins the pilgrims perform a variety of ritual acts or offer ex-votos to the saint in gratitude for help received.

The romarias are mainly financed by offerings from the community. A few days before the festival the organisers arrange for the collection of alms, accompanied by music to encourage cheerful giving.
Some of the larger romarias are widely famed, and offer an excellent opportunity of getting to know the way of life and customs of Portugal. Among the most notable are those of Viana do Castelo, Póvoa de Varzim, Amarante and Loulé.

Associated with the religious ceremonies there are usually **festas** – fairs offering a variety of attractions and entertainments, with dancing and singing, eating and drinking.

The various festas and romarias give visitors an opportunity of seeing a great range of splendid **traditional costumes** (*trajes*). As in many other countries, the women's costumes are particularly fine. Those of the northern provinces of Minho and Douro are notable for their richness of colouring, the brightly coloured embroidered jackets and waistcoats being set off by white blouses and stockings, with head-scarves, kerchiefs and jewelry to complete the effect.

Black costumes, with long gold-embroidered skirts fitting closely on the hips which are reminiscent of Provençal dress, are also found in northern Portugal, and black costumes are common in the Algarve, at the other end of the country. In Alentejo the costumes are adapted to the peasants' hard work in the fields, which is often done by women, wearing trouser-like nether garments, with a kerchief or a floppy hat on their heads. In Ribatejo the *campinos* (cattle-herds) wear breeches, brightly coloured waistcoats and stockings, light-coloured shirts and the stocking caps which are found all over Portugal.

In the little fishing town of Nazaré and the surrounding area young women and girls wear simple coloured dresses with a flower pattern in black or white and a white or black woollen jersey or shawl over their shoulders to protect them from the rough Atlantic winds which often blow in this area.

In the fishing towns and villages on the Atlantic coast visitors will be struck by the number of women clad entirely in black sitting in front of their houses and looking out to sea – where, it may be, some member of the family is pursuing the hazardous trade of a deep-sea fisherman or has perhaps already been lost.

There are great **processions** (*procissões*) in the pilgrimage centre of *Fátima* twice a year (on 13 May and 13 October), with smaller pilgrimages on the 12th and 13th of every month. There are also processions in many towns and villages at Easter, carrying figures connected with the story of the Passion.

Particularly notable is the *Festa dos Tabuleiros*, celebrated at *Tomar* in alternate years. White-clad girls walk in procession through the town bearing on their heads the elaborate tower-like structures known as *tabuleiros*, each incorporating thirty loaves of bread and a decoration of ears of corn, flowers and foliage. The tabuleiro is usually as tall as the girl carrying it.

The procession is supposed to commemorate a 14th c. ceremony during which the Order of the Holy Ghost distributed food to the poor.

Portugal has also preserved many **traditions** frequently of pagan origin, and numerous everyday habits and customs which the outsider may find quaint or antiquated. Among these for example, is the way in which the fishermen of Nazaré launch their boats into the heavy surf and haul them ashore on their return by their own muscle-power or with the help of oxen.

Other local customs are evinced by women sitting outside their houses doing embroidery or pillow-lace work, women selling shellfish in the street, fishermen and fisher women mending nets or setting out fish to dry in the sun on special racks, people grilling sardines on little charcoal stoves outside their houses (producing the penetrating aroma which pervades whole villages and will be one of every visitor's memories of Portugal) and women water-sellers who carry the precious fluid in jugs on their heads. (Heavy loads are frequently carried on the head in this way, giving the women a marvellous poise and dignity.)

Another old Portuguese tradition is the **bullfight** (*tourada*), which is very different from the Spanish *corrida*. In Portugal the bull is not killed – in the arena, at any rate – and there are no *picadores* to soften the bull up.

The central character in a Portuguese bullfight is the **cavaleiro**, a kind of mounted torero clad in an elegant costume of the time of Louis XV – a legacy from the days when all cavaleiros were noblemen. After some demonstrations of *haute école* horsemanship the bull is released into the arena and the cavaleiro begins his *faena* (the Portuguese borrow the Spanish word for the occasion), dexterously avoiding the bull's charge and planting *farpas*, or *bandarilhas* in its neck. In order to avoid injury to the valuable horse the bull's horns are blunted by leather pads (*emboladas*).

Unmounted aides – *Peoes de brega* – sometimes enter the ring to allow the cavaleiro a short breathing-space, although this detracts from the aficionados' assessment of his performance. After the cavaleiro has planted all his farpas he withdraws from the contest and leaves the field to eight *forcados*, on foot and unarmed, who tease the bull into charging them. The full brunt of the charge is borne by the leading forcado who is supposed to cling to the bull's neck until his colleagues can come to his assistance. The first attempt is often spectacularly unsuccessful but the forcados never give up. The purpose of the exercise is to bring the bull to a standstill. This phase of the fight is known as the *pega* (i.e., catching the bull).

Traditional costumes, Viana do Castelo

When the bull has been defeated the *campinos* enter the arena with a small herd of oxen or young bulls, and after a brief period of hesitation the bewildered beast joins the herd and leaves the arena with them.

Spanish-style bullfighting is also very popular in Portugal and can be seen in most *touradas* together with the Portuguese variant. The bull's horns are not blunted and the beast is stronger than its Spanish counterpart because it has not suffered the heavy bleeding caused by the Spanish picador's lance. In Portugal the bull's life is spared. Just before the climax of the fight the *toureiro* or *espada* exchanges the sword for a *bandarilha* which he uses for a "mock execution". As a bravado he may dispense with the bandarilha and just tap the bull's neck with his bare hand, thus getting within closer range of the bull's horns. Most Portuguese *espadas* regularly fight and kill bulls in Spain.

The bullfighting season in Portugal is from Easter to October. Bullfights are held not only in the special bullrings (*praças de touros*) in the larger towns but also in market squares and sports grounds in smaller places.

Mounted bullfighting is also practised in Spain and the South of France, where it is known as the *rejonea*. This is very similar to the Portuguese form, except that there are no *forcados*. In the rejonea the bull is often killed in the arena, usually by a torero on foot, rarely by the rider. In Spain, too, the bull's horns are usually not padded, increasing the hazard for both horse and rider.
Portuguese cavaleiros occasionally appear in rejoneas outside Portugal.

Bullfight fever in Vila Franca

Calendar of Events
(A selection of events of particular interest)

January

Northern Portugal

Vila Nova de Gaia (Oporto)	Festa de São Gonçalo e São Cristóvão
Vila de Feira (Aveiro)	Festa de São Sebastião or Festa das Fogaceiras

February

Northern Portugal

Ovar (Aveiro)	Festas do Carnaval de Ovar

Central Portugal

Nazaré (Leiria)	Festas do Carnaval de Nazaré

Southern Portugal

Mourão (Évora)	Festa da Senhora das Candelas
Loulé (Faro)	Festas do Carnaval de Loulé

March

Northern Portugal

Ovar (Aveiro)	Procissão dos Terceiros (procession)
Póvoa de Lanhoso (Braga)	Festas de São José

Central Portugal

Lisbon (Lisboa)	Procissão do Senhor dos Passos da Graça (traditional procession)

Southern Portugal

Loulé (Faro)	Romaria da Senhora da Piedade (church festival)

March–April

Northern Portugal

Aveiro (Aveiro)	Feira de Março (industrial and trade fair)

April

Northern Portugal

Ovar (Aveiro)	Festas da Semana Santa (Holy Week celebrations, with fireworks)
Braga (Braga)	Festas da Semana Santa (Holy Week celebrations)
Póvoa de Varzim (Porto)	Festas da Semana Santa (Holy Week celebrations)
Fão, Esposende (Braga)	Romaria ao Senhor Bom Jesús de Fão (church festival, with processions and fireworks)

Central Portugal

Idanha-a-Nova (Castelo Branco)	Romaria à Senhora do Almurtão (the most interesting church festival in Beira Baixa, with folk celebrations and religious ceremonies)

May

Northern Portugal
Barcelos (Braga)	Festas das Cruzes (an impressive popular festival, with processions and fairs)
Guimarães (Braga)	Festas das Cruzes (religious festival with a long tradition; fireworks, procession)
Viana do Castelo (Viana do Castelo)	Festa da Senhora das Rosas (religious celebration, with processions and popular festival)
Alvarães (Viana do Castelo)	Festa da Santa Cruz or Festa dos Andores Floridos (procession with flower-decked figures of saints)

Central Portugal
Vila Franca de Xira (Lisboa)	Agrinxira (industrial and agricultural show)
Monsanto (Castelo Branco)	Festa das Cruzes or Festa do Castelo (religious celebrations, popular festival, folk events)
Leiria (Leiria)	Feira de Maio (May Fair, with exhibition of regional products, including handicrafts)
Fátima (Santarém)	Primeira Peregrinação Anual (first annual pilgrimage)

Southern Portugal
Alte (Faro)	Festa da Fonte Grande or Festa do Primeiro de Maio (popular festival, with folk events and a profusion of flowers)
Sesimbra (Setúbal)	Festa do Senhor das Chagas (fishermen's procession, popular festival)

Azores
Ponta Delgada (São Miguel)	Festas do Senhor Santo Cristo dos Milagres (a great festival in which both natives and immigrants join; religious celebrations, sporting contests and other events)

June

Northern Portugal
Amarante (Porto)	Romaria de São Gonçalo (church festival, with folk events, bullfights and fireworks)
Matosinhos (Porto)	Festas do Senhor de Matosinhos (folk festival, bull-running, fireworks, fair)
Quintela (Viseu)	Romaria da Senhora da Lapa (church festival, processions)
Vila Praia de Âncora (Viana do Castelo)	Folk Festival
Amares (Braga)	Festas de Santo António (processions, folk events)
Vila Verde (Braga)	Festas de Santo António (procession, folk festival, show of agricultural produce and livestock)
Penafiel (Porto)	Festa do Corpo de Deus (processions in traditional costume, with a profusion of flowers)
Monção (Viana do Castelo)	Festa do Corpo de Deus (religious festival, traditional folk events)
Barcelinhos (Braga)	Festas de São João (procession, fireworks, regional folk events, pottery fair)
Braga (Braga)	Festas de São João (traditional festival, folk events, processions)
Oporto (Porto)	Festas de São João (traditional festival, folk events, processions)
Vila do Conde (Porto)	Festas de São João (popular festival, folk events in traditional costume, and many other events)
Viseu (Viseu)	Cavalhadas de Vil de Moinhos (religious service with horses, medieval games, folk events)
Póvoa de Varzim (Porto)	Festas de São Pedro (popular festival, folk dances, processions)
São Torcato (Braga)	Romaria de São Torcato (church festival, processions, folk events)

Central Portugal
Santarém (Santarém)	Feira Nacional de Agricultura (National Agricultural Show)
Lisbon (Lisboa)	Festas dos Santos Populares (popular festival, fairs, great number of events)
Figueira da Foz (Coimbra)	Festas de São João (midnight procession in traditional costume, dancing in Casino, folk events)
Sintra (Lisboa)	Feira Grande de São Pedro (large regional show – agricultural produce, antiques, handicrafts, regional cuisine)

Southern Portugal
Reguengos de Monsaraz (Évora)	Festas de Santo António (festival in honour of the town's patron saint; bullfights, Alentejo male-voice choirs)
Évora (Évora)	Feira de São João (one of the most important fairs in southern Portugal; show of handicrafts, folk displays)
Montijo (Setúbal)	Festas de São Pedro (popular festival, with bullfights; the fishermen distribute sardines to visitors)

Madeira
Ribeira Brava	Festas de São Pedro (religious ceremonies, processions, folk dancing)

Azores
Ribeira Grande (São Miguel) — Cavalhadas de São Pedro (medieval equestrian contests)

July

Northern Portugal
Maia (Porto) — Romaria da Senhora do Bom Despacho (church festival, pilgrimage, folk events, fireworks)

Santo Tirso (Porto) — Festas de São Bento (show of stoneware, folk festival)

Paredes (Porto) — Festas do Divino Salvador (procession, animal contests, fireworks)

São Torcato (Braga) — Festival Internacional de Folclore (International Folk Festival, with the best Portuguese and foreign folk groups competing)

Vila do Conde (Porto) — Feira de Artesanato (handicraft fair, with products from all over Portugal)

Lousada (Porto) — Festas do Senhor dos Aflitos (processions, folk displays)

Gulpilhares (Vila Nova de Gaia) — Festival Internacional de Folclore (International Folk Festival)

Central Portugal
Vale de Maceira (Coimbra) — Romaria da Senhora das Preces (church festival, with popular celebrations and fair)

Vila Franca de Xira (Lisboa) — Festas do Colete Encarnado (contests, folk events, bullfights)

Estoril (Lisboa) — Feira de Artesanato (craft fair, folk events, local dishes)

Ançã (Coimbra) — Romaria de São Tomé e São Tiago (festival in honour of the town's patron saints; dancing and other folk events, equestrian contests)

Southern Portugal
Faro (Faro) — Feira da Senhora do Carmo (show of regional handicrafts, folk displays)

Setúbal (Setúbal) — Feira de Santiago (show of local agricultural and industrial products and handicrafts, folk displays, bullfights)

August

Northern Portugal
Meadela (Viana do Castelo) — Festas de Santa Cristina (traditional costumes, folk events, processions)

Terras do Bouro (Braga) — Festas de São Brás (processions, parades, bull-running)

Mirandela (Bragança) — Festas da Senhora do Amparo and Feira de Santiago (religious ceremonies, popular festival, cultural and sporting events)

Neves (Viana do Castelo) — Festa da Senhora das Neves (religious ceremonies, popular festival, fireworks, folk festival, show of handicrafts)

Guimarães (Braga) — Festas Gualterianas (popular festival, with regional dishes and wines, fireworks, folk events)

Caminha (Viana do Castelo) — Festas de Santa Rita de Cássia (processions in traditional costumes, water sports contests, fireworks)

Portuzelo (Viana do Castelo) — Festas de Santa Marta do Portuzelo (fairs, folk festivals with Portuguese and foreign groups)

Baião (Porto) — Festas de São Bartolomeu (religious ceremonies, folk dancing and singing, traditional equestrian contest, bullfights)

Ponte da Barca (Viana do Castelo) — Festas de São Bartolomeu (processions)

Monção (Viana do Castelo) — Festas da Virgem das Dores (processions, show of handicrafts, popular festival, fireworks)

Oporto (Porto) — Festa de São Bartolomeu and Cortejo de Papel (popular festival, procession with paper figures satirically representing prominent figures, religious ceremonies)

Viseu (Viseu) — Feira de São Mateus (show of agricultural produce, wine, livestock and handicrafts, folk festival, bullfights)

Arga de São João (Viana do Castelo) — Romaria de São João de Arga (church festival with splendid processions, folk singing and dancing)

Central Portugal
Peniche (Leiria) — Festas da Senhora da Boa Viagem (traditional fishermen's festival in honour of their patroness; processions of boats, folk events, fireworks, popular festival)

Batalha (Leiria) — Festas da Senhora da Vitória (popular festival, with fairs and folk events)

Coruche (Santarém) — Festas da Senhora do Castelo (folk events, bullfights, bull-running)

Alcobaça (Leiria) — Feira de São Bernardo (industrial and agricultural show, with folk events and handicrafts)

Gouveia (Guarda) — Festas do Senhor do Calvário (processions, dog races, folk festival)

Rio Caldo (Braga) — Romaria a São Bento da Porta Aberta (church festival)

Torno (Porto) — Romaria à Senhora Aparecida (church festival, processions)

Castelões
(Aveiro)

Romaria da Senhora da Saúde da Serra (pilgrimage and festival, mainly religious celebrations)

Póvoa de Varzim
(Porto)

Festas da Senhora da Assunção (traditional fishermen's festival, procession of decorated boats on sea, bullfights, fireworks, folk festival)

Esposende
(Braga)

Festa da Senhora da Saúde e Soedade (traditional fishermen's festival, water sports contests on Rio Cávado, folk events, processions)

Vila Boas
(Bragança)

Romaria à Senhora da Assunção (church festival, many events)

Caldas de Vizela
(Braga)

Festas de Vizela (many events, processions, traditional costumes, folk festival)

Viana do Castelo
(Viana do Castelo)

Festas da Senhora da Agonia (one of the most characteristic Portuguese pilgrimages; processions, costume festival, folk festival, popular festival with fireworks, fairs)

Miranda do Douro
(Bragança)

Festas de Santa Bárbara (popular festival with folk dances by men)

Mar
(Braga)

Romaria a São Bartolomeu do Mar (religious ceremonies, traditional celebrations, popular festival)

Southern Portugal
Beja
(Beja)

Feira de Agosto or Feira de São Lourenço e Santa Maria (large fair with show of handicrafts, diverse events, bullfights)

Alcochete
(Setúbal)

Festas do Barrete e das Salinas (a typical local festival, with blessing of the salt-works, bullfights and popular celebrations)

Azores
Ponta Delgada
(São Miguel)

Festas do Divino Espírito Santo (a traditional island festival)

Madeira
Monte

Festa da Senhora do Monte (processions, traditional costumes, folk dancing and singing)

September

Northern Portugal
Guimarães
(Braga)

Peregrinação à Senhora da Penha (pilgrimage)

Monte Farinha
(Vila Real)

Romaria da Senhora da Graça (church festival)

Gavieira
(Viana do Castelo)

Romaria da Senhora da Peneda (church festival, traditional costumes)

Lamego
(Viseu)

Romaria da Senhora dos Remédios (pilgrimage, folk festival, processions, sporting events)

Vila Praia de Âncora
(Viana do Castelo)

Festas da Senhora da Bonança (fishermen's festival in honour of their patroness; processions and blessing of boats, popular festival, folk events, fireworks)

Praia da Torreira
(Aveiro)

Romaria de São Paio da Torreira (traditional "holy bath", processions to sea, blessing of boats, popular festival, fireworks)

Póvoa
(Bragança)

Romaria à Senhora do Nazo (pilgrimage, fair)

Póvoa de Varzim
(Porto)

Festas da Senhora das Dores (religious ceremonies, festival)

Ponte de Lima
(Viana do Castelo)

Feiras Novas and Festas da Senhora das Dores (fairs, processions, folk festival, procession in traditional costumes, fireworks on Rio Lima)

Cabeceiras de Basto
(Braga)

Feira e Festas de São Miguel (popular festival, religious ceremonies, traditional contests)

Buçaco
(Aveiro)

Festa da Senhora da Vitória (festival commemorating the battle of Buçaco; processions in uniforms of the period, popular celebrations)

Vila Nova de Famalição
(Braga)

Feira Grande de São Miguel (agricultural show, handicrafts, folk events)

Arouca
(Aveiro)

Feira das Colheitas (fair; local handicrafts, folk events)

Central Portugal
Rio Maior
(Santarém)

Frimor (annual industrial and agricultural show, local handicrafts, folk events, bull-running)

Arganil
(Coimbra)

Feira de Montalto (fair, with a large number of events)

Nazaré
(Leiria)

Romaria da Senhora de Nazaré (church festival, with processions, traditional costumes, folk events, fair, fireworks, bullfights)

Castelejo
(Castelo Branco)

Romaria de Santa Luzia e Santa Eufémia (church festival with folk events)

Elvas
(Portalegre)

Festas do Senhor Jesús da Piedade and Feira de São Mateus (a very typical Alentejo festival; processions, popular celebrations, bullfights)

Reguengo de Fétal
(Leiria)

Festas da Senhora do Fétal or Festas dos Caracóis (popular festival, processions)

Southern Portugal
Palmela
(Setúbal)

Festa das Vindimas (vintage festival, bullfights, fireworks)

Many places in the *Algarve*, with grand finale in Vilamoura

Festival de Folclore do Algarve (Algarve Folk Festival, with folk groups from mainland Portugal and the islands)

Moita (Setúbal)	Festas da Senhora da Boa Viagem (great procession, with blessing of boats; popular festival, bullfights, fireworks)
Viana do Alentejo (Évora)	Romaria da Senhora de Airès (church festival, bullfights)

October

Northern Portugal

Vieira do Minho (Braga)	Feira da Ladra (festival and fair, with agricultural and livestock show, large programme of events)
Gondomar (Porto)	Romaria da Senhora do Rosário and Feira das Nozes (procession, "folk night", fair)
Chaves (Vila Real)	Feira dos Santos (annual fair)

Central Portugal

Vila Franca de Xira (Lisboa)	Feira de Outubro (October Fair)
Fátima (Santarém)	Última Peregrinação Anual (last great pilgrimage to Fátima)

Southern Portugal

Moura (Beja)	Festa da Senhora do Monte do Carmo (processions, folk events)
Faro (Faro)	Feira de Santa Iria (annual fair)
Castro Verde (Beja)	Feira de Outubro (October Fair)

November

Northern Portugal

Cerdal (Viana do Castelo)	Feira dos Santos (traditional fair)
Penafiel (Porto)	Feira de São Martinho (fair; regional dishes)

Central Portugal

Cartaxo (Santarém)	Feira dos Santos (fair, with bullfights)
Golegã (Santarém)	Feira de São Martinho – Feira Nacional do Cavalo (livestock show; equestrian contests, bullfights, large number of events)

Southern Portugal

Algarve	Algarve Car Rally

December

Northern Portugal

Freamunde (Porto)	Romaria de Santa Luzia and Feira dos Capões (church festival and fair)

Madeira

Funchal	Festas de São Silvestre or Festas do Fim do Ano (a famous New Year's Eve celebration, with a magnificent firework display at midnight)

Public Holidays

1 January (Ano Novo)
25 April
1 May
Corpus Christi (Corpo de Deus)
10 June (Camões Day)
15 August (Assumption)
5 October (Republic Day)
1 November (All Saints)
1 December (Independence Day)
8 December
  (Immaculate Conception)
25 December (Natal)

Shopping and Souvenirs

In Portugal many craft products are still in everyday use. This is true particularly of the **pottery**, produced in forms and styles which vary from region to region and covering a wide range of types, from the blackish ware made for daily use to decorative pieces painted in lively colours. The gaily coloured cock of Barcelos, one of the most popular products, has become a symbol and emblem for the whole of Portugal.

A particular type of ceramic product is the *azulejo*, a decorative glazed tile (usually blue) whose origins go back to Moorish times (see p. 31). The azulejos sold nowadays, however, tend to be mass-produced.

In the coastal regions beautiful *lace* is made; in the inland parts of the country there are hand-woven textiles (blankets, etc.).

Other popular souvenirs are example of the *filigree work*, made from gold or silver wire, which in some areas form part of the traditional local costumes. There are also attractive woodcarvings, wickerwork and wrought-iron articles to be obtained.

Many visitors like to take home Portuguese *spirits and liqueurs*. The best known brands of *port*, however, can be bought outside Portugal at prices little higher than in the country itself.

Opening Times

Shops are open Monday to Friday from 9 a.m. to 1 p.m. and from 3 to 7 p.m.; on Saturdays only 9 a.m. to 1 p.m. Shopping complexes are usually open Monday to Friday from 10 a.m. until the late evening; and tobacconists and foodshops are also open until late in the evening and on Sundays.

Banks are open Monday to Friday from 8.30 to 11.45 a.m. and from 1 to 2.45 p.m.

Museums are normally open Tuesday to Sunday from 10 a.m. to 5 p.m.; some close at lunchtime.

Information

Direcção-Geral do Turismo
(Directorate-General of Tourism)

Avenida de António Augusto de Aguiar 86, P-1000 **Lisboa** (Lisbon); tel. (01) 57 53 88.
Information bureau,
Palácio Foz,
Praça dos Restauradores;
tel. (01) 36 70 31.

Portuguese National Tourist Office,
New Bond Street House,
1–5 New Bond Street,
London W1Y 0DB;
tel. (01) 493 3873.

Portuguese National Tourist Office,
919 North Michigan Avenue, Suite 3001,
Chicago, IL 60611;
tel. (312) 266 9898.

Portuguese National Tourist Office,
3250 Wilshire Boulevard, Suite 1305,
Los Angeles, CA 90010;
tel. (213) 380 6459.

Portuguese National Tourist Office,
548 Fifth Avenue,
New York, NY 10036;
tel. (212) 354 4403.

Portuguese National Tourist Office,
390 Bay Street,
Toronto, Ontario M5H 2Y2;
tel. (416) 364 8133.

Office National du Tourisme Portugais,
1801 McGill College Avenue, Suite 1150, **Montreal**, P.Q. H3A 2N4;
tel. (514) 282 1264.

Within Portugal information can be obtained from the *Comissões Regionais de Turismo* (Regional Tourist Boards), *Comissões Municipais de Turismo* (Municipal Tourist Boards) and *Delegações de Turismo* and *Juntas de Turismo* in many towns and resorts.

Automóvel Club de Portugal (*ACP*)
(Portuguese Automobile Club)

Head office:

Rua de Rosa Araújo 24–26,
P-1200 **Lisboa**;
tel. (01) 56 39 31.

Branch offices in Aveiro, Braga, Caia, Castelo Branco, Coimbra, Faro, Valença do Minho, Vilar Formoso.

The Automóvel Club de Portugal (ACP) operates a breakdown service. If the breakdown occurs between Coimbra and the Algarve, telephone Lisbon 77 54 75, 77 54 02 or 77 54 91; If N of Coimbra, telephone Oporto 92 71, 92 72 or 92 73.

Diplomatic and Consular Offices in Portugal

United Kingdom

Embassy:
Rua São Domingos à Lapa 35–37,
Lisbon;
tel. (01) 66 11 91.

Consulates:
c/o Agencion Passos Freitas,
Rua da Sé,
Funchal, Madeira;
tel. (00 11) 2 74 69.

Avenida da Boavista 3072,
Oporto;
tel. via operator.

Rua do Dr. Bruno Tavares Carreiro 26,
Ponta Delgada, Azores;
tel. (04 86) 2 52 15.

Rua de Santa Isabel 21/I,
Portimão;
tel. (00 82) 2 30 71.

Rua do General Humberto Delgado 4,
Vila Real de Santo António;
tel. (0 81) 4 37 29.

United States

Embassy:
Avenida do Duque de Loulé 39,
Lisbon;
tel. (01) 57 01 02.

Consulates:
Apartado 88, Rua de Júlio Dinis 826–30,
Oporto;
tel. (02) 6 30 94.

Avenida Dom Henrique,
Ponta Delgada, Azores;
tel. (via operator) 2 22 16.

Canada

Embassy:
Rua de Rosa Araújo 2, 6th floor,
Lisbon;
tel. (01) 56 25 47.

Airlines

Air Portugal (*TAP*),
Praça Marquês de Pombal 3,
P-1200 **Lisboa**;
tel. (01) 53 88 52.

Desks at all airports in Portugal.

In the United Kingdom:
19 Regent Street, **London** SW1;
tel. (01) 839 1031.

Rotunda (8th floor),
New Street, **Birmingham**;
tel. (021) 643 5264.

St Andrew's House (15th floor),
141 West Nile Street, **Glasgow**;
tel. (041) 332 6767.

Room 25, Level 7,
International Airport, **Manchester**;
tel. (061) 499 2161.

In the United States:
521 Fifth Avenue,
New York, NY;
tel. (212) 556 8470.

In Canada:
1010 Sherbrook Street West, Suite 2005,
Montreal, P.Q.;
tel. (514) 849 6163.

60 Bloor Street West, Suite 206,
Toronto, Ontairo;
tel. (416) 964 7702.

British Airways

Avenida da Liberdade 23–27,
Lisbon;
tel. (01) 36 09 31.

Rua de Júlio Dinis 778/II,
Oporto;
tel. (02) 69 45 75.

c/o TAP, Rua D. Francisco Gomes 8,
Faro;
tel. (00 89) 2 50 21.

Portuguese Railways

Companhia dos Caminhos de Ferro Portugueses,
Rua de Vitor Cordon 45,
P-1200 **Lisboa**;
tel. (01) 32 62 26.

Radio Messages for Tourists

In cases of extreme emergency the Portuguese radio service (RDP, Dadiodifusão Portuguesa) will transmit messages for visitors to Portugal. Information from the police and motoring organisations.

The Portuguese radio also transmits daily bulletins of news and information for tourists (in English at 8.15 a.m., French at 8.30 and German at 8.45) on 1034 and 782 kHz (medium waves) and 94·3 MHz (VHF).

International Telephone Dialling Codes

From the United Kingdom to Portugal	**010 351**
From the United States or Canada to Portugal	**011 351**
From Portugal to the United Kingdom	**00 44**
From Portugal to the United States	**097 1**

In making an international call the zero prefixed to the local dialling code should be omitted.

Many of the smaller exchanges in Portugal are not yet accessible by subscriber trunk dialing.

Emergency Call

For **police** or **ambulance** the emergency number anywhere in Portugal is **1 15**

Baedeker's Travel Guides

"The maps and illustrations are lavish. The arrangement of information (alphabetically by city) makes it easy to use the book."

—*San Francisco Examiner-Chronicle*

What's there to do and see in foreign countries? Travelers who rely on Baedeker, one of the oldest names in travel literature, will miss nothing. Baedeker's bright red, internationally recognized covers open up to reveal fascinating A-Z directories of cities, towns, and regions, complete with their sights, museums, monuments, cathedrals, castles, gardens and ancestral homes—an approach that gives the traveler a quick and easy way to plan a vacation itinerary.

And Baedekers are filled with over 200 full colour photos and detailed maps, including a full-size, fold-out roadmap for easy vacation driving. Baedeker—the premier name in travel for over 150 years.

Please send me the books checked below:

☐ **Austria**......................$16.95
0–13–056127–4

☐ **Caribbean**.....................$16.95
0–13–056143–6

☐ **Costa Brava**....................$11.95
0–13–055880–X

☐ **Denmark**......................$16.95
0–13–058124–0

☐ **Egypt**........................$16.95
0–13–056358–7

☐ **France**.......................$16.95
0–13–055814–1

☐ **Germany**......................$16.95
0–13–055830–3

☐ **Great Britain**..................$16.95
0–13–055855–9

☐ **Greece**.......................$16.95
0–13–056002–2

☐ **Greek Islands**..................$11.95
0–13–058132–1

☐ **Ireland**......................$16.95
0–13–058140–2

☐ **Israel**.......................$16.95
0–13–056176–2

☐ **Italy**........................$16.95
0–13–055897–4

☐ **Japan**........................$16.95
0–13–056382–X

☐ **Loire**........................$11.95
0–13–056375–7

☐ **Mediterranean Islands**.......$16.95
0–13–056862–7

☐ **Mexico**.......................$16.95
0–13–056069–3

☐ **Netherlands, Belgium and Luxembourg**.......................$16.95
0–13–056028–6

☐ **Portugal**.....................$16.95
0–13–056135–5

☐ **Provence/Côte d'Azur**.........$11.95
0–13–056938–0

☐ **Rail Guide to Europe**..........$16.95
0–13–055971–7

☐ **Rhine**........................$11.95
0–13–056466–4

☐ **Scandinavia**...................$16.95
0–13–056085–5

☐ **Spain**........................$16.95
0–13–055913–X

☐ **Switzerland**...................$16.95
0–13–056044–8

☐ **Turkish Coast**.................$11.95
0–13–058173–9

☐ **Tuscany**......................$11.95
0–13–056482–6

☐ **Yugoslavia**...................$16.95
0–13–056184–3

Please turn the page for an order form and a list of additional Baedeker Guides.

A series of city guides filled with color photographs and detailed maps and floor plans from one of the oldest names in travel publishing:

Please send me the books checked below:

☐ **Amsterdam**......................$11.95
   0–13–057969–6

☐ **Athens**...........................$11.95
   0–13–057977–7

☐ **Bangkok** $11.95
   0–13–057985–8

☐ **Berlin**..............................$11.95
   0–13–367996–9

☐ **Brussels** $11.95
   0–13–368788–0

☐ **Budapest**.........................$11.95
   0–13–058199–2

☐ **Cologne** $11.95
   0–13–058181–X

☐ **Copenhagen**......................$11.95
   0–13–057993–9

☐ **Florence**...........................$11.95
   0–13–369505–0

☐ **Frankfurt**..........................$11.95
   0–13–369570–0

☐ **Hamburg**..........................$11.95
   0–13–369687–1

☐ **Hong Kong** $11.95
   0–13–058009–0

☐ **Istanbul**...........................$11.95
   0–13–058207–7

☐ **Jerusalem** $11.95
   0–13–058017–1

☐ **London** $11.95
   0–13–058025–2

☐ **Madrid** $11.95
   0–13–058033–3

☐ **Moscow**...........................$11.95
   0–13–058041–4

☐ **Munich**............................$11.95
   0–13–370370–3

☐ **New York**..........................$11.95
   0–13–058058–9

☐ **Paris**...............................$11.95
   0–13–058066–X

☐ **Prague**.............................$11.95
   0–13–058215–8

☐ **Rome**...............................$11.95
   0–13058074–0

☐ **San Francisco**....................$11.95
   0–13–058082–1

☐ **Singapore**.........................$11.95
   0–13–058090–2

☐ **Stuttgart**..........................$11.95
   0–13–058223–9

☐ **Tokyo** $11.95
   0–13–058108–9

☐ **Venice** $11.95
   0–13–058116–X

☐ **Vienna** $11.95
   0–13–371303–2

PRENTICE HALL PRESS
Order Department—Travel Books
200 Old Tappan Road
Old Tappan, New Jersey 07675
In U.S. include $1 postage and handling for 1st book, 25¢ each additional book.
Outside U.S. $2 and 50¢ respectively.

Enclosed is my check or money order for $_____

NAME_____

ADDRESS_____

CITY_____STATE_____ZIP_____